9/02

MUSIC EDUCATION

MUSIC EDUCATION

Source Readings from Ancient Greece to Today

SECOND EDITION

Edited by

MICHAEL L. MARK

ROUTLEDGE

NEW YORK   LONDON

Published in 2002 by
Routledge
29 West 35th Street
New York, NY 10001

Published in Great Britain by

Routledge
11 New Fetter Lane
London EC4P 4EE

Routledge is an imprint of the Taylor & Francis Group.

Printed on acid-free, 250-year-life paper.
Manufactured in the United States of America.
10 9 8 7 6 5 4 3 2 1

Library of Congress Cataloging-in-Publication Data
Music education : source readings from Ancient Greece to today /
edited by Michael L. Mark.
        p. cm.
    Includes bibliographical references.
    ISBN 0-415-93678-0   —   ISBN 0-415-93679-9 (pbk.)
    1. Music—Instruction and study—History—Sources.
    2. Music—Philosophy and aesthetics.
    I. Mark, Michael L.

    MT2 .M94 2002
    780'.71—dc21   2001048186

Contents

Introduction

Because music has been valued for a variety of reasons by every culture and society throughout Western history, music education has always been a necessary component of children's education. Despite the vast amount of historical evidence, the question "Why is music education important?" invariably arises as our society continually evolves and its cultural needs change. The music educator knows intrinsically why music and music instruction are necessary, as does every person who has come under the spell of the art. Few, however, are aware of the vast body of historical justification, rationales, and philosophies that illuminate why society has always valued music education and why it still does. The words of Heitor Villa-Lobos, for example, illustrate the vision of music education as a vital force in a particular society. Villa-Lobos, a composer of international stature, was the General Director of Music Education in Brazil. The following statement was an invocation to St. Cecilia, patron saint of music, and was read on a 1939 radio broadcast.

> Divine Protector, who has given to Brazil the gift of music, who has exalted the birds, the rivers, the waterfalls, the winds, and the people of this land into an incomparable symphony whose melodies and harmonies have contributed to the formation of Brazil's soul! Illumine those who cultivate Brazilian music! Encourage the musicians disappointed in their musical life! Enlighten public opinion so as to make the appreciation of Brazilian art possible! Gratify the wish of those who believe music to be of national importance, educating the soul as gymnastics strengthen and develop the body! Lend faith to those who trust that the day will come when music becomes the Sonorous Flag of Universal Peace![1]

The readings in this book are the words of educators, government officials, psychologists, scientists, musicians, philosophers, and of organizations of music educators and of advocates of music education. They were selected as the most representative of their particular times and societies. Most are excerpts, selected to provide enough information not only to clarify the subject matter, but to retain the flavor and unique characteristics of the entire work. I hope that I have chosen wisely enough to allow the readings to express the thoughts and intentions of the many writers accurately. I strongly encourage readers to pursue in their entirety the works that interest them the most. They will be amply rewarded for their time and effort.

The readings exhibit a variety and diversity of writing and editorial styles. No attempt has been made to impose any artificial consistency of style on this collection. Unless otherwise noted, methods of documentation, numbering systems, spelling, punctuation, and other such matters of style are reproduced as per original sources. Archaic grammatical structures and spellings may sometimes appear incorrect, but they add to the unique flavor of each reading.

MLM

Note

1. Nicholas Slonimsky, *Music of Latin America* (New York: Thomas Y. Crowell Company, 1945), 122.

PART I

EUROPEAN VIEWS

Greece and Rome

Athens was the setting in which philosophers created belief systems that were instrumental in shaping Western culture. Greek philosophers recognized that we live in an orderly universe. As rational beings, we have the opportunity to seek truth and virtue, and we are responsible for our own individual satisfaction and happiness. Music and music education were visible manifestations of both societal orderliness and individual pleasure.

With the downfall of Athens and the ascendancy of Rome, there was a new, lasting influence on Western culture. The Romans, like the Greeks before them, strove for perfection in all aspects of society. They developed a system of government that made possible the attainment of excellence in the arts, athletics, commerce, and the military. It was Rome's governmental structure, however, rather than its contribution to the arts, that was its most meaningful historical contribution. The Roman excerpts that follow exemplify contradictory aspects of Roman society. The study of rhetoric was of great importance to the Roman citizen, whose skill as a rhetorician would help him rise in the government. Most Romans, however, were not citizens, and their opportunities were severely limited. St. Augustine's writing is that of a Christian intellectual who found comfort, satisfaction, and joy in his religion and in music.

Plato
Protagoras

Plato's (427–ca. 347 B.C.) imaginary ideal state emphasized education and the arts. His system of education included music and gymnastics to help children understand an idealized Hellenic community life and to prepare them to be active participants in it. Gymnastic games, he said, "develop the civic virtues of disciplined courage, self-control, friendly cooperation, and loyalty to the group and its ideals" (*Republic*, Laws). The Greek word for *music* meant the arts in general and included literature and dancing as well as music. Music was a crucial component of Plato's plan for citizenship education. This reading is in the form of an imaginary dialectic between Socrates (Plato's teacher) and his pupil Glaucon.

. . . When they send the children to school, their instructions to the masters lay much more emphasis on good behavior than on letters or music. The teachers take good care of this, and when boys have learned their letters and are ready to understand the written word as formerly the spoken, they set the works of good poets before them on their desks to read and make them learn them by heart, poems containing much admonition and many stories, eulogies, and panegryics of the good men of old, so that the child may be inspired to imitate them and long to be like them.

The music masters by analogous methods instill self-control and deter the young from evil-doing. And when they have learned to play the lyre, they teach them the works of good poets of another sort, namely the lyrical, which they accompany on the lyre, familiarizing the minds of the children with the rhythms and melodies. By this means they become more civilized, more balanced, and better adjusted in themselves and so more capable in whatever they say or do, for rhythm and harmonious adjustment are essential to the whole of human life. . . .

Republic: III

. . . Education in music is most sovereign, because more than anything else rhythm and harmony find their way to the inmost soul and take strongest hold upon it, bringing with them and imparting grace, if one is rightly trained, and otherwise the contrary. And further, because omissions and the failure of beauty in things badly made or grown would be most quickly perceived by one who was properly educated in music, and so, feeling distaste rightly, he would praise beautiful things and take delight in them and receive them into his soul to foster its growth and become himself beautiful and good. The ugly he would rightly disapprove of and hate while still young and yet unable to apprehend the reason, but when reason came the man thus nurtured would be the first to give her welcome, for by this affinity he would know her.

I certainly think, he said, that such is the cause of education in music.

It is, then, said I, as it was when we learned our letters and felt that we knew them sufficiently only when the separate letters did not elude us, appearing as few elements in all the combinations that convey then, and when we did not disregard them in small things or great and think it unnecessary to recognize them, but were eager to distinguish them everywhere, in the belief that we should never be literate and letter-perfect till we could do this.

True.

And is it not also true that if there are any likenesses of letters reflected in water or mirrors, we shall never know them until we know the originals, but such knowledge belongs to the same art and discipline?

By all means.

Then, by heaven, am I not right in saying that by the same token we shall never be true musicians, either—neither we nor the guardians that we have undertaken to educate—until we are able to recognize the forms of soberness, courage, liberality, and high-mindedness, and all their kindred and their opposites, too, in all the combinations that contain and convey then, and to apprehend them and their images wherever found, disregarding them neither in trifles nor in great things, but believing the knowledge of them to belong to the same art and discipline?

The conclusion is inevitable, he said.

Then, said I, when there is a coincidence of a beautiful disposition in the soul and corresponding and harmonious beauties of the same type in the bodily form—is not this the fairest spectacle for one who is capable of its contemplation?

Far the fairest.

And surely the fairest is the most lovable.

Of course.

The true musician, then, would love by preference persons of this sort, but if there were disharmony he would not love this.

No, he said, not if there was a defect in the soul, but if it were in the body, he would bear with it and still be willing to bestow his love. . . .

While badness could never come to know both virtue and itself, native virtue through education will at last acquire the science of both itself and badness. This one, then, as I think, is the man who proves to be wise and not the bad man.

And I concur, he said.

Then will you not establish by law in your city such an art of medicine as we have described in conjunction with this kind of justice? And these arts will care for the bodies and souls of such of your citizens as are truly well-born, but those who are not, such as are defective in body, they will suffer to die, and those who are evil-natured and incurable in soul they will themselves put to death.

This certainly, he said, has been shown to be the best thing for the sufferers themselves and for the state.

And so your youths, said I, employing that simple music which we said engendered sobriety will, it is clear, guard themselves against falling into the need of the justice of the courtroom.

Yes, he said.

And will not our musician, pursuing the same trail in his use of gymnastics, if he please, get to have no need of medicine save when indispensable?

I think so.

And even the exercises and toils of gymnastics he will undertake with a view to the spirited part of his nature to arouse that rather than for mere strength, unlike ordinary athletes, who treat diet and exercise only as a means to muscle.

Nothing could be truer, he said.

Then may we not say, Glaucon, said I, that those who established an education in music and gymnastics had not the purpose in view that some attribute to them in so instituting, namely to treat the body by one and the soul by the other?

But what? he said.

It seems likely, I said, that they ordained both chiefly for the soul's sake.

How so?

Have you not observed, said I, the effect on the disposition of the mind itself of lifelong devotion to gymnastics with total neglect of music? Or the disposition of those of the opposite habit?

In what respect do you mean? he said.

In respect of savagery and hardness or, on the other hand, of softness and gentleness?

I have observed, he said, that the devotees of unmitigated gymnastics turn out more brutal than they should be and those of music softer than is good for them.

And surely, said I, this savagery is a quality derived from the high-spirited element in our nature, which, if rightly trained, becomes brave, but if overstrained, would naturally become hard and harsh.

I think so, he said.

And again, is not the gentleness a quality which the philosophical nature would yield? This if relaxed too far would be softer than is desirable but if rightly trained gentle and orderly?

That is so.

But our requirement, we say, is that the guardians should possess both natures.

It is.

And must they not be harmoniously adjusted to one another?

Of course.

And the soul of the man thus attuned is sober and brave?

Certainly.

And that of the ill-adjusted is cowardly and rude?

It surely is.

Now when a man abandons himself to music, to play upon him and pour into his soul as it were through the funnel of his ears those sweet, soft, and dirgelike airs of which we were just now speaking, and gives his entire time to the warblings and blandishments of song, the first result is that the principle of high spirit, if he had it, is softened like iron and is made useful instead of useless and brittle. But when he continues the practice without remission and is spellbound, the effect begins to be that he melts and liquefies till he completely dissolves away his spirit, cuts out as it were the very sinews of his soul and makes of himself a "feeble warrior."

Assuredly, he said.

And if, said I, he has to begin with a spiritless nature he reaches his result quickly, but if high-spirited, by weakening the spirit he makes it unstable, quickly irritated by slight stimuli, and as quickly quelled. The outcome is that such men are choleric and irascible instead of high-spirited, and are peevish and discontented.

Precisely so.

On the other hand, if a man toils hard at gymnastics and eats right lustily and holds no truck with music and philosophy, does he not at first get very fit and full of pride and high spirit and become more brave and bold than he was?

He does indeed.

But what if he does nothing but this and has no contact with the Muse in any way? Is not the result that even if there was some principle of the love of knowledge in his soul, since it tastes of no instruction nor of any inquiry and does not participate in any discussion or any other form of culture, it becomes feeble, deaf, and blind, because it is not aroused or fed nor are its perceptions purified and quickened?

That is so, he said.

And so such a man, I take it, becomes a misologist and a stranger to the Muses. He no longer makes any use of persuasion by speech but achieves all his ends like a beast by violence and savagery, and in his brute ignorance and ineptitude lives a life of disharmony and gracelessness.

That is entirely true, he said.

For these two, then, it seems there are two arts which I would say some god gave to mankind, music and gymnastics for the service of the high-spirited principle and the love of knowledge in them—not for the soul and the body except incidentally, but for the harmonious adjustment of these two principles by the proper degree of tension and relaxation of each.

Yes, so it appears, he said.

Then he who best blends gymnastics with music and applies them most suitably to the soul is the man whom we should most rightly pronounce to be the most perfect and harmonious musician, far rather than the one who brings the strings into unison with one another.

That seems likely, Socrates, he said.

And shall we not also need in our city, Glaucon, a permanent overseer of this kind if its constitutions is to be preserved?

We most certainly shall.

Such would be the outlines of their education and breeding. . . .

Aristotle
Politica, Book VIII

Aristotle (384–322 B.C.) was born in Stagira, a city in the Hellenic part of Thrace. He established a school in Athens, the Lyceum, where he taught and developed methods for empirical research which he carried out himself. Aristotle's work contrasted sharply with that of Plato, a generalist who conceptualized broad, sweeping visions of the ideal society. Aristotle was concerned with minutae, as evidenced by his research based on the observation of nature.

No one will doubt that the legislator should direct his attention above all else to the education of youth; for the neglect of education does harm to the constitution. The citizen should be molded to suit the form of government under which he lives. For each government has a peculiar character which originally formed and which continues to preserve it. The character of democracy creates democracy, and the character of oligarchy creates oligarchy; and always the better the character, the better the government.

Again, for the exercise of any faculty or art a previous training and habituation are required; clearly therefore for the practice of virtue. And since the whole city has one end, it is manifest that education should be one and the same for all, and that it should be public, and not private—not as at present, when every one looks after his own children separately, and gives them separate instruction of the sort which he thinks best; the training in things which are of common interest should be the same for all. Neither must we suppose that any one of the citizens belongs to himself, for they all belong to the state, and are each of them a part of the state, and the care of each part is inseparable from the care of the whole. In this particular as in some others the Lacedaemonians are to be praised, for they take the greatest pains about their children, and make education the business of the state.

That education should be regulated by law and should be an affair of state is not to be denied, but what should be the character of this public education, and how young persons should be educated, are questions which remain to be considered. As things are, there is disagreement about the subjects. For mankind are by no means agreed about the things to be taught, whether we look to virtue or the best life. Neither is it clear whether education is more concerned with intellectual or with moral virtue. The existing practice is perplexing; no one knows on what principle we should proceed—should the useful in life, or should virtue, or should the higher knowledge, be the aim of our training; all three opinions have been entertained. Again, about the means there is no agreement; for different persons, starting with different ideas about the nature of virtue, naturally disagree about the practice of it. There can be no doubt that children should be taught those useful things which are really necessary, but not all useful things; for occupations are divided into liberal and illiberal: and to young children should be imparted only such kinds of knowledge as will be useful to them without vulgarizing them. And any occupation, art, or science, which makes the body or soul or mind of the freeman less fit for the practice or exercise of virtue, is vulgar; wherefore we call those arts vulgar which tend to deform the body, and likewise all paid employments, for they absorb and degrade the mind. There are also some liberal arts quite proper for a freeman to acquire, but only in a certain degree, and if he attend to them too closely, in order to attain perfection in them, the same evil effects will follow. The object also which a man sets before him makes a great difference; if he does or learns anything for his own sake or for the sake of his friends, or with a view to excellence, the action will not appear illiberal; but if done for the sake of others, the very same action will be thought menial and servile. The received subjects of instruction, as I have already remarked, are partly of a liberal and partly of an illiberal character.

The customary branches of education are in number four; they are (1) reading and writing, (2) gymnastic exercises, and (3) music, to which is sometimes added (4) drawing. Of these, reading and writing and drawing are regarded as useful for the purposes of life in a variety of ways, and gymnastic exercises are thought to infuse courage. Concerning music a doubt may be raised—in our own day most men cultivate it for the sake of pleasure, but originally it was included in education, because nature herself, as has been often said, requires that we should be able, not only to work well, but to use leisure well; for, as I must repeat once again, the first principle of all action is leisure. Both are required, but leisure is better than occupation and is its end; and therefore the question must be asked, what ought we to do when at leisure? Clearly we ought not to be amusing ourselves, for then amusement would be the end of life. But if this is inconceivable, and amusement is needed more amid serious occupations than at other times (for he who is hard at work has need of relaxation, and amusement gives relaxation, whereas occupation is always accompanied with exertion and effort), we should introduce amusements only at suitable times, and they should be our medicines, for the emotion which they create in the soul is a relaxation, and from the pleasure we obtain rest. But leisure of itself gives pleasure and happiness and enjoyment of life, which are experienced, not by the busy man, but by those who have leisure. For he who is occupied has in view some end which he has not attained; but happiness is an end, since all men deem it to be accompanied with pleasure and not with pain. This pleasure, however, is regarded differently by different persons, and varies according to the habit of individuals; the pleasure of the best man is the best, and springs from the noblest sources. It is clear then that there are branches of learning and education which we must study merely with a view to leisure spent in intellectual activity, and these are to be valued for their own sake; whereas those kinds of knowledge which are useful in business are to be deemed necessary, and exist for the sake of other things. And therefore our fathers admitted music into education, not on the ground either of its necessity or utility, for it is not necessary, nor indeed useful in the same manner as reading and writing, which are useful in moneymaking, in the management of a household, in the acquisition of knowledge and in political life, nor like drawing, useful for a more correct judgment of the works of artists, nor again like gymnastic, which gives health and strength; for neither of these is to be gained from music. There remains, then, the use of music for intellectual enjoyment in leisure; which is in fact evidently the reason of its introduction, this being one of the ways in which it is thought that a freeman should pass his leisure; as Homer says, "But he who alone should be called to the pleasant feast," and afterwards he speaks of others whom he describes as inviting "the bard who would delight them all." And in another place Odysseus says there is no better way of passing life than when men's hearts are merry and "the banqueters in the hall, sitting in order, hear the voice of the minstrel."

It is evident, then, that there is a sort of education in which parents should train their sons, not as being useful or necessary, but because it is liberal or noble. Whether this is of one kind only, or of more than one, and if so, what they are, and how they are to be imparted, must hereafter be determined. Thus much we are now in a position to say, that the ancients witness to us; for their opinion may be gathered from the fact that music is one of the received and traditional branches of education. Further, it is clear that children should be instructed in some useful things—for example, in reading and writing—not only for their usefulness, but also because many other sorts of knowledge are acquired through them. With a like view they may be taught drawing, not to prevent their making mistakes in their own purchases, or in order that they may not be imposed upon in the buying or selling of articles, but perhaps rather because it makes them judges of the beauty of the human form. To be always seeking after the useful does not become free and exalted souls. Now it is clear that in education practice must be used before theory, and the body be trained before the mind; and therefore boys should be handed over to the trainer, who creates in them the proper habit of body, and to the wrestling master, who teaches them their exercises. . . .

It is an admitted principle, that gymnastic exercises should be employed in education, and that for children they should be of a lighter kind, avoiding severe diet or painful toil, lest the growth of the body be impaired. The evil of excessive training in early years is strikingly proved by the example of the Olympic victors; for not more than two or three of them have gained a prize both as boys and as men; their early training and severe gymnastic exercises exhausted their constitutions. When boyhood is over, three years should be spent in other studies; the period of life which follows may then be devoted to hard exercise and strict diet. Men ought not to labor at the same time with their minds and with their bodies; for the two kinds of labor are opposed to one another; the labor of the body impedes the mind, and the labor of the mind the body.

Concerning music there are some questions which we have already raised; these we may now resume and carry further; and our remarks will serve as a prelude to this or any other discussion of the subject. It is not easy to determine the nature of music, or why any one should have a knowledge of it. Shall we say, for the sake of amusement and relaxation, like sleep or drinking, which are not good in themselves, but are pleasant, and at the same time "make care to cease," as Euripides says? And for this end men also appoint music, and make use of all three alike—sleep, drinking, music—to which some add dancing. Or shall we argue that music conduces to virtue, on the ground that it can form our minds and habituate us to true pleasures as our bodies are made by gymnastic to be of a certain character? Or shall we say that it contributes to the enjoyment of leisure and mental cultivation, which is a third alternative? Now obviously youths are not to be instructed with a view to their amusement, for learning is no amusement, but is accompanied with pain. Neither is intellectual enjoyment suitable to boys of that age, for it is the end, and that which is imperfect cannot attain the perfect or end. But perhaps it may be said that boys learn music for the sake of the amusement which they will have when they are grown up. If so, why should they learn themselves, and not, like the Persian and Median kings, enjoy the pleasure and instruction which is derived from hearing others (for surely persons who have made music the business and profession of their lives will be better performers than those who practice only long enough to learn)? If they must learn music, on the same principle they should learn cookery, which is absurd. And even granting that music may form the character, the objection still holds: why should we learn ourselves? Why cannot we attain true pleasure and form a correct judgment from hearing others, like the Lacedaemonians? For they, without learning music, nevertheless can correctly judge, as they say, of good and bad melodies. Or again, if music should be used to promote cheerfulness and refined intellectual enjoyment, the objection still remains—why should we learn ourselves instead of enjoying the performances of others? We may illustrate what we are saying by our conception of the Gods; for in the poets Zeus does not himself sing or play on the lyre. Nay, we call professional performers vulgar; no freeman would play or sing unless he were intoxicated or in jest. But these matters may be left for the present.

The first question is whether music is or is not to be a part of education. Of the three things mentioned in our discussion, which does it produce? Education or amusement or intellectual enjoyment, for it may be reckoned under all three, and seems to share in the nature of all of them. Amusement is for the sake of relaxation, and relaxation is of necessity sweet, for it is the remedy of pain caused by toil; and intellectual enjoyment is universally acknowledged to contain an element not only of the noble, but of the pleasant, for happiness is made up of both. All men agree that music is one of the pleasantest things, whether with or without song; as Musaeus says, "Song is to morals of all things the sweetest." Hence and with good reason it is introduced into social gatherings and entertainments, because it makes the hearts of men glad: so that on this ground alone we may assume that the young ought to be trained in it. For innocent pleasures are not only in harmony with the perfect end of life, but they also provide relaxation. And whereas men rarely attain the end, but often rest by the way and amuse themselves, not only with a view to a further end, but also for the pleasure's sake, it may be well at times to let them find a refreshment in music. It sometimes happens that men make amusement the end, for the end probably contains some element of pleasure, though not any ordinary or lower pleasure; but they mistake the lower for the higher, and in seeking for the one find the other, since every pleasure has a likeness to the end of action. For the end is not eligible for the sake of any future good, nor do the pleasures which we have described exist for the sake of any future good but of the past, that is to say, they are the alleviation of past toils and pains. And we may infer this to be the reason why men seek happiness from these pleasures. But music is pursued, not only as alleviation of past toil, but also as providing recreation. And who can say whether, having this use, it may not also have a nobler one? In addition to this common pleasure, felt and shared in by all (for the pleasure given by music is natural, and therefore adapted to all ages and characters), may it not have also some influence over the character and the soul? It must have such an influence if characters are affected by it. And that they are so affected is proved in many ways, and not least by the power which the songs of Olympus exercise; for beyond question they inspire enthusiasm, and enthusiasm is an emotion of the ethical part of the soul. Besides, when men hear imitations, even apart from the rhythms and tunes themselves, their feelings move in sympathy. Since then music is a pleasure, and virtue consists in rejoicing and loving and hating aright, there is clearly nothing which we are so much concerned to acquire and to cultivate as the power of forming right judgments, and of taking delight in good dispositions and noble actions. Rhythm and melody supply imitations of anger and gentleness, and also of courage and temperance, and of all the qualities contrary to these, and of the other qualities of character, which hardly fall short of the actual affections, as we know from our own experience, for in listening to such strains our souls undergo a change. The habit of feeling pleasure or pain at mere representations is not far removed from the same feeling about realities; for example, if any one delights in the sight of a statue for its beauty only, it necessarily follows that the sight of the original will be pleasant to him. The objects of no other sense, such as taste or touch, have any resemblance to moral qualities; in visible objects there is only a little, for there are figures which are of a moral character, but only to a slight extent, and all do not participate in the feeling about them. Again, figures and colors are not imitations, but signs, of moral habits, indications which the body gives of states of feeling. The connection of them with morals is slight, but in so far as there is any, young men should be taught to look, not at the works of Pauson, but at those of Polyhnotus, or any other painter or sculptor who expresses moral ideas. On the other hand, even in mere melodies there is an imitation of character, for the musical modes differ essentially from one another, and those who hear them are differently affected by each. Some of them make men sad and grave, like the so-called Mixolydian, others enfeeble the mind, like the relaxed modes, another, again, produces a moderate and settled temper, which appears to be the peculiar effect of the Dorian; the Phrygian inspires enthusiasm. The whole subject has been well treated by philosophical writers on this branch of education, and they confirm their arguments by facts. The same principles apply to rhythms; some have a character of rest, others of motion, and of these latter again, some have a more vulgar, others a nobler movement. Enough has been said to show that music has a power of forming the character, and should therefore be introduced into the education of the young. The study is suited to the stage of youth, for young persons will not, if they can help, endure anything which is not sweetened by pleasure, and music has a natural sweetness. There seems to be in us a sort of affinity to musical modes and rhythms, which makes some philosophers say that the soul is a tuning, others, that it possesses tuning.

And now we have to determine the question which has been already raised, whether children should be themselves taught to sing and play or not. Clearly there is a considerable difference made in the character by the actual practice of the art. It is difficult, if not impossible, for those who do not perform to be good judges of the performance of others. Besides, children should have something to do, and the rattle of Archyles, which people give to their children in order to amuse them and prevent them from breaking anything in the house, was a capital invention, for a young thing cannot be quiet. The rattle is a toy suited to the infant mind, and education is a rattle or toy for children of a larger growth. We conclude then that they should be taught music in such a way as to become not only critics but performers.

The question what is or is not suitable for different ages may be easily answered; nor is there any difficulty in meeting the objection of those who say that the study of music is vulgar. We reply (1) in the first place, that they who are to be judges must also be performers, and that they should begin to practice early, although when they are older they may be spared the execution; they must have learned to appreciate what is good and to delight in it, thanks to the knowledge which they acquired in their youth. As to (2) the vulgarizing effect which music is supposed to exercise, this is a question which we shall have no difficulty in determining, when we have considered to what extent freemen who are being trained to political virtue should pursue the art, what melodies and what rhythms they should be allowed to use, and what instruments should be employed in teaching them to play; for even the instrument makes a difference. The answer to the objection turns upon these distinctions; for it is quite possible that certain methods of teaching and learning music do really have a degrading effect. It is evident then that the learning of music ought not to impede the business of riper years, or to degrade the body or render it unfit for civil or military training, whether for bodily exercises at the time or for later studies.

The right measure will be attained if students of music stop short of the arts which are practiced in professional contests; and do not seek to acquire those fantastic marvels of execution which are now the fashion in such contests, and from these have passed into education. Let the young practice even such music as we have prescribed, only until they are able to feel delight in noble melodies and rhythms, and not merely in that common part of music in which every slave or child and even some animals find pleasure.

From these principles we may also infer what instruments should be used. The flute, or any other instrument which requires great skill, as for example the harp, ought not to be admitted into education, but only such as will make intelligent students of music or of the other parts of education. Besides, the flute is not an instrument which is expressive of moral character; it is too exciting. The proper time for using it is when the performance aims not at instruction, but at the relief of the passions. And there is a further objection; the impediment which the flute presents to the use of the voice detracts from its educational value. The ancients therefore were right in forbidding the flute to youths and freemen, although they had once allowed it. For when their wealth gave them a greater inclination to leisure, and they had loftier notions of excellence, being also elated with their success, both before and after the Persian War, with more zeal than discernment they pursued every kind of knowledge, and so they introduced the flute into education. At Lacedaemon there was a choragus who led the chorus with a flute, and at Athens the instrument became so popular that most freemen could play upon it. The popularity is shown by the tablet which Thrasippus dedicated when he furnished the chorus to Ecphantides. Later experience enabled men to judge what was or was not really conducive to virtue, and they rejected both the flute and several other old-fashioned instruments, such as the Lydian harp, the many-stringed lyre, the *heptagon*, *trigonon*, *sambuca*, and the like, which are intended only to give pleasure to the hearer, and require extraordinary skill of hand. There is a meaning also in the myth of the ancients, which tells how Athene invented the flute and then threw it away. It was not a bad idea of theirs, that the Goddess disliked the instrument because it made the face ugly; but with still more reason may we say that she rejected it because the acquirement of flute playing contributes nothing to the mind, since to Athene we ascribe both knowledge and art.

Thus we reject the professional instruments and also the professional mode of education in music (and by professional we mean that which is adopted in contests), for in this the performer practices the art, not for the sake of his own improvement, but in order to give pleasure, and that of a vulgar sort, to his hearers. For this reason the execution of such music is not the part of a freeman but of a paid performer, and the result is that the performers are vulgarized, for the end at which they aim is bad. The vulgarity of the spectator tends to lower the character of the music and therefore of the performers; they look to him, he makes them what they are, and fashions even their bodies by the movements which he expects them to exhibit.

We have also to consider rhythms and modes, and their use in education. Shall we use them all or make a distinction? and shall the same distinction be made for those who practice music with a view to education, or shall it be some other? Now we see that music is produced by melody and rhythm, and we ought to know what influence these have respectively on education, and whether we should prefer excellence in melody or excellence in rhythm. But as the subject has been very well treated by many musicians of the present day, and also by philosophers who have had considerable experience of musical education, to these we would refer the more exact student of the subject; we shall only speak of it now after the manner of the legislator, stating the general principles.

We accept the division of melodies proposed by certain philosophers into ethical melodies, melodies of action, and passionate or inspiring melodies, each having, as they say, a mode corresponding to it. But we maintain further that music should be studied, not for the sake of one, but of many benefits, that is to say, with a view to (1) education; (2) purgation (the word *purgation* we use at present without explanation, but when hereafter we speak of poetry, we will treat the subject with more precision); music may also serve (3) for intellectual enjoyment, for relaxation and for recreation after exertion. It is clear, therefore, that all the modes must be employed by us, but not all of them in the same manner. In education the most ethical modes are to be preferred, but in listening to the performances of others we may admit the modes of action and passion also. For feelings such as pity and fear, or, again, enthusiasm, exist very strongly in some souls, and have more or less influence over all. Some persons fall into a religious frenzy, whom we see as a result of the sacred melodies (when they have used the melodies that excite the soul to mystic frenzy), restored as though they had found healing and purgation. Those who are influenced by pity or fear and every emotional nature, must have a like experience, and others in so far as each is susceptible to such emotions, and all are in a manner purged and their souls lightened and delighted. The purgative melodies likewise give an innocent pleasure to mankind. Such are the modes and the melodies in which those who perform music at the theatre should be invited to compete. But since the spectators are of two kinds—the one free and educated, and the other a vulgar crowd composed of mechanics, laborers, and the like—there ought to be contests and exhibitions instituted for the relaxation of the second class also. And the music will correspond to their minds; for as their minds are perverted from the natural state, so there are perverted modes and highly strung and unnaturally colored melodies. A man receives pleasure from what is natural to him, and therefore professional musicians may be allowed to practice this lower sort of music before an audience of a lower type. But, for the purposes of education, as I have already said, those modes and melodies should be employed which are ethical, such as the Dorian, as we said before; though we may include any others which are approved by philosophers who have had a musical education. The Socrates of the *Republic* is wrong in retaining only the Phrygian mode along with the Dorian, and the more so because he rejects the flute; for the Phrygian is to the modes what the flute is to musical instruments—both of them are exciting and emotional. Poetry proves this, for Bacchic frenzy and all similar emotions are most suitably expressed by the flute, and are better set to the Phrygian than to any other mode. The dithyramb, for example, is acknowledged to be Phrygian, a fact of which the connoisseurs of music offer many proofs, saying, among other things, that Philoxenus, having attempted to compose his *Mysians* as a dithyramb in the Dorian mode, found it impossible, and fell back by the very nature of things into the more appropriate Phrygian. All men agree that the Dorian music is the gravest and manliest. And whereas we say that the extremes should be avoided and the mean followed, and whereas the Dorian is a mean between the other modes, it is evident that our youth should be taught the Dorian music.

Two principles have to be kept in view, what is possible, what is becoming: at these every man ought to aim. But even these are relative to age; the old, who have lost their powers, cannot very well sing the high-strung modes, and nature herself seems to suggest that their songs should be of the more relaxed kind. Wherefore the musicians likewise blame Socrates, and with justice, for rejecting the relaxed modes in education under the idea that they are intoxicating, not in the ordinary sense of intoxication (for wine rather tends to excite men), but because they have no strength in them. And so, with a view also to the time of life when men begin to grow old, they ought to practice the gentler modes and melodies as well as the others, and, further, any mode, such as the Lydian, above all others appears to be, which is suited to children of tender age, and possesses the elements both of order and of education. Thus it is clear that education should be based upon three principles—the mean, the possible, the becoming, these three.

Quintilian
Instituto Oratoria:
Is Knowledge of a Variety of Subjects
Necessary for the Future Orator?

Marcus Fabius Quintilian was born about 35 A.D. His appointment as professor of rhetoric by the Emperor Vespasion was an official recognition of the responsibility of the government in public instruction. He was a pleader (attorney) as well as a teacher, and thus was able to incorporate practical experience in his teaching. The importance of the *Instituto Oratoria* can be appreciated when one realizes that rhetoric was the most essential part of Roman education.

9. For myself I could be perfectly satisfied by the judgment of the ancients. Who does not know that Music, to speak of it first, even in those bygone days commanded not only so much attention but also so much veneration that the same men were adjudged musicians and prophets and philosophers, Orpheus and Linus, to take no other examples. According to the tradition of later times these two were both the sons of gods, and the former, because he soothed savage boorish hearts with a love for his music, was

spoken of as having drawn not only the wild creatures but even rocks and forests in his train.

10. Similarly, too, Timagenes tells us that amongst all the humane studies Music stood out as the most ancient; and most famous poets, too, bear witness, for in their writings the praises of heroes and of gods were sung at royal banquets to the music of the lute. Does not the great bard Lopas in Virgil sing of "the wandering moon and the labors of the sun" and so forth? Assuredly the illustrious poet thus openly proclaims that music is linked with a knowledge even of things divine.

11. Now if that is granted, it will also be required for the training of the orator—if indeed, as we have said, that province as well which the orators abandoned and the philosophers seized upon, belonged really to us and if eloquence cannot be complete without a knowledge of all such things.

12. Yet no one has really doubted that men famous on account of their wisdom have been keen students of music. Pythagoras and his followers have rendered popular a view undoubtedly inherited by them from antiquity, namely, that the universe itself is constructed in accordance with a law which was afterwards imitated by the music of the lyre, and, not content with that concord of different elements to which the name *harmony* is given, they gave a kind of music to the celestial motions. . . .

17. So far I seem to be sounding the praises of the fairest of the arts without linking it up with the orator. Let us therefore pass over the further point that grammar and music were once closely associated. Indeed, Archytas and Evenus thought that grammar was subordinate to music. That the same men were teachers of both subjects is proved by Sophron, a writer of mimes to be sure, but one so much admired by Plato, that the philosopher is believed to have had his works under his head in his dying hour.

18. Eupolis bears like testimony, for in his plays Prodamus is a teacher both of music and of letters, while Maricas, who in the play represents the demagogue Hyperbolus, confesses that he knows nothing of music except the letters of the alphabet. Aristophanes, too, in more than one of his plays shows that it was the ancient practice to combine these subjects in the education of boys, and in Menander's play *The Changeling*, the old man, in explaining to the father who is claiming his son the items of expenditure incurred in the boy's education, says that he has paid large sums to musicians and teachers of geometry.

19. This, too, was the origin of the ancient practice of passing the lyre round at banquets after the feasting was over, and on one such occasion when Themistocles admitted that he could not play it, "he was," to use the words of Cicero, "accounted but ill-educated."

20. At the banquet of the ancient Romans, too, it was customary to have music upon stringed instruments and flutes; and the verses of the dancing

priests of Mars have their tunes. All these practices were instituted by Numa, and they prove conclusively that, even amongst those whom we regard as savage and warlike, music did not fail to receive all the attention which the circumstances of the age allowed.

21. Finally it passed into a familiar Greek proverb, that those who lack education have no dealings either with the Graces or with the Muses.

22. But let us now explain the advantages which the future orator may look for from the study of music, in his own peculiar sphere.

Music has two modes of expression, namely, through vocal utterance, and through the gestures of the body, in both of which the orator aims at a certain fitting harmony. The theory of vocal utterance is divided by the musician Aristoxenus into rhythmic and metric, the former concerned with the modulation of the voice, the latter with melody and the actual sounds produced. Are not all these things, then, necessary for the orator? One has a bearing upon gesture, another upon arrangement of words, and a third upon the inflexions of the voice which in pleading, as elsewhere, extend over an extremely wide range.

23. The alternative view would be that it is only in songs and the lyrical portions of comedy that structure and the smooth joining of words are demanded, but that in pleading these things are unnecessary, or else that arrangement and melody are not employed in a speech as they are in music to suit the requirements of the material in hand.

24. In the case of singing by utterance and by modulation sublimity is given to noble themes, sweetness to pleasant ones, and smoothness to passages that lack emotion, and the whole art of music lies in the sympathetic expression of the moods attendant upon the words which are sung.

25. And yet in pleading, too, the raising or dropping of the voice and its inflexions all aim at rousing certain feelings in the audience, and we seek to stir now the passion now the pity of a juryman by varying modulations (to employ the same word again) of arrangement and of utterance, knowing that instruments that lack the power of speech can bring men's minds under the influence of entirely different emotions.

26. Again, fitting and seemly movements of the body . . . are necessary for the orator and can only be learned from music. No small portion of the art of pleading lies in the skilful use of gesture, and I have set aside a special part of my work for that subject.

27. Come, now, is it not the case that the orator will give attention, first and foremost, to his voice? And what is so peculiarly within the province of music? We must not, however, anticipate this part of the subject either: let us in the meantime be content with a single example, that of Gaius Gracchus, the foremost orator of his age, who when he was making speeches had standing behind him a musician with a pitch-pipe . . . to give him the notes to which his voice had to be attuned.

28. This he was careful to do, even in his wildest harangues, not only in those earliest days, when he struck terror into the aristocrats, but afterwards, too, when he came to be afraid of them.

For the sake of less learned critics, "men of a duller Muse," as the saying goes, I should like to remove all doubts as to the usefulness of the study of music.

29. Surely they will admit that the budding orator must read the poets. But surely this is not possible without some knowledge of music? Even if one is blind enough mentally to be doubtful about other kinds of poetry, the necessity will at least be admitted in the case of the lyrical poets. This argument would require to be developed, if I were advocating this as a new study.

30. But since it has been recognized from early times, from the days of Chiron and Achilles right down to our own, amongst all who have not shirked the normal course of education, it is not for me to cast doubts upon its value by too anxious a defense.

31. It will, I believe, be sufficiently clear from the examples just quoted what sort of music I approve and to what extent, but still I think I ought to declare even more explicitly that I do not recommend the music of the modern stage, effeminate as it is and feeble in its wanton measures, a type of music which has gone far towards robbing us of any manly vigor that still remained in our midst; what I recommend is the music in which the praises of brave men were sung and in which brave men sang themselves in days gone by. Nor would I have my pupils play upon those psalteries and lutes which no modest maiden would ever handle, but I wish them to acquire a knowledge of those laws of harmony, which are so useful in stirring and in soothing the emotions.

32. It is recorded that once when certain youths had been worked up to the point of assaulting with violence a respectable home, Pythagoras bade the musician change her strain to a slow spondaic measure, and in that way succeeded in calming their passions. Chrysippus, too, assigns a tune of an appropriate character to the lullaby sung by nurses to soothe young children.

33. There is also a theme for declamation in the schools, invented with considerable ingenuity, in which a flute-player figures, who had played a Phrygian tune to a priest at a sacrifice and when the priest was driven mad and threw himself over a cliff, was brought to trial as being responsible for his death. Now if such a case is worthy of a pleader's skill and if it cannot be handled without a knowledge of music, how can even the most unfriendly critics fail to admit that his art too is necessary for our purpose?

St. Augustine
Confessions

Aurelius Augustinus was born in 354 A.D. in what is now Algeria. He received a Roman education, and then was sent to Carthage to study rhetoric. Later, he became a teacher of rhetoric at Carthage, Rome, and Milan. During his youth he was a pagan and lived a dissolute life. He had strong feelings of guilt and was ready to reform when he came under the influence of St. Ambrose and read Christian literature. In 387 he converted to Christianity. He was ordained to the priesthood in 392. In 396 he founded a monastery in Hippo (Algeria), and in 396 became bishop of Hippo. He died in 430 during the sacking of Hippo by the Vandals.

Augustine was a prolific writer and had germinal influence on Christianity. It was he who developed the intellectual framework that allowed Christianity to become the predominant European religion. He wrote on a wide variety of subjects, and although his attention to education was a relatively minor part of his total effort, his thoughts influenced European education throughout the Middle Ages. During that time education was, for the most part, a function of the church rather than of the secular state.

Augustine's educational beliefs are revealed in *De Magisero* (*The Teacher*), but it is his thoughts on music and his reaction to it that are of central interest here. In the *Confessions* he discusses several aspects of the weakness of the flesh, one of which is music. The following excerpts reveal his belief concerning the function of music and the danger that it represented to the devout Christian.

Book 10: Chapter XXXIII

The pleasures of the ear did indeed draw me and hold me more tenaciously, but You have set me free. Yet still when I hear those airs, in which Your words breathe life, sung with sweet and measured voice, I do, I admit, find a certain satisfaction in them, yet not such as to grip me too close, for I can depart when I will. Yet in that that they are received into me along with the truths which give them life such airs seek in my heart a place of no small honour, and I find it hard to know what is their due place. At times indeed it seems to me that I am paying them greater honor than is their due— when, for example, I feel that by those holy words my mind is kindled more religiously and fervently to a flame of piety because I hear them sung than if they were not sung: and I observe that all the varying emotions of my spirit have modes proper to them in voice and song, whereby, by some secret affinity, they are made more alive. It is not good that the mind should be enervated by this bodily pleasure. But it often ensnares me, in that the bodily sense does not accompany the reason as following after it in proper order, but having been admitted to aid the reason, strives to run before and take the lead. In this matter I sin unawares, and then grow aware.

Yet there are times when through too great a fear of this temptation, I err in the direction of over-severity—even to the point sometimes of wishing that the melody of all the lovely airs with which David's Psalter is commonly sung should be banished not only from my own ears, but from the Church's as well: and that seems to me a safer course, which I remember often to have heard told of Athanasius, bishop of Alexandria, who had the reader of the psalm utter it with so little modulation of the voice that he seemed to be saying it rather than singing it. Yet when I remember the tears I shed, moved by the songs of the Church in the early days of my new faith: and again when I see that I am moved not by the singing but by the things that are sung—when they are sung with a clear voice and proper modulation—I recognize once more the usefulness of this practice.

The Middle Ages

T he Roman Empire had ruled much of Europe, and its downfall signaled the beginning of the Middle Ages. It was a time of withdrawal from the greater world by the regions of Europe that had been part of the Roman Empire, and it is indicative of the slowdown of progress that Boethius's work, which summarized the musical practices of the past, became the accepted text on music for centuries to follow. During this long period Christianity continued to spread and to gain strength. This was also the time when civil and religious authority were amalgamated, as exemplified by the excerpts from Charlemagne's edict. His pronouncement indicates the influence of Christianity on him and his empire, and the importance of music in Christian education.

Boethius
De Institutione Musica, Book I

Boethius, Roman statesman and scholar, was born in Rome about 480 A.D. He became consul in 510, and then counselor to the Emperor Theodoric. Boethius summarized ancient Greek thought on music in his *De Institutione Musica* (*The Principles of Music*), in which he described the Pythagorian unity of mathematics and music and the Platonic concept of the relationship between music and society. Liberal higher education in the time of Boethius and during the Middle Ages and the Renaissance consisted principally of two bodies of studies: the trivium (grammar, rhetoric, and logic) and the quadrivium (arithmetic, geometry, astronomy, and music). The term *quadrivium* was introduced by Boethius in his *De Institutione Musica*, the major musical treatise of its time, which remained the principal source of information about music as a mathematical subject for over a millennium. It was used as a text at Oxford University as late as the eighteenth century.

Introduction: That music is related to us by nature, and that it can ennoble or debase our character.

. . . When we compare that which is coherently and harmoniously joined together in sound—that is, that which gives us pleasure—so we come to recognize that we ourselves are united according to this same principle of similarity. For similarity is pleasing, whereas dissimilarity is unpleasant and contrary.

From this same principle radical changes in one's character also occur. A lascivious mind takes pleasure in the more lascivious modes or is often softened and moved upon hearing them. On the other hand, a more violent mind finds pleasure in the more exciting modes or will become excited when it hears them. This is the reason that the musical modes were named after certain peoples, such as the Lydian mode, and the Phrygian mode; for the modes are named after the people that find pleasure in them. A people will find pleasure in a mode resembling its own character, and thus a sensitive people cannot be united by or find pleasure in a severe mode, nor a severe people in a sensitive mode. But, as has been said, similarity causes love and pleasure. Thus Plato held that we should be extremely cautious in this matter, lest some change in music of good moral character should occur. He also said that there is no greater ruin for the morals of a community than the gradual perversion of a prudent and modest music. For the minds of those hearing the perverted music immediately submit to it, little by little depart from their character, and retain no vestige of justice or honesty. This will occur if either the lascivious modes bring something immodest into the minds of the people or if the more violent modes implant something warlike and savage.

For there is no greater path whereby instruction comes to the mind than through the ear. Therefore when rhythms and modes enter the mind by this path, there can be no doubt that they affect and remold the mind into their own character. This fact can be recognized in various peoples. For those peoples which have a more violent nature delight in the more severe modes of the Thracians. Gentler peoples, on the other hand, delight in more moderate modes, although in these times this almost never occurs. Indeed today the human race is lascivious and effeminate, and thus it is entertained totally by the representational and theatrical modes. Music was prudent and modest when it was performed on simple instruments; but since it has come to be performed in various ways with many changes, it has lost its mode of gravity and virtue, and having almost fallen into a state of disgrace, it preserves almost nothing of its ancient splendor. For this reason Plato prescribed that boys must not be trained in all modes but only in those which are vigorous and simple. Moreover, it should be especially remembered that if some melody or mode is altered in some way, even if this alteration is only the slightest change, the fresh change will not be immediately noticed; but after some time it will cause a great difference and will sink down through the ears into the soul itself. Thus Plato held that the state ought to see that only music of the highest moral character and prudence be composed, and that it should be modest, simple, and masculine, rather than effeminate, violent, or fickle.

. . . There can be no doubt that the unity of our body and soul seems to be somehow determined by the same proportions that join together and unite the harmonious inflections of music, as our subsequent discussion will demonstrate. Hence it happens that sweet melodies even delight infants, whereas a harsh and rough sound will interrupt their pleasure. Indeed this reaction to various types of music is experienced by both sexes, and by people of all ages; for although they may differ in their actions, they are nevertheless united as one in the pleasure of music . . . and someone who cannot sing particularly well will nevertheless sing to himself, not because it is pleasant for him to hear what he sings but because it is a delight to express certain inward pleasures which originate in the soul, regardless of the manner in which they are expressed. . . . It appears to be beyond doubt that music is so naturally a part of us that we cannot be without it, even if we so wished.

For this reason the power of the mind ought to be directed toward fully understanding by knowledge what is inherent in us through nature. Thus just as erudite scholars are not satisfied by merely seeing colors and forms without also investigating their properties, so musicians should not be satisfied by merely finding pleasure in music without knowing by what musical proportions these sounds are put together. . . .

Charlemagne
Admonitio generalis: 70, 72, 80

As ruler of the Carolingian Empire, Charlemagne's (727–814) lands encompassed what are now Belgium, Holland, France, Switzerland, and large portions of Italy, western Germany, and Spain. He took it upon himself to reverse the decline in education in monastaries and abbeys, where the sons of nobility were taught. The members of the clergy were required to prepare themselves to teach and to establish schools in which would be taught reading, writing, music, arithmetic, grammar, and religious doctrines. The following excerpt is part of a proclamation by Charlemagne.

70. To priests: That bishops, throughout their jurisdictions, diligently examine the priests, as to their orthodoxy, their [way] of baptizing and celebrating Mass; that they may hold to the true faith and follow the Catholic form of baptism; to find out if they understand the Mass prayers well; if they chant the Psalms devoutly, and according to the proper division of the verses; if they themselves understand the Lord's Prayer, and impart an explanation of it to all, so that every one will know what he is asking of

God; that the Gloria Patri be sung with all honor by every one; that the priest himself, together with the holy angels, and the people of God, sing the Sanctus, Sanctus, Sanctus all together. . . .

72. That there should be schools for boys who can read. The Psalms, the notation, the chants, and arithmetic and grammar [ought to be taught] in all monasteries and episcopacies. Correct the Catholic books carefully; because it often happens that while they rightly wish to ask something of God, they make a bad prayer by reason of uncorrected books. And do not permit your students to spoil [the text] either in reading or in writing. If there be need of copying a new Gospel book, or Psalter, or Missal, have grown men write them out with all care. . . .

80. To all clerics: That they should learn the Roman chant thoroughly, and employ it in the correct manner at the night Office and the day Office [which includes the Mass], just as our royal father, King Pippin, decreed when he suppressed the Frankish chant, out of unanimity with the Holy See and peaceful concord in the Church of God.

St. Odo of Cluny
Enchiridion musices

Odo of Cluny was canon and a choir singer at St. Martin of Tours and later served as abbott in French monasteries. He became head of the abbey of Cluny in 927. *Enchiridion musices* presents the first systematic use of letters to represent pitches, a practice that became standard in the Middle Ages.

Prologue

You have insistently requested, beloved brothers, that I should communicate to you a few rules concerning music, these to be only a sort which boys and simple persons may understand and by means of which, with God's help, they may quickly attain to perfect skill in singing. You asked this, having yourselves seen and heard and by sure evidence verified that it could be done. For indeed, being stationed among you, with God's help alone I taught certain actual boys and youths by means of this art so that some after three days, others after four days, and one after a single week of training in it, were able to learn several antiphons and in a short time to sing them without hesitation, not hearing them sung by anyone, but contenting themselves simply with a copy written according to the rules. With the passage of not many days they were singing at first sight and extempore and without a fault anything written in music, something which until now ordinary singers had never been able to do, many continuing to practice and study singing for fifty years without profit.

When you were earnestly and diligently inquiring whether our doctrines would be of value for all melodies, taking as my helper a certain brother who seemed perfect in comparison with other singers, I investigated the Antiphoner of the blessed Gregory, in which I found that nearly all things were regularly set down. A few things, corrupted by unskilled singers, were corrected, both on the evidence of other singers and by the authority of the rules. But in the longer melodies, beloved brothers, we found sounds belonging to the high modes and excessive ascents and descents, contrary to the rule. Yet, since universal usage agreed in defending these melodies, we did not presume to emend them. We noted them as unusual, however, in order that no one inquiring into the truth of the rule might be left in doubt.

This done, you were kindled by a greater desire and insisted, with vehement entreaties and urgings, not only that rules should be made, but also that the whole Antiphoner should be written in useful notes and with the formulas of the tones, to the honor of God and of His Most Holy Mother Mary, in whose venerable monastery these things were being done.

Deriving confidence, therefore, from your entreaties, and complying with the orders of our common father, I am neither willing nor able to discontinue this work. For among the learned of this age the doctrine of this art is very difficult and extensive. Let therefore whoever pleases cultivate the field further with unwilling labor and wall it in. He who of himself perceives this little gift of God will be satisfied with a simple fruit.

Later European Views

The history of Europe from the time of Martin Luther best makes evident the value that Western cultures and societies have placed on music. Philosophers, churchmen, politicians, educators, and others whom we recognize as historically significant figures have left testimony of why their people needed to be musically educated. In some cases, even the method of music education was prescribed. Many of the reasons for the strong European musical cultures that exist today can be found in these readings.

Frank Ll. Harrison
Music Education for Religious Conversion

One of the historic purposes served by music education is religious conversion, clearly seen in the practices of the Spanish conquerors of Mexico. The Spanish, wishing to replace the indigenous native culture with their own, desired to make the Indians more subservient to the civil and religious authority of Spain.

Throughout the sixteenth century music served as a valuable tool in the cultural encounters and peaceful exploration of the Americas. It was the task of those entrusted with this work to explore and define the geographical and social nature of the territory concerned and devise a workable strategy for changing the culture of its inhabitants into one more closely corresponding to that of the European explorers. . . .

No less important were the contributions of Pedro de Gante, whose school in Texcoco . . . was the first designed to teach European culture to the Aztecs. Gante stressed music as an important component of the curriculum. In his *Historia* Motolinía added the names of Arnaldo de Basaccio and the aged Juan Caro to that of the Netherlander Pedro de Gante (Ghent), for all three men were central to the teaching of European music in Mexico.

Studying this early stage of Christian missionary work, we can discern two attitudes toward music: one adopted by the secular clergy, the other by the religious orders. Juan de Zumárraga, the first Franciscan bishop of Mexico City, from 1528 to 1548, was keenly aware of the power of music. In a letter dated April 17, 1540, he wrote, "Indians are great lovers of music, and the religious who hear their confessions tell us that they are converted more by music than by preaching, and we can see they come from distant regions to hear it." This aspect of the process of encounter involved integral transference of the whole apparatus of Spanish church music to New Spain. Initially, indigenous, mission-trained people participated in this transference, especially in the western provinces. But gradually, they were marginalized by the *encuentro*, and the process of European musical transmission rested entirely with Spanish immigrants.

. . . Bernardino de Sahagún's most striking production was his *Psalmodia Cristiana Mexicana, ordenada en cantares o psalmos, para que cantan los Indios en los areytos que hacen en las Eglesias*, printed in 1583 in Mexico City. This work documented the other side of peaceful exploration—penetration and transformation of native musical culture. A key to this process is another tome written in Spanish and Nahuatl, *Historia general de las cosas de Nueva España*, in which Sahagún linked music, the Nahuatl language, and Christian doctrine and ritual. . . .

Martin Luther
Luther on Education: Studies and Methods

Martin Luther was born in 1483 in Eisleben, Germany. Although ordained a priest, his theological beliefs deviated from the accepted theology of the Catholic Church and in 1517 he posted his *Ninety-five Theses*, signaling the beginning of the Protestant Reformation. Luther loved music and was an accomplished flutist and lutenist. Believing that music exerted a beneficial influence on one's character, he valued music education and felt that teachers should be musicians. Luther influenced Germany's musical culture by popularizing church music, much of which he wrote himself, and the schools that were established under his influence included music as part of the curriculum.

Satan is a great enemy to music. It is a good antidote against temptation and evil thoughts. The devil does not stay long where it is practiced.

Music is the best cordial to a person in sadness; it soothes, quickens, and refreshes his heart.

Music is a semi-disciplinarian and school-master; it makes men more gentle and tender-hearted, more modest and discreet.

I have always loved music. He that is skilled in this art is possessed of good qualities, and can be employed in anything. Music must of necessity be retained in the schools. A school-master must be able to sing, otherwise I will hear nothing of him.

Music is a delightful, noble gift of God, and nearly related to theology. I would not give what little skill I possess in music for something great. The young are to be continually exercised in this art; it makes good and skillful people of them.

With those that despise music, as all fanatics are wont to do, I am not pleased; for music is a gift bestowed by God and not by man. So it also banishes Satan, and renders men joyful; it causes men to forget all wrath, uncharity, pride, and other vices. Next to theology, I esteem and honor music. And we see how David and all the saints clothed their pious thoughts in verses, rhymes, and songs; because in times of peace music rules.

Preface to Georg Rhau's Symphoniae incundae

Luther's best known statement about music is the preface to the *Symphoniae incundae* (*Delightful Symphonies*) of 1538. Here, the word *symphony* means any music for several vocal or instrumental parts. Georg Rhau was a printer in Wittenberg who was also a musician and composer. A follower of Luther, he made important contributions to the young Lutheran church by publishing twelve collections of music for the Lutheran church. *Symphoniae incundae* was the first.

Greetings in Christ! I would certainly like to praise music with all my heart as the excellent gift of God which it is and to commend it to everyone. But I am so overwhelmed by the diversity and magnitude of its virtue and benefits that I can find neither beginning nor end or method for my discourse. As much as I want to commend it, my praise is bound to be wanting and inadequate.

. . . It was not without reason that the fathers and prophets wanted nothing else to be associated as closely with the Word of God as music. Therefore, we have so many hymns and Psalms where message and music join to move the listener's soul, while in other living beings and [sounding] bodies music remains a language without words. After all, the gift of language combined with the gift of song was only given to man to let him know that he should praise God with both word and music, namely, by proclaiming [the Word of God] through music and by providing sweet melodies with words. For even a comparison between different men will show how rich and manifold our glorious Creator proves Himself in distributing the gifts of music, how much men differ from each other in voice and manner of speaking so that one amazingly excels the other. No two men can be found with exactly the same voice and manner of speaking,

Martin Luther

although they often seem to imitate each other, the one as it were being the ape of the other.

But when [musical] learning is added to all this and artistic music which corrects, develops, and refines the natural music, then at last it is possible to taste with wonder (yet not to comprehend) God's absolute and perfect wisdom in His wondrous work of music. Here it is most remarkable that one single voice continues to sing the tenor, while at the same time many other voices play around it, exulting and adorning it in exuberant strains and, as it were, leading it forth in a divine roundelay, so that those who are the least bit moved know nothing more amazing in this world. But any who remain unaffected are unmusical indeed and deserve to hear a certain filthy poet or the music of the pigs.

But the subject is much too great for me briefly to describe all its benefits. And you, my young friend, let this noble, wholesome, and cheerful creation of God be commended to you. By it you may escape shameful desires and bad company. At the same time you may by this creation accustom yourself to recognize and praise the Creator. Take special care to shun perverted minds who prostitute this lovely gift of nature and of art with their erotic rantings; and be quite assured that none but the devil goads them on to defy their very nature which would and should praise God its Maker with this gift, so that these bastards purloin the gift of God and use it to worship the foe of God, the enemy of nature and of this lovely art. Farewell in the Lord.

John Calvin
Commentaries: Ethics and the Common Life

John Calvin (1509–1564), French Protestant reformer, theologian, and educator, was born a Catholic but taught Lutheran doctrine and opposed the Catholic church. He fled France and eventually settled in Geneva, Switzerland, where he established himself as a political, religious, and educational leader. Calvin taught that the church should control education. His curriculum included the vernacular, the Bible, arithmetic, reading French, Latin, and Greek, rhetoric, logic, elocution, and music.

. . . Although the invention of the lyre and of other musical instruments serves our enjoyment and our pleasures rather than our needs, it ought not on that account to be judged of no value; still less should it be condemned. Pleasure is to be condemned only when it is not combined with reverence for God and not related to the common welfare of society. But music by its nature is adapted to rouse our devotion to God and to aid the well-being of man; we need only avoid enticements to shame, and empty entertainments which keep men from better employments and are simply a waste of time.

Richard Mulcaster
The Elementaire

Richard Mulcaster (1530–1611) was the headmaster of the Merchant Taylor's School of London, of which the poet Edmund Spenser was a graduate. He believed that the education of children should be carried out in accordance with the child's interests and abilities, and that the curriculum should include music. He also believed in the development of good health and intellectual capacities, universal education, and instruction in English (much instruction at that time was in Latin). Mulcaster's ideas influenced other educators in Europe and America, and the Boston Latin Grammar School, the oldest public school in the United States (founded in 1635), reflected his educational aims and ideals.

. . . As for knowledge, whereby to encrease the childes understanding, that is assigned to the teacher alone, as proper to his office without participation of anie parent, tho a wise and a learned parent be the verie best part of the verie best teacher. . . . I ented to handle all those things which young children are to learn of right, and maie learn at ease, if their parents will be carefull, a little more then ordinarie. The thinges be five in number, infinite in use, principles in place, and these in name, *reading, writing, drawing, singing,* and *playing.* . . .

. . . When the childe shall have the matter of his *Reading,* which is his first principle so well proined and so pikked, as it shall catechise him in relligion trewlie, frame him in opinion rightlie, fashion him in behavior civillie, and withall contain in som few leaves the greatest varietie of most syllabs, the chefe difference of most words, the sundrie pronouncing of all parts, and branches of everie period, doth not *Reading* then which is the first principle seme to season verie sure? enriching the minde with so precious matter, and furnishing the tung with so perfit an utterance? When the argument of the childes *Copie,* and the direction of his hand, whereby he learns to write shalbe answerable to his reading, for choice of good matter, and reverence to young yeares, neither shall offer anie thing to the eie, but that maile beawtifie the minde, and will deserve memorie, will not *uniting* season well, which so useth the hand, as it helpeth to all good? When the *pen* and *pencil* shalbe restrained to those draughts, which serve for present semelinesse, and more cunning to com on, for the verie necessarie uses of all our hole life, doth not that same liquor, wherewith theie draw so, deserve verie good liking, which will not draw at all but where vertew bids draw? When *Musik* shall teach nothing, but honest for delite, and pleasant for note, comlie for the place, and semelie for the person, sutable to the thing, and serviceable to circumstance, can that humor corrupt, which bredeth such delite, being so everiewhere armed against just chalenge, of either blame or misliking? . . .

John Amos Comenius
On Education

John Amos Comenius (1592–1670) was born in Bohemia to a family that belonged to the Protestant sect called the Brethren of Unity. His life was a series of tragedies caused by the plague and the persecution of Protestants by Ferdinand of Austria. A minister and an educator, Comenius's purpose was to reform society to bring about harmony among Christians. He wrote several books that influenced education in Europe, America, and Asia. *The Gate of Languages Unlocked* went through 106 editions, eighty of them during his lifetime. There were 116 editions of *The World Through Sense Pictures*, the last nine in the twentieth century.

School of Infancy: Activity and Expression 10, 11, 12

10. Music is especially natural to us; for as soon as we see the light we immediately sing the song of paradise, thus recalling to our memory our fall, A, a! E, e! I maintain that complaint and wailing are our first music, from which it is impossible to restrain infants; and if it were possible, it would be inexpedient, since it contributes to their health; for as long as other exercises and amusements are wanting, by this very means their chests and other internal parts relieve themselves of their superfluities. External music begins to delight children at two years of age; such as singing, rattling, and striking of musical instruments. They should therefore be indulged in this, so that their ears and minds may be soothed by concord and harmony.

11. In the third year the sacred music of daily use may be introduced; namely, that received as a custom to sing before and after dinner, and when prayers are begun or ended. On such occasions they ought to be present, and to be accustomed to attend and conduct themselves composedly. It will also be expedient to take them to public worship, where the whole assembly unites in singing the praises of God. In the fourth year it is possible for some children to sing of themselves; the slower ones, however, ought not

to be forced, but permitted to have a whistle, a drum, or pipes, so that by whistling, drumming, and piping they may accustom their ears to the perceptions of various sounds, or even to imitate them. In the fifth year it will be time to open their mouths in hymns and praises to God, and to use their voices for the glory of their Creator.

12. These things parents, in singing or playing with children, may easily instill into their minds; the memory is now more enlarged and apt than previously, and will, with greater ease and pleasure, imbibe a larger number of things in consequence of the rhythm and melody. The more verses they commit to memory, the better will they be pleased with themselves, and the glory of God be largely promoted. Blessed is the home where voices resound with music.

The Great Didactic

Sketch of the Mother School

1. It is when it first comes into being that a tree puts forth the shoots that are later on to be its principal branches, and it is in this first school that we must plant in a man the seeds of all the knowledge with which we wish him to be equipped in his journey through life. A brief survey of the whole of knowledge will show the possibility of this, and this survey can easily be made if we bring everything under twenty headings. . . .

17. (xvi.) They will take their first steps in music by learning easy hymns and psalms. This exercise should form part of their daily devotions.

Sketch of the Vernacular School

. . . We may define the Vernacular School as follows. The aim and object of the Vernacular School should be to teach to all the young, between the ages of six and twelve, such things as will be of use to them throughout their whole lives. That is to say:

(i.) To read with ease both print and writing in their mother-tongue.

(ii.) To write, first with accuracy, then with speed, and finally with confidence, in accordance with the grammatical rules of the mother-tongue. These rules should be written in a popular form, and the boys should be exercised in them.

(iii.) To count, with ciphers and with counters, as far as is necessary for practical purposes.

(iv.) To measure spaces, such as length, breadth, and distance, with skill.

(v.) To sing well-known melodies, and, in the case of those who display especial aptitude, to learn the elements of advanced music.

(vi.) To learn by heart the greater number of the psalms and hymns that are used in the country. For, if brought up in the praise of God, they will be able (as the Apostle says) to exhort one another with psalms and hymns and spiritual songs, singing to God from their hearts. . . .

John Locke
Some Thoughts Concerning Education

John Locke was born in Wrington, England, in 1632. He was a philosopher who, being charged with educating children of the nobility, found current educational practices unsatisfactory. Locke's close friend, Edward Clarke, requested his advice on the education of his son. Locke obliged with a series of letters written between 1684 and 1691 from Holland, where he was living at the time. Upon his return to England he published the letters, which served as the basis of his book, *Some Thoughts Concerning Education* (1693).

196. Besides what is to be had from Study and Books, there are other Accomplishments necessary for a Gentleman, to be got by Exercise, and to which Time is to be allowed, and for which Masters must be had. *Dancing* being that which gives *graceful Motions* all the Life, and above all things Manliness, and a becoming Confidence to young Children, I think it cannot be learned too early, after they are once of an Age and Strength capable of it. But you must be sure to have a good Master, that knows, and can teach, what is graceful and becoming, and what gives a Freedom and Easiness to all the Motions of the Body. . . .

197. *Musick* is thought to have some Affinity with Dancing, and a good Hand upon some Instruments is by many People mightily valued. But it wastes so much of a young Man's Time to gain but a moderate Skill in it; and engages often in such odd Company, that many think it much better spared: And I have amongst Men of Parts and Business so seldom heard any one commended or esteemed for having an Excellency in *Musick*, that amongst all those things that ever came into the List of Accomplishments, I think I may give it the last Place. Our short lives will not serve us for the Attainment of all Things; nor can our Minds be always intent on something to be learned.

Letter to Edward Clarke

. . . Music I find by some mightily valued, but it wastes so much of one's time to gain but a moderate skill in it, and engages in such odd company, that I think it much better spared. And amongst all those things that ever come into the list of accomplishments, I give it next to poetry the last place. Our short lives will not serve us for the attainment of all things; nor can our minds be always intent on something to be learnt. The weakness of our constitution, both of mind and body, requires that we should be often unbent; and he that will make a good use of any part of his life must allow a large portion of it to recreation. At least this must not be denied to young people unless, whilst you with too much haste make them old, you have the displeasure to see them in their graves or a second childhood sooner than you could wish. And therefore I think that the time and pains allotted to serious improvements should be employed about things of most use and consequence, and that, too, in the methods the most easy and short that could be at any rate obtained, and perhaps it would be none of the least secret in education to make the exercises of the body and the mind the recreation one to another. I doubt not but something might be done by a prudent man, that would well consider the temper and inclination of his pupil; for he that is wearied, either with study or dancing, does not desire presently to go to sleep, but to do something else which may divert and delight him. But this must be always remembered, that nothing can come into the account of recreation that is not done with delight.

Concerning dancing I have (as you know already) a quite other opinion than of music, it being that which gives graceful motions all the life and above all things, manliness, and a becoming confidence to children. I think it cannot be learnt too early, after they are once of an age and strength capable of it. But you must be sure to have a good master that knows and can teach what is graceful and becoming, and what gives a freedom and easiness to all the motions of the body. One that teaches not this is worse than none at all, natural unfashionableness being much better than apish, affected postures; and I think it much more passable to put off the hat and make a leg like an honest country gentleman than like an ill-fashioned dancing master. For as for the jigging part and the figures of dances, I count that little or nothing. . . .

Johann Heinrich Pestalozzi
Letter to Greaves: Training of Eye and Ear Music in Education

Johann Heinrich Pestalozzi was born in Zurich, Switzerland, in 1746. His goal as an educator was to elevate the lowly condition of the common people, peasants in the feudal society that still existed in Switzerland. He devised an educational program that would give dignity and self-respect to the people. Imported to America by several educators, the Pestalozzian method of education was influential in changing education in the New World. Because of Pestalozzi's influence, American schools introduced into the curriculum geography, music, art, and gymnastics. The teaching of arithmetic and reading were revolutionized, and corporal punishment became less prevalent. Pestalozzi was friendly with an Englishman named J. P. Greaves, who was a student of the Pestalozzian method in Yverdon in 1817 and 1818. Pestalozzi wrote Greaves a series of letters the next year. They were translated and published in 1827.

. . . Early Training in: Esthetics

. . . It seems not to be sufficiently understood that good taste and good feelings are kindred to each other, and that they reciprocally confirm each other. Though the ancients have said that "to study those arts which are suited to a free-born mind soothes the character, and takes away the roughness of exterior manners," yet little has been done to give free access to those enjoyments or accomplishments to all, or even to the majority of the people. If it is not possible for them to give much of their attention to subordinate or ornamental pursuits, while so much of their time is taken up by providing for their first and necessary wants, still, this does not furnish a conclusive reason why they should be shut out altogether from every pursuit above the toil of their ordinary avocations.

Yet I know not a more gratifying scene than to see, as I have seen it among the poor, a mother spreading around her a spirit of silent but serene enjoyment, diffusing among her children a spring of better feelings, and setting the example of removing everything that might offend the taste— not, indeed, of a fastidious observer, but yet of one used to moving in another sphere. It is difficult to describe by what means this can be effected. But I have seen it under circumstances which did not promise to render it even possible. Of one thing I am certain, that it is only through the true spirit of maternal love that it can be obtained. That feeling, of which I cannot too frequently repeat that it is capable of an elevation to the standard of the very best feelings of human nature, is intimately connected with a happy instinct that will lead to a path equally remote from listlessness and indolence, as it is from artificial refinement. Refinement and fastidiousness may do much, if upheld by constant watchfulness; a nature, however, a truth, will be wanting; and even the casual observer will be struck with a restraint incompatible with an atmosphere of sympathy.

Music

Now that I am on the topic, I will not let the opportunity pass by without speaking of one of the most effective aids of moral education. You are aware that I mean Music; and you are not only acquainted with my sentiments on that subject, but you have also observed the very satisfactory results which we have obtained in our schools. The exertions of my excellent friend Hans Georg Nägeli, who has with equal taste and judgment reduced the highest principles of his art to the simplest elements, have enabled us to bring our children to a proficiency which, on any other plan, must be the work of much time and labor.

National Songs

But it is not the proficiency which I would describe as a desirable accomplishment in education. It is the marked and most beneficial influence of music on the feelings, which I have always thought and always observed to be most efficient in preparing or attuning, as it were, the mind for the best of impressions. The exquisite harmony of a superior performance, the studied elegance of the execution, may indeed give satisfaction to a connoisseur; but it is the simple and untaught grace of melody which speaks to the heart of every human being. Our own national melodies, which have since time immemorial been resounding in our native valleys, are fraught with reminiscences of the brightest page of our history, and of the most endearing scenes of domestic life. But the effect of music in education is not only to keep alive a national feeling: it goes much deeper; if cultivated in the right spirit, it strikes at the root of every bad or narrow feeling; of every ungenerous or mean prosperity, of every emotion unworthy of humanity. In saying so I might quote an authority which commands our attention on account of the elevated character and genius of the man from whom it proceeds. It is well known that there was not a more eloquent and warm advocate of the moral virtues of music than the venerable Luther. But though his voice has made itself heard, and is still held in the highest esteem among us, yet experience has spoken still louder, and more unquestionably to the truth of the proposition which he was among the first to vindicate. Experience has long since proved that a system proceeding upon the principle of sympathy would be imperfect, if it were to deny itself the assistance of that powerful means of the culture of the heart. Those schools, or those families in which music has retained the cheerful and chaste character which it is so important that it should preserve, have invariably displayed scenes of moral feeling, and consequently of happiness, which leave no doubt as to the intrinsic value of that art, which has sunk into neglect, or degenerated into abuse, only in the ages of barbarism or depravity.

I need not remind you of the importance of music in engendering and assisting the highest feelings of which man is capable. It is almost universally acknowledged that Luther has seen the truth, when he pointed out music, devoid of studied pomp and vain ornament, in its solemn and impressive simplicity, as one of the most efficient means of elevating and purifying genuine feelings of devotion.

We have frequently, in our conversations on this subject, been at a loss how to account for the circumstance that in your own country, though that fact is as generally acknowledged, yet music does not form a more prominent feature in general education. It would seem that the notion prevails, that it would require more time and application than can conveniently be bestowed upon it to make its influence extend also on the education of the people.

Now, I would appeal, with the same confidence as I would to yourself, to any traveler, whether he has not been struck with the facility, as well as the success, with which it is cultivated among us. Indeed, there is scarcely a village school throughout Switzerland, and perhaps there is none throughout Germany or Prussia, in which something is not done for an acquirement at least of the elements of music on the new and more appropriate plan.

This is a fact which it cannot be difficult to examine, and which it will be impossible to dispute; and I will conclude this letter by expressing the hope which we have been entertaining together, that this fact will not be overlooked in a country which has never been backward in suggesting or adopting improvement, when founded on facts and confirmed by experience.

Friedrich Froebel
The Education of Man: Chief Groups of Subjects of Instruction

Friedrich Wilhelm August Froebel was born in 1782 in Oberweissbach, Germany. He taught in a Pestalozzian school in Frankfurt from 1805 to 1807 and then became a private tutor for two years at Pestalozzi's Yverdon Institute. Later, he conducted educational experiments in Thuringia. Froebel organized and directed elementary and secondary schools in Switzerland between 1831 and 1836. It was during this period that he decided that the education of younger children needed his attention, and in 1837 he organized the first school for young children, which he named Kindergarten (children's garden). Froebel's work resulted in the development of kindergartens in the United States and many other countries. His educational theories are explained in his best-known work, *The Education of Man.*

D. Art and Objects of Art

84. If what has been said heretofore concerning the objective and central points, or axes, of human life is surveyed from a common point of view, human aims will present themselves under three aspects. There is either a ten-

dency to inward repose and life, or a tendency to the study and comprehension of the external, or a tendency to direct representation of the internal.

The first is the prevailing tendency of religion; the second, of the contemplation of nature; the third, of self-development and self-contemplation.

Similarly, it will be found that *mathematics* is concerned more with the representation of the external in the internal, with the representation of inner conformity to universal law, with the representation of nature in inner (human) terms. For this reason mathematics mediates between nature and man; it has reference more to the understanding.

Language is concerned more with the outward representation of inner perception, has reference more to reason. There is still wanting for the complete representation of his nature as a whole the representation of inner life as such, of the mind. This representation of the internal, of the inner man as such, is accomplished in *art*.

85. With one exception all human ideas are relative; mutual relations connect all ideas, and they are distinct only in their terminal points.

Therefore, there is in art, too, a side where it touches mathematics, the understanding; another where it touches the world of language, reason; a third where—although itself clearly a representation of the inner—it coincides with the representation of nature; and a fourth where it coincides with religion.

Yet all these relationships will have to be disregarded, when it is considered with reference to the education of man, in order to lead him to an appreciation of art. Here, art will be considered only in its ultimate unity as the pure representation of the inner. We notice at once that art, or the representation of inner life in art, must be differentiated in accordance with the material it uses.

Now, the material, as an earthly phenomenon, may be motion as such, but audible in sound, as tones which vanish while being produced; or it may be visible in lines, surfaces, and colors; or it may be corporeal, massive. Here, too, as in all actual things, there are, however, many transitions and combinations.

Art, as representation by tones, is music, particularly song. Art, as representation by color, is painting. Art, as representation by plastic material, is modeling. The last two are connected by drawing. This, however, may be considered simply as representation by lines, so that painting would appear as representation by surfaces, and modeling as representation by solids.

On account of the mediating quality of drawing, it appears very early as a phase in human development, and we noticed that even at an earlier stage children have the desire to draw . . . . Even the desire to express ideas by modeling and coloring is frequently found at this earlier stage of childhood, certainly at the very beginning of the stage of boyhood . . . .

This proves clearly that art and appreciation of art constitute a general capacity or talent of man, and should be cared for early, at the latest in boyhood.

This does not imply that the boy is to devote himself chiefly to art and is to become an artist; but that he should be enabled to understand and appreciate works of art. At the same time, a true scholastic education will be sure to guard him against the error of claiming to be an artist, unless there is in him the true artistic calling.

A universal and comprehensive plan of human education must, therefore, necessarily consider at an early period singing, drawing, painting, and modeling; it will not leave them to an arbitrary, frivolous whimsicalness, but treat them as serious objects of the school. Its intention will not be to make each pupil an artist in some one or all of the arts, but to secure to each human being full and all-sided development, to enable him to see man in the universality and all-sided energy of his nature, and, particularly, to enable him to understand and appreciate the products of true art.

Like drawing, but in a different respect, representation in rhythmic speech is mediatory. As representation of the ideal world in language, as the condensed representation, as it were, of the ethereal spiritual world of ideas, as the tranquil representation of absolute, eternally moving, and moved life, it belongs to art.

In everything, in life and religion, hence also in art, the ultimate and supreme aim is the clear representation of man as such. In its tendency, Christian art is the highest, for it aims to represent in everything, particularly in and through man, the eternally permanent, the divine. Man is the highest object of human art.

Thus, we have indicated in their totality the object, the aim, and the meaning of human life, as they are revealed even in the life of the boy as a scholar. It still remains to consider the sequences and connections in the development of successive phases of his nature at the scholastic stage, as well as the character, the order, and form of the instruction by which the school seeks to aid the boy in this development.

John Ruskin
On the Relation of National Ethics to National Arts

John Ruskin (1819–1900) was born in London. In his extensive writings, he developed the thesis that aesthetic achievement is based on morality. He said that only a good and well-intentioned man could create a true work of art, and that art is a universal language that speaks to all humanity, not just the con-

noisseur, because it is closely related to all aspects of civilization. The following excerpts are from a lecture presented at the Senate House, Cambridge, on
May 24, 1867.

. . . The proposition, then, which it will be my object to demonstrate in the
present lecture, is that, all Art being the Formative or directing Action of
Spirit, whatever character the spirit itself has must be manifested in the
Energy or Deed of it, and makes the deed itself Bad or Good. . . .

16. I pass to the next greatest art, that of Music. And as in this the relative science is of the highest complexity and interest, I must at once clear
the inquiry from such confusion as the introduction of questions relating to
science instead of art would otherwise cause. To every art there is, of
course, an attached positive science—to language, that of grammar; to
music, that of sound; to painting, that of colour; and to architecture, that of
dynamics. A right ethical state is necessary to the following out any of
these sciences completely, but the connection between morality of temper
and the power of ascertaining an abstract truth such, for instance, as the
relation of the pitch of notes to the length of the string, is not direct and
constant, whereas the connection between morality of temper and right
expression or creation in any of the arts is direct, the one being a function
of the other. It is therefore quite possible for a bad man to be a good gram-
marian, but never a good writer; he may be a good scientific musician,
never a good composer; he may be a dexterous disposer of colours, never a
good painter; and an ingenious builder, but never a good architect.

17. The want of a right ethical state in the investigation of what I may
perhaps be allowed to call the Art Sciences is, therefore, shown rather by a
disturbance of the due relation between the art and its science, than by
errors in the technical knowledge itself. The vanity and insensitiveness
which make knowledge too prominent, or the indolence and want of self-
command which shrink from the labour necessary to acquire it, are both
forms of one and the same egotism, and continually disgrace an art which
otherwise might have been admirable, by the insolent display, or the
equally insolent defect, of disciplined skill. But I shall not confuse the
immediate subject of our inquiry with any investigation of these modes of
technical vice. I suppose in every case the artist to be well trained and duly
informed; and so perfect a master of his science as not to be moved to the
display of it by his vanity; and I confine myself wholly to the examination
of the effect of his ethical state on the forms of production to which he will
determine that such science is to be applied.

18. Now, Music rightly so called is the expression of the joy or grief of
noble minds for noble causes. The last clause of the definition is almost
redundant, for a noble mind does not truly rejoice or grieve but for a noble

cause. Nevertheless, in its encounter with accidents of base evil it is capable of an acute and mortifying pain which cannot be expressed by music; and in its attainment of the various lower forms of material good it may feel for a time great gladness of complacency, not properly expressible by music, so that I leave the second clause of the definition as in some sort necessary to its completeness. I say then that true music is the natural and necessary expression of a kingly, holy passion for a lofty cause; that, in proportion to the royalty and force of our personality, the nature and expression of its joy or suffering becomes measured, chastened, calm, and capable of interpretation only by the majesty of ordered, beautiful, and worded sound. Exactly in proportion to the degree in which we become narrow in the cause and conception of our passions, incontinent in the utterance of them, feeble of perseverance in them, sullied or shameful in the indulgence of them, their expression by musical sound becomes broken, mean, fatuitous, and at last impossible; the measured waves of the air of heaven will not lend themselves to expression of ultimate vice, it must be for ever sunk into discordance or silence. And since, as before stated, every work of right art has a tendency to reproduce the ethical state which first developed it, this, which of all arts is most directly ethical in origin, is also the most direct in power of discipline; the first, the simplest, the most effective of all instruments of moral instruction; while in the failure and betrayal of its functions, it becomes the subtlest aid of moral degradation.

19. I say failure rather than disease of function. For, strictly speaking, the distinction is not between good music and bad music, but between that which is and is not music. And so in all the other arts, strictly speaking, there is no such thing as bad sculpture or bad painting. There is only no sculpture and no painting. . . .

And the worst corruption of music in modern days is not in, as it might at first be supposed, the exaltation of a dangerous sentiment by faithful sound, as in the hymn of the Marseillaise, but it is the idle and sensual seeking for pleasure in the sound only, without any true purpose of sentiment at all, and often without the slightest effort to discern the composer's intention, or understand the relation in a master's work between the syllable and the note. There is no harm but a real discipline in the purposeful expression of any sentiment which can be set to noble sound. But there is infinite harm in an idle and wanton catching of pleasant cadences with only foolish meaning in them, or none. . . .

20. There is, however, a more subtle form of error in musical indulgence, which is that mythically expressed by the Greeks in the contest of the Sirens with the Muses, and with Orpheus, and which is also in the mind of Plato through all the discussion respecting the two modes of harmony in the *Laws*. . . . Many people imagine that when they are drawn by their

delight in the higher forms of musical composition to withdraw themselves for a time from common life and solemnize their hearts by hearing sacred words beautifully sung, there is, at least in the degree in which their true sympathies may be excited, a gain to their moral character. Nay, many of them would probably assure us, and with perfect truth, that they distinctly felt themselves morally stronger and purer after such pleasure. But that greater strength of the soul, though actual and undeniable for the time, is a dearly purchased gain; it is just what the increase of strength by over-exciting stimulant is to the body, and the morbid and momentary increase of moral sentiment is necessarily followed by general dulness of the moral nerve. So far only, however, is this the case as we have completed the religious emotion that it may be a servant to our pleasure. There are doubtless persons so lovely and constant of soul that their profane life is artificial to them, and the sacred one natural; whose thoughts are always at home when at their Father's feet, and whose pure lips are then purest when they utter His name. These, through their inmost being, are incapable of any false delight; to them every pulse of accidental passion joins with and deepens the steady current of their life. But between these and the common hunter after pleasure in pathetic sensation, for whom the strain of the cathedral organ is made an interlude to the music of the ballet that he may excite his palled sensation by the alternate taste of sacred and profane, there is an infinite range of gradually lowered faculty and sincerity, receiving in proportion to the abasement of its temper injury from what, to the highest, brings only good. . . .

32. And even that slight clue we have quitted. There is an impression on the public mind that in order to recover national power in art, some knowledge of its practice should be diffused through the mass of the people.

Now what is really wanted is very nearly the reverse of this. It is not to teach the body of the nation to know something of art, but to teach the artists of the nation to know much of other things. It is not to give a *painter's* education to the populace, but to give a *gentleman's* education to the painter. We have seen that by an artist or painter I mean a person who has the special gift for creative work rooted in affectionateness, in love of justice, and in power of imagination. We must no longer permit the kindest, truest, and most inventive minds in the nation to be the worst educated; and while by their peculiar constitution they are impelled to devote themselves to the finer kinds of manual labour, we must endeavour by the strictest training to inform and influence them with the thoughts which that labour may most usefully express. To understand that the artist is one of the principal officers of public instruction, and to prepare our youth reverently for entrance into the church of painters, as we now prepare them for entrance [into the church of priests], is the first step to the making of art itself a means of popular education. Then there should be National Museums of Art giving authoritative presentation to the people of examples of good work and authoritative instruction in the indisputable methods of it. . .

Herbert Spencer
Literary Style and Music

The philosopher Herbert Spencer was born in Derby, England in 1820. He believed in the individual's preeminence over society and science's over religion. He advocated that government should do no more than necessary to protect the security of citizens and enforce legal contracts. His educational views were presented in four essays: "What Knowledge is of Most Worth," "Intellectual Education," "Moral Education," and "Physical Education." Spencer's thesis is that although all knowledge is of value, some is of greater importance. Spencer helped bring about profound change in English education by changing its focus from traditional humanistic education to a more utilitarian philosophy.

And now, what is the *function* of music? Has music any effect beyond the immediate pleasure it produces? Analogy suggests that it has. The enjoyments of a good dinner do not end with themselves, but minister to bodily well-being. Though people do not marry with a view to maintain the race, yet the passions which impel them to marry secure its maintenance. Parental affection is a feeling which, while it conduces to parental happiness, ensures the nurture of offspring. Men love to accumulate property, often without thought of the benefits it produces; but in pursuing the pleasure of acquisition they indirectly open the way to other pleasures. The wish for public approval impels all of us to do many things which we should otherwise not do—to undertake great labours, face great dangers, and habitually rule ourselves in ways that smooth social intercourse; so that in gratifying our love of approbation we subserve divers ulterior purposes. And generally our nature is such that, in fulfilling each desire, we in some way facilitate fulfilment of the rest. But the love of music seems to exist for its own sake. The delights of melody and harmony do not obviously minister to the welfare either of the individual or of society. May we not suspect, however, that this exception is apparent only? Is it not a rational inquiry, What are the indirect benefits which accrue from music, in addition to the direct pleasure it gives? . . .

Now the hypothesis which we have hinted above is, that beyond the direct pleasure which it gives, music has the indirect effect of developing this language of the emotions. Having its root, as we have endeavoured to show, in those tones, intervals, and cadences of speech which express feeling, arising by the combination and intensifying of these, and coming finally to have an embodiment of its own, music has all along been reacting upon speech, and increasing its power of rendering emotion. The use in recitative and song of inflections more expressive than ordinary ones, must from the beginning have tended to develop the ordinary ones. The complex musical phrases by which composers have conveyed complex emotions may rationally be supposed to influence us in making those involved cadences of conversation by which we convey our subtler thoughts and feelings. If the cultivation of music has any effect on the mind, what more natural effect is there than this of developing our perception of the meanings of qualities and modulations of voice, and giving us a correspondingly increased power of using them? Just as chemistry, arising out of the processes of metallurgy and the industrial arts and gradually growing into an independent study, has now become an aid to all kinds of production; just as physiology, originating from medicine and once subordinate to it, but latterly pursued for its own sake, is in our day coming to be the science on which the progress of medicine depends; so music, having its root in emotional language and gradually evolved from it, has ever been reacting upon and further advancing it. . . .

Probably most will think that the function here assigned to music is one of very little moment. But reflection may lead them to a contrary conviction. In its bearings upon human happiness, this emotional language which musical culture develops and refines is only second in importance to the language of the intellect; perhaps not even second to it. For these modifications of voice produced by feelings are the means of exciting like feelings in others. Joined with gestures and expressions of face, they give life to the otherwise dead words in which the intellect utters its ideas, and so enable the hearer not only to *understand* the state of mind they accompany, but to *partake* of that state. In short they are the chief media of sympathy. And if we consider how much both our general welfare and our immediate pleasures depend on sympathy, we shall recognize the importance of whatever makes this sympathy greater. If we bear in mind that by their fellow-feeling men are led to behave justly and kindly to one another; that the difference between the cruelty of the barbarous and the humanity of the civilized results from the increase of fellow-feeling; if we bear in mind that this faculty which makes us sharers in the joys and sorrows of others is the basis of all the higher affections; if we bear in mind how much our direct gratifications are intensified by sympathy—how at the theatre, the concert, the picture gallery, we lose half our enjoyment if we have no one to enjoy with us; we shall see that the agencies which communicate it can scarcely be overrated in value. The tendency of civilization is to repress the antagonistic elements of our characters and to develop the social ones; to curb our purely selfish desires and exercise our unselfish ones; to replace private gratifications by gratifications resulting from or involving the pleasures of others. And while by this adaptation to the social state the sympathetic side of our nature is being unfolded, there is simultaneously growing up a language of sympathetic intercourse—-a language through which we communicate to others the happiness we feel, and are made sharers in their happiness. This double process, of which the effects are already appreciable, must go on to an extent of which we can as yet have no adequate conception. The habitual concealment of our feelings become such as do not demand concealment, the exhibition of them will become more vivid than we now dare allow it to be; and this implies a more expressive emotional language. At the same time, feelings of higher and more complex kinds, as yet experienced only by the cultivated few, will become general, and there will be a corresponding development of the emotional language into more involved forms. Just as there has silently grown up a language of ideas which, rude as it at first was, now enables us to convey with precision the most subtle and complicated thoughts; so there is still silently growing up a language of feelings which, notwithstanding its present imperfection, we may expect will ultimately enable men vividly and completely to impress on each other the emotions which they experience from moment to moment.

Thus if, as we have endeavoured to show, it is the function of music to facilitate the development of this emotional language, we may regard music as an aid to the achievement of that higher happiness which it indistinctly shadows forth. Those vague feelings of unexperienced felicity which music arouses—those indefinite impressions of an unknown ideal life which it calls up—may be considered as a prophecy, the fulfillment of which music itself aids. The strange capacity which we have for being affected by melody and harmony may be taken to imply both that it is within the possibilities of our nature to realize those intenser delights they dimly suggest, and that they are in some way concerned in the realization of them. If so, the power and the meaning of music become comprehensible, but otherwise they are a mystery.

We will only add that if the probability of these corollaries be admitted, then music must take rank as the highest of the fine arts—as the one which, more than any other, ministers to human welfare. And thus, even leaving out of view the immediate gratifications it is hourly giving, we cannot too much applaud that musical culture which is becoming one of the characteristics of our age.

Education: Intellectual, Moral, and Physical— What Knowledge Is of Most Worth?

. . . The question which we contend is of such transcendent moment, is, not whether such or such knowledge is of worth, but what is its *relative* worth?

When they have named certain advantages which a given course of study has secured them, persons are apt to assume that they have justified themselves: quite forgetting that the adequateness of the advantages is the point to be judged. There is, perhaps, not a subject to which men devote attention that has not *some* value. . . .

. . . "But we that have but span-long lives" must ever bear in mind our limited time for acquisition. And remembering how narrowly this time is limited, not only by the shortness of life, but also still more by the business of life, we ought to be especially solicitous to employ what time we have to the greatest advantage. Before devoting years to some subject which fashion or fancy suggests, it is surely wise to weigh with great care the worth of the results, as compared with the worth of various alternative results which the same years might bring if otherwise applied.

In education, then, this is the question of questions, which it is high time we discussed in some methodic way. The first in importance, though the last to be considered, is the problem—how to decide among the conflicting claims of various subjects on our attention. Before there can be a rational *curriculum*, we must settle which things it most concerns us to know; or, to use a word of Bacon's, now unfortunately obsolete, we must determine the relative values of knowledges.

To this end, a measure of value is the first requisite. And happily, respecting the true measure of value, as expressed in general terms, there can be no dispute. Every one in contending for the worth of any particular order of information, does so by showing its bearing upon some part of life. . . .

How to live? That is the essential question for us. Not how to live in the mere material sense only, but in the widest sense. The general problem which comprehends every special problem is—the right ruling of conduct in all directions under all circumstances. In what way to treat the body; in what way to treat the mind; in what way to manage our affairs; in what way to bring up a family; in what way to behave as a citizen; in what way to utilize all those sources of happiness which nature supplies; how to use all our faculties to the greatest advantage of ourselves and others; how to live completely? And this being the great thing needful for us to learn, is, by consequence, the great thing which education has to teach. To prepare us for complete living is the function which education has to discharge; and the only rational mode of judging of any educational course is, to judge in what degree it discharges such function. . . .

Our first step must obviously be to classify, in the order of their importance, the leading kinds of activity which constitute human life. They may be naturally arranged into: 1. Those activities which directly minister to self-preservation; 2. Those activities which, by securing the necessaries of life, indirectly minister to self-preservation; 3. Those activities which have

Herbert Spencer

for their end the rearing and discipline of offspring; 4. those activities which are involved in the maintenance of proper social and political relations; 5. Those miscellaneous activities which make up the leisure part of life, devoted to the gratification of the tastes and feelings. . . .

And now we come to that remaining division of human life which includes the relaxations, pleasures, and amusements filling leisure hours. After considering what training best fits for self-preservation, for the obtainment of sustenance, for the discharge of parental duties, and for the regulation of social and political conduct; we have now to consider what training best fits for the miscellaneous ends not included in these—for the enjoyments of Nature, of Literature, and of the Fine Arts, in all their forms. Postponing them as we do to things that bear more vitally upon human welfare; and bringing everything, as we have, to the test of actual value; it will perhaps be inferred that we are included to slight these less essential things. No greater mistake could be made, however. We yield to none in the value we attach to aesthetic culture and its pleasures. Without painting, sculpture, music, poetry, and the emotions produced by natural beauty of every kind, life would lose half its charm. So far from thinking that the training and gratification of the tastes are unimportant, we believe the time will come when they will occupy a much larger share of human life than now. When the forces of Nature have been fully conquered to man's use; when the means of production have been brought to perfection; when labour has been economized to the highest degree; when education has been so systematized that a preparation for the more essential activities may be made with comparative rapidity; and when, consequently, there is a great increase of spare time; then will the poetry, both of Art and Nature, rightly fill a large space in the minds of all.

But it is one thing to admit that aesthetic culture is in a high degree conducive to human happiness; and another thing to admit that it is a fundamental requisite to human happiness. However important it may be, it must yield precedence to those kinds of culture which bear more directly upon the duties of life. As before hinted, literature and the fine arts are made possible by those activities which make individual and social life possible; and manifestly, that which is made possible, must be postponed to that which makes it possible. A florist cultivates a plant for the sake of its flower; and regards the roots and leaves as of value, chiefly because they are instrumental in producing the flower. But while, as an ultimate product, the flower is the thing to which everything else is subordinate, the florist very well knows that the root and leaves are intrinsically of greater importance; because on them the evolution of the flower depends. He bestows every care in rearing a healthy plant; and knows it would be folly if, in his anxiety to obtain the flower, he were to neglect the plant. Similarly in the case before us. Architecture, sculpture, painting, music, poetry, &c., may be truly called the efflorescence of civilized life. But even supposing them to be of such transcendent worth as to subordinate the civilized life out of which they grow (which can hardly be asserted), it will still be admitted that the production of a healthy civilized life must be the first consideration; and that the knowledge conducing to this must occupy the highest place.

And here we see most distinctly the vice of our educational system. It neglects the plant for the sake of the flower. In anxiety for elegance, it forgets substance. While it gives no knowledge conducive to self-preservation—while of knowledge that facilitates gaining a livelihood it gives but the rudiments, and leaves the greater part to be picked up any how in after life while for the discharge of parental functions it makes not the slightest provision—and while for the duties of citizenship it prepares by imparting a mass of facts, most of which are irrelevant, and the rest without a key; it is diligent in teaching every thing that adds to refinement, policy, and èclat. However fully we may admit that extensive acquaintance with modern languages is a valuable accomplishment, which through reading, conversation, and travel, aids in giving a certain finish; it by no means follows that this result is rightly purchased at the cost of that vitally important knowledge sacrificed to it. Supposing it true that classical education conduces to elegance and correctness of style; it cannot be said that elegance and correctness of style are comparable in importance to a familiarity with the principles that should guide the rearing of children. Grant that the taste may be greatly improved by reading all the poetry written in extinct languages; yet it is not to be inferred that such improvement of taste is equivalent in value to an acquaintance with the laws of health. Accomplishments, the fine arts, belles-lettres, and all those things which, as we say, constitute the efflorescence of civilization, would be wholly subordinate to that knowledge and discipline in which civilization rests. *As they occupy the leisure part of life, so should they occupy the leisure part of education.*

Recognising thus the true position of aesthetics, and holding that while the cultivation of them should form a part of education from its commencement, such cultivation should be subsidiary; we have not to inquire what knowledge is of most use to this end what knowledge best fits for this remaining sphere of activity. To this question the answer is still the same as heretofore. Unexpected as the assertion may be, it is nevertheless true, that the highest Art of every kind is based upon Science—that without Science there can be neither perfect production nor full appreciation. Science, in that limited technical acceptation current in society, may not have been possessed by many artists of high repute; but acute observers as they have been, they have always possessed a stock of those empirical generalizations which constitute science in its lowest phase; and they have habitually fallen far below perfection, partly because their generalizations were comparatively few and inaccurate. That science necessarily underlies the fine arts, becomes manifest, *a priori*, when we remember that art-products are all more or less representative of objective or subjective phenomena; that they can be true only in proportion as they conform to the laws of these phenomena; and that before they can thus conform the artist must know what these laws are. That this *a priori* conclusion tallies with experience we shall soon see. . . .

To say that music, too, has need of scientific aid will seem still more surprising. Yet it is demonstrable that music is but an idealization of the natural language of emotion; and that consequently, music must be good or bad according as it conforms to the laws of this natural language. The various inflections of voice which accompany feelings of different kinds and intensities, have been shown to be the germs out of which music is developed. It has been further shown, that these inflections and cadences are not accidental or arbitrary; but that they are determined by certain general principles of vital action; and that their expressiveness depends on this. Whence it follows that musical phrases and the melodies built of them, can be effective only when they are in harmony with these general principles. It is difficult here properly to illustrate this position. But perhaps it will suffice to instance the swarms of worthless ballads that infest drawing-rooms, as compositions which science would forbid. They sin against science by setting to music ideas that are not emotional enough to prompt musical expression; and they also sin against science by using musical phrases that have no natural relation to the ideas expressed: even where these are emotional. They are bad because they are untrue. And to say they are untrue, is to say they are unscientific. . . .

Not only is it that the artist, of whatever kind, cannot produce a truthful work without he understands the laws of the phenomena he represents; but it is that he must also understand how the minds of spectators or listeners will be affected by the several peculiarities of his work a question in psychology. What impression any given art-product generates, manifestly depends upon the mental natures of those to whom it is presented; and as all mental natures have certain general principles in common, there must result certain corresponding general principles on which alone art-products can be successfully framed. These general principles cannot be fully understood and applied, unless the artist sees how they follow from the laws of mind. To ask whether the composition of a picture is good, is really to ask how the perceptions and feelings of observers will be affected by it. To ask whether a drama is well constructed, is to ask whether its situations are so arranged as duly to consult the power of attention of an audience, and duly to avoid overtaxing any one class of feelings. Equally in arranging the leading divisions of a poem or fiction, and in combing the words of a single sentence, the goodness of the effect depends upon the skill with which the mental energies and susceptibilities of the reader are economized. Every artist, in the course of his education and after-life, accumulates a stock of maxims by which his practice is regulated. Trace such maxims to their roots, and you find they inevitably lead you down to psychological principles. And only when the artist rationally understands these psychological principles and their various corollaries, can he work in harmony with them.

We do not for a moment believe that science will make an artist. While we contend that the leading laws both of objective and subjective phenomena must be understood by him, we by no means contend that knowledge of such laws will serve in place of natural perception. Not only) the poet, but also the artist of every type, is born, not made. What we assert is, that innate faculty alone will not suffice; but must have the aid of organized knowledge. Intuition will do much, but it will not do all. Only when Genius is married to Science can the highest results be produced.

As we have above asserted, Science is necessary not only for the most successful production, but also for the full appreciation of the fine arts. In what consists the greater ability of a man than of a child to perceive the beauties of a picture; unless it is in his more extended knowledge of those truths in nature or life which the picture renders? How happens the cultivated gentleman to enjoy a fine poem so much more than a boor does; if it is not because his wider acquaintance with objects and actions enables him to see in the poem much that the boor cannot see? And if, as is here so obvious, there must be some familiarity with the things represented, before the representation can be appreciated; then the representation can be completely appreciated, only in proportion as the things represented are completely understood. The fact is, that every additional truth which a work of art expresses, gives an additional pleasure to the percipient mind a pleasure that is missed by those ignorant of this truth. The more realities an artist indicates in any given amount of work, the more faculties does he appeal to; the more numerous associated ideas does he suggest; the more gratification does he afford. But to receive this gratification the spectator, listener, or reader, must know the realities which the artist has indicated; and to know these realities is to know so much science. . . .

Emile Jaques-Dalcroze
Reform of Music Teaching in Schools

Emile Jaques-Dalcroze (1865–1950) began his career as a music teacher in 1891 in Switzerland. He was concerned that music education was not as successful as it should be because of the fragmented approach to teaching that prevented students from comprehending relationships among the various aspects of music. To provide a more comprehensive teaching method, Jaques-Dalcroze designed a curriculum based on solfège, improvisation, and his own creation, eurythmics. He felt that the benefits of the study of music with the use of eurythmics were self-understanding and self-development. He wrote the book *Rhythm, Music, and Education* (1905) to express these ideas.

. . . The educational methods of the last centuries are certainly not calculated to enable our children to comprehend and assimilate modern artistic developments. Our artists have forged new implements of creation; these implements must be adjusted to the hands of amateurs, who must then be trained to handle them, and finally entrusted with them at any age when they are most ripe for 'prentice work, when their hands are flexible and easily adapted to new methods, before the fire of ambition has been snuffed out by disappointment and world-weariness, before they have acquired the habit of doing things in the old way and are thus prevented from successfully coping with the new. . . . Obviously, no evolution, no progress can be accomplished without the co-operation of youth. It is in virgin souls that new ideas take firmest root. "Bend the green twig as you will," runs an old Persian proverb, "only fire can straighten it out again; but you want a mallet to drive a pile." The earlier we instill tastes and convictions in a man, the more sure we may be of durability and solidity. We should regard the child as the man of tomorrow.

The progress of a people depends on the education given to its children. If it is desired that musical taste shall not remain the prerogative of the cultured few, but shall penetrate the real heart of the whole people, I repeat that a genuine musical education—like the teaching of science and morals—should be provided at school.

It is evident that religion has ceased to inspire our teachers to preserve for musical studies the place they formerly occupied in the general education scheme. Many good people find themselves wondering why the schools continue to teach singing at all, since no opportunity is given the children of displaying their attainments either in the churches, on secular holidays, in their recreation, or as a rhythmic assistant and complement to their courses of gymnastics.

These good people, who point out that the teaching of music today serves neither a practical nor an ethical aim—but ministers merely to the annual delectation of school inspectors—have every excuse for losing interest in musical studies, and regarding them as of no importance. But if they would take the trouble to reflect upon the matter, they would recognize that these studies could and should be given a very definite, practical, and ethical aim, and thenceforward they would do their utmost to encourage and stimulate their development.

Private music lessons are virtually confined to the children of well-to-do families, whose parents are actuated generally by snobbishness or by respect for tradition. The music master, for whom such lessons provide a livelihood, can hardly be expected to reject a pupil who shows no aptitude for the work. For the same reason, none of our amateur conservatories will turn a pupil away, be he deaf or idiot. This has the deplorable result of investing a multitude of musical dunces, steeped in affectation, with a reputation for talent—most people being unfortunately under the impression, that they have only to take lessons in order to know something, and that, having "gone in for" a particular subject, they must necessarily understand it. And there is the other side of the picture. While the affluence of some parents enables them to provide a musical education for children utterly unfitted for it—to the serious detriment of the art—poverty alone deters other parents, to its even greater detriment, from making similar provisions for their genuinely talented children. Making music a compulsory school subject is the only sure means of mobilizing the vital musical forces of a country. Were it undertaken in the right spirit, efficiently organized, and confided to intelligent and competent teachers, every child would at the end of two or three years be put to the test: those who showed talent being enabled to continue their studies to the point of attaining the maximum development of their faculties; the remainder, those devoid of all musical taste, being relieved from the burden of lessons of no value to them, and thereby conferring an almost equal benefit on the art, in being debarred from meddling with it, and clogging its progress by ridiculous pretensions. . . . The Coach, in La Fontaine's fable, would probably never have arrived at its destination, had the pretentious fly been joined by others; a swarm of them, with their buzzing and erratic aerial maneuvers, would have exasperated the coachman and distracted the horses. . . . Heaven preserve us from our musical flies.

"Talent," said Montesquieu, "is a gift confided to us by God in secret, and which we display without knowing it."

If every child were compelled by law to pass an examination conducted by artists, and to subject himself for a few years to competent control, no single promising recruit would be allowed to pass into obscurity, neither would the hopelessly unmusical evade detection and its logical consequences.

The classification of capacities and incapacities once established—the former receiving due encouragement, the latter rendered comparatively innocuous—the teaching of music could obviously be practiced on a more effectual basis. The results would now depend on two important factors, with which we shall deal presently at greater length: the method of teaching, and the choice of teachers. Once our educational authorities realize their responsibilities and set about providing a sound primary musical grounding for every moderately gifted child, and a more thorough training for every exceptionally talented one, not only will they have introduced into school life a new element of vitality, recreation, joy, and health, not only will they have recruited to the ranks of art a large number of adepts whose later co-operation must prove invaluable (assuring and strengthening the existing choral societies, and encouraging the formation of orchestras composed entirely of local talent), but they will also have assembled for future purposes a host of embryonic teachers, of proved learning and appreciable talents, and—still more important—*au courant* with the latest methods of instruction.

These advantages should satisfy the most skeptical as to the desirability of reforming the system of musical education in vogue today, even though our motives have no longer the religious and traditional character that actuated our ancestors in the 16th and 17th centuries, in their zest for musical erudition. In those days music was studied with a view to adequate participation in the musical side of religious ceremonies. The acquirement of musical taste was accordingly a result of studies undertaken for this definite purpose. Today, when religious ardor has manifestly ceased to inspire all but the most primitive vocal efforts, it behooves us to inquire whether the retention of any form of musical tuition in the curriculum of our schools is not a mere survival of routine, and, if so, whether it is not time we replaced this tradition (now that its original meaning has disappeared) by a more vital incentive to progress. Whether this take the form of a desire to strengthen musical taste and to prepare for the study of classical and modem masterpieces, or for hygienic considerations, is not (for the moment) material. The essential thing is that we should know exactly why we are to retain music in our current curriculum. We can later—assuming we are satisfied as to the public utility of such retention—proceed to inquire as to whether this generation is in advance of the preceding ones. Should it appear that absolutely no progress has been made, it is our business to ascertain the cause of this *status quo*, and thence set about devising means for securing a better record for the coming generation. The progress of the man is one of the results of his preoccupations as a child. Sound ideas instilled in the schoolroom are transformed later into deeds, provided that a cognizance of their means of accomplishment is accompanied by an estimate of the effort necessary for the purpose, and by genuine love of the art, in whose cause the effort is to be made. By this means alone can we make sure of our country keeping pace with the times, of our choral societies facing the future instead of burrowing in the traditions of the past, and of virtuosity becoming a mere means of expression, instead of the whole end of musical training. By this means alone can we tempt beauty to our firesides, and fill the void caused by the decline of religion. Our professionals, better supported and understood by amateurs, will no longer seek conquests in other lands, preferring to remain in the country which they best understand, and of which consequently they can best sing the beauties.

The time will return when the people express in melody its simple joys and griefs. Children, having relearnt to sing in unison the old songs that charmed their forefathers, will feel inspired to create new ones, and we shall see the end of that lamentable division of singing at our music competitions into two parts: folk-songs and artistic songs. . . .

The teaching of music in our schools fails to produce anything like adequate results, because our educational authorities leave the whole control of the tuition in the hands of stereotyped inspectors. As these are nominated by pure routine, and no attention or encouragement is given to the initiative of any official who may feel tempted to deviate from the beaten track, the consequence is that no innovation of principle or practice has found its way into the curriculum from time immemorial. The theories of Pestalozzi and Froebel on the musical training of young children have been adopted only by private schools. The highly original educational experiments of Kaubert, about the year 1850, received absolutely no recognition in high quarters. The value of Swedish drill was only appreciated after a campaign extending over 15 years. The brilliant system of analyzing and explaining musical rhythm and expression advocated by Mathis Lussy, our compatriot, and one of the greatest of modem theorists, has not, up to the present, attracted the attention of our educational authorities. Not that this is so remarkable, seeing that, so far as I am aware (I can only pray that I am not mistaken!) music is absolutely unrepresented on our public bodies, nor have these latter ever manifested the slightest disposition to confer with professional musicians. I say I can only pray that I am not mistaken, and that by some chance some stray musician has not, in this or that canton, been summoned to take an active or consultative part in the official school-board proceedings, for we should have to conclude, from the actual condition of things, that his influence had been absolutely *nil*. It is preferable to believe that the failure of our public bodies to assure a development of musical studies compatible with the means and powers at their disposal, is not deliberate. "Not deliberate"—that is to say, the result merely of taking no interest in the question, and of never suspecting its importance.

Music, outside of genuine artistic circles, is held in very light repute not only by our educational authorities, but even by painters, sculptors, and men of letters; and it is by no means unusual to find journalists, otherwise full of zeal for the artistic development of their country, treating music as a negligible quantity, and greeting musical events, either with the smiling indulgence of the condescending patron, or with an equally insufferable

Emile Jaques-Dalcroze

affectation of superiority, explicable only in the light of their abysmal ignorance of the art. . . .

And yet our country is among those whose scholastic institutions command almost universal admiration, thanks to their excellent organization generally, and to the enterprise and enlightenment of most of our boards of education. How, then, does it come about that only the teaching of music—and of artistic matters in general—should be neglected and abandoned to routine? The answer is that our scholastic authorities have no understanding of music, and no ambition to acquire one. I shall be told that it is manifestly unnecessary for a geographical expert to be represented on a school board to secure an adequate teaching of geography. Granted; but only because no member of such a board would be found incapable of realizing the value of geography and the importance of obtaining competent instructors in the science. For this purpose he only requires to have received himself a general all-round education, to have a sound judgment, good hearing, and . . . to be able to read. The same applies to other subjects of special training, such as gymnastics . . . There again, it is not necessary to be an expert to recognize its utility and advocate its extension. Indeed, the arguments in favor of the training and hygiene of the body are furnished by the body itself. And the practical means of developing the flexibility, and of securing the balance, of limbs are easy enough to grasp; for that, again, it is sufficient to be able to read intelligently. But music is another matter altogether. Those who have gone through life with an untrained ear cannot be expected to appreciate the necessity of furnishing others with an ear attuned to fine perceptions by the diligent practice of special exercises. Those who themselves cannot distinguish either melodies or harmonies are hardly the best advocates of a system designed to secure these accomplishments for others. And, while they may accept it out of respect for tradition, they will be unable either to select the best method for training the ear, and rendering it capable of analyzing the relations and combinations of sounds, or to appreciate the merits of the experts to whom they may delegate the responsibility of selecting such a method. The spirit of music expresses itself in a language of its own, which our scholastic authorities are unable to read. And unfortunately, they will not allow others to read for them. And yet with them rests the exclusive right of nominating teachers and deciding on methods. . . . That is why music has no share in the general prosperity of our educational system. That is why children learn neither to read, phrase, record, or emit sounds in our schools. That is why our sons and daughters grow up dumb.

"But look here," protests Mr. So-and-So (a familiar and ubiquitous type), "there is surely no need to have a competent general direction to make the teaching effective. At that rate, you would want singing lessons given in our schools by specialists. And yet, as things are, quite ordinary masters produce the happiest results."

I am not denying, Mr. So-and-So, that there *are* good masters in our schools; but there are also bad ones, and this would not be the case—or it would hardly ever be—if we had a competent and well-informed direction, and if the training of teachers were more complete so far as music is concerned. Bad teachers must produce bad pupils. If you take the average of those who are successful at examinations, you may be sure that it is far smaller than it would have been if all the teachers had been well chosen. And that, bear in mind, is the principal count in my indictment. I contend that, on leaving school, the greatest possible number of pupils should have received a musical education adequate for the artistic requirements of modem life, and for the application of natural faculties normally and logically developed. These capable masters you speak of—can't you see what different results they would obtain if their own education had been properly conducted? I am not here going to analyze their methods in detail—indeed they vary according to the country—but I think I may assert, without fear of contradiction, that one and all are based on theory instead of on sensorial experiment. No art is nearer life itself than music. No art has developed and is still developing more rapidly, no art has inspired so many ingenious theorists or so many systems of teaching, growing ever more and more simple, proof positive of their pedagogic value! To choose between these systems is admittedly difficult, and we are not reproving the authorities with having chose wrongly. Our grievance is that *they have neglected to choose at all*, that they have preferred in every case—without a single exception—to retain the methods of the past. What is the infallible criterion of the worth of a system of instruction? Surely the practical results of the system, the technical accomplishments of the pupils who have followed it. . . .

A. S. Neill
Summerhill

Alexander Sutherland Neill (1883–1973) founded Summerhill School in Leiston, Suffolk, England, in 1921. It was an experimental boarding school in which children were free to learn as they wished. They were guided by their own interests, and learned in an atmosphere of permissiveness and freedom.

. . . The most frequent question asked by Summerhill visitors is, "Won't the child turn round and blame the school for not making him learn arithmetic or music?" The answer is that young Freddy Beethoven and young Tommy Einstein will refuse to be kept away from their respective spheres.

The function of the child is to live his own life, not the life that his anxious parents think he should live, nor a life according to the purpose of the educator who thinks he knows what is best. All this interference and guidance on the part of adults only produces a generation of robots.

You cannot *make* children learn music or anything else without to some degree converting them into will-less adults. You fashion them into accepters of the *status quo*—a good thing for a society that needs obedient sitters at dreary desks, standers in shops, mechanical catchers of the 8:30 suburban train—a society, in short, that is carried on the shabby shoulders of the scared little man—the scared-to-death conformist.

PART II

AMERICAN VIEWS, 1700–1950

Music education in colonial America was originally a matter of private initiative, as exemplified by the entrepreneurial singing masters of New England who gradually spread their music to other parts of the country. It became a function of the public schools in 1838, when it was accepted as a curricular subject by the Boston School Committee (board of education), although it was also taught in private singing schools well into the twentieth century. Music has had a strong impact on education throughout the United States, and has generated many writings intended to justify its place in the schools. The writings that follow show an evolution of beliefs in the value and necessity of music education.

Presidential Words

Every President from Washington to today has had something to say about arts education; here are some excerpts.

George Washington, letter to Reverend Joseph Willard, March 22, 1781

The arts and sciences essential to the prosperity of the state and to the ornament and happiness of human life have a primary claim to the encouragement of every lover of his country and mankind.

John Adams, letter to Abigail Adams, May 12, 1780

I must study politics and war that my sons may have liberty to study mathematics and philosophy. My sons ought to study mathematics and philosophy, geography, natural history and naval architecture, navigation, commerce, and agriculture, in order to give their children a right to study painting, poetry, music, architecture. . . .

Thomas Jefferson, letter to James Madison, September 20, 1785

You see I am an enthusiast on the subject of the arts. But it is an enthusiasm of which I am not ashamed, as its object is to improve the taste of my countrymen, to increase their reputation, to reconcile to them the respect of the world, and procure them its praise.

Franklin D. Roosevelt, address at Temple University, February 22, 1936

Inequality may linger in the world of material things, but great music, great literature, great art, and the wonders of science are, and should be, open to all.

Dwight D. Eisenhower, remarks at the opening of new American galleries at the Metropolitan Museum of Art, October 24, 1957

Art is a universal language and through it each nation makes its own unique contribution to the culture of mankind.

John F. Kennedy, remarks on behalf of the National Cultural Center, National Guard Armory, November 29, 1962

Art and the encouragement of art is political in the most profound sense, not as a weapon in the struggle, but as an instrument of understanding of the futility of struggle between those who share man's faith. Aeschylus and Plato are remembered today long after the triumphs of imperial Athens are gone. Dante outlived the ambitions of thirteenth-century Florence. Goethe stands serenely above the politics of Germany, and I am certain that after the dust of centuries has passed over our cities, we too will be remembered not for victories or defeats in battle or politics, but for our contribution to the human spirit. . . .

Lyndon B. Johnson, remarks at the signing of the Arts and Humanities Bill, September 29, 1965

Art is a nation's most precious heritage. For it is in our works of art that we reveal to ourselves, and to others, the inner vision which guides us as a Nation. And where there is no vision, the people perish.

Richard M. Nixon, address at the Annual Conference of the Associated Councils of the Arts, May 26, 1971

We, this Nation of ours, could be the richest nation in the world. We could be the most powerful nation in the world. We could be the freest nation in the world—but only if the arts are alive and flourishing can we experience the true meaning of our freedom, and know the full glory of the human spirit.

Gerald R. Ford, message to the Congress, transmitting Annual Report of the National Endowment for the Arts and the National Council on the Arts, June 23, 1976

Our Nation has a diverse and extremely rich cultural heritage. It is a source of pride and strength to millions of Americans who look to the arts for inspiration, communication, and the opportunity for creative self-expression.

Jimmy Carter, remarks at a White House reception, National Conference of Artists, April 2, 1980

The relationship between government and art must necessarily be a delicate one. It would not be appropriate for the government to try to define what is good or what is true or what is beautiful. But government can provide nourishment to the ground within which these ideas spring forth from the seeds of inspiration within the human mind. . . .

Ronald Reagan, remarks at the National Medal of Arts White House Luncheon, June 18, 1987

Why do we, as a free people, honor the arts? Well, the answer is both simple and profound. The arts and the humanities teach us who we are and what we can be. They lie at the very core of the culture of which we're a part, and they provide the foundation from which we may reach out to

other cultures so that the great heritage that is ours may be enriched by—
as well as itself enrich—other enduring traditions.

Bill Clinton, remarks at a public elementary school in East Harlem, NY,
June 16, 2000

Learning improves in school environments where there are comprehensive
music and arts programs. They increase the ability of young people to do
math. They increase the ability of young people to read. And most important of all, they're a lot of fun.

Remarks at the Concert of the Century for VH-1 Save the Music

. . . Music education is very important to me. When I was a young boy as a
school musician, I started at nine with Ms. Lillian Rutherford and George
Gray learning to sing and play. I learned that music was more than scales or
keys or how to make sure I was always in tune. Music taught me how to mix
practice and patience with creativity. Music taught me how to be both an
individual performer and a good member of a team. It taught me how to work
always to bring mind and body and spirit together and the beauty of music.

And so for all my teachers, for the ones I mentioned, for my junior high
school band directors, Carol Powell and Joel Duskin, for my wonderful
friend Virgil Sperlen, who taught me in high school. Some are still with me,
some have gone on to their reward. I want to say again, I don't think I
would be President if it hadn't been for school music. . . .

My people are Americans and my time is today. Let us promise that we
Americans will keep American music and the spirit it represents, inspiring
our children and their children as we enter the new millennium. . . .

George W. Bush, proclaiming August 2000 to July 2001 The Year of Arts Education
in Texas

Education prepares children for a lifetime of learning and enriches their
quality of life. Although reading, math, and science are critical to a young-
ster's success, arts instruction is also a major building block in school cur-
riculums. Whether involving music, drama, dance, or design, the arts add
joy to a child's life, stimulating creativity and enhancing learning ability.

Arts education in schools takes many forms. Young people may play an
instrument in orchestra, paint a mural, sing in the choir, or act in a play. Regardless of the activities they enjoy, children develop a greater understanding of history, culture, and the rich traditions found in our communities and our society.
Students also learn discipline, focus, and self-confidence and gain knowledge of
how to express themselves both in individual and group activities . . .

Cotton Mather
Preface to The Accomplished Singer

Cotton Mather (1663–1728) was a Puritan clergyman and writer. He is characterized as the typically intolerant and severe Puritan, partly because of his role
in the Salem witch trials. Mather, an intellectual leader, was influential in the
establishment of Yale University and was the first native-born American to
become a fellow of the Royal Society.

1. It is the Concern of everyone that would enjoy *Tranquillity* in this World,
or obtain *Felicity* in the World to come, to follow that Holy Direction of
Heaven, *Exercise thyself in* PIETY. And there is no *Exercise of* PIETY more
unexceptionable than that of making *a joyful* Noise of SINGING in the
Praises of our GOD; That of signifying our *Delight* in Divin Truths by
SINGING of them; That of *Uttering* the Sentiments of Devotion, with the
Voice, and such a *Modulation of the Voice,* as will naturally express the *Satisfac-*
tion and *Elevation* of the Mind, which a Grave SONG shall be expressive of.
'Tis indeed a very *Ancient Way* of Glorifying the Blessed GOD; As *Ancient* as
the Day *when the Foundations of the Earth were fastened,* and *the Corner-Stone thereof*
was laid. The *Morning-Stars* then *Sang together.* And it is as *Extensive* an one; For
it is Remarkable, That All *Nations* make SINGING to be one part of the
Worship which they pay unto their GOD. Those Few *Untuned Souls,* who
affect upon Principle to distinguish themselves from the rest of Mankind,
by the Character of *Non-Singers,* do seem too much to divest themselves of
an *Humanity,* whereof it may be said unto them, *Doth not Nature itself teach it*
you? Be sure, they sufficiently differ from the *Primitive Christians;* For, though
the Eastern Churches were at first Superiour to the *Western,* for the *Zeal* of
the House of GOD in this matter, yet both betimes Concurr'd in it. Not
only *Justin* the *Martyr,* and *Clemens* of Alexandria, as well as *Tertullian,* and several others of the Primitive *Writers,* but also Governour *Pliny* himself will tell
us, what *Singers* to their GOD, the Faithful were then known to be; and how
much they *Worshipped* Him in these *Beauties of Holiness.*

    2. BUT this piece of *Natural Worship* is further Confirmed by a *positive*
Institution of GOD our SAVIOUR for it. The *Sacred Scriptures* with which the
Holy SPIRIT of GOD has Enriched us, have directed us unto this *Way* of
Worshipping. In our Old *Testament* we there find it as a Command of GOD;
but Calculated particularly for Times under the *New-Testament:* Psal. LXVIII.
32. *Sing Praises unto GOD, ye Kingdoms of the Earth, O Sing Praises unto* the Lord.
And Psal. C. 1, 2, *Make a Joyful Noise unto the Lord, All ye Lands,* Come *into his*
Presence with Singing . . . . In our *New-Testament* itself 'tis a Thing so positively
enjoined, that it must be a wonder, if any Christian can make any Question
of it. How plainly is it commanded? James V: 13 Is *any cheerful among you, Let*

him sing Psalms. Yes, in the *Pauline* Epistles, we have it; how frequently, how earnestly inculcated! . . .

3. THE *Sacred Scriptures*, which have *Directed* us to *Sing unto the Lord, and Bless His Name*; have also *supplied* us with an admirable and sufficient *Matter for our Songs*.

WE have a PSALTER [the Bay Psalm Book], whereof the biggest part is of PSALMS, that were Composed by *David*, who being the Last of the Limitations which the Glorious GOD made of the *Line*, wherein the *First Promise* was to be accomplished, GOD for the sake of that *Redeemer*, distinguished him, with doing of amazing Things for him, and by him; whereof This was one, that he was made the greatest *Instrument* for assisting the Devotions of the Church, that ever was in the World. The rest were Composed by other *Holy Men of GOD, who wrote as they were moved by the Holy* SPIRIT . . . .

William Billings
Rules for Regulating a Singing School

William Billings was one of the best known composers and singing school masters of the American colonial period and the early United States.

As the well being of every society depends in a great measure upon GOOD ORDER. I here present you with some general rules, to be observed in a Singing School.

1st. Let the society be first formed, and articles signed by every individual; and all those who are under age, should apply to their parents, masters, or guardians to sign for them: the house should be provided, and every necessary for the school should be procured, before the arrival of the master, to prevent his being unnecessarily detained.

2nd. The Members should be very punctual in attending at a certain hour, or minute, as the master shall direct, under the penalty of a small fine, and if the master should be delinquent, his fine to be double the sum laid upon the scholars. Said fine to be appropriated to the use of the school, in procuring wood, candles, &tc.

3rd. All the scholars should submit to the judgment of the master, respecting the part they are to sing; and if he should think it fit to remove them from one part to another, they are not to contradict, or cross him in his judgement; but they would do well to suppose it is to answer some special purpose; because it is orally impossible for him to proportion the parts properly, until he has made himself acquainted with the strength and fitness of the pupil's voices.

Augusta Brown
The Inferiority of Yankee Music

The most mortifying feature and grand cause of the low estate of scientific music among us, is the presence of common Yankee singing schools, so called. We of course can have no allusion to the educated professors of vocal music, from New England, but to the genuine Yankee singing masters, who profess to make an accomplished amateur in one month, and a regular professor of music, not in seven years, but in one quarter, and at the expense, to the initiated person, usually one dollar. Hundreds of country idlers, too lazy or too stupid for farmers or mechanics, "go to singing school for a spell," get diplomas from others scarcely better qualified than themselves, and then with their brethren, the far famed "Yankee Peddlars," itinerant to all parts of the land, to corrupt the taste and pervert the judgment of the unfortunate people who, for want of better, have to put up with them.

Lowell Mason
Manual of the Boston Academy of Music

Lowell Mason (1792–1872) was one of the most influential figures in the history of music education in the United States. A composer, author, and teacher, he was the key figure in persuading the Boston School Committee to adopt vocal music as a regular subject in the school curriculum (see the Report of Special Committee, Boston School Committee).

4. REASONS WHY VOCAL MUSIC SHOULD BE GENERALLY CULTI-VATED. I. *It* CAN *be generally cultivated.* It is the universal testimony of those who have had experience, that, as a general fact, all have organs adapted to produce and distinguish musical sounds. Every child can vary the tones of his voice; and if he receives early instruction, it will be as easy for him to learn to sing, as to learn to talk or to read. If we had not learned to talk in early life, our organs would have become so rigid and unmanageable, as to render it impossible ever to learn to speak correctly, and perhaps not at all. It is a well known fact, that adults seldom acquire any sounds in a foreign language, which are not in their own. But put a child into a foreign family, and he will soon get all their peculiar tones. He can learn by imitation, while his organs are flexible and pliant. This is true not only of the voice, but also of the ear. What is technically termed a *musical* ear, is chiefly the result of cultivation. It is by experience that infants learn to distinguish sounds; and when their attention is early arrested by musical sounds, the ear

becomes sensitive and active. But neglect the ear, and it becomes dull, and unable to discriminate. . . . Children brough up in musical families and often entertained by musical sounds, so soon acquire a musical sense, as, in some instance, to be regarded as prodigies. Such were Mozart, Crotch, &c. To show that this is the result of cultivation, those children who are taken care of in infancy by singers, usually become so themselves, whether the parents sing or not. It has also been found by teachers of infant schools, that almost all children can sing. In the Boston alms house, in which place, if any where, we should expect to find children neglected.

5. II. *Vocal music* OUGHT *to be generally cultivated.* If we have established the point that it *can* be, few will doubt that it *ought* to be cultivated. Whoever acknowledges the high rank, which music demands, and deserves to hold in Christian devotion, will not consider its cultivation of little moment. If a service is acceptable, it is our *duty* to use every exertion to render it worthy of acceptance. If the sacrifice send up a grateful incense to the throne of God, it should be, as much as possible, "without spot or blemish." The musical talent is one given us by our Maker. It is a responsible and sacred talent; and can we do otherwise than yield to the constraining obligation, "to stir up the gift that is in us!" Few can plead incapacity, and no one has a right to do it, until he had subjected his powers to a rigid examination. No talent however vigorous, springs spontaneously into action. Some labor is necessary to unfold its latent energies, as well as to improve it. Many talents remain actually unknown to their possessor, until circumstances bring them to view. It is not only our duty to improve on our own talents, but also to develop and cultivate those of our children. "Not only should persons make conscience of learning to sing; but parents should conscientiously see to it, that their children are taught this, among other things, as their education and instruction belong to them." The business of common school instruction generally, is nothing else than the harmonious development and cultivation of all the faculties of children; hence, music as a regular branch of education, ought to be introduced into schools. The musical talent ought to be, in the same natural manner, incited, developed, cultivated, and rendered strong. Further reasons will be presented in the following sections. . . .

6. ADVANTAGES OF THE EARLY AND CONTINUED CULTIVATION OF VOCAL MUSIC. I. *It improves the voice,* in speaking and reading, by giving smoothness, volume, and variety to the tones. The voice, like every other faculty, is strengthened by use. If a child lifts a given weight every day, we all know his strength will be gradually increased, provided he is not forced to exert himself beyond his strength. So the voice by constant exercise, will continually improve, provided it is not strained beyond its natural tone. The voice, it is true, may be greatly injured or even destroyed,

by thus *forcing* it, particularly on the high notes; but under proper and judicious direction, it will daily improve by use. This is in strict analogy with the common laws of exercise, applicable alike to the physical, intellectual, and moral powers of man. Children, in their amusements, are often exerting their voices to their utmost extent, and this without injury, because they do not go beyond their natural tones. Criers in the streets of our large cities, acquire an astonishing volume of voice and force of intonation, by this daily practice; yet who ever heard of such persons or any public criers losing their voices, in consequence of such exertion? It is dangerous to use the voice in singing, only when it is dangerous to use it by much talking; that is, when the lungs are affected by a cold or by the consumption. This is the common cause of a ruined voice. Persons who are fond of music, often force the lungs in singing when in a diseased state, and by excessive irritation, bring on permanent disease. Singing not only tends to strengthen the voice, but also gives smoothness and variety to the tones in speaking. It is as necessary to give a pleasing variety to the tones in order to produce good speaking as good singing; and the musical intervals should be as much under the control, in the former case as in the latter. The tones in speaking should have that gradual swell and vanish which give beauty to singing. If our public speakers had early been taught to sing, and continued the practice, we should not hear their too often drawling tones, particularly those of clergymen. A speaker who cannot sing, is generally monotonous and dull. Having defective organs, only three out of about 75 were found, who could not, on the first trial, sing the first four notes of the scale; and two of those three had been in the establishment but a few days. These were allowed to take their seats with the others, and practise as they were able; but no particular attention was paid to them. After a few weeks, they were examined and one of them was found to have become one of the best singers among them, and another had made considerable progress. . . .

7. II. *Vocal Music conduces to health.* It was the opinion of Dr. Rush, that singing by young ladies whom the customs of society debar from many other kinds of healthy exercises, is to be cultivated, not only as an accomplishment, but as a means of preserving health. He particularly insists, that vocal music should never be neglected in the education of a young lady; and states, that besides its salutary operation in soothing the cares of domestic life, it has a still more direct and important effect. "I here introduce a fact," says the doctor, "which has been suggested to me by my profession; that is, the exercise of the organs of the breast by singing, contributes very much to defend them from those diseases, to which the climate and other causes expose them. The Germans are seldom afflicted with consumption: nor have I ever known more than one instance of the

spitting of blood amongst them. This, I believe, is in part occasioned by the strength which their lungs acquire by exercising them frequently in vocal music, which constitutes an essential branch of their education." "The music master of our academy," says Gardiner, "has famished me with an observation still more in favor of this opinion. He informs me, that he had known several instances of persons strongly disposed to consumption, restored to health by the exercise of the lungs in singing." 'In the new establishment of infant schools for children of three and four years of age, every thing is taught by the aid of song. Their little lessons, their recitations, their arithmetical countings, are all chanted; and as they feel the importance of their own voices when joined together, they emulate each other in the power of vociferating. This exercise is found to be very beneficial to their health. Many instances have occurred of weakly children of two or three years of age, that could scarcely support themselves, having become robust and healthy by this constant exercise of the lungs." These results are perfectly philosophical. Singing tends to expand the chest, and thus increase the activity and powers of the vital organs. . . .

8. III. *Vocal music in its elevated form, tends to* IMPROVE THE HEART. This is its proper and legitimate and ought to be its principal object. It can and ought to be made the handmaid of virtue and piety. Its effects in softening and elevating the feelings, are too evident to need illustration. There is something in the nature of musical tones, viewed in their pure and simple, not unnatural state, which is truly heavenly and delightful: and if music of such a character could become universal throughout the nation, it would be a sure and excellent means of national improvement. We speak expressly of music in its elevated and natural form, and not that screaming or screeching at the very extent, and highest pitch of the voice, which is sometimes heard, and called vocal music. Such is not the *music of nature,* and such not the music we hope to be instrumental of diffusing by the publication of this Manual. It is to be regretted that music which is accompanied with vulgar and indelicate associations, as has been too often the case, should find its way into our nurseries and juvenile schools, and even into the drawing rooms of young ladies. The effects of a suitable style of music in connection with judicious words, is now to some extent well known. It tends to produce love to teachers, love to mates, love to parents, and love to God; kindness to dumb animals, and an observance of the works of nature and of the events of Providence; and leads the mind "through nature up to nature's God." Such are its legitimate tendencies; and such we hope to be instrumental in making its ordinary tendencies. In this way, amusement may be blended with instruction; and cheerfulness, happiness, and order introduced into the family and into the school. This is not theory or imagination, but fact; testimony to which has reached our ears, from both teachers

and parents. . . . We can affect the moral character, only through the medium of the feelings. When they are interested, the attention can be fixed, and the mind turned to the most important truths. Most of our feelings are habitual, and connected with our ordinary associations. Hence, a most important part of education is to control and direct the associations. No instrument for this purpose is more powerful than vocal music; hence, parents ought to spare no pains to have their children properly instructed in it. There is a criminal neglect on the part of parents, as is evinced by the character of the music and of the poetry not unfrequently found on the piano forte. Surely they should allow their children to learn none but intelligent pleasing melodies, and good valuable poetry; of which, owing to the corrupt taste, we find a want, notwithstanding we have a multitude of songs and ballads. This defect will be remedied, we doubt not, as soon as the public taste demands it. Only the most choice songs and melodies must be admitted into our families and schools; if, after being learned in youth, they are to live and be sung in a later age. LET ME HAVE THE MAKING OF THE BALLADS OF A NATION AND YOU MAY MAKE THEIR LAWS. . . .

9. IV. *Vocal music tends to produce social order and happiness in a family.* Those parents and children who sing together, have a stronger attachment for each other. The family circle is prized; for here can always be found amusement, and such as does not lead into temptation. They can truly sing, "Home, sweet home." Nothing tends more to produce kindly feelings. It is almost impossible to sing with one, towards whom we indulge unkind feelings; and if we do, such feelings will soon be forgotten. Singing is naturally the overflowing of kind and joyful feelings. Who ever saw children singing together, or parents and children, that were not apparently happy? When singing is employed in the family devotions, it tends to produce a proper frame of mind, and to calm the feelings. It throws a delight and interest into the exercises, which calls up and fixes the attention. In the pious families of the Scotch, singing is a necessary a part of the devotions of a family, as reading the Bible; and in no families in the world, do all the members more heartily unite in these exercises.

When vocal music is properly attended to in schools and in families, its effect will be seen in the house of God; and we then shall not be pained with the profanity we now too often are compelled to witness, both in the choir and in the congregation.

10. V. *The course of instruction pursued in the manual, is eminently* INTELLECTUAL AND DISCIPLINARY, the mind is exercised and disciplined by it, as by the study of arithmetic; and the voice as by reading and speaking. It tends to produce habits of order, both physical and mental. Considered then merely in a literary point of view, and as affecting our habits and man-

ners, it ought to be introduced into every system of education. Sometimes a mind naturally dull, like that of the blind boy, has been awakened by the excitement of music, and thus stimulated to action in other pursuits. The excitement of one dormant faculty may be made the instrument of the excitement of others. We rarely find a singer of a dull disposition; although some, who yielding themselves entirely to an improper indulgence of music, are rendered unfit for almost every thing substantial or useful. This, however, is not the fault of music, but is the result of an improper cultivation of the musical talent, and a want of a proper balance of mind. A man may give himself up entirely to any exciting subject, and be unfit for the common business of life. But in a well balanced mind, music can never do injury. Parents and friends of children will thus see, that by urging the importance of introducing of vocal music into our schools, we are not advocating a waste of time, or the introduction of a study merely ornamental.

11. It is almost the only branch of education, aside from divine truth, whose direct tendency is to *cultivate the feelings*. Our systems of education generally proceed too much on the principle, that we are mere intellectual beings, not susceptible of emotions, or capable of happiness. Hence, we often find the most learned the least agreeable. There is no necessity for this. The feelings may and ought to be cultivated in connection with the intellect. Before our race can be much improved, the principle that the human soul is all mind and no heart, must be discarded; and human beings must be treated as possessing feelings as well as intellects. The feelings are as much the subject of training as the mind; and our happiness depends more on the cultivation of the former than of the latter. The chief object of the cultivation of vocal music is to train the feelings. How this is done, has been exemplified in the preceding sections.

12. *The error of supposing vocal music can be taught in a few months;* or that it is an easy task to learn to sing. This is a fatal mistake; and ruinous to correct execution. No one can learn to sing without active, persevering, and long continued effort. You may as well expect a child to learn to talk or to read, by being taught a few lessons. . . .

The Boston School Committee
Report of Special Committee, August 24, 1837

In 1832, the Boston School Committee (board of education) decided to take no action on a report by a special committee it had appointed to investigate whether vocal music should be added to the public school curriculum. In that year, the Boston Academy of Music was founded; it served as a laboratory for Lowell

Mason to prove the feasibility and value of vocal music instruction. The Academy was very successful, and Mason became a highly reputed teacher of children.

In 1836, the Boston Academy of Music presented a petition to the Boston School Committee, requesting it to reconsider including vocal music in the curriculum. The committee appointed another special committee to make a recommendation on the petition. Its 1837 report resulted in the adoption of vocal music in the curriculum of the Boston schools, with Lowell Mason in charge of several music teachers. The significance of this memorable event was that music was included as a full member of the curriculum for the first time, supported by school taxes just as the other subjects were. This event led the way to the same kind of action by boards of education throughout the country for the next century.

The select Committee of this Board, to whom was referred the memorial of the Boston Academy of Music, together with the two petitions signed by sundry respectable citizens, praying that instruction in vocal Music may be introduced into the Public schools of this City, having had the matter under consideration, ask leave to present the following

Report. The committed have given to the subject that attention which its importance required. They have afforded the memorialists a hearing, and availed themselves of such means of information as it was in their power to obtain. After mature deliberation and a careful scrutiny of arguments and evidence, the Committee are unanimously of opinion that it is expedient to comply with the request of the petitioners. As, however, the subject is one but recently presented to this community, and one therefore upon which much honest difference of opinion, and perhaps some prejudice, may be supposed very naturally to exist, the Committee are desirous to spread before the Board the reasons which have led to their conclusion. If there be weight or value in these reasons, the conclusion grounded on them will not probably be denied; if on the other hand, they be fallacious or unsound, the weakness and the fallacy will both here and elsewhere be exposed. The committee invite the Board to a dispassionate examination of the question. When viewed in all its bearings, it is one, in their opinion, of great public interest. At the same time, it must be admitted, there are peculiar difficulties in the way of its discussion. Music has, in popular language, too generally been regarded as belonging solely to the upper air of poetry and fiction. When, however, it is made the grave subject of legislative enactment, it is necessary to summon it from this elevation, and checking the discursive wanderings of the imagination, consider it in connection with the serious concerns of real life. The Committee will endeavor to discuss the question with the sobriety which the occasion demands. They are well aware that the cause which they support can find no favor from a

Board like this, except so far as it reaches the convictions through the doors, not of the fancy, but of the understanding.

There are two general divisions which seem, in the opinion of the Committee, to exhaust the question. The *first* is, the intrinsic effect of the study of vocal Music, as a branch of instruction in the schools, and on them; and *secondly*, its extrinsic effect as a branch of knowledge without them. Under these two divisions we propose to treat the subject.

There is a threefold standard, a sort of chemical test, by which education itself and every branch of education may be tried. Is it intellectual—is it moral—is it physical? Let vocal Music be examined by this standard.

Try it *intellectually*. Music is an intellectual art. Among the seven liberal arts, which scholastic ages regarded as pertaining to humanity, Music has its place. Arithmetic, Geometry, Astronomy, and Music, these formed the *quadrivium*. Separate degrees in Music, it is believed, are still conferred by the University of Oxford. Memory, comparison, attention, intellectual facilities all of them, are quickened by the study of its principles. It is not ornamental merely. It is not an accomplishment alone. It has high intellectual affinities. It may be made, to some extent, an intellectual discipline.

Try Music *morally*. There is—who has not felt it—a mysterious connection, ordained undoubtedly for wise purposes, between certain sounds and the moral sentiments of man. This is not to be gainsaid, neither is it to be explained. It is an ultimate law of man's nature. "In Music," says Hooker, "the very image of virtue and vice is perceived." Now it is a curious fact, that the natural scale of musical sound can only produce good, virtuous, and kindly feelings. You must reverse the scale, if you would call forth the sentiments of a corrupt, degraded, and degenerative character. Has not the finger of the Almighty written here an indication too plain to be mistaken? And if such be the case, if there be this necessary concordance between certain sounds and certain trains of moral feeling, is it unphilosophical to say that exercises in vocal Music may be so directed and arranged as to produce those habits of feeling of which these sounds are types? Besides, happiness, contentment, cheerfulness, tranquility—these are the natural effects of Music. These qualities are connected intimately with the moral government of the individual. Why should they not, under proper management, be rendered equally efficient in the moral government of the school?

And now try Music *physically*. "A fact, says an American physician, has been suggested to me by my profession, which is, that the exercise of the organs of the breast by singing contributes very much to defend them from those diseases to which the climate and other causes expose them." A musical writer in England after quoting this remark says, "The Music Master of our Academy has furnished me with an observation still more in favor of this opinion. He informs me that he had known several persons strongly disposed to consumption restored to health, by exercise of the lungs in singing." But why cite medical or other authorities to a point so plain? It appears self-evident that exercises in vocal Music, when not carried to an unreasonable excess, must expand the chest, and thereby strengthen the lungs and vital organs.

Judged then by this triple standard, intellectually, morally, and physically, vocal Music seems to have a natural place in every system of instruction which aspires, as should every system of instruction which aspires, as should every system, to develop man's whole nature.

In regarding however the effect of vocal Music, as a branch of popular instruction, on our Public schools, there are some practical considerations which, in the opinion of your Committee, are deserving of particular attention.

Good reading, we all know, is an important object, in the present system of instruction in our schools. And on what does it depend? Apart from emphasis, on two things mainly, modulation and articulation. Now modulation comes from the vowel sounds, and articulation from the consonant sounds of the language chiefly. Dynamics, therefore, or that part of vocal Music which is concerned with the force and delivery of sounds, has a direct connection with the force and delivery of sounds, has a direct connection with rhetoric. In fact, the daily sounding of the consonant and vowel sounds deliberately, distinctly, and by themselves, as the Committee have heard them sounded in the musical lessons given according to the Pestalozzian system of instruction, would, in their opinion, be as good an exercise in the elements of harmonious and correct speech as could be imagined. Roger Ascham, the famous school master and scholar of the Elizabethan age, and surely no mean judge, holds this language. "All voices, great and small, base and shrill, weak or soft, may be holpen and brought to a good point by learning to sing." The Committee after attentive observation, confess themselves of this opinion.

There is another consideration not unworthy of remark. "Recreation," says Locke, "is not being idle, as any one may observe, but easing the weary part by change of business." This reflection, in its application to the purposes of instruction, contains deep wisdom. An alternation is needed in our schools, which without being idleness shall yet give rest. Vocal Music seems exactly fitted to effort that alternation. A recreation, yet not a dissipation of the mine—a respite, yet not a relaxation—its office would thus be, to restore the jaded energies, and send back the scholars with invigorated powers to other more laborious duties.

There is one other consideration to which the committee ask the serious attention of the Board. It is this. By the regulations of the School Committee it is provided, that in all the Public schools the day shall open with becoming exercises of devotion. How naturally and how beautifully vocal Music would mingle with these exercises; and what unity, harmony, and meaning might thus be given to that which at present, it is feared, is too often found to be a lifeless or an unfruitful service, need only be suggested to be understood. The Committee ask the Board to pause and consider whether the importance has been sufficiently looked to, of letting in a predominating religious sentiment, independently of all forms of faith, to preside over the destinies of our schools.

And now before proceeding further, let us consider briefly the objections which have been urged against the adoption of vocal Music in our system of Public Education. The Committee are desirous to give full force to every objection. Nothing in the end is gained by misrepresenting or obscuring an opponent's arguments. Let us pass these objections in review, state them fairly, and give them, if possible, a fair answer.

It is then objected that we aim at that which is impracticable, that singing depends upon a natural ear for Music, without which all instruction will be useless. If musical writers and teachers are to be believed, the fact is not so. Undoubtedly, in this, as in other branches, nature bestows the aptitude to excel on different individuals in very different degrees. Still what is called a musical ear is mainly the result of cultivation. The ear discriminates sounds as the eye colors. They may both be educated. Early impressions can create an ear for Music. It is with learning to sing as with acquiring the pronunciation of a foreign language. Instruction, to be available, must be given while the organs have the flexibility of youth. To learn late in life is, generally, to learn not at all. There may be cases, it is true, of some who form their earliest years defy all efforts of instruction. Like those who come into the world maimed in other senses, they are, however rare. They are the unfortunate exceptions to a general rule. Besides, what on this point is the language of experience? Mr. Woodbridge in his Lecture before the American Institute, says that he was informed by Vehrli, a well known instructor in Switzerland, that out of several hundred poor children committed to his care, he had met with only two who could not be made to sing. Mr. Woodbridge likewise states that he was told by a celebrated musical teacher, in this country, that out of 4000 pupils, not an individual who could not be taught to sing had been found. Thus well attested facts repel this objection.

But it is said, the time spent would be quite inadequate to the end proposed, that the labor of a life is needed to form the musician. The answer to this objection is, that it mistakes the end proposed, which is not to form the musician. Let vocal Music in this respect be treated like the other regular branches of instruction. As many probably would be found to excel in Music as in Arithmetic, Writing, or any other of the required studies, and no more. All cannot be orators, not all poets, but shall we not therefore teach the elements of grammar, which orators and poets in common with all others use? It should never be forgotten that the power of understanding and appreciating Music may be acquired, where the power of excelling in it is found wanting.

Again it is objected, if one accomplishment is introduced into our schools, why not another? If instruction is given in vocal Music, why should it not be given in dancing also? The answer simply is, because Music is not dancing; because Music has an intellectual character which dancing has not; and above all, because Music has its moral purposes, which dancing has not. Drawing stands upon a very different footing. And your Committee cannot help remarking, as they pass, that in their opinion, there is no good reason for excluding the art of linear Drawing from any liberal scheme of popular instruction. It has a direct tendency to quicken that important faculty of observation. It is a conversant with form and intimately connected with all the improvements in the mechanic arts. In all the mechanical and many of the other employments of life, it is of high practical utility. Drawing, like Music, is not an accomplishment merely—it has important uses, and if Music be successfully introduced into our Public schools, your Committee express the hope and the conviction that Drawing, sooner or later will follow.

But the most general objection to the introduction of vocal Music into our Public schools is this. It will, we are told, impair discipline. This, though a common and somewhat plausible, is yet a superficial objection. It probably had its origin in certain vague impressions of what lessons in vocal Music were, when given according to the ancient method of instruction. To those, then, not acquainted with the subject, it may be necessary to state that the Pestalozzian system, as it has been called, has been applied to Music. The works of Nägeli and Pfeiffer, now in general use upon the continent of Europe, are founded on this system. These works were introduced into this country by Mr. William C. Woodbridge, of whose early services cause, it is here fitting to make honorable mention. They led soon afterwards to the formation of the Boston Academy of Music, an instruction destined, it is believed, to achieve great good in this community. One of the objects in forming the Academy was to carry vocal Music, by the aid of its Professors, into the schools, and they have since published a Manual of vocal Music, constructed upon the basis of the works just mentioned. Of this Manual, an eminent musical writer in England says, "it is the best work on the subject in the English language, and it is highly creditable to the new world to have set such a pattern to the old." According to the principles of the Manual, a lesson in vocal Music, as given by the Professors of the Academy, is not unlike a lesson in Arithmetic. Musical takes the place of numerical notation. The blackboard, not the book, is before the pupil, and by the use of his own faculties and senses he goes from principle to principle, till the whole science is evolved. How then can an exercise of this kind be adverse to discipline? On the contrary, it is itself a discipline of the highest order, a subordination of mind, eye, and ear, unitedly tending to one object; while any deviation from that object is at once made known. Melody is concerted action, and is discipline aught else? "Where Music is not, the Devil enters," is a familiar German proverb in regard to schools; and after witnessing the lessons in Music as given according to the Pestalozzian system, the Committee do not hesitate to say, that if any want of discipline follow the introduction of vocal Music into a school, the fault must be with the Master of that school—a it is not in the system.

Your Committee have heard but one other objection, and that scarcely demands a notice. Vocal Music as a school exercise, is, say some, a newly fashioned notion. It is an innovation upon old usages. It is, say they, a new thing. Alas for modern self complacency, and for this objection! What we propose was old three hundred years before the Christian era. The best defence of Music and Drawing, as branches of Public Education, is to be found in Aristotle, and it is a fact worth noting, that these same branches, Music and Drawing, amid all the helps of modern civilization, have just been introduced into the Primary Schools of France. Strange Revolution! Thus the human mind completes its wondrous cycle. Thrones crumble and nations are swept from the face of the earth, yet the good sense of a strong thinker outlives the vicissitudes of fortune and the wreck of matter, and founded on the eternal principles of human nature, endures the same from age to age!

The Committee have this distinctly considered every objection which they have heard urged against the introduction of vocal Music into the Public schools of this City. They have done so from an earnest wish, without prejudice or passion, to approximate to truth. They can sincerely say that they have sought as anxiously to hear objections as to refute them.

Before quitting this division of the subject, it remains to add, that the Committee had recourse to one other source of information. Vocal Music has been adopted, as a branch of instruction, into some of the most respectable private schools in this City. Mr. *Thayer*, Mr. *Fowle*, Mr. *Hayward*, and Messrs. *Cushing* and *Cleveland* have tried it, on a limited scale, for different periods of two to four years. The Committee sought to inform their own minds by availing themselves of the judgment of these gentlemen. Their testimony, on the whole, is of the most favorable character. Differing in somewhat unessential details, all concur in the main point, the utility of the exercise, and are determined to continue in their schools.

Thus tried, tried by the light of general reasoning, tried by the objections of its adversaries, tried by the concurrence of attesting witnesses, the introduction of vocal Music into the Public Schools, judged intrinsically by its effects within and on them, is commended to the favorable consideration of this Board.

The Committee thus far, have confined themselves to the narrowest view of this question. It is necessary to do so, because if it should have appeared that the bringing of vocal Music into the Public schools would in any wise injuriously affect their present welfare, there would have been an end to the whole matter. In that event, the Committee would have gone no further. Those of us who have been reared beneath the generous influences of these free monuments of the wisdom of our fathers, lay filial hands upon them. We wish to strengthen, not destroy. Your Committee have sought only to show that no injury, on the contrary, that much good to the school may be expected from this exercise, and therefore, the remaining branch of the inquiry is before us, and we proceed to consider the expediency of vocal Music as a study in the schools, by its extrinsic influence as a branch of knowledge without them. So highly do your Committee prize this influence, that even if the effect of Music within the schools were of a negative, and not as the Committee have essayed to prove, of a positive character, if vocal Music should merely do no harm, yet still on this the lowest supposition, there would be abundant reason for its introduction. Let us then consider in few words that this extrinsic influence is.

What is the great object of our system of popular Instruction? Are our schools mere houses of Correction, in which animal nature is to be kept in subjection by the law of brute force and the stated drudgery of distasteful tasks? Not so. They have a nobler office. They are valuable mainly as a preparation and a training of the young spirit for usefulness and happiness in coming life. Now the defect of our present system, admirable as that system is, is this, that it aims to develop the intellectual part of man's nature solely, when for all the true purposes of life, it is of more importance, a hundred fold, to feel rightly, than to think profoundly. Besides, human life must and ought to have its amusements. We cannot bring up a race upon Lyceum Lectures solely, wholesome though that food may be. Man must have agreeable excitement. There will be recreation when the toils of the day are ended. What shall that recreation be? So far then as human life is concerned, properly to direct the feelings and amusements, belongs to every system of Public Education. An initiation into the elements of vocal Music at school, in the opinion of your Committee, seems best fitted to supply that direction. "Music," says a modern German writer, "is the gymnastics of affections." Music and the love of it have been and may be perverted—who know it not? Guard it therefore, guide it, lead it into the right channels. But be not guilty of the illogical deduction of arguing from the occasional abuse of one of God's best gifts to its disuse. No. Let all parents understand that every pure and refined pleasure for which a child acquires a relish, is, to that extent, a safeguard and preservative against a low and debasing one. Music when kept to its legitimate uses, calls forth none but the better feelings of our nature. In the language of an illustrious writer of the seventeenth century, "Music is a thing that delighteth all ages and beseemeth all states, a thing as seasonable in grief as joy, as decent being added to actions of greatest solemnity, as being used when men sequester themselves from action." If such be the natural effects of Music, if it enliven prosperity or soothe sorrow, if it quicken the pulses of social happiness, if it can fill the vacancy of an hour that would otherwise be listlessly or unprofitably spent, if it gild with a mild light the checquered senses of daily existence, why then limit its benign and blessed influence? Let it, with healing on its wings, enter through ten thousand avenues of the paternal dwelling. Let it mingle with religion, with labor, with the home-bred amusements and innocent enjoyments of life. Let it no longer be regarded merely as an ornament of the rich. Still let it continue to adorn the abodes of wealth, but let it also light up with common schools and you make it what it should be made, the property of the whole people. And so as time passes away, and one race succeeds to another, the true object of our system of Public Education may be realized, and we may, year after year, raise up good citizens to the Commonwealth, by sending forth from our schools, happy, useful, well instructed, contented members of society.

The subject, in this connection, swells into one of national universality and importance. There are said to be, at this time, not far from *eighty thousand* common schools in this country, in which are to be found the people who in coming years will mould the character of this democracy. If vocal Music were generally adopted as a branch of instruction in these schools, it might be reasonably expected that in, at lest, two generations we should be changed into a musical people. The great point to be considered in reference to the introduction of vocal Music into popular elementary instruction is, that thereby you set in motion a mighty power which silently, but surely in the end, will humanize, refine, and elevate a whole community. Music is one of the fine arts. It therefore deals with abstract beauty, and so lifts man to the source of all beauty, from finite to infinite, and from the world of matter, to the world of spirits and to God. Music is the great handmaid of civilization. Whence come these traditions of a referred antiquity, seditions quelled, cures wrought, fleets and armies governed by the force of song—whence that responding of rocks, woods and trees to the harp of Orpheus—whence a City's walls uprising beneath the wonder-working touches of Apollo's lyre? These, it is true, are fables, yet they shadow forth, beneath the veil of allegory, a profound truth. They beautifully proclaim the mysterious union between Music, as an instrument of man's civilization, and the soul of a man. Prophets and wise men, large minded law-givers of an olden time understood and acted on this truth. The ancient oracles were uttered in song. The laws of the twelve tables were put to Music, and got by heart at school. Minstrel and sage are, in some languages, convertible terms. Music is applied to the highest sentiments of man's moral nature, love of God, love of country, love of friends. Woe to the nation in which these sentiments are allowed to go to decay! What tongue can tell the unutterable energies that reside in these three engines, Church Music, National Arts, and Fireside Melodies, as a means of informing and enlarging the mighty heart of a free people!

Foreign examples are before us. In Germany, the most musical country in the world, Music is taught like the alphabet. In Switzerland and Prussia, it is an integral part of the system of Instruction. Regenerated France has, since the revolution of July, appropriated the same idea. Her philosophic statesmen are trying to rend the darkness, and prepare their country for the future that is before her. "We cannot," says M. Guizot, "have too many co-operators in the noble and difficult enterprise of amending popular Instruction." England still halts in the march of reform. We ask the attention of the Board to the following passage from a work of extraordinary eloquence and power recently published, in England, written by Mr. Wyse, a member of the British Parliament. "Music, says this writer, even the most elementary, not only does not form an essential part of education in this country, but the idea of introducing it is not even dreamt of. It is urged that it would be fruitless to attempt it, because the people are essentially anti-musical. But may they not be anti-musical because it has not been attempted? The people roar and scream, because they have heard nothing but roaring and screaming, no Music from their childhood. Is harmony not to be taught? is it not to be extended? is not a taste to be generated? Taste is the habit of good things—'Je ne suis pas la rose, mais j'ai vecu avec elle'—it is to be taught. But the inoculation must somewhere or other begin. It is this apathy about beginning that is censurable, not the difficulty of propagating when it has once appeared. No effort is made in any of our schools, and then we complain that there is no Music among scholars. It would be just as reasonable to exclude grammar and then complain that we had no grammarians." With these sentiments your Committee heartily concur. Let us then show this apathy no longer. LET US BEGIN. Prussia may grant instruction to her people as a boon or royal condescension. The people of America demand it as their right. Let us rise to the full dignity and elevation of this theme. We are legislating not about stocks or stones, or gross material objects, but about sentient things, having that in them which, while we are legislating grows, and still will grow when time shall be no more. From this place first when out the great principle, that the property of all should be taxed for the education of all. From this place, also, may the example, in this country, first go forth, of that education rendering more complete, by the introduction, by Public authority, of vocal Music into our system of popular instruction. "The true grandeur of a people," says Cousin, "does not consist in borrowing nothing from other, but in borrowing from all whatever is good and in perfecting whatever it touches." Rome grew to greatness, by adopting whatever she found useful among the nations whom she conquered. The true policy of the American legislator on the subject of education is, to gather whatever of good, or bright, or fair, can be found from all countries and all times, and wield the whole for the building up and adorning of the free institutions of our own country.

The Committee here quit the subject. In its innermost circle, it embraceth a school; in its outermost circumference, it compasseth round a nation.

The Committee have thus endeavored, in sincerity and simplicity, to discuss this question. They clam no exemption from mortal frailty. They may be wrong. If, however, they have erred in attaching so much importance to vocal Music as a part of Public Education, they can only say they err with Pythagoras and Plato, Milton and Luther, Pestalozzi and Fellenberg. Finer spirits than these the world hath not bred. In such company there will be consolation.

Before closing this Report, the Committee must be pardoned one allusion. They hail it, as a star of good omen to this cause, that the President of the Boston Academy of Music is this year the Chairman of this Board also. May its auspicious influence continue to be shed in both these spheres!

And now, in conclusion, the Committee feel constrained in candor to confess that they are not practical musicians. If this take from the worth of the opinions they have expressed, it must be so—the result cannot be helped. Perhaps, however, they have been, on that account, the more unprejudiced, as being freed thereby from that amiable esprit de corps which sometimes unintentionally biases the judgment. Whichever way the scale incline, let the truth prevail.

In this spirit, and as embodying the plan, which, in accordance with the principles of this Report, they are about to present, the Committee ask the Board to adopt the subjoined Resolutions.

Resolved, That in the opinion of the School Committee, it is expedient to try the experiment of introducing vocal Music, by Public authority, as part of the system of Public Instruction, into the Public schools of this City.

Resolved, That the experiment be tried in the four following schools, the Hancock school, for Girls, in Hanover street; the Eliot school, for Boys, in North Bennet street; the Johnson school, for Girls, in Washington street; and the Hawes school, for Boys and Girls at South Boston.

Resolved, That this experiment be given in charge to the Boston Academy of Music, under the direction of this Board, and that a Committee of five be appointed from this Board to confer with the Academy, arrange all necessary details of the plan, oversee its operation, and make quarterly report thereof to this Board.

Resolved, That the experiment be commenced as soon as practicable after the passing of these resolutions, and be continued and extended as the Board hereafter may determine.

Resolved, That these regulations be transmitted to the City Council, and that they be respectfully requested to make such appropriation as may be necessary to carry this plan into effect.

All which is submitted, by the Committee, to the judgment of this Board and the final judgment of our constituents.

T. Kemper Davis, Chairman
In School Committee, August 24, 1837

The foregoing Report was read and laid upon the table, and ordered to be printed; and that each member of this Board, and of the City Council, be furnished with a copy.

Attest, S. F. McCleary, Secretary

Samuel Caldwell
Superintendent's Report (1843), Buffalo (NY) Public Schools

Samuel Caldwell was superintendent of the Buffalo Public Schools in 1842–1843.

In July last, by direction of the Council, a teacher of Vocal Music was employed for the term of six months. He is required to visit each school twice a week, and devote half an hour to instruction and practice in Singing in each and every visit. The gentleman employed has thus far devoted himself assiduously and faithfully to this business, perambulating the City from District to District, in sunshine and in storm; and it is gratifying to me to be able to state that in most of the Schools he is a welcome visitor, and a valuable coadjutor in the work of education. The progress the children have already made in acquiring a knowledge of music, and the decided testimonials of public approbation have resulted in the re-employment of the Teacher for another term of six months. The experiment of introducing music as a branch of education into our public schools has thus been made, although singing was introduced as a recreation into several of the schools soon after the free school system were established. Whenever the teacher was able to lead in music, he found the children ready to follow; and thus to some extent music was introduced before the present teacher commenced his labours, and many of the children were able to sing before music was taught as an elementary study. The success of the experiment has thus far exceeded the anticipations of its friends, and little doubt now exists of its becoming a permanent branch of juvenile instruction.

Horace Mann
Report for 1844: Vocal Music in Schools

Horace Mann (1796–1859) graduated from Brown University, where he taught for two years—his only teaching experience. Mann was elected secretary of the Massachusetts State School Board when it was established in 1837, and in that position he dramatically advanced the quality of public education. Among other things, he was responsible for improved methods of instruction in all subjects, and the introduction into the curriculum of vocal music, history, geography, physiology, and hygiene. Mann's Annual Reports to the Board of Education are fascinating reading for the student of the history of education.

There are about five hundred schools in the State where vocal music is now practiced. Half a dozen years ago, the number was probably less than one hundred. . . .

The pre-adaptation of the human mind to seek and to find pleasure in Music, is proved by the universality with which the vocal art has been practiced among men. Each nation and each age steps forward as a separate witness, to prove the existence of musical faculties and desires, in the race; and their testimony is so unanimous and cumulative that no tribunal can withstand its force. In cultivating music, therefore, are we not following one of the plainest and most universal indications of nature; or rather of that Being by whose wisdom and benevolence nature was constituted? The Creator has made the human soul susceptible of emotions which can find no adequate expression but in song. Amongst all nations, joy has its chorus, and sorrow its dirge. Patriotism exults over national triumphs, in national songs; and religion yearns, and vainly strives to pour out its full tide of thanksgivings to its Maker, until the anthem and the hallelujah take the rapt spirit upon their wings and bear it to the throne of God.

Nature not only points, as with her finger, towards the universal culture of the musical art, but she has bestowed upon all men the means of cultivating it. The voice and the ear are universal endowments—or at most, the exceptions are few, and there is abundant reason to believe that these exceptions are not inherent in the nature of things, but only punishments for our infraction of the Physical Laws; and that the number of exceptions may be gradually reduced, until the calamity of privation shall be wholly removed—and removed too, not by any repeal of the laws that inflict it, but only by obedience to their requirements. Substantially, then, the voice and the ear are universal endowments of nature, and thus the means of enjoying the delights and of profiting by the utilities of music, are conferred upon all.

Of what other, among that beautiful sisterhood, called the Fine or the Elegant Arts, can this be said? Doubtless there is an instinct pointing to architecture, painting, sculpture, etc., as well as an instinct of music. Men might have reared arches, columns, and temples, as embodiments of their emotions of grandeur and sublimity, had no necessity of shelter ever prompted the erection of a human habitation. So painting and sculpture might have arisen to commemorate the lineaments or the deeds of the departed great and good, or to solace or to inspire their bereaved survivors. But how costly, for instance, are architectural gratifications. What years of labor, what expenditure of means, must precede the enjoyments they confer. In any previous age, and even in the present, how small is the portion of the human family to which the sight of a splendid edifice is accessible. But the pleasure resulting from the use of the human voice in song, is the common patrimony of mankind. The inmate of the lowliest dwelling as well as the master of the lordliest castle may enjoy them. He whose hard lot deprives him not only of the embellishments but even of the common comforts of life, may regale himself with unpurchased "wealth of song." The pleasures of music attend their possessor not only in the hours of prosperity, but in those of sorrow. Music may be a companion in the lone vigils of pain, or in the deeper solitude of bereavement. It may support and console, when no other of the benignant family of the Arts could give balm or anodyne to the wounded spirit.

In one respect, Vocal Music holds signal pre-eminence over Instrumental. The latter is too expensive a luxury to be within the reach of a great portion of mankind. But the instruments of vocal music levy no contributions upon another's skill, or our own money. They are the gratuity of nature, and in this respect, the common mother has rarely been unmindful of any of her children. Of the implements or contrivances by which many pleasures are produced, it is the vaunted recommendation, that they can be compacted in a small space and carried about by the traveler, on his person, or in his equipage, without cumbersomeness. But, in this respect, we can say of this simple yet most exquisite mechanism—the organs of the human voice—what can be said of no contrivance or workmanship, prepared by human skill and designed for human enjoyment. No one can carry about his person or transport from place to place, a column, a statue, or a painting, however beautiful, or however essential to his enjoyment, it may be; but the apparatus for singing is the unconscious companion of all, and we can often use it without hindrance when engaged in active occupations. Present at all times, unburdensome, as a means of gratuitous solace, an inexpensive luxury—what other of the refining arts offers inducements for cultivation so universal, or rewards that cultivation with bounties so generous and manifold?

Nature has drawn broadly the lines of another great distinction, which redounds with equal force, in favor of the vocal art. I refer to an organic difference, established in our spiritual constitution, between the gratifications of the intellect, and the pleasures of taste or sentiment. The intellectual powers are progressive in their nature. For stimulus they demand novelty. If fresh exertions are not rewarded by fresh truths, all exertion will soon cease. The mental athlete can no longer find pleasure in tossing the playthings of feathery lightness, that amused his childhood. He demands a solidity that will cohere in his grasp and a might that will match his strength. The philosopher cannot return to toys and he presses onward to the discovery of new truths. The ratiocinative mind so long accustomed to logical processes that it has acquired an almost intuitive power of discerning remote conclusions on an inspection of premises, can no longer treat in those infantile steps by which the consecutive stages in an argument or demonstration were once passed over. . . .

There is still another attribute or quality of music too important to be unnoticed in the developing its relations to mankind. It does not require any degree of perfection as a science, in order to become pleasing as an art. Doubtless in this, as in all other things, those who understand the subject best will enjoy it most; but still, proficiency is not indispensable to pleasure; and those who possess the art at all, realize an enjoyment fully proportioned to the degree of art they possess. It is not so in regard to many, and perhaps, most other human attainments; for a high degree of excellence in them must be reached before their rewards can be received. In music, however, a reward is bestowed corresponding with the degree of advancement gained, however, limited that advancement may be. The ear of a musical amateur is pained at the rude carol of a rustic, but why should that rustic troll his song with such unwearying perseverance, if it were not joyous and exhilarating to himself? When the connoisseur pours out his condemnation or ridicule upon the unartistic specimens of the cottage, he is selfishly thinking of his own pleasure, instead of benevolently sympathizing with that of others. Were his heart as well cultivated as his ear, he would think with gratitude upon their resources of pleasure, instead of looking with disdain upon their want of skill. Probably their imperfect skill comes much nearer to a requital than he does, for the cost and the pains expended in acquiring it. This characteristic of the musical art, to bestow at least a proportionate gratification, from the rudest beginnings to the highest excellence, is another of the bounties offered by nature upon its universal diffusion.

But we are not left to speculation and inference as to the beneficial effects of vocal music in public school. The universal practice of music in most of the schools of the German states, for a long series of years, in an experiment sufficient of itself to settle the question of its unity. Probably it is not the least efficient among the means by which the schools of Prussia are kept in such admirable order, with so rare a resort to corporal punishment. In that kingdom no person could be approved as a teacher—no individual, indeed, would ever think of presenting himself as a candidate for teaching, even in the obscurest school and at the lowest salary—who was not master both of the theory and practice of vocal music, and also a performer upon one or more instruments. Aided by these influences, which conspire of course with other springing from the mildness and amiability of the teachers' character, and from their strong love of children, their high sense of duty, and emphatically, from their richly replenished and well disciplined minds, the Prussian teachers rarely have occasion for resorting to coercive measures; and thus the Prussian schoolroom becomes the abode of peace and love, a bright spot where the sun of affection is rarely obscured even by a passing cloud. The whole country, indeed, is vocal with music. It adds zest to all social amusements. It saves the people from boisterous and riotous passions. Pervading all classes, it softens and refine the national character. It is the recreation of the student after his severe mental exertion, and it cheers on the laborer sweating at his toil. . . .

But we have evidence nearer home of the beneficial effects of music in schools. Six years ago, by a vote of the Boston school committee, provision was made, for giving, at the public expense, stated and regular instruction in vocal music, in all the Grammar and Writing schools of the city. The practice has continued without interruption to the present time. At the period of its introduction, greater doubts were entertained by many intelligent people, as to the expediency of the measure. Some of the teachers themselves were alarmed, lest consequences unfavorable to the schools should follow in its train. But, after a trial of several years, the opinion of the same gentlemen was asked respecting its practical results; and, I believe with an entire unanimity, they awarded a favorable decision. Those who, in the beginning, had entertained distrust and apprehension respecting the

Horace Mann

adoption of the measure, with a creditable frankness, avowed themselves satisfied, and declared in its favor. From what I know of public opinion among the friends of education, in Boston, I do not believe it would now be possible to revoke the order by which music was introduced into its schools. Provision for instruction in the art of vocal music, in the above named schools, may therefore be regarded as a part of the generous policy of the city towards them, for an indefinite future period. . . .

. . . To be more specific in presenting the claims of this subject to the attention of our community, I may say,

1st, that Vocal Music promotes health. It accomplishes this object *directly*, by the exercise which it gives to the lungs and other vital organs; and *indirectly*, by the cheerfulness and genial flow of spirits, which it is the especial prerogative of music to bestow. Vocal music cannot be performed without an increased action of the lungs; and by increased action of the lungs necessarily causes an increased action of the heart and of all the organs of digestion and nutrition. The singer brings a greater quantity of air in contact with the blood. Hence the blood is better purified and vitalized. Good blood gives more active and vigorous play to all the organs of absorption, assimilation, and excretion. The better these functions are performed, the purer and more ethereal will be the influences which ascend to the brain. The latter is an organ so exquisitely wrought, that its finest productions are dependent upon the healthfulness of the vital processes below. A fit indigestion annihilates a statesman's power, though a nation perishes for want of his counsels; and a fever disarms a warrior, before whom legions have trembled. But, on the other hand, energy and electric celerity of movement are generated in a well-formed brain, when it is supplied with healthful and highly oxygenated blood. Spontaneous effusions of serenity, of cheerfulness, and of strength, are the natural results of wisely-managed physical organs; and these qualities serve to invigorate the health that produced them. Thus, by the action and reaction of the material and spiritual natures upon each other, a joyous and tuneful elasticity is dispensed to every part of the complex system of man. The scientific physiologist can trace the effects of singing, from the lungs into the blood; from the blood into the processes of nutrition, and back again into the blood, and into the nerves; and finally from the whole vital tissue into the brain, to be there developed into the flower and fruit of cheerfulness, increased health, increased strength, and a prolonged life, just as easily and as certainly as a skillful manufacturer can trace a parcel of raw material which he puts into his machinery, through the successive states of being broken down, cleansed, softened, changed into new forms, and made to evolve new qualities, until it comes out at last, a finished and perfect product. In both cases, there may be various conspiring or disturbing forces, tending to aid or to defeat the result, but still, from beginning to end, the connection between cause and effect is as distinctly traceable, as is a broad white line running across the black surface.

In our climate the victims of consumption are a host. It is a formidable disease to males and still more to females. About twenty per cent of the deaths that occur, are caused by consumption; and this estimate includes infancy and childhood as well as adult age. Restricting the computation to adult life, probably one half or nearly one half of all the deaths that occur, are caused by this terrible disease alone. Vocal music, by exercising and strengthening the lungs, and by imparting gaiety to the spirits, would tend to diminish the number of that sad procession whom we daily see hastening to an early tomb.

2d [sic], Vocal Music furnishes the means of intellectual exercises. All musical tones have mathematical relations. Sounds swelling from the faintest to the loudest, or subsiding from the loudest until "There is no space 'twixt them and silence," are all capable of being mathematically expressed. The formulas, 2, 4, 8, 16, 32, 64, 128, etc.; or 128, 64, 32, 8, 4, 2 are no more significant to the mathematician, of certain fixed, natural, unalterable relations between numbers, then the tones of musical chords are to the scientific musician. Hence the intellect can be exercised on the relations of tones, as well as on the numbers, quantities, or magnitudes of arithmetic, algebra, or geometry; and while music furnishes problems sufficient to task the profoundest mathematical genius that has ever existed, it also exhibits scientific relations so simple as to be within the schoolboy's comprehension. Music, therefore, has this remarkable property—emotions—to the head or to the heart, tasking all the energies of the former, or gratefully responding to all the sentiments of the latter.

3rd, But the social and moral influences of music far transcend, in value, all its physical or intellectual utilities. It holds a natural relationship or affinity with peace, home, affection, generosity, charity, devotion. There is also a natural repugnance between music and fear, envy, malevolence, misanthropy. . . .

Dr. Chalmers observes, "It says much for the nature and original predominance of virtue—it may be determined another assertion of its designed preeminence in the world, that our best and highest music is that which is charged with loftiest principle, whether it breathes in orisons of sacredness, or is employed to kindle the purposes and to animate the struggles of resolved patriotism; and that, never does it fall with more delightful cadence upon the ear of the delighted listener, than when, attuned to the home sympathies of nature, it tells, in accents of love and pity, of its woes, and its wishes for all humanity. The power and expressiveness of music may well be regarded as a most beauteous adaptation of external nature to the moral constitution than that which is so helpful as music eminently is to his moral culture. Its sweetness sounds are those of kind affection. Its sublime sounds are those most expressive of moral heroism; or most fitted to solemnize the devotion of the heart and prompt the aspirations and the resolves of exalted piety. . . ."

One of the most delightful attributes or characteristics of music is, its harmonizing, pacificating tendency. It may be employed as a grand mediator or peacemaker between men. Harmony of sound produces harmony of feeling. Can it have escaped the observation of any reflecting man, when present at a crowded concert, or at any numerously attended musical festival, what a heterogeneous mass of human beings was before him? Competitors in business; rivals, almost sanguinary, in politics; champions of hostile creeds; leaders of conflicting schools in art or philosophy—in fine, a collection and full assortment of contrarieties, and antagonisms—and yet the whole company is fused into one by the breath of song! For the time being, at least, enemies are at peace; rivals forget their contests; partisans lay aside their weapons; and the bosoms that harbored acrimonious or vindictive feelings over which time seemed to have no power, are softened into kindness. All respond alike, all applaud in the same place; and men whose thoughts and feelings, an hour before, were as far asunder as the poles, or as the east is from the west, are brought as near together in feeling as they are in space. Who will deny homage to an art that can be made men brethren, even for an hour?

If music has such power over men, is it not evident that it will have still greater power over children? I have heard of a family whose custom it was, on the express or manifestation of ill-nature or untowardness by any one of the members, for all the rest to join instantly in song; and thus the evil spirit was exorcised at once. Neither child or man can be long angry *alone*. All but madmen will yield their passions, if they receive no sympathy from others while expressing them, or if they are not kept alive by an answering passion in an opponent. How extensively may this principle be applied in the management and discipline of children in school; and surely music is one of the best instrumentalities for so benign a purpose.

But, grant the expediency of introducing vocal music into our Common Schools, and the question arises, what measures can be adopted to accomplish that end? Unhappily, there are but few persons in our community competent to teach the art even of vocal music. We are an un-musical, not to say, an anti-musical people. No hereditary taste for the art has descended to us. Our Pilgrim Fathers were too stern a race, and their souls were occupied by interests too mighty and all-absorbing, to afford them either leisure or inclination to cultivate music as a refinement or an embellishment of life. Hence, throughout New England, since the first settlement of the colonies, a high degree of musical skill has been a rare accomplishment; and with the exception of church music, the mass of the population have been strangers, if not worse than strangers, to the art. . . .

In our large cities and towns, it is obvious, that there is sufficient pecuniary ability to employ a teacher of music expressly for the schools. It would be better were all our teachers competent, as some of them are, to give instruction in this art. One of the finest resources for the infusion of good feeling and for the expulsion of bad, would then be at the command of the teacher, at all times; and he might invoke its aid on any and every emergency. It is the common testimony of teachers, that occasionally there are days, when the cordiality and kindness that should characterize all schools, seem to have departed; when the nerves of the pupils appear to be on the surface, and all movements wound them. On such occasions, the tranquilizing influences of song are gratefully remedial. Its timely service is worth more to the school than the singing of an entire day, when a more auspicious spirit prevails. In most cases, with competent teachers, music would nearly or quite supersede the necessity of coercion, and thus work a vast economy of blows and tears. But where music has been taught to the pupils by a master of the art, the teacher, though not an adept himself, can superintend the exercises, and thus make it an auxiliary in the government of his school. . . .

A question is sometimes asked, whether if music cannot be taught scientifically, in our schools, it would be expedient to have it taught by rote. The answer to this question is found in the fact, that most if not all the social and moral effects of music will be realized, when it is practiced as an art, as fully as though it were studied as a science. Its adaptation to the intellect depends on its scientific relations; its adaptation to the intellect depends on its scientific relations; its adaptation to the universal heart of mankind depends on its power to soothe, to tranquilize, or to enliven; to express the highest and most rapturous joys which ever thrill the human soul, or to pour a delicious oblivion over the wounded spirit. . . .

Rev. A. D. Mayo
Methods of Moral Instruction in Common Schools

Reverend A. D. Mayo was a prolific writer and lecturer on American society during the last quarter of the nineteenth century.

MUSIC AND MORALS. It is unnecessary to tell a people whose hearts are yet thrilling in the great International Jubilee that Music is one of the most subtle and powerful methods of moral instruction. There is nothing in this world like the singing of children; and no where do children sing as in our common schools. In the home, the choir, the concert, the Sunday school, we oftenest hear the harmony of children trained in similar conditions of society. But when a hundred little ones, called to the school-house from the palace and the cellar, from all civilized lands, representing every human grade of culture and faith, unite in a patriotic song, or a grand, simple religious hymn; then voices are heard calling out from that deep of music to the far-off future, and he must be indeed a barbarian who is not moved out of himself thereby.

A rigid reform is demanded in the selection of music for our common schools. A great deal of it is puerile, too much is beyond the capacity of children, some of it can be accounted for only by the perverse desire of the special teacher to exhibit his musical menagerie. We need more songs of home, of country, of simple praise to God and love to man. We need less drill over the science of music and more actual singing that shall knit together the souls of the scholars into a loving community.

I know not how I should have lived through ten years of the strange experiences and crushing and confusing toils of professional life in a great western city, could I not have been almost every day lifted up and cheered by the wonderful singing of the children in the Cincinnati Common Schools. For often, when every thing in that turbid drift of humanity we call society in the valley of the Ohio seemed whirling beyond my power, and I would not see ahead the length of the ship I steered, on passing a school-house, a wave of song would come surging out through an open window, hushing the noisy street, attesting the hurrying crowd; as if the gates of the better-land had swung half-open for a moment we heard the dwellers within chanting, "Glory to God in the Highest, and on earth peace, good will to men." Marry your highest moralities to childhood's music, and young America may yet sing itself within sight of the millennium in this New World.

William L. Tomlins
The Power of Music Education

William L. Tomlins taught in New York City and Chicago, where he became director of the Apollo Club, a highly respected chorus. William Bailey Birge said of Tomlins, "The new interest in chorus singing was largely set in motion by the work of William L. Tomlins with children." This reading is from about the year 1900.

The trouble with our common school education is that it is concerned too exclusively with the things of knowledge, and that it leaves the deepest powers in the children undeveloped. This unused part is his spirit; the realm of Motive and Creative Life. The boy whose powers are merely physical is but a fraction of his true self. Add his mental powers and still you have only half your boy, for besides what he knows and does there is what he *is*. To fully fit your child for life, then, you must complete him; body, mind, and spirit. Already his physical and lower-mind powers are active. Now awaken his intellectual and spiritual ones. Make him alive in his inner and innermost being, and soon he will pulse with the great world-life all about him, soon he will be filled with the joy of living, tireless in energy, just as when—a little fellow—he was in touch with his little play-world.

In bringing this three-fold power of the child into the harmonious expression you complete the circle of his individuality. Almost instantly there will come to him the awareness of this fuller life within and all around him. It is simply a question of completeness; of a complete bell which rings out its life, as against a cracked one which cannot and whose voice is but a dead chink.

The effects of this transformation come quickly to view and are seen in self-reliance, initiative, purposefulness, and many other things which make for character building. In a word, the child's powers are approached from within as well as without, and thereby he is lifted so above and beyond his former powers as to be out of all comparison with them.

Samuel Winkley Cole
The Purpose of Teaching Music in the Public Schools

Samuel Winkley Cole was an influential author and professional leader during the early decades of the twentieth century.

What then is the purpose of teaching music in the public schools? I answer: the creation of a musical atmosphere in America; the establishment of a musical environment in every home; the development of a national type of music. . . . In short, the real purpose of teaching music in the schools is to lay the foundation for all that we can hope or wish to realize, musically, in the United States of America. . . . To sum it all up: the real purpose of teaching music in the public schools is not to make expert sight-singers nor individual soloists. I speak from experience. I have done all these things, and I can do them again; but I have learned that, if they become an end and not a means, they hinder rather than help . . . a much nobler, grander, more inspiring privilege is yours and mine: to get the great mass to singing and to make them love it.

A. E. Winship
The Mission of Music in the Public Schools (1905)

A. E. Winship was editor of the *New England Journal of Education*.

If the mission of the school is to teach the three R's then music has no mission in the public schools. With all due regard to the eminent personal success that stands behind some very clever words already spoken in this convention, I hesitate not to say that few arguments are as vague and vicious, trite and tricky, as a spectacular plea for the three R's. . . .

Is music a fad or has it a mission?

What is the real, vital mission of the public school? Is it not to do for the children as a whole what they will find, all in all, beneficial thru life, not simply in business, not simply in the earning of a living, but at a work and at play, in the home and in society, in the using of money as well as in the getting of it, in enjoying life as well as in being able to live, in getting genuine pleasure out of others, in giving pleasure to others, and in keeping youths and adults from going wrong physically, intellectually, and morally? Music does much for the disposition and for the character. It provides recreation and utilizes leisure; it may be a limitless blessing to the home; the church could hardly exist without it. The child taught to discriminate between music and vulgar noise will not be tempted by the trashy shows that are, perhaps, the worst curse that afflicts the city life of the poor and the weak.

In one city in the West a cheap show settled down in the town. Children's matinee tickets were sold to the stores for two and a half cents, to be given as premiums. The demoralization of the school threatened. The wise and energetic superintendent forced the teaching of school music, introduced chorus work and started an orchestra in every school, openly attacked the cheap music, and literally drove the show out of business. The public schools can revolutionize the entertainments of most cities if they really appreciate the possibilities in good music. Isn't this a mission worthwhile?

School music must be devotional, patriotic, intellectual, and inspirational.

There is no more perfect mechanism than the mechanics of music, but there is no music in that which is merely mechanical. There is nothing so inspirational as music, but there is no worthy music in anything merely inspirational.

The school music must be devotional—will be this under any reasonable conditions. It will inevitably breathe a religious spirit into the day. It is the one phase of religious activity that does not end to be dogmatic, denominational, or sectarian. It is religious naturally as a breath from heaven, as pure as the flake of wafted snow ere it touches the earth, as tonic to the souls as a breath from the Wasatch range. In the present skeptical state of the public mind toward dogmatism, and its almost reverential attitude toward the public school, it is worth all the teaching of music costs and more to breathe into the life of childhood and youth a reverence that need not be dogmatic, a religion that need not be sectarian.

Patriotism is devotion with a human christening. It idealizes, almost defies, one's country. It enkindles the worshipful side of our being humanward. The only thing that will keep Canada from joining the United States is the fact that every child has sung "God Save the Queen (or King)" each school day of his life. It has closed every school day even known by a Canadian. This will make "America" impossible to them, even tho the tune may be the same. We do not sing "America," The Star-Spangled Banner," "Dixie," and the state hymns as much as we ought, but every child learns them in the schools and sings them on every star occasion. Sometime he will do this daily. The schools of Canada make any anti-British sentiment impossible; "America" in the schools makes any anti-American sentiment impossible. No teaching of history will do for patriotic sentiment what a daily school song can do.

Music has an intellectual mission. It makes intellectual activity graceful and refreshing. The old idea was that nothing was intellectual that did not come hard. Friction was an indication of power. The squeak of the mind was supposed to voice activity. Grinding was the characterization of conquest. Drill, a simpler word for boring, was deified.

All that is in the past. Nothing that tires or can tire is power today. Tireless stream, frictionless electricity, even wireless telegraphy are symbolic of mental action. When a mind snaps, when the nerves are prostrate, when the brain sags, there has been a wrong use. Rhythm is the best mental action. Genius is the power to be carried to limitless height, depth of breath without friction in the flight or leap.

Music is one rhythmic art. Its mathematics are more exact than logarithms, its science keener than chemistry, its art richer than that of the sculptor and painter, and yet the mind obeys the laws of mathematics and chemistry, and art in music as easily as sound flies above the ocean more readily than the heavy cable drags it beneath the sea.

Music, rightly taught, does more for mental development than the mystic symbols of algebra or the planting of Greek roots in the brain soil.

It is not enough that the school sings. It must know what it sings, why, and how. Music is the most exact science, the most nearly fathomless philosophy, the most exhaustless psychology, the most brilliant art.

A. E. Winship

The public school has a phase of its mission to teach the possibilities of music, to teach the Psalms of Israel, of the masters, and the masterpieces. It is a crime against heaven and earth to teach of the warriors and the triumphs thru courage, and not to teach of men like Handel and Haydn, Mendelssohn and Beethoven, Mozart and Wagner, the story of whose lives is more fascinating than that of Xenophon or Caesar.

Music is the noblest inspiration. It comes nearest crossing the threshold of eternity. For music the very gate of heaven stands ajar.

There is no occasion to be less accurate or rapid in number work, to read less intelligently or write less distinctly in order for public-schools music to make us more devout, more patriotic, more intellectual, more inspired in our love for man and our adoration of Jehovah.

Horatio Parker, Osbourne McConathy, Edward Bailey Birge, and W. Otto Miessner
The Progressive Music Series (1916)

The *Progressive Music Series* was one of the most prominent basal music series based on progressive education theories. Recognizing the need for children to participate, it emphasized singing, rhythm activities, and dramatization. It was divided into three major parts in correlation with the three learning stages in children recognized by progressive education theory: the sensory, associative, and adolescent periods. Musical materials and experiences appropriate for each period were included. Major emphasis was on music appreciation, to be developed through rote singing, sight singing, music theory and history, and listening.

I. Aims of School Music Instruction

The general aim of education is to train the child to become a capable, useful, and contented member of society. The development of a fine character and of the desire to be of service to humanity are results that lie uppermost in the minds of the leaders of educational thought. Every school subject is valued in proportion to its contribution to these desirable ends. Music, because of its powerful influence upon the very innermost recesses of our subjective life, because of its wonderfully stimulating effect upon our physical, mental, and spiritual natures, and because of its well-nigh universality of appeal, contributes directly to both of these fundamental purposes of education. By many of the advanced educators of the present day, therefore, music, next to the "three R's," is considered the most important subject in the school curriculum.

Although the beneficent influences of music study reach our in number-less directions, it is generally agreed that the primary aim of music instruction in the public schools should be the development of a lasting love for the best in music, and an intelligent appreciation of it. To achieve these desirable results, the course in music may be organized under four separate though closely related lines of study, namely, Music Appreciation, Voice Culture, Sight Reading, and Interpretation. So interdependent are these several departments of the subject that a lesson in any one of them almost inevitably must include something of the others. Nevertheless clarity of purpose on the part of the teacher will be greatly enhanced by having the various aspects of her work distinctly differentiated in her mind as she conducts her class in its study of music.

Frances Elliott Clark
Music in General Education

Frances Elliot Clark (1860–1958) was a major influence in the development of music appreciation in schools. After serving as a music supervisor, she accepted a position with the Victor Talking Machine Company. There she created recordings and materials for use in the public schools, thus making possible effective classroom instruction in listening. Clark was the first president of the Music Educators National Conference (1907–1909), then called the Music Supervisors National Conference; and was also president of the Music Section of the National Education Association; and the National Federation of Music Clubs.

We who were pioneers in the work know the struggles we had and what difficulties have been overcome in bringing school music to a point of recognition by either the musicians or the educators. In the long pull of securing attention from school people, as being a factor in education and making our work really worthwhile as teachers of music, we older supervisors have borne the burden of the heat of the day bringing the work from its humble beginnings to its present place in the sun.

Standards have been raised, work has improved, opportunities have multiplied, the field has been enlarged, recognition has come; and now to the younger, better educated, better equipped, better paid supervisors of today, the door is wide open, the vista so alluring and so assured that we of yesterday wish we might begin all over again for the very joy if it.

The great war, whose shadow is still over us, settled a few things in the educational world, as in the commercial, financial, and other realms. It was not the over-scientific, over-specialized education of the military caste of the enemy that won the war . . . but the compelling heart power of the appeal from stricken countries . . . sentiment and sympathy, love and law, soul and spirit, took our whole people into it, like the wing sweep of an avenging angel, in righting a great world wrong. It was not our military prowess . . . nor yet our commercial instincts, but the keen sense of righteousness and honesty learned in our public schools.

And so it comes about . . . a swinging back of the pendulum from the over-emphasis placed upon the industrial and vocational training, commercial and utilitarian courses, to a saner mixture of the cultural subjects that make for right understanding and right living, and sensible serving in the upbuilding of the community, the state, and the nation, to those things that bring a realization of the spirit of "All for Each and for All."

School music has more to offer in the service of this newly awakened sense of the need of closer relationship of all classes, more to offer to the newly organized centers of communal thought, more to give toward building and keeping a high morale, a better spirit of happiness and joy in life, than any other one branch of study in the curriculum.

Music has at least as much to offer in mental discipline, in stirring the powers of discrimination, coordination, selection, and judgment, as any other one subject—and, next to reading, better stimulates the imagination. It correlates with other branches better than any other, save reading and writing, and even as a vocational subject it is second only to those of the most populous trades, while as a socializing function it has absolutely no peer.

The hour of music as education has struck. Not music for fun nor entertainment, nor as a pastime or accomplishment, nor yet as an art, standing alone—although at times it may be any or all of these—*but as one of the great vital forces of education.*

It only remains for the school music supervisors to rise to their new duties and opportunities to make school music in every city, village, and rural community the very heart of the school life, the focal point of all neighborhood activities, and a part of all civic work. It must be made a dynamic force in the life of every child everywhere, country as well as city, through being not a highbrow appendage, a beautiful but useless fringe on the garment, but a real servant of education.

The doors are open. Every great national musical or educational organization is behind the work of community music. High schools almost everywhere are giving credit for music courses, school orchestras multiply and will lead on directly to the municipal orchestra. Much hearing of the best music is raiding the standards of taste and appreciation. The field is ripe for the harvest and the laborers all too few . . . .

We of yesteryear builded better than we knew. We have not toiled in vain. And so, as we call upon the younger music educators to take up the advanced work which we with prophetic eye see in the aurora of the new day, let us bid them Godspeed.

Hannah Matthews Cundiff and Peter W. Dykema
The School Music Handbook (1923)

The *School Music Handbook* was written as a text for pre-service and in-service music educators and as a resource book for supervisors, administrators, school board members, and members of the public who wished to know more about music in the schools. It included a discussion of practically every topic with which music teachers dealt at that time in American schools.

If our country is to become truly musical it must be through the work of the public schools in the impressionable days of youth.

Why do we want American to be a music loving land? Because we are convinced that the nation with a love of music and an appreciation of it, possesses the greatest resource of happy and wholesome living.

Present day education can only hope to find its application in a more or less distant future, and while we work to shorten the span as much as possible, today's efforts can only find fruition in the days to come. While we cannot know the specific problems of those days, our present problem is to fit for life, as life seems to be tending. We know that labor, physical and manual, is becoming more dignified and respected and better paid. We know, too, that working hours are becoming shorter and that people are finding themselves with leisure and with money to spend on amusement for that leisure. How this time and money will be spent depends upon the tastes of the people. What the tastes of the people shall be depends upon the habits formed n their impressionable days—their school days.

Education should fit people for living day be day a full satisfying life. Such a life includes plenty of work with a certain spirit of play entering into that work, and a generous amount of play with a touch of the work spirit blending with the play.

How shall the play hours of the American people be spent? Education will be the deciding factor. Satisfaction in sordid things is best replaced by intimate acquaintance with things of true worth. Educators are realizing this and the schools are fast becoming the centers of many influences which are reaching out and enriching home and civic life. Prominent among these influences is music.

Judging by the number of popular songs, marches, and dances that may be heard from one end of our land to the other within a month's time we might assume that we are a musical nation. Unfortunately the compositions enjoyed by our general public are not music of a high type, nor is the satisfaction they give deep and genuine. Undeveloped taste is the secret of such perverted satisfaction, and music in the public school is the correction for it. The time is coming we hope, when an intimate knowledge of some of the great music of the world, some of the literature, the paintings, the sculpture, will be a part of the education of the mass of people, thus affording our wide land a fuller, more joyous life. True art is universal in its appeal provided always that its medium has become familiar.

The place of music in the public schools is widely acknowledged as of deep significance. Its possibilities and obligations are more and more the subject of serious consideration. Let us examine briefly some of the phases of music which the schools should offer.

1. Since singing must ever be the universal medium of musical expression, our schools must provide for the correct use of the singing voice in free and spontaneous sing, caring for it from its first use, through its changes and development into maturity.

2. Since power to interpret the printed page is the only means of independence in selection of music and in its performance, our schools must provide for independent reading.

3. Since there are many who have the desire and the ability to express themselves musically through some instrument other than the vocal organ, our schools must provide for class instruction in violin, cornet, drums, piano, and such other instruments as can be successfully taught to groups of young people.

4. Since vocational education is established as indispensable, our high schools must provide adequate training for that large number of young persons who wish to make music a profession, as well as for those who choose to become stenographers, mechanics, or other business or professional workers. Credits must be arranged for graduation in music courses as well as in other special courses.

5. Since the great majority of persons are unlikely to be creators of performers of music, but are entitled to love and appreciate it, and since appreciation of music is dependent upon contact with good music and upon training in musical judgment and discrimination, our schools must provide opportunity to hear good music of various sorts. This is now possible in rural districts and in the crowded cities as well, through the use of the mechanical inventions now on the market. In this phase of music in the schools is found the means by which the large part of the public is to benefit. In addition to the pleasure of self-expression in group singing, our people should take pleasure in listening to really good music. To bring this about is one of the chief functions of music in the schools.

America now has more concert performers of all kinds than can be supported with our present music ideals. Even in such a center as New York the people who come in touch with fine music are a small percent of the public at large. The big public, the mass of the people should be music-lovers, enjoying well written and well performed compositions. To this end the schools must work, so that our public may come to that point of intelligent listening where in forming an audience they "assist" as the French say, instead of merely attending.

6. Since education is now recognized to be work while largely in proportion to its linking up with the daily life, our schools must give children such music as they can take into their homes. A considerable portion of the songs they sing should be songs that they will enjoy singing in the home and that are already known by the older members of the family, or may be easily learned by them. The school program must provide time for committing to memory many good songs and must set up the habit of family singing. In like manner the work done in instrumental music must stress the home side, and set up the ideal of family orchestral groups.

7. Since cooperation and service are the basis of democracy, our schools must foster their growth. Group activities in which one thinks not only of himself but of his relation to the whole, seeking to do his bit in such manner that the unified effort of all shall succeed, at times finding himself in prominence, at others subordinated, employ qualities which are necessary in citizenship and should be cultivated in our boys and girls. Choral work, orchestras, and bands develop this group interest and should be recognized as valuable features of school life.

8. Since each member of a democracy is most valuable as he makes best use of his own peculiar talents, music instruction should, in so far as it legitimately can do so within the limits of its program allotment, stimulate the creative spirit through original musical expression. While it is to be devoutly hoped that by this means unusual talent may be discovered and directed, the main object of creative work is to quicken the appreciative spirit of the entire group.

9. Finally, since the main springs of actions rise usually from feeling rather than thought, and since music properly taught can exercise a potent influence over the emotional life, we may rightly expect from school music important moral discipline.

By bearing in mind such considerations as these we shall begin to be really musical, and to feel in our daily life the joys and benefits of music's influence.

Walter Damrosch, George Gartlan, and Karl W. Gehrkens
General Directions to Teachers (1922)

The *Universal School Music Series* (from which this excerpt is derived) was a group of textbooks written by Damrosch, Gartlan, and Gehrkens to encourage children's creativity. It characterized progressive education as it applied to teaching and learning music and contained much music meant to stimulate the aesthetic instincts of children. It was the intention of the authors to "give the children, abundantly, while they are still in school, the joyful experience of hearing and sharing in the rendition of beautiful music." There was an emphasis on song singing and listening lessons in order to achieve the general objective, which was appreciation. In keeping with the progressive education of philosophy, the *Universal School Music Series* attempted to promote social and patriotic values by means of music with appropriate texts.

I. Music as a School Subject

Music is one of the most valuable subjects in the school curriculum, and the influence of music in the lives of both children and adults is more potent than that of almost any other educational activity. Music affects human beings favorably, both in their intellectual and emotional lives. Because of its power to "tone up" the mind and body, its beneficial effect in causing increased quickness of perception, its potency to socialize, its possibilities in preparing one for a worthy use of leisure time, and above all, because of its influence in causing an immeasurable increase in human happiness—for all of these reasons, music has come to be more and more commonly regarded as an indispensable subject in all types of schools; and a larger and larger place is being accorded it.

In the individual school room the teacher is to approach the children's musical activities from two standpoints:

1. The *work lesson*, during which certain ground is to be covered, certain problems mastered, certain musical effects listened to; and during which both teacher and pupil shall bring to bear upon the task the keenest concentration of which they are capable.

2. The *recreational music period*, during which everyone will sing favorite songs, hear phonograph selections, or listen to vocal or instrumental solos.

During the first-named type of musical activity—the work lesson—the pupil is to acquire the technique which will make the second type—the recreational—more and more enjoyable as he goes on through the grades. Such is the primary function of the work lesson, but be it noted that such an exercise has a valuable by-product in the form of mental training. Indeed, music is as valuable for mental training as any other subject in the curriculum. The teacher will find that the prosecution of musical activity in this manner requires application as intensive as any other work that the pupil will do in all his life; and the formal music period should, therefore, be placed on the day's program at an hour when the pupil's minds are alert.

The recreational music period is usually short, and properly follows a period of intense work on arithmetic or some other taxing subject. It is informal and friendly, and as one of its chief values is that it makes the entire school happier and therefore affects the discipline favorable; it also unifies the sentiment of the room and intensifies group feeling; and it relaxes both mind and body, besides making easier for both teacher and children a zestful attack upon the next job in the day's work. The wise teacher knows that both time and nerves are conserved by a few minutes of recreational music two or three times daily, entirely apart from the formal music period.

II. Points Applying To All Grades

1. Community Songs. One of the most noticeable shortcomings of our American social life has been our inability to engage in satisfactory song-singing at social or other gatherings. Perhaps the chief reason for this deficiency is that few of us know the words of our songs. It is our aim to meet this need at least partially, by suggesting that all children in the public schools commit to memory each year the words of two or three well-known songs. The words of these songs are then to be reviewed each succeeding year and sung at frequent intervals, so that by the end of the eighth year each pupil should be able to sing from memory fifteen or twenty songs suitable for group-singing. In order to distinguish this material from the rest these songs will be referred to in this series as "patriotic and home songs," and every grade teacher is urged not only to see that each child shall learn the words of the songs designated for the current grade (this, in general, to be done as part of the required language works, and outside of the formal music period), but also to see that the songs taught in preceding years shall be reviewed from time to time throughout the year, and thus kept in repertoire.

Buescher Saxophones
Commercial Interests and Music Education

This is an advertisement for Buescher saxophones, published during the Jazz Age in 1928. The saxophone had only recently become a popular instrument, and manufacturers were trying to enlarge their market to include adult beginners, along with the well-established market of professional, military, and school ensembles. Saxophone advertisements often suggested that women play the instrument.

Sister Susie and the Steno Job

She finished high school *with honors!* Then Business College gave her training in six months and she started out to beat typewriters for a living. Fine!

But Susie was temperamental. Grinding drudgery *might do* for the type of girl whose only aim is an early marriage. For Susie it was *killing*. So Sister Susie "took up the saxophone."

Now Susie was just an *average* girl. You could never call her *gifted* or *talented*. But within a week she was playing tunes and in six months she could handle her saxophone *like a veteran*.

Then things happened. First, a little club orchestra. Next, a local sextette. Then some home town "entertainment"—a sharp-eyed scout from a well-known booking office—a contract—and little Miss Susie hit the *"big time" vaudeville*, drawing down as much cash weekly as the salaries of *half a dozen stenographers*.

Only Buescher assures success!

Will Earhart
A Steadfast Philosophy: "To Justify or Not to Justify"

Will Earhart was born in Franklin, Ohio, in 1871. He did not complete high school, having been expelled for a prank, but he became a music teacher one year later. From 1889 to 1912 he was music supervisor in Richmond, Indiana, where he developed a school music program that included all of the elementary and high school grades. The high school orchestra that he founded in Richmond in 1909 was probably the first such ensemble to grow to full symphonic size. In 1900, Earhart added harmony and music history as electives, but he changed them to music appreciation in 1901. In 1905, years ahead of his time, he succeeded in persuading the school board to award credit for participation in the orchestra. He demonstrated in Richmond that a music program of high quality could be developed as a part of the school curriculum. In 1912 Earhart became Director of Music for the Pittsburgh schools. His influential books and articles were written over a span of fifty years, and he was a leader in many professional activities, including those of the Music Supervisors National Conference (later the Music Educators National Conference).

Certain assumptions must be made, if we are to clear the ground of our argument from confusion. The first is that music, as we shall speak of it, is assumed to be taught successfully. This is no small assumption, for by "successfully" I mean that music shall be taught in such a way that the ends sought by all the arts, namely, enrichment of the personality by means of beautiful moments of experience, shall be attained. The second is that all other subjects of the curriculum shall be conceived as being taught successfully in the manner and degree prescribed for music; that is to say, these other subjects also shall be conceived as making in fact the contributions to human living included within their intentions. In short, we accept the ideals of purposes and attainments held on both sides. Only thus can we conceive the various subjects in their true character, and at the same time rid ourselves of fruitless bickering over methods of teaching and comparisons of teachers with one another.

With the ground thus cleared, the argument for music, as I see it, may be presented in three sections.

I. Aesthetic

Reality and Aesthetic Responses: If we look at the moon and say that it is round, we think we register a "fact." If we regard it and say that it is beautiful, we think we register something less valid. But since the factual, as the affective, merely records a transaction between a certain type of organism (ourselves), something outside the factual is nothing more than a subjective registration—precisely as is the beautiful. What would the multiple eye of the house fly apprehend as the reality "out there"? What is red light to the ants that Sir John Lubbock saw it slay as though it were some deadly Martian ray? What, now, is matter? What is mathematical reality, under modern physics and Einstein? We can know of all that is outside ourselves only that which we register, and the nature of that registration is prescribed by what WE are. "Round" and "beautiful" are thus equally valid testimony to something that, so far as we can know it, has occurred in us.

The Depth of the Factual Compared with the Aesthetic: The aesthetic appears to involve us more deeply than does the factual. If only half alive, we can see the factual aspects of matter. The dying man can see that "the casement window slowly grows a glimmering square." Square, indeed, but without depth or meaning. Dr. Richard Cabot points out that in our "devitalized" moments, as when we struggle to consciousness after a disturbed night, a baby is a lump of flesh, a picture is but pigment smeared on canvas. Only when we are most alive, when we respond in greatest depth and volume, is the factual submerged and integrated in the tide of response that we know as aesthetic. Had I time, I should endeavor to prove that the factual (alias the rational) deals characteristically with matter, and for purposes of our material well-being.

II. Intellectual and Educational

So far as the rational enters into the intellectual—and there are many who yet naively suppose that the rational is all there is of intellectual action— music engages the intellect only in connection with staff-notation, names, dates, acoustics, and other such factual aridities. But if we turn to all that part of the mind that is not concerned with business, manufacture, science—in brief, with the exact and quantitative—we may find music richly present. I cannot elaborate this view here, but in the 1931 Yearbook is one attempt by me to do so, and in the February 1933 issue of the *Music Clubs Magazine* is another. Suffice it to say here that music is conceived in the mind, is held in memory of the mind, is subjected to reflective, creative, ideational processes in the mind, comes forth as great mental achievements from the mind—for who would say that a Beethoven Ninth Symphony is less great as a mental product than a St. Paul's Cathedral, or a play such as *Hamlet* (not to mention a Chrysler car!)—and in fact can be found only in occasional and brief and precarious existence in the universe outside of the mind. As stuff for the mind to deal with, it is therefore quite as nutritive as scientific matter—say, as the natural history of the lobster. Not the stuff of thought, but the depth and energy of the function of thought is thus the measure of mental and educational worth.

III. Social

The factual, the rational, the utilitarian, the materialistic, the technological, all have this in common: They aim to do something to our material environment that will enable us to attain a condition wherein we will find ourselves leading the better life. What they are concerned with, therefore, is means toward an end. Factories, automobiles, concrete roads, are not the better life, but somehow we think that we may overtake the better life if we pursue it by means of these.

In contrast, art is a present salvation. The sunset, the song, the upthrown Gothic arch, the painter's dream, are present goods, doing something to bring sensitivity, humaneness, harmony, sweetness, purity, unselfishness, nobility, into our living.

By the first of these vaguely held concepts of life, man has been made a producer, a producer of many things, in ever increasing quantity. He has, indeed, almost come to measure the progress of his society in terms of tonnage.

But Henderson says: "If man is the highest product of creation, then civilization must be judged, not by what man produces, but by the manner of man produced."

Dr. William John Cooper, former United States Commissioner of Education, lately stated in Pittsburgh that technological progress would result soon in a 30-hour work week, filled with mechanical actions that required little training. He said that in view of this prospect the prime concern of education was with those factors that would minister to human betterment and happiness, and as examples of such factors, he emphasized only health, education, music, and art.

So, our civilization seems destined to move, whether we wish it or not, from one that conceived progress in terms of Man as a Producer to one that conceive Man as the Product and Education must reflect the world.

As the movement advances, we may expect that music, already amiably accepted because of the persistence in society of certain ineradicable humane instincts, will become fully justified in the consciously accepted creeds of people.

In order to leave no doubt, I would say in closing that I, myself, think a place for music in our public schools is justified.

John Dewey
The Aesthetic Element in Education (1897)

John Dewey, a noted American philosopher, put forth the project method of learning, in which students learned experientially. His ideas formed a signifi-cant part of the basis of the progressive education movement. Dewey believed that the public school should be a microcosm of society. The arts played an important role in his plan for education.

I interpret this title to mean a certain phase of all education, rather than a particular group of studies.

I. Responsiveness, an emotional reaction to ideas and acts, is a necessary factor in moral character.

II. It is also a necessary element in intellectual training, as supplying a delicacy and quickness of recognition in the face of practical situation.

III. The significance of the aesthetic element is that it trains a natural sensitiveness and susceptibility of the individual to usefulness in these directions. The individual has a natural tendency to react in an emotional way; but this natural disposition requires training. In some, who are natu-rally obtuse or thickskinned, it requires to be brought out; in others, who are naturally more sensitive, it may assume a morbid and exaggerated form, unless made to function in definite ways.

IV. The factors in aesthetic experience which are especially adapted to afford the right training are balance and rhythm. Balance implies control or inhibition which does not sacrifice a fullness and freedom of the experi-ence. It is opposed both to random, undirected action and to repressed, or undeveloped, action. Rhythm involves regularity and economy in the sequence of actions. Both balance and rhythm are forms of variety in unity: rhythm being temporal, balance spatial.

V. The aesthetic element thus should combine freedom of individual expression and appreciation with the factor of law and regularity in what is expressed. It is possible to extend the idea of artistic production to all kinds of work.

VI. Modern theory and practice in education have laid relatively too much stress upon the volitional training in practical control and intellectual training in the acquisition of information, and too little upon the training of responsiveness. We need to return more to the Greek conception, which defined education as the attaching of pleasure and pain to the right objects and ideals in the right way. This ideal over-emphasized the emotional element, but we have now gone to the opposite extreme.

Art as Experience: The Act of Expression

. . . Finally, what has been said locates, even if it does not solve, the vexed problem of the relation of aesthetic or fine art to other modes of production also called art. The difference that exists in fact cannot be leveled, as we have already seen, by defining both in terms of technique and skill. But neither can it be erected into a barrier that is insuperable by referring the creation of fine art. Conduct can be sublime and manners gracious. If impulsion toward organization of material so as to present the latter in a form directly fulfilling in experience had no existence outside the arts of painting, poetry, music, and sculpture, it would not exist anywhere; there would be no fine art.

The problem of conferring aesthetic quality upon all modes of production is a serious problem. But is a human problem for human solution; not a problem incapable of solution because it is set by some unpassable gulf in human nature or in the nature of things. In an imperfect society—and no society will ever be perfect—fine art will be to some extent an escape from, or an adventitious decoration of, the main activities of living. But in a better-ordered society than that in which we live, an infinitely greater happiness than is now the case would attend all modes of production. We live in a world in which there is an immense amount of organization, but it is an external organization, not one of the ordering of a growing experience, or that involves moreover, the whole of the live creature, toward a fulfilling conclusion. Works of art that are not remote from common life, that are widely enjoyed in a community, are signs of a unified collective life. But they are also marvelous aids in the creation of such a life. The remaking of the material of experience in the act of expression is not an isolated event confined to the artist and to a person here and there who happens to enjoy the work. In the degree in which art exercises its office, it is also a remaking of the experience of the community in the direction of greater order and unity.

Oscar Handlin
John Dewey's Challenge to Education (1959)

Oscar Handlin was a distinguished American historian.

. . . Often, however, simple instruction in the correct procedures seemed inadequate. It was not enough to teach children who lived in slums that "a healthful, beautiful location, good construction, perfect drainage, perfect plumbing, and perfect sanitary conditions generally, are indispensable to the house beautiful"; or to illustrate the proper mode of dining with quotations from Homer, Plutarch, and Boswell. It was essential, in addition, that the students' tastes be bent toward desirable, and therefore previously defined, goals.

The function of the school was also to soften and ennoble its charges. "Beware of the boy who was never in love with his schoolmistress; he will become a man who will bear vigorous watching, even in the pulpit." That end could be attained through the development of an appreciation of the higher aspects of culture. Domestic science, for instance, led to an awareness of the artistic elements in decoration and to an understanding of the beauties of English, French, German, and Italian furniture. Students were thus to be exposed to the noble, gentle styles of life so different from their own.

The development of high school education in music was particularly enlightening from this point of view. The underlying emphasis at the start, and for a long time thereafter, was upon singing for an uplifting purpose. "We need more songs of home, of country, of simple praise to God and love to man." Singing was important because of its subject matter. It dealt with "such subjects as Love of Country, Home-loving, the Golden Rule, etc." These, the teachers knew, will surely develop like sentiments in the children who sing them. Since music regulated the emotions, "the habitual use of vocal music by a family" was "an almost unfailing sign of good morals and refined tastes."

Furthermore, music also had value "as a disciplinary study"with power "to develop the mind and will of the child." It taught patriotism, morality, temperance, and obedience to the law. Singing was even "to some degree a safeguard against those diseases which affect the breathing organs." The need for proper attention to music was particularly great in the United States. "The social results of a developed rhythmical sense in considerable masses of people . . . are far-reaching. It cultivates a feeling for order and regularity. . . . It gives . . . a measure of values. . . . With our heterogeneous population, our widespread opposition of social classes, and the dreadful monotony of living among the lower classes . . . it surely is worth our while to cultivate in all classes in every kind of social group the feeling for order and symmetry." A "refined sense of harmony" was also essential. "The street noises that assault our ears and exhaust our nerves; the hideous architecture of our great cities, and the deadly architectural monotony of our factory towns; the excesses of public advertising; and our widespread disregard for the natural beauties of land, river, and sea—what are these but the inevitable outspeaking of a people to whom life has not yet become harmonious?"

In the logical progression of this argument, music had become not that which people enjoyed, but that which was good for them. A little story made this unmistakably clear. The young girl, sent by the town's subscriptions to study at the Conservatory in Boston, returns to Auroraville. Asked to play "Home Sweet Home" or "Rocked in the Cradle of the Deep," she refuses: "You see, I have really learned what is good music." The townspeople are antagonized when she plays instead Moszkowski's Sonata, an "unmelodious incomprehensive clatter." They withdraw their support. But she persists; and in time they acknowledge that they were wrong and she was right. "The people of no town were ever prouder of a native who had won distinction than the Auroraville people now are of that brilliant performer on the piano, Miss Hettie Ketchum."

The result, in the schools, was a steady shift in emphasis to courses that would identify good music and bring "added culture and refinement" into children's nature. It followed also that musicians had to avoid the opprobrium "of being deficient in general culture."

So too, the teaching of art was desirable because it encouraged accuracy of observation and contributed to success in later life. But the objects had to be carefully chosen; in a defective painting, the effect was "exactly like that of powder and rouge on a woman's face." "The purification and elevation" of "a vitiated and crude public taste" was "manifestly to be achieved by the systematic education of the youth" in the appreciation of great art, "however difficult that might be. . . ."

Karl W. Gehrkens
The Ultimate Aim of Music Teaching in the Public Schools

Karl W. Gehrkens was the editor of the *Music Supervisors Journal* during the second decade of the twentieth century, and served in several leadership positions in the music education profession through the 1930s.

The ultimate aim of music teaching in the public schools is to cause children to know, to love, and to appreciate music in as many forms as possible, and thus to bring added joy into their lives and added culture and refinement into their natures.

The specific means for accomplishing these aims may vary considerably in various places, but it is the sense of this body of music supervisors that the most direct approach is at present to be found in the expressive singing by the children themselves of a large amount of the best music available, and it is their belief that in this singing the art side and the science side of music need not necessarily be antagonistic, as some have seemed to assume, but may each contribute something to the sum total of musical influence that we are seeking to exert upon the child. It is our belief, also, however, that when the science side is emphasized, it should always be as a means to an end and never as an end in itself. In other words, that although skill in sight singing, keenness in analysis in ear training, and some knowledge of theoretical facts may all be desirable, yet these technical aspects of musical study must never be allowed to interfere with the legitimate working out of those emotional and aesthetic phases of music which constitute the real essence of the art; in other words, that it is the art side of music with its somewhat intangible influence which we are seeking to cultivate rather than the science side with its possibilities along the line of mental training and its more easily classified results.

Peter W. Dykema and Karl W. Gehrkens
High School Music: Our Educational Philosophy

Peter W. Dykema taught at Teachers College, Columbia University. Karl W. Gehrkens taught at the Oberlin Conservatory. Both held many leadership positions in professional associations. It was Gehrkens who created the slogan "Music for every child, every child for music" (1923).

Introduction
Our educational philosophy

Why teach music to high school students? In fact, why democratize music at all? Because participation and growing skill in music is a joyful and satisfying experience which lifts the individual to a higher level of satisfaction than is provided by most of life and therefore increases the sum-total of human happiness. Such in brief is the philosophy that underlies this book.

The older education frequently emphasized the hardness of things. An experience was supposed to be educational in proportion as it was difficult. If it was disagreeable as well as difficult, so much the better. The teacher usually dominated the pupil, therefore anything like original expression on the child's part was "bad." To a very large extent both pupil and teacher were at the mercy of rules and textbooks in the school, and of puritanical, merciless convention in the community. Things were "so" because the teacher said so; and if the pupil had the temerity to challenge the teacher's statement the latter had only to refer to "the book" where what he said was to be found in print. And whatever was printed in a book must be right!

Is it strange that under such circumstances the pupil often disliked school, disliked the teacher, disliked books—was glad when the end of the school day or the school year came? Probably the teacher was often glad too, but of course he didn't dare admit it.

Such frequently was school life in "the good old days," and such it still is today in a great many places. But the leaven of Rousseau, of Pestalozzi, of John Dewey has at last begun to work, and already we have hundreds of schools where both pupils and teacher are striving together happily at tasks that both enjoy doing because these activities are felt to have a real connection with life:"there is some sense to them." The teacher stimulates and guides, but does not dominate. Originality of expression is encouraged, and the pupils write stories, invent melodies, originate patterns and designs, create beautiful and useful objects out of wood or iron. Boys and girls are encouraged to engage in free bodily movement, especially rhythmic movement, and there is abundant opportunity for free play. The problems of home and community are brought to school for discussion and possible solution. Experimentation is the order of the day. Both pupils and teacher are happy, and often there is real regret when it is time to go home—especially when the home is not "ideal" in atmosphere. There were a few modern schools of this type a generation—yes, even a century—ago. Today the number is increasing rapidly, and in another fifty years the senseless, old-fashioned type of public school education will, we trust, have entirely disappeared.

To be sure, not all schools that call themselves "modern" are of this happy, productive type. Some schools that call themselves "progressive" are actually *retrogressive*, assuming as they do that the child is to be allowed, yes encouraged, to do anything he wants to do at any time. Is it not true that thoughtful consideration for others is still the most important single trait that school and home, working as a team, must inculcate in each individual child? Should not the theory of free expression on the child's part be based on the ideal that he may express himself only when he does not by so doing infringe on the rights of others; that in developing his original ideas he must bear in mind that every other child has an equal right to develop *his* ideas? And must he not learn to do things even if they are hard, provided there is some valid reason for doing them? Must he not, on occasion, do certain things because these things have to be done at fixed times so that there may be order rather than chaos in the school? Some modern teachers apparently do not realize the importance of these things and some allegedly progressive schools do not practice them. But are they not true nevertheless?

The authors of this book believe that school ought to be a place where a group of pupils, under the wise and friendly guidance of a teacher, work hard at doing things most of which are palpably useful and sensible, many of which are extremely interesting, and a few of which are so fascinating that at least some of the pupils would rather do them than anything else in the world. Of course there is play too, but often it is hard to tell which is work and which is play. In a music class the singing of an attractive new song for the first time may be play. But now the teacher says, "Do it again and get the dotted-eighth rhythm exactly right"; or, "Once more, and with better tone quality"; or, "Sing the fourth measure again and watch the into-nation; no, the F-sharp is still a little flat; that's better, now repeat it, and lis-ten!"—and that is probably work. However, when, a week later, some pupil says, "May we sing the song again that we learned last week?"; and the song is sung joyfully and perfectly—that is probably play again. It does not much matter what is called play and what work; but certainly the school must provide experiences in which the student does a certain thing because that is the thing to be done at that time, and sticks to it until it is finished—work; and other experiences in which there is usually a little less formality and which are engaged in largely for the fun of it—play.

The emphasis in the genuinely progressive school is, then, upon what the pupil does rather than on what the teacher does. The pupil initiates many of the activities and the teacher merely helps him to do more per-fectly what he himself has come to feel a need for doing. If the teacher sees that the pupils are not having a sufficient number of "good" wants or needs, he manipulates the situation so that certain things which the pupil had not thought of are brought to his attention; or he makes certain other things that are already in the pupil's consciousness more alluring so that he will be more strongly attracted to them. Thus, if the orchestra is short of violas and no one offers to take up this interesting but usually unpopular instrument, the conductor may arrange to have some fine viola player present a group of solos at an assembly period, the effect of such an experience probably being that several violinists ask for the privilege of playing viola—espe-cially if the school offers to lend them the instruments.

The teacher is kindly in his attitude and sympathetic with the pupil when he has difficulties; but he is firm too, and he insists that when a worthwhile task has once been started, it must not be left until it is finished. In the end the pupil sees that the teacher's "severity" is wise and kind, and he therefore does not think of it as unfriendly. So the days and the years go by, the pupils working happily, learning facts and skills, acquiring self-dis-cipline and regimentation, developing ideals and attitudes, becoming well-

Peter W. Dykema and Karl W. Gehrkens

adjusted personalities. And at last it is the ideals and attitudes that best survive the ravages of time. Key signatures and symphony themes may be forgotten; skill in playing violin or oboe may be lost; but an ideal of good tone, of perfect intonation, and an attitude of love and enthusiasm for fine music—these will endure as long as life itself shall last.

"Yes, but what of music study in this new type of school," you ask, "what place has it in modern education?" to which we reply confidently, "A very important place."

The older school attempted to "store" the memory and to "train" the intellect. If it set itself any other goal it was to teach conventional morality—but in the main this was done only theoretically. The modern school attempts to develop the entire personality as a unified whole: mind, body, feelings and attitudes, will power—even memory. "Special" subjects like music, art, and physical education had but a limited place in the schools of yesterday. In the schools of today they have a much larger place; and in the schools of tomorrow they will achieve the distinction of being no longer called "special," that is, "irregular," or "unimportant," but will be recognized as the very core of the educational experience.

The genuinely progressive school is a happy place; and no subject has more to do with making it happy than music. It is a place where original expression is encouraged; and what subject lends itself better to creative effort than music, unless possibly English? It is a place where physical expression is made much of; and what more joyful or more educational type of physical activity can be imagined than folk dancing, free rhythmic response, and eurythmics? It is a place where the child learns to subordinate his personal desires to the best interests of the group, because in the end this will best serve his own interests also; and what more powerful agency is there for this purpose than ensemble singing or playing, activities in which the individual is constantly having to subordinate himself to the total effect?

The modern school aims to provide experiences that will carry over into adult life, and here music can be a vital influence. To be sure, most of the pupils will never become professional musicians, but it is not the professional musician of whom we are thinking just now. Our main concern is to afford the great masses of people the satisfaction of participation in music. . . .

"But," you are saying, "when are these authors ever going to get to their philosophy? Here I almost skipped this introduction because I was afraid of impending long words and high-sounding phrases that would mean nothing to me; and about all I get is anecdotes about busy doctors and bored middle-aged housewives who liked music well enough as children so that when they grew up they decided to continue playing and singing." To which the authors reply with a chuckle that this is exactly what they are trying to tell you, that this is their philosophy: Music must be made so delightful, so satisfying an experience during school days that a very large number of children will learn to love it so deeply and to play and sing so well that when school days are over they will still want to continue to play and sing and listen—perhaps even create. They will want to keep on studying, too, so as to achieve more and more skill, and therefore greater and greater satisfaction from their own performance. Because they love music they will want to associate with other people who also love it. In the end music becomes for them a release from dullness and frustration, even from pain: an exalter of the human spirit; a stimulant toward a more friendly attitude as they mingle with other human beings; a necessary part of normal, happy living.

How badly the world needs all this! How self-centered, how grasping and selfish many of us are. How intent on material gain. How anxious to outshine our neighbors with our larger cars, our more complicated households, our sons and daughters at expensive colleges. How mechanized we have become, how naively do we put our trust in science and machinery; and how desolate and helpless does the human being feel when he finds that in the end machinery is heartless, that it can give but scant comfort to the yearning spirit of man when he is alone or confronted by disaster. How obsessed we are by bigness; and how vain and inglorious a thing is size when pain and disaster come, when the soul craves reassurance and serenity.

But how satisfying a thing is beauty, and especially beauty in the guise of music. What a comfort to be able to play the piano when one is low in spirit. What a satisfaction to sing or whistle or play the violin when one is happy. How thrilling to join three other string players and read Haydn quartets for an evening. What a relief to sing in the church choir after a hard day's work. What a joy to attend a symphony concert or a piano recital, and, because the ears have been trained to hear, to be able to forget oneself almost completely while listening to the music. Pain and sorrow and disillusionment are lost sight of; the joy of being alive is exalted; and one is transported for awhile to a different world—the world of ecstacy.

This is the function of music in life—to provide nurture for the spirit of man—which the ravages of the machine age are inexorably starving. To be happy, to be satisfied, man must express himself in some way; and here, in music, we have the ideal medium of expression. Money, position, power—in the end these will all fail us, and the men and women who make such things their principal goal will be lonely and disillusioned, often bitterly unhappy. It is only from the things of the spirit that lasting satisfaction eventuates, and among these music must be conceded to have a highly important place, possibly the most important. This is our philosophy. This is our creed. And the music teacher, if he is to be successful in any real sense, must believe in music as an exalter of the human spirit, as a life-giving force in education.

Peter W. Dykema and Karl W. Gehrkens

He must come to realize that music is taught for what it can contribute to the child rather than for what the child can contribute to music. So it is not merely *public school music* that we are advocating, nor even—to adopt the broader terms—*school music* or *music education*. It is education through music, to borrow the title of Charles Hubert Farnworth's epoch-making book; it is music at the center of human life; music that changes life, that changes the child so that he still remains changed when he has become a man; music that awakens in each individual a craving for artistic expression and provides him with a type of experience that satisfies this craving; music that makes the individual more friendly, more capable of working harmoniously with others, that causes him to listen to the effect of the whole and to subordinate his own egoistic desires to the total ensemble; music that is so genuine, so thoroughly fine that because of its beauty and purity it reaches down deep into the soul; music that lifts the individual human being above the humdrum of daily life, soothing him when the pain of existence would otherwise be too intense, and, at other times, affording a medium for expressing his joy at being alive—it is this kind of *education through music*, this kind of music as a part of normal living, that we advocate—in school, in home, in church, in community.

James L. Mursell and Mabelle Glenn
The Psychology of School Music Teaching:
The Aims of School Music (1938)

James L. Mursell was Professor of Education at Teachers College, Columbia University. Mabelle Glenn was Supervisor of Music in Kansas City, Missouri. Both were influential authors.

I. Music Education as Progressive Reconstruction of Experience

John Dewey has defined all education as the reconstruction of experience. By this he means that it is neither the storing up of information, not the reaction of fixed habits. Rather it is the opening up to the individual of new and ever wider avenues for experience and action. Every subject in a curriculum may be educative or non-educative, according to the fundamental philosophy on which its treatment is based. It is educative only in so far as it becomes an opportunity for wider and characteristically human experience. For instance, if mathematics, history, and literature are taught merely on a basis of information or of skill, they lose their value. Essentially they are great fields of human enterprise and endeavor, wide realms in which men have discovered possibilities of experience and action. Exactly the same thing holds in music. If it is taught as a drill subject, or as an information subject, then it has no real place in the school curriculum. Its justification, and its educative value, depend wholly on its being treated as a field of vital and inspiring experience. . . .

3. The idea of music education as a reconstruction of experience leads us directly back to a point on which we have insisted again and again—namely, that the heart of music education is appreciation. If we fail to create appreciation, we become at once just trainers, mere teachers of tricks, and we cease to be educators. Appreciation precisely means experience with the beauty and the power of music, and we have seen how all parts of the program must be organized to produce just this result.

II. Music Education as Discipline

While we insist that music education is entirely different from training, so that its chief agency is not drill but appreciation, this does not mean for a moment that we want to make everything easy, to eliminate all challenge, and all stress and strain. To remove essential difficulties from any subject is to vitiate it. But wrongly to understand, and wrongly to handle the difficulties of any subject, is to kill it. What we believe is that the enjoyment and creation of music should be made so attractive, so alluring, that difficulties become challenges, and hard work, a joy. This is the disciplinary value of music, as well as of any other subject. . . .

III. Music Education as an Enterprise in Fuller Living

Another idea on which Dewey insists is that education is not a process of preparation for life. It is life itself. The ultimate justification for music in the schools is not the idea that children will use it at some time in the future, so that it is wise to prepare them for so doing. It is that music properly taught has an immense and potent appeal to the child, that it offers him a wide opportunity, *here and now*, for fuller living and that this opportunity ought to be his. Notice that we say music *properly taught*. If it is handled as a drill subject, with primary emphasis on such things as note reading, theory, or technique, it will not have this value. Such an approach always involves two difficulties. (1) It means that we have to create interest and motivation artificially, by some sort of sugar-plum incentives, as for instance, by greatly over-emphasizing social motivation. But when music is taught in terms of appreciation, it tends to become its own motive. (2) Instead of having reasons for what we do, we have to invent excuses. The love of music justifies itself. Its value is obvious and undeniable. But the value of knowing note names, understanding musical theory, or developing technique, as ends in themselves, is far from self-evident. So when teachers aim at these things, they have to concoct reasons. The most commonly used of these—the claim that such studies train the mind—has already been discussed and dismissed. But also we have feeble efforts to show that children may sometime, somewhere use a certain skill or trick—efforts always dubious and debatable. *Educational procedures which cannot justify themselves in the here and the now, in terms of a happier and fuller life for the child, are always open to the most serious question.* What we want is a program that will not aim at drill, and at the same time will not shirk difficulties; one that will seek to give the child an opportunity to become, at his own level, a *child musician*—that is, to find in music an opportunity for happiness and a fuller life.

But we may be asked, what about the vocational and avocational emphasis in school music? Should we not hold that school music aims to help some few into professional careers, and to open for many a worthy avocation? Our answer is that school music, just like every other educative subject, has nothing at all directly to do with preparation. *But it has everything to do with helping the child to discover music for himself, and to discover himself musically.* If this is achieved, then the later uses to which music will be put will very largely take care of themselves. The real problem for the vocational adviser is the person who has not found himself, and has no idea of what he really likes, or how he wishes to shape his life. Finding one's self is the basis of finding work and leisure time pursuits.

In a very real sense, an educative process has no aim or end except more education, more growth, more life. We see this in grade school singing, where we said that each song should be at once a goal and a stepping stone. Here we have a principle as broad as humanity, and to it we should cling. Help the child to live music, and you have educated him musically. Train him in a bag of tricks, and you have wasted both his time and your own.

So here for the third time we are brought in our discussion of aims, to the leading concept of appreciation. A scheme of music education that is to be in truth an adventure in fuller living, must center about the understanding love of music, and must be informed in all its parts by the spirit of appreciation.

IV. Music Education as an Agency for Creative Democracy

Dewey insists that the true essence of democracy is not its political structure. Its vital characteristic is a wide and intimate sharing of experience, a social situation where lives may meet and may mutually refresh, instruct, inspire, and encourage one another. This was exemplified in the most perfect of all democracies, that of ancient Athens, a state where men of many temperaments and many minds, met and mingled together in a rich community of living. In that state too, we see the creative force of the democratic ideal, embodying itself in matchless masterpieces of art, contributed for the common good, and deriving their meaning and vitality from their expression of the common aspiration. But such a creative sharing is simply impossible without a wealth of experience to be shared. This was the true social meaning of the great literary, dramatic, and artistic manifestations of Athenian genius. They provided the means whereby men's minds might come together, the focal points for the community of will and enterprise and patriotic love. Ancient Athens was a democracy founded in part on music, though certainly the art meant less to a classical civilization than it does to us in this age. Today we are beginning to see in music an agency for humanizing and ennobling modern social life, with all its stress and strain, and all its anti-human, anti-democratic subdivisions of function.

We see the social power and richness of music. But we must not think that to capture this power, we must slight music and intrinsic musical value, and emphasize a spirit of "get-together." Davison tells us how, during the way, those camps which emphasized mere "get-together" and let music slip, found infinitely less value in their community singing than those in which musical values themselves were assiduously cultivated. What we mean is that we must have faith in music, that we must make music the main thing, and let it do its own work, which it assuredly will. We see this strange uniting power in music most perfectly in the amateur ensemble group, where each individual finds his work enriched by that of all the others, and where he himself contributes to a corporate undertaking. It is no accident that philosophers have thought of the harmony of the heavens as a celestial music, or that theologians have pictures the chief joy of the redeemed as participation in an anthem old and yet ever new. Music has an enriching and creative mission for democracy in bringing men more closely face to face.

Here too we see the ultimate mission of school music. There have been times when music was an aristocratic art, the peculiar possession of the few. But these have always been decadent times for music. The art has been continually refreshed by the streams of folk music. Its greatest servants have always tended to universalize its appeal. When they have expressed themselves about their lives and work, they have many times shown the intimate sense of a mission to all mankind. Thus we have the stupendous words of Beethoven, words which no man not conscious of a godlike power dare utter: "I am the Bacchus who presses for humanity the delicious wine of life."

In American school music we see an art movement which is vital because of its true, democratic instinct and impulse. To have this movement thwarted by drill-masters and led into blind alleys by pedants and technicians would be a tragedy which we ought not even to contemplate. We should have gone far beyond such immaturity and mechanistic crudity. To teach America the achievement of loving music wisely is the ultimate aim of school music. This the school music teacher should dedicate himself to the task of conveying the power and glory of music to all the children of our schools, with a creed which is nobly summarized in these words:

"Thou lovely art, my joy and consolation,
Whose wondrous power drives all our care away,
Thou hast my heart throughout my life's duration,
The world rejoices in they magic sway.
I've sounded all the forms of human pleasure;
But thou art better than all else to me.
A foretaste thou of heaven's richest treasure.
Thou hold art, I give my life to thee."

Hazel Nohavec Morgan
Statement of Belief and Purpose (1947)

Hazel Nohavec Morgan edited the first two source books of the Music Educators National Conference. This essay appeared in the first source book, *Music Education Source Book.*

Throughout the ages, man has found music to be essential in voicing his own innate sense of beauty. Music is not a thing apart from man; it is the spiritualized expression of his finest and best inner self.

There is no one wholly unresponsive to the elevating appeal of music. If only the right contacts and experiences are provided, every life can find in music some answer to its fundamental need for aesthetic and emotional outlet. Education fails of its cultural objectives unless it brings to every child the consciousness that his own spirit may find satisfying expression through the arts.

The responsibility of offering every child a rich and varied experience in music rests upon the music teacher. It becomes his duty to see that music contributes its significant part in leading mankind to a higher plane of existence.

The Music Educators National Conference, in full acceptance of its responsibilities as the representative and champion of progressive thought and practice in music education, pledges its united efforts in behalf of a broad and constructive program which shall include:

(1) Provision in all the schools of our country, both urban and rural, for musical experience and training for every child, in accordance with his interests and capacities.
(2) Continued effort to improve music teaching and to provide adequate equipment.

(3) Carry-over of school music training into the musical, social, and home life of the community, as a vital part of its cultural, recreational, and leisure-time activities.

(4) Increased opportunities for adult education in music.

(5) Improvement of choir and congregational singing in the churches and Sunday schools; increased use of instrumental ensemble playing in connection with church activities.

(6) Encouragement and support of all worthwhile musical enterprises as desirable factors in making our country a better place in which to live.

Music Educators National Conference
A Declaration of Faith, Purpose, and Action

Resolutions Adopted by the Music Educators National Conference, Cleveland, April 1, 1946, as published in the first source book.

We, the members of the Music Educators National Conference, reaffirm our conviction that music is a beneficent agent for making life more satisfying. In peace as well as in war, music is one of the most important sources of spiritual sustenance.

We reaffirm our faith in the value of music in education, and particularly in its importance in the development and control of attitudes, feelings, and emotions.

We believe in America; we believe that music is helping to strengthen the power and ideals of our country. We believe it is our responsibility to bend every effort to the end that this power of music shall reach into the whole life of America, through every community, and contribute its full share to our national welfare and development.

I. *Music in the Elementary and Junior High School Grades.* We recommend that increasing emphasis be placed on the program of music education in the elementary and junior high school grades; that teacher-training institutions implement this progress by stressing this phase of teacher preparation; and that maintenance of standards be supported by city and county supervisory service.

II. *State Music Supervision.* We further recommend that each State Department of Public Instruction include a State Supervisor of Music on its staff.

III. *String Instrument Promotion.* In the stress and strain of modern living it is becoming obvious that the patient, time-consuming endeavor needed by pupils for the development of string instrument performance is being neglected. We recommend that all music educators become aware of this trend and use their influence to encourage the interest of young folk in the string instruments, and make every effort to nurture this interest.

IV. *Music in the Senior High Schools.* We commend highly the attention now being given to the glee clubs, choruses, choirs, orchestras, and bands in the high schools. However, these elective subjects reach only a small percentage of high school students throughout the nation. To provide appropriate musical experience for a larger portion of pupils we urgently recommend that more offerings in general music courses be included in the curriculum.

V. *Skill in Reading Music.* Despite the growing tendency to give less time and attention to acquiring skill in reading music, we reaffirm our belief in the importance of an ability to perform music easily and accurately from the printed page.

VI. *Time Allotment.* A well-rounded program of music activities in the elementary school should include singing, listening, creating, playing, rhythmic expression, dramatizations, and music reading. We recommend a minimum allotment of one hundred minutes per week as essential to the effective realization of such a program.

VII. *Technological Aids in Music Education.* We believe that recordings, radio, television, the stroboscope, the mirroscope, films, and other audio-visual devices are capable of supplying effective teaching aids. We recommend that music educators investigate, study, and become aware of the valuable potentialities of all such equipment.

VIII. *Music Teaching as an Exponent of Democratic Processes.* While we are training thousands of young men for military duty, we must also train the younger millions to embrace the ideals and democratic processes for which civilization strives. To that end each one of us is under the necessity of searching out procedures of teaching that will make our classroom the highest example of a functioning democracy.

IX. *The Broadening Scope of Music Experience.* Lines of separation between popular entertainment music, on the one hand, and the music of standard concert and opera repertoires, on the other, are slowly but surely becoming less marked. Furthermore, there is a tendency in music education to view and estimate the total music curriculum in relation to the total social and cultural scene of life.

Both the so-called popular and so-called high-brow music of today stem from the cultural level of this period in our national growth, and in music, as elsewhere, we are a nation uneasy in our diversity of contrasts.

It follows that bases of judgment and choice of values for our young people are the more imperative. We, therefore, recommend that music educators seriously study ways and means of achieving a combination of the dynamic factors embodied in the music of today and the enduring music of the past in programs that remain consistent with the aims of music education.

X. *International Cultural Relations Through Music.* A world at peace is the dearest hope of the millions of people n every country on earth. Music is the universal language and should be utilized at its highest potential power to help win and sustain world-wide peace.

We, the members of the Music Educators National Conference, therefore, urge the adoption of the bill now pending before Congress authorizing the cooperation of the United States in the United Nations Educational, Scientific and Cultural Organizations.

We further urge that our Executive Committee set up a special committee with delegated power to proffer to the President of the United States and to the Secretary of State our full cooperation in this international project, and that the members of this special committee use their every effort to see that music is adequately represented on the proposed commission and on the proposed committee to be appointed by the Secretary of State.

XI. *Providing Music Material is a Social Responsibility.* Since the foundations of democracy are rooted in broad education, the providing of material for the educational process is a matter of public concern. Music education is highly dependent upon adequate variety of books, music, instruments, records, and other aids, many of which cannot equal in sales the figures reached by purely entertainment products.

As educators, we maintain that approved educational material is so vital that all producers of such material, and the manufacturers of phonograph records in particular, are obligated to plan their products not entirely as commercial outputs which, piece by piece, are to be evaluated as to their revenue-producing possibilities, but also as long-view educational outputs for influencing that richer outlook on life which tends to perpetuate our democracy.

James L. Mursell
Principles of Music Education (1936)

James L. Mursell's writings on psychology influenced the teaching of music.

Social Principles—The Place of Music in Social Life

. . . The vitality of any scheme of education turns on the extent to which it is an agency for favorable social adjustment. Persons responsible for any such scheme should be concerned critically, and anxiously with the uses to which learners will put the things they are taught—the effect that those things have upon them in social living. Emphatically, this is true of the music program. It should be organized deliberately to produce palpable practical results in pupils' lives both now and later on. We may perhaps state its most characteristic and basic aim in terms of use as follows: The music program should aim at the promotion of active and intelligent musical amateurism.

We often hear that music education is part of the equipment of human beings for leisure. And it seems to follow that with the increase of leisure we should seek an increasing emphasis upon music in the schools. Unquestionably, this argument is sound up to a certain point. But it is open to a serious objection, which has been urged recently in influential quarters. For it is pointed out that the mere increase of leisure does not necessarily involve a demand for music. Many other activities can be imagined that might fill the growing amount of free time in a satisfactory manner. So we must show that music is, for various reasons, a peculiarly desirable leisure pursuit. To define our argument more precisely, it is that music indeed represents a worthy use of leisure, because it can be used with beneficial effects in a variety of social situations, because it is open to many persons, and because it is intrinsically enjoyable. A sound program of music education will be organized to capitalize all these values. Let us consider some of the social situations in which music may be used with beneficial effects.

Music Is a Pursuit Available in a Variety of Significant Social Situations

a. Music is an important agency for the enrichment of home life. Concretely, this means a heightened interest in listening, a more discriminating use of mechanical music, of course including the radio, and performance by members of the family for home enjoyment. It should be one of the aims of the program of music education to promote such activities. That program should be regarded, in part, as a training for more worthy home membership.

b. The music program should have definite outcomes in the church and the Sunday school. One of its effects should be an increased interest and participation in congregational singing, church choirs, and the musical aspects of worship generally. Here, again, we must insist in the necessity of definite planning, if these social benefits are to be realized.

c. The music program should be planned for definite outcomes in secular community music. Both rural and urban community life can be enriched and bettered measurably by setting up and maintaining a variety of musical activities. And the school music program should find much of its vitality in sustaining them. Musical organizations that exist largely for their own sakes or for general recreative purposes, such as choirs, orchestras, small ensembles, music clubs, study groups, groups active in promoting concert courses, and the like, can serve a valuable social purpose. One of the principal aims of the music program should be to further such organizations by interesting the pupils in them.

In general, the music work in the schools gains most of its significance and value from its social effects, and these effects should be a main conscious concern for the music educator, and should not be left to chance. . . .

Music in the Schools—The Substance of a Hope

These words are written under the shadow of stupendous and fateful happenings [World War II]. The attack has fallen upon us. Our complacencies have vanished. What seemed to many our security has, in one blinding flash, been revealed for the delusion that it always was. In years gone by we have often been told that ours was a changing world, and that with this fact we must reckon. Yet to many of us such words had an academic ring, and it seemed that we might heed them or not as we pleased. No longer is this so. This reality of which we have been warned is now brought home to all of us with inescapable force. We are in the grip of a mighty tide, sweeping us onward towards unknown destinies. Now we know it.

Is this a time to write a book about the teaching of music? Yes, it is! For it is a time to remind ourselves where true and lasting values lie. We cannot foresee the shape of things to come; but we all do our part in creating them, whether for weal or woe. None of us can wish to deal in trivialities in days like these, or in the days that are sure to come. But music is not numbered among the trivial things of life. It is one of the most perfect of all expressions of what is best and purest in the human spirit. And now, in the midst of so much evil, we and our children supremely need its eloquent reminder that goodness also is mighty and enduring. In the midst of so much doubt, confusion, conflict, and hate we and our children need its testimony to eternal values. . . .

I

Each and every worker in the field of music education is the representative of a hope and the exponent of a faith. He is so whether he knows it or not. This he can never understand too clearly or remember too often, for it is the very heart of his responsibility. At first sight the idea may seem obscure. Certainly one does not often come upon it in educational discussions. But it is none the less fact, and a critically important one. To appreciate it we need only raise a single question: How is it that we have music education in the schools at all?

The development of music in American public education is an exceedingly remarkable phenomenon—much more so than we usually recognize, perhaps because we are so accustomed to it. Programs of work in music, albeit often imperfect ones, are almost universally accepted in our thousands of school systems, and taken seriously as an integral part of the curriculum. Enormous numbers of children are being reached and influenced more or less effectively. A remarkable range and variety of musical activities are being carried on. A great deal of the work being done, particularly by high school orchestras, bands, and choral organizations, is of an impressive excellence. A new profession is coming into existence, equipped with sound and practical techniques for teaching music better, in the main, than it has ever been taught before. Universities, colleges, and conservatories are making an important place in their budgets and time schedules for training this new personnel. And publishing firms are finding it worth their while to invest large sums of money in producing teaching materials of a very superior excellence both as regards content and format. What is still more remarkable, all this has come about within the lifetime of many men still active in the field. Music has become a far more notable curricular success and has been carried much further in the American schools than in those of any other country.

Now such a development does not take place by chance. And anyone able for a moment to take the viewpoint of an outsider who retains the capacity for surprise and curiosity can hardly avoid asking what brought it about. . . .

Teachers and educational workers often fail to appreciate the part played by public opinion in shaping the curriculum of the American schools. This leads to a lack of realism, and an imperfect understanding of their own responsibilities and opportunities. The curriculum as actually taught is by no manner of means the exclusive creation of educational philosophers and psychologists, or of planning boards and commissions, or of groups of teachers in individual schools. Such planning agencies of course have their effect. They are important sources of leadership, suggestion, and criticism. They may start the ball rolling by introducing new procedures and devices such as the use of projects or mastery units, or the adoption of integration or the core curriculum. But they are not prime movers. The program of studies as it works out from day to day in actual practices is the resultant of many forces and many pressures, often more or less conflicting. The complete making of a curriculum does not take place inside any committee room, but rather in and through a working adjustment between the school and its constituency. And by far the strongest influence in determining what shall be taught and what shall not is public opinion operating over long periods of time.

For instance, science was not brought into the curriculum because educational authorities wanted it. Some indeed favored it, but others in positions of great influence bitterly resisted its introduction for long enough. It arrived and gained support because the public became convinced that their children should not grow up lacking contact with it—because they saw in it certain possibilities and values for better living from which they thought their children would benefit. . . .

This, of course, is exactly how music came to be established in schools. Lowell Mason introduced it in Boston, and after the sundry vicissitudes, it commended itself to the citizens. Other early leaders set up music programs here and there, also with successful results and increasing acceptance. Various educational statesman, among them Eliot of Harvard, gave it a few kind words, which helped things along. But this did hardly more to cause the development than a weather forecast does to cause a fine day. The public was given more and more convincing samples. Exposition, discussion, and publicity did their part. Planning became more and more effective, as the trial and error—or rather the trial and success—process worked along. But the dynamic which carried everything before it was a rising tide of public good will, a belief that music was a good thing for young people, a hope that from it certain values might enter the lives of the rising generation. And every present-day worker in the field of music education is a beneficiary and a representative of this hope, and has a central responsibility for helping to make it good.

Among the many implications of this idea, the following call for special comment.

1. Every teacher should be conscious that his work is conducted in, and indeed made possible by a nexus of personal and social relationships. What he is able to do depends in the long run upon the wishes and attitudes of his pupils, of their parents, and of the school constituency. He has in mind certain standards: he proposes to use certain types of materials or certain methods, or to promote certain activities. Are they wise? Are they feasible? The ultimate answer cannot be found in the internal logic of his subject. As a matter of fact, this can be utilized to prove almost anything one wishes to prove. Should we have a great deal of folk music? Should we cling to Bach and eschew jazz, or even Gilbert and Sullivan? Should we exalt the standard instruments, and have nothing to do with harmonica bands? A decision cannot be reached by deductions from the nature of music itself; for the art of music has many aspects and can be approached and treated successfully in many ways. The criterion is what the public with which he is dealing—and of course that public includes the pupils—can be led to accept. For he is not a representative of music per se but rather a servant of the community whose business it is to promote the acceptance and enjoyment of music by human beings. . . .

2. The proper line for the teacher to take may be summed up as follows. (a) He must discriminate between well-intentioned and sinister and selfish pressures. The latter it is his responsibility to fight, even if so doing costs him his job, though it usually need not do so if he fights wisely. For instance, it is one thing when the local Rotary Club wants to promote a marching band, and quite another when some commercial house with head offices in a faraway city tries to insist on the exclusive use of its products, or to push one of its own candidates into a position of influence in a school system. These last are insolent and flagrant invasions, and well merit the

James L. Mursell

stinging repudiation which a high-minded school-man who has won the support of his public can well administer. (b) He must realize that lay initiatives, while praiseworthy and desirable, are nearly always limited. They make fine starting points, but unsatisfactory policies. The psychology promoted by the W.C.T.U., the health education pushed by the insurance companies, the drawing introduced by the Boston business men did not work out any too well. And while the American Bar Association had a fine idea—to develop better citizenship—it was not very effectively applied by making youngsters study that complicated and subtle legal document, the Constitution, which has often seemed to baffle much older heads. So also in music, when Rotary pushes for a marching band and a drum majorette, or Kiwanis begins to ask why there is no high school glee club, the music teacher should thank Heaven for so much public interest. He may think that an orchestra and an a cappella choir would be much better, in which he may be right or wrong. But instead of deploring low popular taste, he should set himself to use live popular interest; and in moulding it, he may himself be moulded. (c) The music teacher is not merely teaching music. He is not merely teaching boys and girls. He is at the center of a nexus of community desires and interests to which he must respond, and on which he must exert influence. He stands for the community as a whole, in terms of a special kind of work. In this sense he is a public person, and his work, which extends far beyond the classroom, is a public service, and can only be done with real success when so regarded.

3. What about those situations where the constituency seems quite indifferent to its schools, and where it seems a mockery to talk about music teaching or anything else meeting and fulfilling a public wish, because the public apparently has no wishes? They are, of course, crucial for the whole approach here suggested.

One should recognize that such situations are educationally limiting and defective, and teachers should consider it a primarily obligation to rectify them. Neither music nor any other subject can be taught as it should be if it is handled within the isolated limits of the classroom and the school. This is because the teaching of a subject means a great deal more than trying to get children to learn this and that which is considered desirable. Rather it is an affair of influencing the lives—the thoughts, the interests, the feelings, the action of choices—of human beings. The music program which makes no impression upon the school constituency, and which is treated with blank indifference, lacks a most essential element of vitality. For the interest, the pride, and the faith of the constituency in what the school is doing for its children is an indispensable motive force for effective work. Where it is lacking, one of the first necessities is to set about building it. This is not done merely by publicity, although publicity of various sorts may help.

Chiefly it means organizing a program with a real human interest and appeal, a program which matters, a program with a high sales potential. The question to ask oneself is this: What kind of musical activities will, over a period of years, create a snowball effect of increasing interest and cooperation, so that as time passes, all concerned will become more and more aware that something worth-while is happening? This is how various subjects and various activities actually have established and maintained themselves in the American schools. It is by all means the sound and constructive line for educational planning. And there is no field where it has more obvious possibilities than music. . . .

II

The proposition, then, is this. The music teacher has a job because the American public, by and large, has come to want music for its children. . . .

A broad interpretation of the cultural life of this country makes it reasonably clear why the American public has supported music in the schools, what benefits it believes can and should come from musical activities, and what sort of program of music education is likely to be found acceptable.

1. There are convincing reasons for believing that the first great benefit which the public hopes may come to their children from the study of music in the schools is a feeling for ideal values and for the uplifting power and message of beauty.

A desire for something called *culture*—that much maligned word—has always been a strong motive in American life. Often it has expressed itself in crude and inadequate forms, and without much clear understanding of what was really involved. But it has been powerful and constant just the same. This is a major social fact. . . . .

Workers in the field of music education would be very foolish not to take this popular impulse seriously, or to fail to shape up their work with reference to it. It is one of their chief sources of support. Above all, they should not let themselves be scared out by the thought that their subject may be classed among the "fads" and "frills." It is the makers and user of this phrase, not the exponents of aesthetic and ideal values, who are out of step with American cultural trends.

Here enters the job of educational leadership in transforming a popular demand, not always wisely expressed or well understood but real and vital just the same, into a coherent and constructive program of action. What should workers in music education do about it? They should squarely and courageously emphasize, first and foremost, the aesthetic values of the art of music. In doing so they are acting in terms of a valid interpretation of a widespread and powerful popular demand. We all know that music may be taught in such a way that its aesthetic values are reduced to the vanishing point, and indeed it often is. Worthless materials may be used; routine procedures maybe be followed; emphasis may center narrowly upon technical skills; the great literature of the art may never been opened up; nothing may be done to inspire and stimulate children to love and appreciate the beauty and expressive possibilities of the art. Teachers who do such things, and they are not a few, may justify themselves by all sorts of excuses. They may say that children need discipline, that minds must be trained by hard work, that unappetizing drudgery must precede the flowering of interest and inspiration. But they may be quite sure that over a period of years the public, although it will not know exactly what the matter is, will come to be quite aware that it is not getting what it wants.

Moreover, a forthright emphasis upon the aesthetic values of music is the best possible way of convincing all reasonable persons that the art is neither a fad, or a frill, not a mere adornment of leisure. When a child comes really to love music, that love obviously penetrates and influences the whole of his life. His parents may not be able to state in a list of points just what good it does him. But they will be unable to doubt that good accrues. . . .

2. The second great benefit which it seems reasonable to believe that the public hopes music may confer upon their children is that for many of them it would constitute itself as an independent and continuing interest, and so an agency for personal growth and self-fulfillment. The belief that the schools ought to take cognizance of, respect, and promote individual interests is a major trend of popular thought and desire in this country—a trend extending back over many years. Education workers may safely build upon it, and indeed should do so. They need fear a hostile reaction only to its perversions.

One of the most widely mishandled of all educational topics is the place and function of interest. Judging from various recent and noisy discussions one would think that it is a novel invention of extremist progressives, who claim—or so it is alleged—that a child's education should be determined by his whims. This is a complete historical misconception. The battle now going on may seem exceedingly startling, but the doctrine that education should take organized cognizance of individual interests extends back for many years. As long ago as 1850, and even before that, the public was beginning to demand that the schools make it possible for a person to study more or less whatever he wanted to study. The old prescribed sequence of subjects which everyone was compelled to follow irrespective of his wishes, came under increasing fire, and schools which tried to maintain it found themselves under more and more impossible competition. The educators, as they always have and always must, began to respond to popular pressure. More and more new subjects were introduced. And the whole development reached its peak at Harvard, where after a couple of decades of the regime of Eliot, almost no required courses remained. The proponents of the free elective system were putting into effect a popular wish, a "common sense" about how education ought to be run. They did not themselves set up the principle that the curriculum a student follows should be determined simply by his interests. But they acted as if they believed it, and the public gave them support. . . .

We now see that one thing the schools should do is to bring children at as early an age as possible into contact with many phases of human life and culture. As they began to manifest preferences and interests, these should be made, as far as possible, foci of mental development. The assumption always is that such preferences should be marked enough to deserve respect, that they should grow more and more serious as times goes on, and that they should to the point where the individual will follow along his chosen line largely on his own initiative. Interest in this sense is something quite different from whim, except perhaps in its very earliest stages. It is a continuous movement of the mind in the direction of independent mastery and self-initiated work. It depends to some extent on guidance, but its whole tendency is to take the individual out of leading strings as soon as may be. Such interests are of momentous importance. They may lead directly towards a career, and in fact often have. They may culminate in effective and constructive hobbies. Their value in stabilizing a person on his course through life is self-evident. Indeed it is not necessary to argue long in their defense. Their development and promotion should, without question, be a major concern of the American school system. The whole position is thoroughly consistent with the evolution of our educational thought and practice.

So the worker in the field of music education should have no qualms at all about saying that one of his chief aims is to arouse a living and continuing interest in the art of music, and in setting out to do so in the more realistic possible way. In this he is following an educational policy which has ninety-year endorsement from the American people, and which is thoroughly sound in principle. . . .

3. Yet another hope and wish which workers in the field of music education should set themselves to fulfill is that their subject may constitute for young people the tonic of a demanding and disciplinary experience. In this matter our social and educational attitudes involve a serious and baffling contradiction. On the one hand there is a widespread feeling that discipline is important in the development of every child, that he ought to be confronted with exacting and serious tasks which he should not be permitted to shirk. This expresses itself in criticisms of certain modern tendencies in the schools, which seem to put a premium on making everything easy and pleasant, and to make little of definite and rigorous responsibilities. But so

James L. Mursell

long as we are absolutely committed to the idea that everyone has a right to go to school and stay there, we can expect little effective support for the application of really stringent pressures. People do a great deal of talking. They feel a certain admiration for various instructors who are said to have "high standards," which usually means piling on more than the average amount of work and producing a somewhat unusually large crop of "flunks." But if a teacher or a principal undertook to apply the sort of drastic measures which are common enough in Europe—if, for instance, he proposed to drop all pupils who did not show seriousness of purpose, or who failed to reach a certain percentage on an examination—there would almost surely be an outcry, and he would either back down or lose his job. It is hopeless to expect educators to apply stringent pressures when they have every reason to doubt that the public will support them. Apparently the American people want discipline for their children, but do not want and will not stand arbitrary imposition.

Yet there is a constructive outcome, and its nature is perfectly clear. Discipline is altogether desirable. No one achieves very much, or gets very far, or develops very soundly without hard work. The systematic avoidance of difficulty can lead on to weakness and futility. Yet even though imposed discipline may not be so poisonous as some people claim, it clearly has very limited values. And in any case, as a matter of practical politics, public school teachers cannot go very far along this line. Therefore the only alternative is to seek disciplinary values in tasks which are undertaken because the pupil himself wishes to see them through. The idea is perfectly sound and unanswerable in theory. A person will work harder, learn more about the meaning of real effort, and get far richer and more solid values from a self-imposed undertaking than he will ever get from the stringencies of a taskmaster. The trouble arises when we try to apply the notion to the work of the school. It is very difficult to do so on a large scale. Our conventional techniques of teaching and management all imply an outwardly imposed discipline which is not, and indeed cannot be, carried far enough to be very effective. But one of the fields where we come nearest to being able to put our principle into operation in a thoroughgoing way is music.

For instance, whenever a group or an individual is learning to perform a composition, the goal of interpretation, and of the creation of controlled and authentic musical effects, may be set up. Every artist knows perfectly well that such a goal is exceedingly exacting. Yet it is not set up by the teacher, but by the situation. It does not call for the achievement of a stated percentage on an arbitrarily marked examination, but the attainment of a standard of excellence objectively apparent to all concerned. Of course it requires the use of materials which have a real interpretive challenge, and of techniques of teaching which confront the learners with interpretive problems and demands. But, to repeat, all this is in the logic of the situation itself, and not imposed from the outside. Or again, working for public performance releases a very powerful disciplinary influence which can and should be widely used. . . .

4. Yet another hope which can and should be fulfilled through the agency of music is that the schools afford young people constructive and convincing experiences of a democratic type. We live in times when this has become a painful live issue. Yet there is considerable confusion in handling it. The public desires and believes that the schools should do their utmost to support the democratic way of life. But often this works out simply as the study of history, of social trends, and of our great political documents. Such plans are excellent as far as they go; yet it is quite clear that what can be done for the support of democracy merely by talking about it is rather limited. Also, unfortunately, it is all too clear that our schools, as at present organized and operated, afford rather meager experiences of the democratic process itself. This is not because we want things that way, or are insincere in our protestations, but because we lack the operative techniques to conduct the whole great enterprise of public education or on a thoroughgoing democratic basis. Putting the point bluntly, we don't know how.

But in the field of music, within certain limits, we do know how. There are three chief ways in which music can be an agency for the sort of social outlook and attitude we desire. In the first place, material can be selected with this aim in mind. Neither instrumental nor vocal music was created in a social and cultural vacuum. It arose under very definite conditions, and as an expression of certain aspirations and certain attitudes towards life. It has symbolic force. In studying it, children can come to at least some fellow-feeling with the hopes and emotions of others, and the meanings of their own corporate life can be reinforced. In a very real sense, music can make the whole world kin. Certainly it can be used for propaganda purposes, as examples from abroad make only too evident. But this is both a perversion of its nature, and also indeed a testimony to its power. The music teacher who fails to select material and also to handle and present it with attention to the human ramifications and meanings of the art is certainly foolish.

Then there is a more direct type of social influence which music can exert. It is an art of group activity, and hence affords foci of very cogent experience in human relationship and collaboration. Here, clearly, is a remarkable opportunity which should not be ignored. The teacher should think of an ensemble group as learning not only music, but also orderly democratic behavior and he should shape up his procedures and disciplinary arrangements with this latter end in view. There is much in the professional tradition of ensemble music which is not educationally desirable or appropriate. The ordinary professional ensemble is about as clear-cut an example of dominance and subordination as one can find. The orchestra is the conductor's instrument, and is so regarded by all concerned. We should not be content to duplicate this situation in school music. Once more the problem is essentially a practical one. Traditionally successful methods cannot be jettisoned unless we have others to take their place. How can a choir, an orchestra, or a band work together as a group of collaborators seeking to achieve an interpretation which is a common desire, rather than as so many efficient slaves of the baton? This may seem a difficult question; yet various approaches to the problem may suggest themselves without too much difficulty. Certainly it is something to be worked for and experimented with; for clearly we have no finer opportunity for providing a unique experience of democratic control for a given end than that presented by ensemble music.

Lastly, music may be an agency for democratic living by providing rich and significant experiences and activities in which all may share. No one will wish to deny that differences in musical ability exist. No tests or other pretentious apparatus are needed to demonstrate such a truism. But in the first place such differences, so far as we know, have almost nothing to do with differences of racial, social, or economic status. The Negro, the Indian, the Mexican, the child from a poor home or an underprivileged neighborhood is not handicapped musically by nature. Musical activities can cut across such distinctions; and there is apt to be less prejudice here than in most other doings in the schools. . . .

5. Yet another hope to the fulfillment of which the teaching of music in the schools can and should be keyed, is to provide young people with a means of recreation which can last throughout their lives. Music has always served this purpose in human affairs. It has certainly done so in our country, as the great body of American folk and popular music recognized in recent years amply attests. In times past there was not much artistic sophistication or trained skill. The type of music popularly used and enjoyed was not particularly high, and the range of musical experiences available was decidedly limited. Mostly it was an affair of singing songs, often of a somewhat commonplace kind, at formal and informal social functions. Yet the spontaneity of such activities, and the universality with which they are carried on and enjoyed is clear evidence of the deep appeal of the musical art, and of the willingness indeed the eagerness, of men and women to engage in it. Even the most detached observer of life as it has been lived in the United States would say that it supplied something that human creatures obviously want, that it gave them a sense of relaxation, renewal, and togetherness which is perfectly summed up in the literal meaning of the word *re-creation*. Here is something which everyone in the field of music education would do well to ponder. It indicates a tangible service which he can offer, and a very practi-

cal justification for his work. For clearly, if the right kind of educational direction can be put behind this natural human impulse to use music for release and enjoyment, it can be made far more effective. And there is today a need for such service which hardly existed in former times, simply because we have a far simpler leisure than former generations enjoyed. It is a great mistake, as the whole course of this argument has indicated, to think of the value of music as confined to leisure time. But it would be a still greater mistake not to give very serious and realistic heed to the leisure time uses of the art. . . .

III

. . . Instead of asking what our aims should be, it is so much better to ask what the public wants and hopes of us, what wishes it has been led to entertain, clearly or dimly, explicitly, or vaguely. If we can make even a good guess at this, we have a commission with some steam and urgency about it. Curiously enough, the public is often a great deal more sensible about what the schools should try to do, at least in matter of broad policy and outcome, than are the specialists. It is apt to want perfectly defined, concrete, understandable things, while the specialist has an axe to grind and produces a whole array of excuses for doing so which often fail to make sense. The hopes and wishes and regard to music education which this admittedly somewhat conjectural but by no means wholly subjective or arbitrary analysis of public opinion brings to light are a case in point. These are the kinds of things we should try to do. It will require a good deal of revision of our ways, works, and thoughts, but the undertaking is by no means impossible; and assuredly it is educationally sound, and will elicit the all-important popular support.

PART III

AMERICAN VIEWS SINCE 1950

A merican education began to undergo profound change in the early 1950s when it became apparent that the schools were not preparing students adequately to allow the nation to continue its international leadership position in the emerging technological age. Technological supremacy was especially crucial during the Cold War because there was a continual threat of military conflict with the Soviet Union. As the nation's attention began to focus more intensely on mathematics and science education, both educators and scientists became concerned about a school curriculum that neglected the arts in favor of what were known as core subjects. The likelihood of an unbalanced curriculum came to the attention of the American Association of School Administrators, who stated:

> . . . We believe in a well-balanced school curriculum in which music, drama, painting, poetry, sculpture, architecture, and the like are included side by side with other important subjects such as mathematics, history, and science. It is important that pupils, as a part of general education, learn to appreciate, to understand, to create, and to criticize with discrimination those products of the mind, the voice, the hand, and the body which give dignity to the person and exalt the spirit of man.[1]

Scientists agreed. The White House Panel on Educational Research and Development stated:

> Certain members of the Panel were convinced that there was a degree of correlation between excellence in scientific achievement and the breadth of an individual's human experience. The best scientists, it was thought, were not necessarily those who had devoted themselves singlemindedly to their own field; somehow, familiarity with the arts and humanities sharpened a good scientist's vision.[2]

Even more than educational administrators and scientists, music educators themselves were concerned about the future of their discipline. Their uncertainty turned out to be a positive motivating force for the profession, which began an ongoing period of introspection, assessment, and planning. One particular fortuitous aspect of this time of change was the development of an intellectual community within the music education profession. There had been a richness of intellectual leaders in the past, but nothing that could be identified as a community of intellectuals. In 1953, Allen Britton, of the University of Michigan, established the *Journal of Research in Music Education*, a highly respected scholarly journal that offered scholars a publication outlet directly related to their professional interests. During the 1950s and 1960s, a group of scholars focused their research on philosophical issues, resulting in the philosophy of aesthetic education. These two developments created a community that made possible unprecedented opportunities for scholarly dialogue and discourse that has increased steadily to the present. This community has examined the music education profession from many viewpoints and has helped enable music education to evolve through the second half of the twentieth century into a healthy, dynamic component of American education.

Five factors emerged, each developing its own raison d'etre for music education: philosophy, evolving societal needs for educational change and improvement, new music program developments, and innovative explorations of the relationship between music, mind, and brain. The fifth factor, advocacy, developed in parallel with the others. Its role has been to inform the public, policy makers, and educators why music education is necessary and valuable, using the information and data developed in the above four areas.

Notes

1. American Association for School Administrators, *Official Report for the Year 1958; including a Record of the Annual Meeting and Work Conference on "Education and the Creative Arts"* (Washington, DC: American Association of School Administrators, 1959), 248–249.

2. Irving Lowens, "MUSIC: Juilliard Repertory Project and the Schools," *The Sunday Star* (Washington, DC), May 30, 1971, E4.

Philosophy of Music Education

usic education needed visionary intellectual leadership to make it an integral part of the dawning new
curriculum of the 1950s. Some of the readings that
follow are statements of belief that reflect the thinking of earlier
times; they might not be considered philosophy, as defined by
Harry S. Broudy: ". . . a reasoned justification for a set of beliefs
rather than a mere assertion of these beliefs." They are included
in the philosophy section to emphasize the transitional nature
of the 1950s. These writings, among others, were the platform
from which music educators began their journey to the philosophy of aesthetic education.

Professional leaders began to discourage music educators
from promoting the nonmusical benefits of music education,
referring to them in their writings and addresses as "ancillary,"
"instrumental," and "utilitarian" values. Gradually, music educators began to support the position that the value of music education was to be found in the music itself. This clearly was part
of the progression toward the development of the philosophy of
aesthetic education. Charles Leonhard wrote:

> While reliance on statements of the nonmusical value of
> music may well have convinced some reluctant adminis-
> trator to more fully support the music program, those val-
> ues cannot stand close scrutiny, because they are not
> unique to music. In fact, many other areas of the curricu-
> lum are in a position to make a more powerful contribu-
> tion to these values than is music.[1]

Allen Britton agreed: "Many who seek to justify the present
place of music in American schools tend to place too heavy a
reliance upon ancillary values which music may certainly serve
but which cannot, in the end, constitute its justification."[2] A
small group of music educators turned to the field of philosophy,
studying the writings of such aestheticians as Leonard Meyer
and Suzanne Langer. They began the development of what
would become known as aesthetic education. The 1970 publication of Bennett Reimer's book, *A Philosophy of Music Education*,[3]

provided a bible for the philosophy, and the release of the second edition in 1989 indicates that the philosophy of aesthetic education remains influential. The philosophy of aesthetic education remained virtually unchallenged until the 1990s, when the community of music education philosophers expanded and new publication outlets became available to them. A new philosophical movement, praxialism, developed. The praxial philosophy of music education has become the subject of a considerable amount of research and scholarly writing.

Notes

1. Charles Leonhard, "The Philosophy of Music Education—Present and Future," in *Comprehensive Musicianship: The Foundation for College Education in Music* (Washington, DC: Music Educators National Conference, 1965), 42.

2. Allen Britton, "Music in Early American Public Education: A Historical Critique," in *Basic Concepts in Music Education*, ed. Nelson Henry (Chicago, IL: National Society for the Study of Education, 1958), 195.

3. Bennett Reimer, *A Philosophy of Music Education* (Englewood Cliffs, NJ: Prentice-Hall, 1970).

D. A. Clippinger
Collective Voice Training: A View of Aesthetic Education (1925)

D. A. Clippinger was a teacher of singing and conductor of the Chicago Madrigal Club. He also wrote *The Clippinger Class-Method of Voice Culture.*

There came a time when it began to dawn upon man that some things were more satisfactory than others. Some voices sounded better than others. The aesthetic sense, the sense of discrimination and judgment which is the basis of what we call artistic taste, became operative. At that moment the voice teacher came automatically into being and has since developed an industry rivaled only by that of automobiles and Standard Oil.

Michael L. Mark
Historical Precedents of Aesthetic Education Philosophy

Michael L. Mark is professor of music emeritus at Towson University.

Music education leaders in the 1950s had become sensitive to the fact that much of the intellectual support system for their profession consisted of rationales, rather than philosophy. It was then that they began to use terms like "ancillary," "instrumental values," and "utilitarian" in their writings and addresses to describe nonmusical benefits of music education. Advocates like Charles Leonhard and Allan Britton wrote about the futility of basing music programs on nonmusical values. At that time, some music educators began to advocate proactively that the value of music education was to be found in the music itself, which clearly was part of the progression toward the development of the philosophy of aesthetic education. Earlier, in the 1930s, music education scholars like James L. Mursell had advocated that the purpose of music education should be aesthetic development, but it was Charles Leonhard who coined the phrase "aesthetic education" in a 1953 article in the journal called *Education*. George Heller wrote in his biography of Charles Leonhard that Leonhard "began his essay with a plea for music educators to emphasize the aesthetic value of music, rather than the instrumental or ancillary values."[1] Leonhard also pioneered the development of music teacher education programs based on aesthetic principles.

The movement to a new philosophy was fueled by the publication of two landmark books: *Foundations and Principles of Music Education* by Charles Leonhard and Robert House was published in 1959, and *Basic Concepts in Music Education*, published in 1958 as the fifty-seventh yearbook of the National Society for the Study of Education. The Leonhard and House book articulated an early version of the philosophy of aesthetic education. *Basic Concepts in Music Education* presented contemporary philosophical, sociological, psychological, and historical views of music education. The committee that oversaw the book's publication, the Music Educators National Conference Committee on Basic Concepts, called upon scholars from several disciplines to contribute to an appropriate intellectual foundation for the profession. One of them was Harry Broudy, a philosopher who is well known to music educators. He had written an article in 1957 for the *Music Educators Journal* on whether music education actually needed a philosophy. In it, he pointed out that the search for a true philosophy would require music educators to delve more deeply than had been attempted to that time, and he discussed some of the disciplines with which music education philosophers would need to familiarize themselves. He said, "We are here flirting with aesthetics, ethics, metaphysics, epistemology, and theology—fearful names for philosophical inquiry and diagnosis."[2]

The dawn of the era of aesthetic education philosophy in the 1950s carried different, and perhaps even greater, significance than simply the beginning of a new intellectual phase for music education. The philosophy that we know as aesthetic education was probably the first true American philosophy of music education; it did not replace an older one. To understand what this means, we must recognize whose philosophy had supported music education and who spoke for music education in the past. Throughout Western history, music education has always had philosophical bases on which to operate, but they were societal or educational philosophies, rather than philosophies of music education. Those societies and eras that are the milestones of the Western cultural heritage—the ancient Hebrew, Greek, and Roman civilizations, the Middle Ages, the Renaissance, the Age of Enlightenment, the beginnings of American democracy—all relied on music to fulfill functions that required the participation of large numbers of citizens. Because there were often specified musical roles for adults, it was a given that music education was also a societal imperative. In these societies, the role of music education was both prominent and respected.

For the most part, those historical figures who left writings about the role of music education were not music educators. Their interests in music education usually were related to the preservation and advancement of their own societies. They were philosophers, religious leaders, nobles, civic officials, and others who were concerned with matters far beyond who was to receive music instruction, what music was to be taught, and who was to teach it. They include such historical figures as Plato, Aristotle, St. Augustine, Boethius, Charlemagne, Martin Luther, John Calvin, John Amos Comenius, John Locke, Johann Heinrich Pestalozzi, John Ruskin, and Herbert Spencer. The writings of these leaders contained references to music education because of its important role in helping to maintain society in the ways they thought important.

From the early days of American democracy, our own societal leaders continued the tradition of writing about music education. Thus, we find written support for the teaching of music by Cotton Mather, the Boston School Committee, Horace Mann, and many others. In the nineteenth century, music educators began to contribute their writings as well. The written words of Lowell Mason, George Root, Luther Whiting Mason, and other leading figures of the music education profession began to form a new kind of literature—the justification of music education by music educators. By the twentieth century, a fairly substantial body of these writings had accumulated. Now, the thoughts of Will Earhart, Walter Damrosch, Karl W. Gehrkens, Osbourne McConathy, W. Otto Miessner, Peter Dykema, Hazel Nohavec Morgan, Russell V. Morgan, Frances Elliott Clark, and many others were available in books, articles, and published addresses. In addition, a new category of music education authors emerged in the twentieth century. Their reflections on music education were written from the viewpoints of psychology and philosophy. Thus, we have the words of such figures as John Dewey, Max Schoen, James L. Mursell, and Robert Lundin. By the middle of the twentieth century, there was a large and convincing body of literature that illuminated the benefits of music education in schools and rationalized reasons for its support.

This impressive library remains of historical interest. It represents the ideas of some of the best thinkers of earlier times about music education. However, although they often used the word "philosophy," there is little actual philosophy in this body of literature, as we might define it today. For the most part, what has been referred to as philosophy were actually rationales. The word *rationale* can be defined in a number of ways, but for the purpose of this paper, it is a statement of belief and justification that is not grounded in the rigorous method of systematic inquiry employed by philosophers. Perhaps simple and appealing rationales, being persuasive to both the public and to music educators, were all that was needed prior to the era of aesthetic education. . . . By the middle of the twentieth century, however, American society was entering a new period, one that required a more highly educated populace. No longer would rationales suffice. Now, a true philosophy of music education was needed, one developed by means of authentic philosophical inquiry.

Notes

1. George Heller, *Charles Leonhard: American Music Educator* (Metuchen, NJ: The Scarecrow Press, 1995), 86.
2. Harry S. Broudy, "Does Music Education Need A Philosophy?" *Music Educators Journal* 44/2 (November–December 1957), 28–30.

Russell V. Morgan
Music: A Living Power in Education (1953)

Russell V. Morgan was Supervisor of Music in Cleveland, Ohio, and president of the Music Educators National Conference.

Basic Philosophy for Music Education

The many fields of knowledge that we have are but windows through which the human soul can look out upon a significant and beautiful universe. As fine as music is, it is only one window, and a good life calls for a broader vista than one single direction. I claim that music always has been a highly significant emotional and aesthetic stimulus in human life and that to weave it into the fabric of American life would do much to create a thrilling and hopeful dawn for humanity in this new world.

Whenever some cataclysmic event occurs in world history, humanity instinctively thinks of it as an opportunity to change the purposes and practices of life. At times there seems basis for hope that there will be a revolution in the lives of people. History does not give us any foundation for such a belief. On the contrary, most of the patterns of living have been an evolution of gradual change in outlook, activity, and basic philosophy. There are in existence many great principles having eternal truth which must not be forgotten but used as a foundation for ever-expanding development.

Music and a New World

It is evident that America has placed too much emphasis on its remarkable material achievement in the scientific field, with the projection of that human search for knowledge, until it has reached the present state of using atomic powers for better or for worse. The human spirit is presently appalled by the fact that advancement of knowledge is not necessarily for the good of humanity. It is my personal belief that we will realize more and more than it is the *will* and *purpose* of humanity that is the greatest concern of the present day, and that this should be the directing force for the enormous potential power at our command.

Perhaps today's condition is to be expected when we realize that the aim of education has been primarily concerned with only the intellectual phase and has been seemingly blind to the necessity of developing the spiritual, emotional, and aesthetic aspects of human life. If we, as music teachers, can help in blending the direction of our educational program toward greater emphasis upon these spheres of human growth, there is the possibility of developing a people who will wholeheartedly and effectively use all of our material resources and scientific knowledge for the good of humanity.

Cesar Franck, in a moment of true insight, made this statement: "Music is both craft and an art." No one would deny the necessity for craftsmanship in music or any other of the avenues of activity about us, but it would be tragic if, in our concern for the development of technical proficiency, we do not develop a program for balancing that craftsmanship with the *spirit* of art.

Properly taught, music can provide a remarkable example of true democracy wherein both the individual and society have due regard for each other. The dignity and worth of the individual must always be protected, and yet it is necessary that the individual feel his responsibility to society as a whole. This is true democracy, the American way of life, and we in the music education field can do much to develop a true balance in this matter for our young people.

One thing greatly needed in America is a crusade urging students to use their talents for the betterment of the community in which they live. There is altogether too much thought of their being developed so that they may go to some far-off place and become famous. Perhaps it will be difficult to change this thinking so long as emphasis is placed more upon the former than on the music to be performed. It is to be hoped that the day will come when people will be far more interested in knowing *what* opera, symphony, string quartet, or oratorio is to be performed than in *who* is the conductor or soloist.

We have made great strides in America. Consider the fact that we have some four hundred organized symphony orchestras with paid conductors and many thousands of choruses and choirs which show an increasing respect for good musical literature and good performance. Perhaps the need now is to broaden our activities to include more interest in such things as chamber music, home ensembles, and group music wherever it can operate to the betterment of human living.

It would be foolish to think of music as the only saving force in the world. The many fields of knowledge that we have are but windows through which the human soul can look out upon a significant and beautiful universe. As fine as music is, it would be only one window, and a good life calls for a broader vista than one single direction. I do claim that music always has been highly significant emotional and aesthetic stimulus in human life, and that to weave it into the fabric of American life will do much to create a thrilling and hopeful dawn for humanity in this new world.

Many of us teachers have a positive genius for completely separating our philosophies of music education and our actual practices in music education. Everyone will agree that our practice should be merely the expression of our philosophy, but all too often I have seen communities of teachers spend hours of hard and thoughtful work in preparing a philosophy as a foundation for a course of study. Then I have observed these same people reverently place that philosophy on a shelf and go on about the work-a-day business of teaching school, without bothering to develop procedures that will actually bring that philosophy to the children in the classroom. Both philosophy and the practice of implementing it are obvious needs.

Permanent Values

The contemporary period at any point in the history of the world has seemed to be chaotic and confusing to those who were living at that time. As we gain historical perspective, the confusion and uncertainty resolve into a clarified picture in which much of the activity disappears permanently and only a few important and significant items remain. There are deeply significant events occurring today, side by side with those chattering inconsistencies which seem to overpower us and blind us to the really good things.

There are some values which are permanent. Theses are the enrichments that come to human life through activity in and understanding of the fine arts.

First to be mentioned is the development of integrity and ideals within the individual. We all recognize the tremendous urge toward accomplishment and social responsibility that comes from well-directed experiences in music and the other arts.

Second, there is the development of an attitude that will place opportunity above security. One of the marks of energetic youth is the desire to seek out new and better ways rather than to be confined to a security that sooner or later becomes dull and commonplace to the one who chooses it.

Third, I believe that the aesthetic and emotional enjoyment of the fine arts will always have an important place in living, and that those who have equipped themselves with this power to understand and appreciate music, literature, and art have achieved one of the great fundamentals for a happy and successful life.

Fourth, a recognition that power and ability can come only through a slow, solid growth and that the exercise of patience in waiting for fruition is of utmost importance.

Every student who has taken hold of these fundamental ideas may feel that he has been equipped with the power to help himself in reaching an understanding of what this life is all about. Temporary adjustments are needful. Humanity turns from certain demands for artistic performance only to emphasize its desire for an artistry in some new form of expression, but to discover new avenues and to adjust the eternal values of artistic effort into channels of activity that humanity demands at the present moment. The real challenge in all fields of fine arts today is to discover how best to bring satisfaction to our fellow beings through permanent aesthetic values, for from the very beginning this has been one of the greatest hungers of mankind.

Everyone is aware that we have been going through a striking period of renaissance in the field of music. There are many reasons for this. Perhaps the greatest of all is the prevalence today of radio and television and many fine musical programs available through these media. We have heard and seen great singers, players, and orchestras. They have set up for us standards of taste and discrimination that have acted in a miraculous way toward bringing the finest expression in the arts to an interested and appreciative audience. Side by side with the great expansion of musical opportunity for the listener has been the development of a program of music education in our schools that will help make all citizens appreciate more richly and fully the beauty that is theirs for the asking.

A Social Attitude toward Music Education

One sometimes senses a line of battle drawn sharply between two opposing social concepts, one insisting that the worth of our educational process is measured by the products men are taught to produce and the other holding to the proposition that the purpose of education is to develop men possessing the power to live richly.

The social objective can cause real harm if it ignores the artistic qualities in performance. There are enthusiastic exponents of the social values who fail to realize that activity is not necessarily purposeful per se. These individuals, believing in the good of musical participation, seem not to see the necessity of guarding musical quality. While granting that it is proper for the social aim to come first, it can still be insisted that unless artistic values raise consistently, the whole activity will disintegrate and become worthless.

It is my personal conviction that the first purpose of music education is to enrich the lives of human beings, both as individuals and in groups. In order to carry out this intention, however, we need to use a constantly higher quality of musical literature and an improving skill and understanding if interest is to be maintained and a permanent enrichment of personality assured. This is the true social attitude which music educators should maintain.

The social and artistic values must be reconciled and made to serve each other rather than remain in seeming conflict. Art values that do not enrich humanity are worthless, but it is just as clear that the social purpose of music cannot be realized unless artistic values serve as a guiding factor.

A strong development of social values can be secured through proper music instruction. The music class is a practical situation in which the individual contributes to the welfare of the group and the group activity increases the social and artistic equipment of the individual. Each boy and girl must participate to the fullest extent of his or her ability in order that the group result may be acceptable. The individual receives inspiration and good from the contributing activity of all his co-workers. As a member of a musical organization, he is conscious of the failure in the group result if any individual member does not contribute his best. In other words, the student learns that the good of the group depends upon his individual contribution and, at the same time, that his own good depends on every other member contributing his share.

A child may experience keen delight in contact with some musical beauty and, though that child may never again hear music, the expansion of soul caused by that brief glimpse into the infinite will remain throughout life. So let us feel confidence in teaching well done, though the individual may never continue the activity in adult life. However, a proper basic philosophy gives us hope that many will be impelled to draw continually closer to the source of beauty and live much more richly than they otherwise would.

Earl E. Harper
Music in American Education:
Moral and Spiritual Values in Music Education (1954)

Earl E. Harper was president of Evansville College and editor of several Methodist hymnals.

I. If moral and spiritual values are to be found in music education, they must be found in the music educator.

It is true that the work of the artist is of the nature of revelation. What he reveals to his fellow men through his art may be truth so exalted that neither he nor any other man can verbalize it, much less incarnate it. The old adage, "Practice what you preach," is often construed to mean that we should not preach "more than we can practice." I disagree emphatically.

The prophet is a *speaker for* rather than a *speaker before*. But the prophet is a *speaker for* the divine. Therefore the truth he proclaims is always beyond us. In the light of truth revealed or proclaimed we should have the moral courage and spiritual audacity to declare that we aim at standards of character, personality, and achievement, which we have not reached and may never reach.

Some years ago, prior to the recent successful conquest of Mt. Everest, an organization of mountain climbers was making a supreme effort finally to send two of their number to what has been called "the top of the world." The time came for the last assault. Upward into the cloud and mist these two brave men climbed. They were never seen again. No one knows whether they reached the top or not. But a great thing was said about them by their comrades. When they had descended from their tragically futile mission, they said, "When last we saw our friends they were headed for the top and still climbing."

That man or woman who, through carelessness, indifference, self-indulgence, weakness, or perhaps cowardice, turns back from continuing effort to achieve his ideals actually joins the ranks of those who stand against what he believes.

The truth which preachers of religion proclaim will endure in spite of moral failure among those who preach. Nevertheless, when the proclamation of a spiritual ideal has been identified with a man whose lifework is religious ministry, if that man makes a moral shipwreck of his own life, he becomes a traitor to truth.

It is presumable that educators are all united in agreement that moral and spiritual values are vitally important in the culture of individuals and the civilizations of nations.

Most of us are so convinced of the necessity of moral life and spiritual inspiration in human experience that if we should conclude that music education, or education in the fine arts generally, does not offer us a work which we can do and through which we can express, manifest, and measurably implement our ideals, then we will get out of it.

The first question we must ask ourselves concerning any cherished ideal is whether we believe in it to the point of complete personal dedication.

II. Moral and spiritual values are most important of all values in personal life, and in the corporate life of men and women banded together in a profession, a state, a nation, or a world order.

There is a distinction with a difference between moral and spiritual values. Moral values have to do with the rules and practice of daily life. Spiritual values have to do with the genesis of and authority for these rules.

Moral values issue in ethical codes. Spiritual values involve not only motivation to live by these codes, but they tap the mainsprings of dynamic power without which men cannot long endure the struggle to live ethically, righteously, and justly, with major emphasis upon self-sacrifice to mankind.

Moral values may be validated dialectically by our study of history. Spiritual values are rooted and grounded in man's faith in a divine intelligence creatively responsible for and regnantly powerful in the universe.

A structured statement of moral values may be likened to an intelligently devised, ingeniously constructed, and marvelously complicated machine. Spiritual values represent the power which makes the machinery operate. An excellent framework of ethical standards expressed in a beautifully articulated code is possible without reference to religion–spiritual values.

The tide of human reverence and devotion to religious ideals ebb and flow as time moves on. The present day is one of terrible concern about moral standards and almost desperate turning to spiritual ideals. Moral degradation comparable to that of Sodom of the Old Testament, the Roman Empire of the early Christian era, or of Central Europe in the interval between the first and second world wars, threatens us in the United States of America today. Faced with increasing moral bankruptcy in the areas of juvenile delinquency, crime in its many ugly aspects, national and political disharmony, and international tension, strain, and fear, men are anxiously asking whether divine help cannot be invoked to solve the problems which mortal intelligence faces with deepening hopelessness.

III. The most important thing in the life and work of a man or woman is his or her basic total philosophy of life.

No man or woman in any walk of life is engaged in work more naturally adapted to the realization, proclamation, and promotion of moral and spiritual values than are music educators.

First, there are great disciplinary values inherent in your relation as educators to the youth whom you teach. The conductor of a musical organization must carry out his work with an innate sense of command, and with acknowledgment on the part of the personnel involved that he has authority. This can and too often does breed a petty tyranny.

We should continuously remind ourselves that we live in an age or increasing leisure time. There are those who exclaim that this means correlatively advancing culture. The plain truth is that additional leisure in many instances means a new crime wave. What is important is the use which is made of this time. No more enjoyable, attractive, or worth-while engagement of time and attention of people, and especially youth, freed from labor has been discovered or can be imagined than music as a recreational experience.

Second, to the great extent that the vast literature of the art of music interprets reality in human life, we are dealing with works of art which proclaim moral and spiritual values.

We do not need to use works of art to point morals. Through art life finds interpretation. And when works of art are presented in any medium which thus interprets life, they preach their own sermons. Sometimes, perhaps, we are so harmed with the artistic masterpiece as entertainment that we fail to realize the profound truth involved.

In public concerts and in our recorded programs in music rooms we can and do bring responsive audiences the sacred orations of Bach, Handel, and Haydn, the magnificent symphonic psalms of Honegger and Vaughan Williams, and the requiems of Brahms, Verdi, and Cesar Franck. In our lounges, halls, and galleries we hang paintings and place sculptured figures which interpret man's desire and quest for spiritual enlightenment through the ages. Men and women of all faiths and no faith find in these common inspiration.

Third, of all of the fine arts, music has been and continues to be the greatest instrument of man's quest for moral and spiritual values in life.

Evidence of the truth of this assertion is to be found in the fact that men, whatever may be their religious faith, spend from one-third to one-half of all the time they are engaged in corporate worship participating in or listening to singing and the playing of instruments. Added emphasis to this truth is the fact that an enormous portion of all the money men give to and spend on the religious quest through organized religion is spent in one way or another for music. The creation of a Commission on Church Music and Worship, or Worship and the Fine Arts, by nearly every religious faith and denomination, and the establishment of a Department of Worship and the Arts as a major subdivision of the National Council of Churches of Christ in the United States of America give practical emphasis and bear eloquent testimonial to the importance of music in the realization, proclamation, and promotion of moral and religious values in human life.

Perhaps we cannot hope to add to the sum total of human wisdom concerning music as a bridge from the world of the sense to the world of the spirit, but we can remind ourselves of certain important facets of religious life and worship which are involved.

First, music as a marvelously effective means of spiritual impression. From the time "Jubal struck his chorded shell" and men, listening, felt that no less than a God must dwell in its hollow, this great art has somehow made men feel that their lives are more than mortal, that a divine spirit impinges upon them wherever they are and whatever they are doing.

Second, music, whether instrumental, in prelude, offertory, response, and postlude; or vocal, as a setting for anthem, hymn, chant, or introit, is an incomparable means of spiritual expression. Even the stranger in a worshiping congregation as he stands to sing a hymn engages actively and vocally in prayer, praise, and meditation and exhortation.

Third, music as a universal language of the spirit brings men of all faiths into spiritual unity in a consummate realization that there are great universal fundamentals of faith which are common to all, whether they are Hebrews, Roman Catholics, Protestants, or followers of ethnic religions.

Music educators find a great avocational employment of their talents and techniques, fraught with a sense of dignified and helpful service, in the musical ministry of religion. And so important has this aspect of the ministry become that more and more opportunities open every day for a professional career in this artistic religions service.

Conclusion. I have asked you to consider the fact that if moral and spiritual values are to be found in music education they must be found in the music educator; that moral and spiritual values are ultimate values, transcendent, but permeative of the entire structure of life and education; and that in the art of music, educators have a matchless opportunity to lead those whom we educate into an experience of discipline, high moral purpose and conduct, and spiritual growth.

"Art in its nobler form is one of the great quickeners of moral endeavor. This power it holds in no small degree due to the fact that it contains a transcendent element. The artistic impulse is not content until it has created something more perfect than yet finds embodiment in our experience; it strives to suggest that 'eye hath not seen or ear heard.' Herein it is at one with the moral impulse, which is not satisfied to leave things as it finds them, but seeks to remould them into a more perfect order. Both the moral and artistic are alike haunted by a vision of ideal perfection. Art, no less than reflection, may recall us to our better selves by suggesting in forms of beauty those ideals for which it is alike our duty and our joy to strive."

Members of the music education profession, if you accept and discharge the *responsibilities* which rest upon you in your life and work, you will bring moral guidance to the people of our land which will impart happiness and stability into the social life of America, and measurably strengthen our democracy to meet the fierce frontal attacks and insidious undermining influences which threaten it. If you do this, you will deserve to be numbered with the prophets, priests, and seers as benefactors of the race.

But if you realize the *possibilities* of your work in revitalizing the spiritual life of mankind and in assisting man to tap the ultimate source of spiritual values and inspiration, you will deserve to be canonized with the saints.

Benjamin C. Willis
Music in American Education (1954)

Benjamin C. Willis was general superintendent of schools, Chicago.

The Stake of Music in Education

The stake of music in education can be analyzed from many viewpoints. The discussion here is limited to three aspects: (1) The artistic implications of music in education; (2) the general educative value of music in education; and (3) the place of music in education from a functional standpoint.

Artistic Implications

From the artistic standpoint, music, as it is taught in the schools of the United States, incorporates artistic values in its methods and techniques.

Because of this the results of the teaching and guidance in the field of music show a technical proficiency unmatched by any other country in the world. From this we are grateful to you, the music educators, and to your great organization which has been so largely responsible for this whole development.

I earnestly encourage you to continue this endeavor for proficiency in music education. In this sense we want you to be a tightly compartmentalized part of education because only in this way can we hope to have a continuance of the great work you have started—the fine performance of these musical groups. To this end you must not only insist on your rights as *music educators*, but you must continue to emphasize also the necessity of certain areas of specialization within your ranks. Some of you will necessarily devote your energies to the business of increasing your stature as specialists in one of the several areas of your profession as conductors of bands, orchestras, or choirs. All of this is quite necessary to insure competence on these areas for your students. But I very strenuously urge you *not* to carry these ambitions of specialization beyond reasonable limits. The borders within your own field of specialization cannot be defined for you. We can only advise you.

If music is to be made a thing of beauty and joy forever in the lives of all children, then the ideal of cooperation and of unity must direct the field of music education in America. Those of us in administration and in general education must be very sure that our music programs are controlled by persons who are dedicated to the stake of *music in education* and not to the individual *music specialist's stake in education*. Therefore, as you develop these fine bands and orchestras and choruses which we want so much, be sure that you always keep foremost in your mind the *importance* of maintaining the integrity of your total profession—music education—and the relative *unimportance* of over-emphasizing compartmentalization *within your own field*.

The General Educative Values of Music

All are aware these days of the growing necessity to make as complete as possible the education of our boys and girls. The responsibility is great to the millions of pupils in our elementary schools in developing, through well-planned experiences, their native love and interest in music. Then, as they grow toward maturity, they will gain in the ability to utilize these experiences in the enjoyment of creating and listening to good music.

You will agree that while children are in elementary school their education should be as effective as it is possible to make it. The man or woman who is in the field of music education and who does not have the needs of this large group of the school population in mind, is, in my opinion, not a true educator.

Then there are the thousands and thousands of students whose formal education terminates in high school. They also need as complete an education as possible before embarking on their individual careers. Many of these high school students have never had an opportunity to participate in your bands, your orchestras, your choruses, and yet, all of you would agree that they are entitled to music as an essential part of their secondary school education. It would be a sad commentary on our position as educators if we failed to provide adequate music education for these young citizens. They are entitled to the immediate and future benefits which participation in musical activities provides.

Similarly, colleges and universities must be continually on the alert and must be evaluating their curricula to see that their graduates are properly equipped in all phases of education. The day for defending the place of music in our college curriculum is past. Something more than earning a living and specializing in professions is involved, for educators now recognize that it is necessary to provide for the college student a variety of rich musical experiences so that he may derive both immediate and future satisfaction from music.

Business and professional leaders are deeply interested in the training given students for their careers—in the pure sciences, the natural sciences, business education, and so on. However, there is a growing conviction that the liberal arts are basic and that by no means should they be neglected in the anxiety to turn out graduates who are qualified only in the techniques of their chosen occupations. Business, industry, and the professions need people who can think beyond the business office, the laboratory, the ship, and the sales meeting; people whose education is sufficiently balanced to meet the challenges of civic, social, and vocational life.

Music is a vital part of a balanced education. It has a very real stake in the education of our students, from elementary school through college.

Administrators need your help in this great task and responsibility. We need musicians who are educators. We need music educators who can tell us not only *what is good music* but *what music is good for.* Here is your real and live and challenging responsibility. You can reach only a small portion of this large aggregate of our school population to whom I refer through participation in your bands, orchestras, and choruses.

By all means continue your pursuits in this direction, but widen your concepts of your responsibility to the masses of our school population. Realize the educational value of music activities at every school level and strive earnestly to make them available for *all* pupils. You cannot do this alone but administrators cannot do it without you. Working together it can be accomplished.

The Functional Value of Music

Any subject has a functional value when it contributes to the general well-being of the individual and when it helps him to participate fully and more effectively in the life of the society in which he lives and works. Certainly music has functional value, and this is related to the important responsibility it has in education for citizenship.

Music education always has had an important place in the curriculum of democracies. Over two thousand years ago music was a part of the education of every Greek citizen. Those of us who believe that music has a stake in American education today have our convictions considerably strengthened when we read the sections of Plato's *Republic* (Books 2 and 3) in which he expresses this program of education: "Gymnastics for the body and *music for the soul*." Greek music, art, and poetry were bound up with civic life, closely allied to the religious festivals which were then the heart and soul of the nation. So today it does not seem too much of a boast to say that one of the most important contributions music education makes in *our* curriculum is one of *education for citizenship*.

Guiding Principles

There are specific contributions which music can make in educating for citizenship. Some guiding principles on which administrators and music educators can build a music education program which will contribute to the development of desirable citizenship traits are:

(1) Music offers an opportunity for self-expression through a group activity. Thus, it has a socializing value which is beneficial for the uninhibited students who may, through this one avenue of participation in a school activity, learn the all-important principles of good citizenship—self assurance, self-realization, personal security, and respect for the achievements of others. Certainly through encouraging individual initiative and group cooperation, music education is helping to develop good citizens.

(2) Music offers an opportunity to develop moral and spiritual values and to satisfy aesthetic needs. Young people are expressing, creating, or enjoying beauty when they are singing a song, playing a tune, or just listening. Likewise, music provides a wholesome means of enjoying leisure and can be a powerful influence for good. Youngsters participating in good music are not likely to be numbered among our juvenile delinquents. As music educators you have the privilege of helping these people live well-adjusted lives and thus become better, happier citizens.

(3) Music provides a medium through which boys and girls can make direct contributions to their community during their school days and thus acquire a consciousness of the responsibility of the individual to the community. This is borne out of the fact that in most of the communities in the United States it is the school music groups—the bands, orchestras, and choruses in elementary schools, high schools, and colleges—which furnish the focus for the music life of the community. These activities provide an

outlet for self-expression and for belonging, which are two basic human needs, and at the same time build that spirit of cooperation upon which democracy depends for its very existence.

(4) Music offers a medium for understanding other people, their culture, and their problems. This is not to say that the mere singing and playing of music of various countries by our boys and girls makes them necessarily understand those countries. The people of some countries have been playing each other's music for centuries and at periodic intervals these people have been at war with each other. However, music is a universal tool of communication; it transcends the boundaries of nations; it promotes the brotherhood of man.

With good teaching, teaching with imagination the music of other countries in our classrooms, and through our classrooms reaching our homes and communities, we contribute enormously to the stature of our future citizens who want to live in a peaceful world with the citizens of other countries.

(5) Through music the student is led to a realization that the arts, of which music is one, have been of indisputable importance throughout all history. As a matter of fact, the arts are the permanent purveyors of history from one civilization to another. An understanding of the thoughts, ideals, and aspirations of preceding generations is needed to build a background for good citizenship.

At the risk of under-emphasizing many of the other important functions of music in the curriculum at all levels of education today, I believe I would put *education for citizenship* as its most important function. This concept is a very logical and necessary base from which many of the other values to be derived from music as a part of education, can follow. This is *music's most important stake in education*.

Music educators who are teaching music as a fundamental part of our American way of life and who are analyzing the challenge of music in education for citizenship are making notable and invaluable contributions to the all-round education of our boys and girls.

Educators of this type are needed and can be used in all levels of music education from preschool through college and the university. Such educators are not committed to a program of idealisms which claim that music does all things for all people. Instead, they do their utmost to help young people in the schools to become as literate as possible in the field of music. Well-balanced individuals—musicians and educators—have a keen realization that music is a means through which boys and girls can learn to play and work together; that it is a means through which better citizens can be developed; that music contributes to the richness of family life; that it offers many vocational opportunities for our young citizens. In the

hands of these persons the stake of music in education, which is considerable, will be assured.

Harry S. Broudy
A Realistic Philosophy of Music Education (1958)

Harry S. Broudy was professor of education at The University of Illinois at
Champaign-Urbana.

1. . . . . although the world comes to each person filtered through his own
sense organs, nervous system, and a particular pattern of space, time, and
history, he does not create the objects that he apprehends; nor are they
merely ideas in his or anyone else's mind. If three of us hear *Yankee Doodle*
and disagree on its pitch or rhythm, we do not conclude that *Yankee Doodle*
has no single pitch or rhythm. On the contrary, we try to find the peculiarities in each individual that would explain his hearing them differently.

The realist does not insist that every quality of music must lie wholly in
the object, where they indeed appear to be. The objectivity of pitch, timbre,
tempo, and formal design is easier to defend than are certain "expressive"
qualities, such as nobility, religiousness, strivingness, dignity, sublimity.
Clearly the "humanness" of these latter qualities makes it seem plausible to
believe that they are creations or projections of the human consciousness
onto the patterns of sound that we call music. Yet, even here realism is reluctant to give up objectivity altogether. Plato and even the more moderate
Aristotle would try to find some correspondence between the structure of
the music and its fitness to express human passions and aspiration. Thus, the
Phrygian mode was held to be appropriate to the mood of courage.

2. Why is realism so concerned with whether the qualities of music are
in the object or added to it by the listener? For one thing, if there is no
sense in which the musical object is independent of the listener, then it
makes little sense to talk about standards for music; one can only talk about
standards for listeners. If enjoyment, as such, is to be the sole standard of
listening, then the child, the symphonic musician, and the music critic
might all be listening to *Peter and the Wolf* with equal enjoyment. It would
seem that those who are willing to affirm this have to explain why music
education is necessary. Those who are reluctant to accept this conclusion
are assuming standards of listening other than enjoyment as such, or they
are assuming that knowledge or skill can affect the quality of enjoyment.

For another matter, realism holds that, in knowing or hearing anything,
we do not alter it.[1] Musically, this means that our previous experience or

---

expectations do not create or change the sound patterns emanating from the voice or instrument, however much or little they affect our interpretation of these patterns. In other words, they would hold that a piece of music, although related in many ways to the culture in which it was composed and the experience of its auditors, nevertheless has musical qualities and structure independent of these and peculiar to itself which can be progressively explored in any culture and at any time by the musically cultivated person.

3. However, we cannot banish relativity altogether. As has been mentioned, it is doubtful whether music would be "expressive" to any but human beings. It seems more in accord with experience to say that if music has a given structure of tonality and rhythm, it *invites* appropriately tuned human beings to apprehend them as being expressive, that is, as sounding sorrowful, joyful, noble, dignified, or sublime. Music is alleged to have charms even for the subhuman organism, but, although a lullaby may make a tiger gentle, it is doubtful that for a tiger the music expresses gentility or anything else.

Realism in company with other philosophic systems has the problem of accounting for the fact that what people like and what is judged good music do not always agree. If we are to dispute about taste, then we have to be able to say that there is a standard for the cultivation of the listener as well as for the construction of the music.

Theoretically, realism provides for this by the hypothesis that the virtues, that is, the excellences of the mind, of the will, of the senses, of the body—all are signs of perfecting and perfection. In other words, although music, structurally and qualitatively, is what it is apart from the listener, it takes a "tuned" man, that is, a man cultivated in music, to discern the goodness of the music. Therefore, the standard of both music and men is the connoisseur.

4. In both Plato and Aristotle and the long tradition they founded, music, although delightful to the ear and charming on that account alone, derived its significance elsewhere. First, music was made up of tones that bore certain mathematical relations to each other. For Pythagoras and Plato, mathematics was the science of measure and, therefore, of order. The orderliness of the cosmos was attested by the mathematical relations the planets bore to each other. Hence, the audible music of men was somehow the representative of the inaudible but more perfect music of the celestial spheres. Music revealed a reality deeper than itself, and the more reality it disclosed, the better it was.[2] Second, Plato and Aristotle believed that music could be used in character training because it affected the emotions directly. Thus, Plato was concerned lest certain softening musical modes, such as the Lydian and Ionian, would undermine the hardiness of the

guardians.[3] Aristotle felt that the emotion induced by music and poetry could knock out of the person the more harmful forms of that emotion (catharsis).[4] Good music, therefore, could mean more metaphysically significant music or music that helped build better character.

This brings us to the problem as to whether art can refuse to be evaluated in other than artistic terms. The ancients recognized the difference between music that was good musically and that which was good morally or intellectually. Plato was adamant on this point: aesthetic experience had to be judged by its *effects* on the whole life of a person or a society as well as by artistic standards alone. The musician may resent this as an infringement on his artistic autonomy, but the educator cannot have a curriculum made up of discrete, unorganized types of experiences. We shall argue that the expressive qualities of music as distinguished from the more specifically musical characteristics are the ones that bring music into relation with the other areas of life and that one meaning of "greatness" in music is the way in which it does so.

Problems in the Philosophy of Music Education

We shall now turn to a set of topics or problems that face any philosophy of music education, if by philosophy is meant a reasoned justification for a set of beliefs rather than a mere assertion of these beliefs. A philosophy of music education, we submit, is to be assessed in terms of its answers to certain questions. Although, in what follows, we cannot speak for any or all realists, we present it as an approach that does differ from both idealistic and pragmatic approaches and which may not be uncongenial to many realists.

1. What are the components of the musical experience?
2. How is musical experience related to other types of experience?
3. Which phases of musical experience can we hope to improve by instruction?
4. What principles can justify our setting up standards for musical judgment and music education?
5. What can we meaningfully demand as outcomes of music education in the public school?
6. What does our philosophy seem to signify in the way of a program of general music education and the training of teachers of music? . . .

General-education Program in Music

From what has been said, the following points can be made with respect to (a) a program of music education for general education, and (b) the qualities needed by a teacher in such a program.

1. As regards the program, the key concept we have employed is that of connoisseurship. Growth in taste and appreciation has been held to be correlative with growth in musical skill, knowledge, and the ability to comprehend and discriminate the musical qualities. If this is so, then the program can be formal, systematic, and deliberately instituted and conducted, for both knowledge and skill can be taught systematically. It also makes sense to speak of a method of teaching music if there are skill and knowledge to be taught, and if there are gradations of this knowledge and skill in the learner.

The concept of connoisseurship encourages the use of materials that the experts of successive ages have regarded as good and important. It does not exclude the contemporary and experimental, but it does evaluate them in terms of musical *knowledge* and *cultivated* taste.

Further, this view sees value in having the learner aware of the continuity of the musical tradition. Thus, the study of a twelfth-century chant aids the listener when he hears it used or simulated in a contemporary work; and its presence in the contemporary work expands the understanding of it in its original form.

2. As regards the qualification of the music teacher, the concept of the connoisseur likewise provides a few guiding principles.

If there can be method in the teaching of music, it makes sense to ask that teachers master it. This means that the teacher will not be left to blunder through some impromptu pattern of music instruction as best he can. Nor can he rely upon enthusiasm, love of children, or even on love of music itself to make up for deficiencies in method.

The teacher cannot use a tradition of connoisseurship in music of which he is ignorant. There is a selected body of knowledge about music—historical, theoretical, and technical—that ought to be part of the educated person's experience. In the teacher, this ought to be underlined and augmented with respect to the requirements of music-teaching at various levels of instruction.

Finally, if the justification for shaping preferences is the faith of the teacher that the learnings he is "forcing" upon the pupil will enhance the pupil's enjoyment of music and life, then this phenomenon of effort and reward must have *come to pass in his own experience.* Otherwise, his standards are secondhand and conventional, and his faith unfounded. To demand that elementary-school teachers achieve this order of musical experience and cultivation is asking a great deal, but is the conclusion escapable—even if it should be objected that the other arts will make similar demands upon them?

On the other hand, the music-teaching specialist will have to be *generally* educated as well as musically cultivated. The problem of maintaining the delicate balance between technique and knowledge, performance and

Harry S. Broudy

appreciation, skill and enjoyment will never be solved by the ignorant lay-
man or the overspecialized expert.

Notes

1. Philosophically, this point gets its emphasis from the insistence of the experimen-
talists that the situation as given to us is transformed in the process of our inquiry into
it, e.g., John Dewey, *The Quest for Certainty* (New York: Minton, Balch & Co., 1929, 85ff.).
In Aristotelian realism it is held that during the act of knowing, the mind and the object
become formally, although not numerically or existentially, identical.

2. Julius Portnoy, *The Philosopher and Music* (New York: Humanities Press, 1954), 14–36.

3. "Rhythms and music in general are imitations of good and evil characters in men"
(Plato, *Laws*, VII, 798.)

4. *Politics*, VII, 134.

C. A. Burmeister
The Role of Music in General Education (1958)

C. A. Burmeister was Chairman of the Music Education Department at Northwestern University.

Significant Contributions of Music to General Education

Previous attempts to support the place of music in the curriculum have
largely treated music as the instrument to goals that are not unique to music
and, for the most part, are better arrived at by other means, for example,
health, social competency, and lofty ideals. As has been indicated in other
chapters of this yearbook, notably those by McMurray and Broudy, it must
be shown that music is central in the core of common experiences required
of all. The alternative is to limit music to the status of an additional peripheral subject designed to accommodate exceptional talents or special interests and to help prepare for vocational-professional life. If it can be shown
that music plays or should play a considerable role in the lives of all men,
then its place in general education is assured.

It should not be denied that music plays some part in the realization of
many of the goals of general education, such as those mentioned in the preceding paragraph. Also, it must be admitted that music is not unique in that
it is the sole means by which a given goal may be achieved. Nevertheless,
there are ways in which music makes a significant contribution to the general
education of man and in which music is unexcelled as a means of attaining a

specific goal. Three areas in which music makes contributions which are unique in that sense are: (1) aesthetic growth; (2) productive use of leisure time; (3) emotional development.

No one seriously doubts that music belongs in general education. The problem is one of clarifying how the work of the music specialist fits that of other educational specialists to produce a well-rounded educative product. According to McMurray . . . the primary aims of music education would be: (1) to help everyone to further awareness of patterns of sound as an aesthetic component in the world of experience; (2) to increase each person's capacity to control the ability of aesthetic richness through music; (3) to transform the public musical culture into a recognized part of each person's environment.

Broudy . . . also argues that the place of music in a specific curriculum should be based on aesthetic considerations. He advances a realistic view that since perfection lies in the direction of form, then the ability to detect aesthetic form (that arrangement of elements that attracts, holds, and directs the interest of the listener) is the heart of music education.

Somewhat akin to the unique contributions of music education to aesthetic growth are the unique contributions to preparation for increased leisure time. It would seem that any activity which is deliberately designed to help all to live fuller lives would be assured of consideration. According to Ulich, no consideration of general education would be complete which did not recognize that a common core of experience for all individuals should include contact with useful, practical work, sports, and all those activities which appeal to the emotions. It should be noted that play is a common element in work, in sports, and in art, which is perhaps the most sublime form of play. Music as play must be considered in this context because of its universality in the experiences of all men.

A third, and perhaps the most important, unique contribution of music to general education stems from a fallacy in educational thought noted in these words from the report of the Board of the Boston Academy of Music of 1835: "Now, the defect in our present system, admirable as that system is, is this, that it aims to develop the intellectual part of man's nature solely when, for all the true purposes of life, it is of more importance, a hundred-fold, to feel rightly than to think profoundly."

Add these words which supply a current urgency: "For in their emotions men are united, whereas the inevitable differences of intellect separate men from one another."

In other words, general education aims at developing an individual capable of making reasoned decisions based on intellectual growth. Yet, experience has demonstrated that the emotions largely determine in what directions and to what extent the intellect will be permitted to act. There-

C. A. Burmeister

fore, those activities which affect the emotional life of the individual right-fully belong in general education—and as has been indicated, they assume a priority of consideration not generally accorded them.

It is not within the scope of this chapter to show in detail how music affects behavior. This would involve elaboration of the theory that the musical stimulus entering the organism by means of the auditory nerve encounters no cortical resistance before stimulating the thalamus, or primitive forebrain, which is held to be the seat of the emotions. The stimulated thalamus initiates psychophysical reactions such as altered respiration, heartbeat, and blood pressure, and bombards the cortex with urgent demands which are interpreted by the cortex in terms of feelings. Because of these effects, which have been demonstrated empirically . . . it is possible to say that, while music is not the only activity which relates directly to emotional growth and development, it does possess these unique attributes:

1. Music is the most subtle, pervasive, and insistent of all the arts.
2. It requires no intellectualization to work its effects.
3. Its effects cannot be denied by the auditor. It is impossible to direct or divert the psychophysical effects of the sheer potency of tone by an act of the will.
4. Special abilities are not necessary. All can share in a response to music.

In the plainest language possible, we like music because it makes us feel good. Given proper guidance, that liking may be developed into refined aesthetic sensitivity. If the activities which foster that development continue to make us feel good, it cannot be anything but beneficial to our emotions. And if the fun in being musical is not thwarted in the process, music will have made a significant contribution to general education.

Charles Leonhard and Robert W. House
The Objectives and Processes of Education (1959)

Charles Leonhard is professor of music emeritus at the University of Illinois at Champaign-Urbana. Robert W. House is professor of music emeritus at the University of Minnesota, Duluth. Leonhard and House: *Foundations and Principles of Music Education* (New York: McGraw-Hill, 1959). Reprinted with permission of The McGraw-Hill Companies.

Chapter 1: The Objectives and Processes of Education

Introduction. It is the viewpoint of this book that music education has a highly important function in the education program and that music education must be shaped logically and realistically within the framework of the total program of the school. It is believed that the primary purpose of the music education program is to develop the aesthetic potential, with which every human being is endowed, to the highest possible level.

Music education has a truly unique mandate in contemporary American education—to provide varied, significant, and cumulative musical experience for every American child. If this mandate is to be fulfilled, school music experiences must be of such quality as to enable every child to:

1. Establish working standards in his valuation of music
2. Bring imaginative vision to all his experience with music
3. Develop the resources for the heightened quality of symbolic experience available through music
4. Attain the highest level of musical understanding of which he is capable
5. Gain sufficient proficiency in singing and in playing an instrument to make it possible for him to be an active participant in music throughout his life

Music has intrinsic value; it requires no external justification. Dewey provided a clear-cut focus for music education in saying:

> They [the arts] reveal a depth and range of meaning in experiences which otherwise might be mediocre and trivial. They supply, that is, the organs of vision. Moreover, in their fullness they represent the concentration and consummation of elements of good which are otherwise scattered and incomplete. They select and focus the elements of enjoyable worth which can make any experience directly enjoyable. They are not luxuries of education but emphatic expressions of that which makes any education worthwhile.[1]

Clearly music merits full rights in the curriculum; it can and should be taught as music, and for its own sake.

The point of view presented in this book is that the music program should be dedicated to the development of musical responsiveness and musical understanding on the part of all pupils in the school. The task of the school music program is essentially to organize a favorable musical environment in which every pupil can undergo the maximum musical growth consistent with his ability and his interests. The school must be especially concerned that it provide musical experiences which have significance in the daily living of the pupils both while they are in school and when they are away from school.

Charles Leonhard and Robert W. House

These experiences fall into two broad categories, general music and musical specializations. The former consists of a planned sequence of musical experiences selected for their value in promoting musical responsiveness, broad musical understanding, and over-all musical competence; these experiences should be available to all pupils throughout their period of schooling. The musical specializations properly represent a natural and desirable outgrowth of significant and successful general music experiences. All aspects of the program should be considered as means to musical development of the pupils and never as ends in themselves.

This view of the purpose of music education differs markedly from views exemplified in many current programs of music education. The music education scene includes several different kinds of programs which fail to take into account the nature of the aesthetic experience and the importance of aesthetic experience in the life of the human being. These faulty programs include the following:

1. Programs with undue emphasis on performance. In these programs every effort is made to discover as early as possible students with superior performance facility. They are started early on some specialized aspect of music with a consequent neglect of their broad musical development. Students who cannot or will not conform to the rigidly prescribed pattern are gradually lopped off and little attention is given to meeting their musical needs.

2. Programs aimed principally at the musical entertainment of students. Here standards in literature and performance have little importance, and no one cares whether musical learning takes place or not, just so long as everybody is happy. Students make little progress from year to year, and contact with music is superficial, rewarding only for the moment and seldom leading anywhere.

3. Programs emphasizing music as an instrument for achieving unmusical ends such as health, citizenship, and so on. Such programs ignore the unique values inherent in the musical experience and attempt to justify music by preposterous and unconvincing claims concerning the utility values of music.

4. Programs in which music loses its identity through specious integration with other subject areas of the school. This condition is especially prevalent in elementary schools having a fused, core, or other type of integrated curriculum and an inadequate staff of specialized music personnel. Although it is true that music can illuminate some other subject matter, the music program which fails to stand on its own feet and provide for cumulative musical learning denies the importance of musical experience itself, musical learning, and musical independence.

5. Programs aimed largely at securing public approbation. Here the music program is viewed as a public relations arm of the school. Principal

attention is given to the preparation of performing groups likely to gain popular approval. No request for a performing group is denied even though the excessive number of appearances interferes seriously with the education of students not only in music but in other phases of their schoolwork. Excesses in this direction occur in schools at all levels but reach most damaging proportions in some college music schools where students may be absent for weeks on extended tours. Viewed objectively, such practices constitute unjustified exploitation of students.

Because of the vitality of the musical art and the devotion of thousands of music educators to their profession, music education has undergone startling development and has made outstanding accomplishments in the United States. Looking at the situation dispassionately, however, one cannot be complacent about the position of music education in American schools. Alarming cutbacks in music programs have already occurred in many parts of the country. In the eyes of many school administrators and many laymen, music remains an educational frill, an adjunct rather than an integral part of the general education program. As a result, when the educational program must be cut, music seems to them to be a logical place in which to begin.

Furthermore, objective evaluation of the products of music education indicates that the program has many shortcomings and is in urgent need of improvement. Some of the more obvious indications of the need for reappraisal of the program are the small percentage of student participation in secondary school music programs, the low level of musical competence and interest shown by many elementary classroom teachers and prospective teachers who are products of music-education programs, the low level of accomplishment outside of performance shown by freshman music majors in colleges and universities, the small impact of the music program on adolescents compared with the impact of the latest popular music trend, and the small demand for good music programs on radio and television.

This situation is due in large measure to the failure of music education to develop a sound theoretical and philosophical orientation for the music program. Most music-education professional literature gives assent to the importance of music in education and attempts to justify it by showing a more or less tenuous connection between music and the general objectives of education. While music can make contributions of varying importance to the achievement of such objectives as health, citizenship, command of fundamental processes, and so on, the weakness of attempts to justify music in this way lies in the fact that none of these objectives is unique to music and that many other areas of study point more directly and convincingly to their attainment than does music.

The practicing music educator, confronted with this hazy and unconvincing theoretical justification for music in general education, almost inevitably either favors unmusical ends at the expense of musical ones or emphasizes performance for the few and neglects the general musical education of the many. This, in turn, reinforces the impression of the administrator and the public that music has little or no value outside of performance.

To consolidate the position of music education in American schools and to ensure further progress, music educators on all levels need to develop these fundamental qualifications:

1. They must understand the total work of the school and the interrelatedness of all aspects of the school program.
2. They must be well informed about the general objectives of the school.
3. They must understand the unique contribution that music can make to the total function of the school.
4. They must be able to work and communicate with administrators in other areas of the school.

The primary purpose of this book is to assist music educators and prospective music educators in developing these essential understandings. The present chapter presents a short summary treatment of the objectives of education and a discussion of the processes involved in education. All phases of the music-education program are treated in subsequent chapters. . . .

Chapter 4: Philosophical Foundations of Music Education

Why should music be included in the school curriculum?

Music has been included in the curricula of schools from the beginning of recorded history, and widely varying reasons for its inclusion have operated at different times. Much of the time music has been justified for the extrinsic value of musical activity, and participation in music has been considered instrumental to achieving ends essentially unmusical. Plato, for example, held that the great value of music lay in its usefulness in achieving social results which he considered desirable. He went so far as to proscribe the use of certain modes as immoral and lascivious. The Romans included music as one of the seven liberal arts because the mathematical aspects of music seemed fit for celestial beings, along with arithmetic, geometry, and astronomy. During the Renaissance and Reformation, Protestant elementary schools brought music into the curriculum to develop religious feelings and to save souls. Children in these schools sang hymns to further the religious objectives of the schools. Music was used in the eighteenth century to heighten the nationalistic spirit and feelings of patriotism. In American music education, instrumental values have tended to dominate the thinking of music educators and administrators from Lowell Mason to the present day. Typical of claims made for music are the following:

> Music education includes activities and learning which develop the social aspects of life.
> Music education develops the health of the student.
> Music education aids in the development of sound work habits.
> Music education instills wholesome ideals of conduct.
> Music education aims to develop good citizenship.
> Music education improves home life.

Although all of these claims have an instrumental conception of the value of music behind them, they are not all equally farfetched. Music can be a social asset, provide a focus for group work, and represent a rewarding endeavor in the home. Some of the other claims, however, border on the ridiculous. Musicians have never been known to have better health than other people, and their posture and health habits are not demonstrably superior. The claim for the development of work habits depends upon a highly specific view of transfer of training which has long since been proved unsound. The claim for developing wholesome ideals of conduct apparently stems from a notion that music has a transcendental "goodness" about it which may rub off onto musical participants. The idea that music contributes to development of citizenship seems extremely naïve, since music groups do not demand a democratic way of life. On the other hand, they are likely to be the most authoritarian groups in which one ever finds himself.

The authors cannot accept an instrumental view of the function of music in the life of the human being or in the school program. While certain values of this kind may accrue, they do not provide the raison d'être for the music program. Furthermore, reliance on instrumental values inevitably perverts and distorts the art of music and debases its true and enduring values.

Reliance on the instrumental values of music has provided music education with a flimsy, unconvincing argument, because none of the claimed values are unique to music and the musical experience. Even if music did develop better health, a good physical education and health program would undoubtedly be more efficient. Developing wholesome ideals of conduct, at best a peripheral accomplishment of music participation, can take place more directly through religious training and other facets of the school program. Likewise, the development of citizenship can best be achieved through civics classes, history classes, and citizenship-education projects. And no reasonable person can believe that work habits developed in music are more likely to operate in other fields of endeavor than those developed in shop, home economics, and algebra class.

Charles Leonhard and Robert W. House

In addition and most regrettably, reliance on instrumental values of music has provided cover for appallingly scanty musical achievement, minimal musical learning, and shockingly low musical standards. The music teacher who teaches little or no music is often excused on the grounds that the children are happy, or are good group members, or will not beat their wives when they grow up and marry. These results are all well and good, but they are not a direct corollary or outcome of musical experience and have little or no relevance for conducting and evaluating the music program.

Does the rejection of instrumental values as the basis for the inclusion of music in the school weaken the case for music and leave it unsupported in the scramble for curricular time? By no manner of means. Actually, it strengthens the place of music by enabling us to emphasize its positive values and to show the unique role of music education as a part of aesthetic education.

Man is unique among all earthly living creatures in the extent and quality of his potential. He has physical, intellectual, ethical, and aesthetic potentials. If any aspect of his potential is neglected and undeveloped, he never attains his true stature as a human being. Responsibility for developing his physical potential is shared by the home, medical services, and the school physical and health education program. The focus of most of the school program is on developing his intellectual potential. The school, the home, the church, and the community agencies share responsibility for developing his ethical potential. Although other agencies such as the home, mass media of communication, and community influences contribute to his aesthetic development, the school has primary responsibility for helping him attain stature in this realm of meaning in which life gains some of its most worthwhile and enduring values. Through aesthetic education he finds true self-realization, insight into life values which are timeless, culturally significant, and personally satisfying. He discovers means for satisfying a basic and pervasive need of all human beings, namely, the need for symbolic experience.

Music has unique qualities that make it the most desirable medium of organized aesthetic education. Human beings are universally responsive to music and can find satisfaction and meaning through experience with it. Although there are wide variations in musical capacity and sensitivity, every person can find satisfaction and enjoyment not only as a consumer but also as a producer of music on some level and in some medium. Music is unique among the arts in lending itself to group participation. For instance, while the consumption of plastic art is an individual matter, everyone within hearing of a musical performance can perceive its meaning. Likewise, the performance of music is in large part a group proposition. Thus, music fits into the scheme of education more neatly than any other form of artistic endeavor and must perforce carry the major load of aesthetic education in all organized general education. Herein lies the major case for the inclusion of music in general education. Who can assail the importance of aesthetic experience in the life of the human being? Who can deny the cultural pervasiveness of the musical art? Who can doubt the cultural significance of music from the beginning of recorded history and the richness of the musical cultural heritage? Who can negate the fact that music lends itself admirably to organized instruction and group participation within the school framework? Who can fail to recognize the urgent necessity for aesthetic education in this modern day when there is a constant tendency to emphasize the material, the technological, and the intellectual aspects of life to the detriment of the spiritual and human values?

We are now in a position to state in summary form the basic tenets of our philosophy of music education. They grow out of the preceding discussion, and we believe them to be logically, musically, and educationally sound.

1. Art is the result of man's need to transform his experience symbolically.
2. Aesthetic experience grows out of and is related to ordinary experience. Aesthetic quality is the source of man's highest satisfaction in living, and while all experience that is carried on intelligently has aesthetic quality, man's most valued experience is in connection with art objects consciously and feelingfully conceived and contemplated.
3. All human experience is accompanied by feeling. Music bears a close similarity to the forms of human feeling and is the tonal analogue of the emotive life.
4. Music is expressive of the life of feeling in that its movement symbolizes the movement of feeling alternating between struggle and fulfillment, intensity and release, rise and fall, movement and repose, and even, finally, life and death.
5. The import of music is not fixed; it is subjective, personal, and creative in the best sense of the word. We can fill the forms of music with any feelingful meaning that fits them.
6. Since the appeal of music is to the life of feeling, every musical experience and all experience with music must be feelingful experience.
7. Music attains significance only through its expressive appeal, and all work with music must be carried with full cognizance of its expressive appeal.
8. Every person has the need to transform experience symbolically and the capacity for symbolic experience with music.
9. The only sound basis for music education is the development of the natural responsiveness that all human beings possess.
10. The music-education program should be primarily aesthetic education.

11. Every child must be given the opportunity to develop his aesthetic potential to the highest possible level through expressive experience with music, including vocal and instrumental performance, listening, and composition appropriate to his developmental level.

12. Music education should be cosmopolitan, employing all kinds of music and giving recognition to the value of all kinds of music.

13. While no type of music can be ignored in the music program, major attention should be given to providing musical experience that is educative in that it leads to an aesthetic response to great music, to the clarification of musical values, and to the development of musical independence.

14. All instructional material should be musical material of the highest possible quality; all teaching should have as its primary objective the illumination of the art of music and should emphasize musical values and not extramusical values.

15. Through extensive experience with music certain instrumental values inevitably accrue. These include the development of resources for worthwhile use of leisure time, the opportunity to participate with peers in a worthwhile group endeavor, resources for enriched home and community life, and the opportunity to discover unusual talent. Results in these areas can occur, however, only when the primary emphasis is placed on providing musical experience that is worthwhile in itself.

Note

1. John Dewey, *Democracy and Education* (New York: The Macmillan Company, 1916), 279. Reprinted by permission of the publisher.

Abraham A. Schwadron
Aesthetics and Music Education (1967)

Abraham A. Schwadron was professor of music at the University of California, Los Angeles. Earlier, while writing this book, he taught at Rhode Island College.

Preface

It has become apparent that critical problems confronting music educators today will not be solved by reiterating well-meaning, but vague, references to desirable skills, curricula, and budgets. While these matters are important, it is paramount to provide a firm philosophical framework for contemporary music education through more penetrating and fundamental concerns. This calls for a renewed emphasis on value education, for philosophical examination of strengths and weaknesses—for critical probings into the aesthetics of music.

That the study of aesthetics is largely neglected in the education of music teachers is both regrettable and paradoxical. Too often the educator tends to regard aesthetic (as well as philosophical) inquiry either as a tedious and quarrelsome rehash of classical and scholastic arguments or as an esoteric discussion having little "down to earth" substance. On the other hand, the teacher of music refers freely to his particular field of endeavor as "aesthetic," or simply as that which deals with the "beautiful." He nobly defends the musical arts on grounds rooted in "aesthetic experiences." Yet, when confronted by students, by administrators, and by the lay public with the task of elucidating on the practice he preaches, he undergoes understandable difficulty.

Just what are our beliefs concerning the nature and values of the musical arts? On what bases are these beliefs derived? What do we mean by "good music" and "good taste"? The problems of why, what, and how music should be taught are inherently bound in meaningful answers to such questions. . . .

The role of music education in uplifting musical tastes and in stimulating artistic integrity has reached a significant level of concern. Philosophical concepts and educational objectives must be re-examined and renewed with aesthetic conviction.

The fact that educators are generally uninformed about philosophy and aesthetics points to the "almost systematic neglect of philosophy and whole realms of aesthetic value in the teacher education program in music";[1] and consequently, in the actual practice of music education. The importance of this book rests on this consideration as well as upon the self-searching needs and professional standards of the music educator in an effort to understand the aesthetic, to identify with the practical, and to speculate with the potential. As a result the music educator should be in a better position to use aesthetic inquiry as a source of ideas and as a logical tool for sorting out values. . . .

Chapter 4: Recommendations

The value of aesthetic inquiry lies not only in the discovery of ideas but also in some form of critical application. In chapters two and three we explored the ways in which the dimensions of aesthetics permeate and give direction to the philosophy and practice of music education. In this chapter we will review and synthesize leading ideas by stating foundations, by interpreting issues, and by suggesting some avenues for research.

Abraham A. Schwadron

I. Education provides the means whereby individual and mass musical discrimination can be realized. The development of musical skills, values, attitudes, tastes, and habits are basic to such a purpose.

II. Music education functions most effectively when both intellectual and emotional factors are considered coordinates in the development of aesthetic perception. The capacity for understanding both form and content are basic to the cultivation of musical tastes and values.

III. If aesthetic experiences contribute to a better-ordered society, then educational conditions must be fostered so that such experiences may occur more often and at more subtle levels of response. In the development of music curricula and programs, public education must center its attention on the bulk of the masses rather than on the talented few.

IV. Since no single theory of aesthetics would be universally agreeable for the needs of contemporary music education, a broad aesthetic outlook, encompassing the wealth of theories, would then be most desirable. To avoid eclecticism, which offers no factual knowledge of its own, specific theoretical understandings should be utilized when they are relevant and, hence, of value to intended purposes.

V. Music education should function within the framework of those principles of general education that outline democratic education—equal opportunity, common education, academic freedom, concensus of opinion, etc. Accordingly, educators must accept the idea of a plurality of values as basic to the pluralistic character of society and to aesthetic education. Education, as opposed to inculcation, should lead to the development of personal artistic criteria which may differ from individual to individual.

VI. The goal of raising the general level of aesthetic understanding toward more significant musical experiences requires a commitment to values which transcends mere pleasurable likes and dislikes. Educators who seek discriminative levels must be prepared to distinguish, and to guide others to distinguish, differences between mundane musical delight and artistic significance.

VII. Aesthetic music education requires an application of information from many disciplines. Such an approach enhances its academic nature and warrants its recognition in a liberal core of cultural studies, notably the humanities.

VIII. The most immediate musical needs of society are primarily consumer-oriented. To educate the masses for levels of musical understanding the guidance and connoisseurship of the expert is necessary.

IX. Music education must recognize its artistic responsibility not only to the contemporary composer, but also to the aesthetic conscience of society.

Our philosophy should recognize the school as a logical agency for socio-musical change and for critical examination of aesthetic needs.

X. The aesthetic event is a connotative complex of associations made concrete by the individual. But these connotations are intracultural, not universal; conditioned, not innate; dynamic, not fixed; personal, not public. Unlike other art forms, the musical experience may also be meaningful in a symbolic manner without reference to extramusical events. When educators rely on referential ideas foreign to music, promote unfounded notions of universal meanings, and avoid abstract symbolized meanings, then the responsibility of education for aesthetic perception is neglected. While direct image-connotation and specific referential meaning is not recommended, comprehension of the materials of music is.

> The listener who can thus think of music in its own terms, rather than through eternal translation into something of words or mental images, is the one who most readily can approach the greatest art products in substantially the same spirit of understanding that is brought to the folk dance or popular song.[2]

Musical understanding results from learning, and may be approached fundamentally by grasping combinations of sounds and the successive patterns by which these sounds become interrelated. Isolated tones become meaningful when associated with other tones. Problems in the perception of rhythm, harmonic progression, texture, and formal design require similar modes of studied relationships. Habits of concentrated attention to stimulate memory and frequent comparisons to motivate critical attitudes are then essential to the task of coordinating the intellect with sense perception.

While this approach to aesthetic education would normally result in an awareness of musical factors that commonly characterize Western music, aesthetic systems of other cultures should also be introduced. Studies of intracultural variations in musical expression broaden cultural and aesthetic understandings and stimulate discriminate attitudes.

Notes

1. Charles Leonhard, "Research: Philosophy and Esthetics," *Journal of Research in Music Education* III (Spring 1955), 24.

2. Oscar Thompson, "The Language of Music," *Perspectives on Music*, ed. Leroy Ostransky (Englewood Cliffs: Prentice-Hall Inc., 1963), 25.

Abraham A. Schwadron

Gerard L. Knieter
The Nature of Aesthetic Education (1971)

Gerard L. Knieter is professor of music at California State University, North-ridge. He was chair of the Department of Music Education at Temple University when he wrote this essay.

Education is concerned with the shaping of behavior. In the arts we are concerned with man's aesthetic behavior. Hence, we must be able to identify that aspect of personality that is concerned with aesthetic behavior. *Aesthetic sensitivity is man's capacity to respond to the emotional values and cognitive meanings of art.* It is a quality of personality that is universal among men and provides the fundamental source out of which the expressive potential develops. While some writers have identified particular arts as universal, what is operationally universal is man's capacity to respond to both internal and external artistic stimuli.

Aesthetic experience is a phenomenon that has enjoyed intensive consideration by aestheticians, philosophers, and, more recently, educators and psychologists. Elaborate systems of description have emerged that tend to obscure the simple fact that the aesthetic experience is the result of a natural process. Rather than presenting a particular theory of aesthetic experience, essential characteristics of the aesthetic experience should be identified.

Characteristics of the aesthetic experience

The aesthetic experience involves focus. An aesthetic encounter is highly directional; it involves an energy flow from the respondent to the work of art. As a result of this quality of involvement the respondent appears to receive stimulation from the work of art. What is vital to note in this characteristic is that the aesthetic experience is not a vicarious encounter. Merely exposing a respondent to works of art in a casual manner (hearing music piped into the elevator or supermarket, walking through a hallway with paintings in view, being aware of people dancing while one is otherwise engaged) does not provide appropriate stimulation to qualify as an aesthetic experience. The need for investing psychological energy indicates that programs of aesthetic education require structure rather than random activities.

The aesthetic experience involves perception. Perception may be viewed as the process through which data from the senses are utilized. A percept is that which is known of an object, a quality, or a relationship as a result of sensory experience. It is a state of awareness rather than an image or a memory. Percepts tend to be organized around a series of related sensations that are actuated from either internal or external stimuli. When a pattern of percepts becomes organized it may give rise to the development of a concept.

A concept is a generalization involving a class of ideas, a stable percept, or assorted data. It is usually organized as a result of a group of related sensations, percepts, and images. The current stress on teaching music through concepts is dependent upon the listener's ability to discern specific musical qualities and their interrelatedness. Since musical activity requires active sensory involvement, programs of music education as aesthetic education stress perceptual development.

The aesthetic experience involves affect. Two basic types of affective response occur during the aesthetic experience: physiological change and feelingful reaction. Considerable experimentation in the former indicates that music is capable of bringing about changes in blood pressure, respiration, pupil dilation, and psychogalvanic response. In the latter the response may vary from simple feeling to the most complex emotional sets. Part of the joy of music is being able to respond to the expressive content embodied in the very nature of music. It is the aim of music education as aesthetic education to develop this capacity for affective responsiveness in order to actualize man's deepest humanistic potential.

The aesthetic experience involves cognition. Since man learns from experience, and since music is a part of his experience, he has naturally developed (consciously or unconsciously) some degree of comprehension in musical matters. For the aesthetic experience to take place the respondent cannot simply bathe in the "emotional waters." The respondent is acutely conscious while affectively engaged. This intellectual awareness is usually manifested in one or more of the typical cognitive processes: analysis, synthesis, abstraction, generalization, evaluation. It is important for educators to note the significance of the intellectual component of the aesthetic experience since it provides structural linkage with the formal instructional program.

The aesthetic experience involves the cultural matrix. Music does not exist in a cultural vacuum; it has evolved out of a particular history and geography featuring discrete aesthetic value systems. The process by which we acquire our aesthetic values (acculturation) is the same process through which we acquire our social values. Music educators should be alert to the wide variety of musical styles contiguous with contemporary American culture. Since American youth are exploring the musics of China, Japan, India, and Africa on their own, our professional involvement with this music requires considerable extension. Recognizing that any musical aesthetic value system is learned rather than absolute should help us appreciate the importance of exercising judicious restraint when evaluating contemporary music.

The five characteristics of the aesthetic experience have been identified sequentially but occur simultaneously. During the aesthetic experience the respondent feels, thinks, and concentrates. An evaluation is made in light of past experience that is culturally oriented; perceptual acuity is based upon formal and informal learning; affective responsiveness may range from relative indifference to intense anger or rapture. Although the aesthetic experience is a complicated psychological process it is a natural function of human behavior at every stage of life. For music education to be aesthetic education, the curriculum should be organized so that musical study is aesthetically oriented and proceeds systematically in accordance with the developmental level of the student. . . .

Cultivating Aesthetic Sensitivity

Ideas and descriptive statements about aesthetic education are diverse. This plurality is fundamentally healthy since it reflects both the individuality of music educators and the multiplicity of aesthetic theories that account for the art of music. Yet it is necessary for the profession to be precise with respect to aesthetic education so that musicians and educators can communicate with one another. Most simply stated, aesthetic education stresses the cultivation of aesthetic sensitivity. Even greater specificity is possible if concern is extended to both school and society. *Aesthetic education is the process that enables man to develop his capacity for expression in the arts.*

The key concept is *expression* since it accounts for the three modes of behavior that are foundational to music. The first is creation—the process by which music is composed. It is the classical form of creativity, focused on bringing something new into existence. The second is performance—the process of re-creation that transforms the composer's ideas, symbolically recorded in some form of notation, into an aural experience. And the last is the response. As in the case of the aesthetic experience, these three modes of musical behavior overlap. Creation frequently involves performance and response; performance certainly involves response and creative behavior; and response involves the creation of a musical synthesis in the mind of the listener and the performer.

Traditional programs of music education have stressed the first two types of behavior. It is important to emphasize that music education as aesthetic education would continue to develop opportunities for creation and performance even beyond the levels that already have been achieved in the schools. The third mode—response—is the one that has suffered. The musically talented have received almost all of the school's attention. Eighty to ninety percent of the American population have received inept general music instruction, and have therefore invested their resources into commercial entertainment and spectator sports. One must acknowledge the fact that the public voluntarily provides financial support for entertainment and sports while symphony orchestras, ballet companies, and theater groups still seek means of survival in the manner of the old European patronage system. To be fair with the community, one might ask why financial support *should* be provided by those who can vividly remember an uninteresting music teacher telling them what they should like and what is good for them.

Unless we begin to develop positive attitudes toward music by the entire community, support for music in the schools is in danger of disintegrating. The point is that aesthetic education does not force a choice between performance and course in music; it seeks to support performance by expanding the development of musically sensitive audiences. Since most of us have been educated as performing musicians, and since we must seek support for our programs from those who are not schooled in this art, imaginative ways of communicating the significance of music must be found. As our understanding of aesthetic education deepens, greater insight into this problem will emerge. . . .

Music Education as Aesthetic Education

Aesthetic education is an approach to education in the arts that emphasizes the development of the aesthetic potential. It suggests a view of the arts that derives meaning from the organic relationship of art and experience. There is no need for a single theory of aesthetics, education, or personality since the individual is encouraged to develop his own critical orientation within the parameters of his education and his society.

Programs of music education become aesthetic education programs when they focus upon the artistic content of music. Such programs are demanding of students and teachers since they require the cultivation of a functional aesthetic literacy m those skills, knowledges, and attitudes that enable the individual to express artistic energies in a productive way. For the nonmusician this means becoming a concertgoer (respondent) who is sensitive and intelligent in musical matters. The same type of aesthetic literacy applies in the fields of theater, dance, and the visual arts.

Programs of music education conceived as aesthetic education stress the sensitive, intelligent, and creative development of musicality through the fundamental avenues of expression: creativity, performance, and response. This means developing a program for all of the students. The musically talented should have opportunities for composition, performance, and theoretical study, and the potential concertgoer should have experiences that emphasize the development of response potential.

The aesthetic approach to music education provides sophisticated opportunities to satisfy the psychobiological need for artistic expression found in all men. It is a study that challenges the intellect, stimulates the emotions, and develops the very basis of what is unique in each man: his creativity.

Gerard L. Knieter

Charles H. Ball
Thoughts on Music as Aesthetic Education (1971)

Charles H. Ball was associate professor of music at George Peabody College for Teachers, Nashville, Tennessee.

Central Ideas of Aesthetic Education

The key idea is that the experience of an art work is the most important element in aesthetic education. Since the perception of aesthetic values is the ultimate goal, the experiencing of aesthetic objects must be the starting point. The purpose of discussion and analysis must always be to increase perception—to improve the quality of the experience. The reverse can easily take place. Factual knowledge that does not contribute to appreciation is wasted.

The second idea is that the elements of music are less important than their uses. A sequence, or a fugal stretto, or a retrograde statement of a set is not as important as the effect that sequence, or fugal stretto, or retrograde statement makes on the listener. Sensitivity to this kind of aesthetic value is a sensitivity to the real artistic quality of a work, and can be built through experiencing and comparing many works. This does not mean, of course, the superficial and frequently invalid comparisons between different arts often found in many humanities, or multiple arts, or even music classes. I am speaking of the comparison of the effective with the less effective, of the natural and logical with the forced and rhetorical. From such comparisons will come the power to make discriminations between the valid and the banal. This is important. It helps avoid wasting precious and limited life-time. It protects one's most valuable possession—the quality of his experience.

This conception of aesthetic education is perhaps best illustrated by listing examples of what I consider to be unaesthetic education.

The first example is the constant and uncritical use of inferior works. This does not imply that only the great masterpieces should be used. Obviously, if techniques of comparison are to be used, some material of lesser quality is necessary. But there is much use of inferior material out of ignorance on the part of the teacher or out of lack of respect and true appreciation for better art.

A second example is the authoritarian demand that the students' taste arbitrarily conform to that of the teacher. This syndrome is usually marked by the use of such words as "master," "genius," "inspiration," and other terms that sicken the stomach and alienate the student.

Third would be the study of art works apart from the experience of them. Talking about music without experiencing it is mere verbiage. The performance program in the schools still offers the greatest potential for aesthetic education in music if handled in the right way.

A further example is a common misconception that arises from unclear goals. For example, we have heard much about the importance of teaching rock in the classroom. To me, this is a misconception of what we should be trying to do. We should not be teaching rock, nor should we be teaching Bach; we should be teaching a sensitivity to the aesthetic qualities of music. If this is our clear goal there is little doubt that both Bach and rock will be used in the classroom, as well as much of what lies between the two. But it will not be done for the sake of pushing one music over another. We will be trying to teach principles and leave the judgments to the students enlightened by such instruction.

If we really value music for what it is, and if we unashamedly teach it as aesthetic education, we have the greatest opportunity to contribute to society that any profession has ever had. We must make our determination and wisdom equal to the opportunity.

Bennett Reimer
A Philosophy of Music Education (*1989*)

Bennett Reimer is professor of music emeritus at Northwestern University.

Preface

In the preface to the first edition of this book (1970) I commented that

> It is very difficult at present to come to an understanding of how music education can become "aesthetic education," because so little has been written directly on this subject. The philosophy offered in this book is an attempt to supply the background of understanding out of which effective action can be generated.

During the next decade or so the music education profession moved massively in the direction of what I and others had defined as aesthetic education. The underlying premises of this philosophical position became so deeply internalized and its characteristic words and phrases became so widely used in our common professional language that it almost seemed to have "always been that way." While many of the concepts of aesthetic education remain imperfectly understood and many of its implications for action remain imperfectly applied, the general view it proposes has become the bedrock upon which our self-concept as a profession rests.

Problems with the term aesthetic education

Although this philosophy has become pervasive in music education in both theory and practice, the term *aesthetic education* and some of the language associated with this concept have caused several problems. While many people are quite comfortable with the terminology, others find it confusing or even threatening. This occurs largely because the word *aesthetic* is borrowed from the field of professional philosophy, and although it is used occasionally in ordinary language it remains for the most part a technical term unfamiliar to those not trained in philosophy. As a result, the impression sometimes given was that aesthetic education is somehow different from music education or a variant of music education or a scholarly, pedantic approach to music education that involves teaching the concepts of that branch of philosophy called aesthetics.

Adding to the confusion was the rise in interest during the 1970s in attempts to forge cooperative arts programs. These were called by a variety of names, one of which was aesthetic education. So it was assumed by some that whenever the term was used, it involved, in some mysterious way, the teaching of all the arts. Since the concept of arts education is itself immensely complicated, the confusion surrounding the term *aesthetic education* was compounded.

Still another difficulty associated with the term is that it suggests to some people a focus on art for art's sake or music for music's sake, which seems to mean that art or music are then unrelated to the everyday lives that we as human beings actually live. Further, such an esoteric or elitist view could certainly not be relevant for the "common people," whose involvements with art are earthy and freewheeling. The term *aesthetic education*, suggesting Mozart string quartets and Couperin harpsichord pieces and other ornaments for the musically genteel, could not possibly pertain to the more rough and tumble world of music as it really exists for the majority in our culture.

All these misconceptions (for that is what they are) have to some degree impeded the growth of a shared philosophical view that could give our profession a more solid base on which to build. They have been "glitches in the system." But the underlying, essential thesis of aesthetic education, below any confusion the term might cause, is not any longer controversial for the vast majority of music educators. That thesis, simply put, is that while music has many important nonmusical or nonartistic functions, its musical or artistic nature is its unique and precious gift to all humans. Music education exists first and foremost to develop every person's natural responsiveness to the power of the art of music. If that goal is primary, others can be included whenever help-ful. But when music itself, with its universal appeal to the human mind and heart, is bypassed or weakened in favor of nonmusical emphases that sub-merge it, we have betrayed the art we exist to share. It is that simple.

It is also that complex. What, precisely, is musical or artistic about music? What is not? How can we keep the two in fruitful balance? What does musical teaching do that nonmusical teaching does not? Is all music valid as music or only some music? What is good music? Why does music as an art matter so much to us, so that we claim it should be taught to all children? . . .

Chapter 2: Alternative Views about Art on Which a Philosophy Can Be Based
The uses of aesthetics

In the long, complex history of aesthetics thousands of views have been expressed about art. To one who examines these views with any degree of objectivity, it becomes evident that here, if no place else, is a perfect exam-ple of truth being relative. So strong is this impression, so overwhelming its effect, that one is tempted to throw up one's hands in despair, turn one's back on the entire field of aesthetics, and proclaim that in music education one might as well do whatever strikes one's fancy, since there probably exists plenty of justification for whatever this happens to be.

To yield to this temptation, however, is to give oneself up to ineffectual-ity. Of course there is no immutable truth in aesthetics. Of course there is no single or simple answer to every question. Of course there is no one guideline which will insure satisfactory results of action. The question is, can one accept this condition and at the same time develop a point of view which helps one's efforts to be as consistent, as effective, as useful for one's purposes as intelligence and modesty allow?

There is really no alternative but to answer "yes." Everything we do in this world is done in the face of imperfect and partial knowledge. But it is possible—in fact, it is necessary—to adopt some working premises and to use them (not be used *by* them) as guidelines to action, knowing full well that they may be altered or even dropped as conditions change. To refuse to work from a critically accepted position about the nature of one's subject is to avoid one of the central imperatives of human life, which is to carve out, from all existing possibilities, the most reasonable possibilities for one's purposes. Not to do so dooms one to intellectual and operational paralysis. To do so blindly and irrevocably ensures the same fate. Searching out a convincing, useful, coherent point of view, adopting it as a base of opera-tions, examining it and sharpening it, tightening it while using it, opening it to new ideas and altering it as seems necessary, can help one to act with purpose, with impact, with some measure of meaningfulness.

The problem, of course, is to determine the best possible point of view. Several principles can help us do so. First, the field of aesthetics must be approached in a highly selective way. It would be beside the point (and quite impossible) to investigate indiscriminately the writings of every aesthetician in history, or every aesthetician of this century, or every aesthetician alive today, looking for leads to a philosophy of music education. Instead, the search must start with an acquaintance with the field of music education: its problems, its needs, its history, its present status. Aesthetics must be used by music educators to serve their own purposes. Otherwise they are likely to lose themselves in the history and problems of aesthetics, never to emerge with a workable philosophy. A philosophy should articulate a consistent and helpful statement about the nature and value of music and music education. Only those portions of aesthetics useful for this purpose need be used. Aesthetics must never be the master of music education—it must be its servant.

Second, the point of view adopted should be sufficiently broad to take into account all major aspects of music and music education but sufficiently focused to provide tangible guidelines for thought and action. No single aesthetician has supplied the breadth of conception needed for our purpose, although, as will be seen, some have been of unusual help. It will be necessary to identify an aesthetic position which includes major thinkers and which also has an identifiable structure of ideas which can be handled without being overwhelming in complexity.

Third, the point of view should be particularly pertinent to the art of music but at the same time capable of yielding equally valid insights into the nature of all the arts. Some aesthetic theories are heavily slanted toward the nonmusical arts, and while they offer insights into music, they do so only secondarily. An example would be the psychoanalytic theory of Carl G. Jung, which is immensely fruitful with ideas about literature, poetry, and the visual arts, but which has little to say about music.[1] Obviously this situation should be reversed for our purposes, although a view confined to a single art, even music, would be unacceptable also.

Fourth, the view being sought must contain rich implications for education. It would be of little use to adopt a theory which offered few leads to teaching and learning music and the other arts, no matter how strong the theory might be in other matters. Existentialist aesthetics, for example, has provided powerful insights into the nature of art and its role in human life.[2] But helpful as these insights are, they do not seem to lend themselves directly or abundantly to problems of mass education. It would be difficult, therefore, to depend on this particular view for a philosophy of music education.

Finally, any aesthetic position to be used as a basis for a philosophy must be relevant to the society in which we live and to the general conditions under which American education operates. Important as Marxism-Leninism has been in history, for example, it is quite peripheral to our concerns. The same can be said about Freudian aesthetics and Oriental aesthetics and medieval aesthetics. All of these, and others, can be of use for particular purposes, but they cannot be the foundation on which our philosophy is to be built.

Of all existing aesthetic viewpoints,[3] one in particular fulfills the principles just outlined and does so with unusual power. This view is presented by Leonard B. Meyer as one of three related aesthetic theories: referentialism, absolute formalism, and absolute expressionism. An explanation of each of these theories will set the stage for the choice to be made as to which will best serve as the basis for a philosophy, and for our systematic examination of the implications of using this theory as a base of operations for music education.

Chapter 10: Toward the Transformation of Music Education

Forging a new vision

It is feasible for music education to strengthen itself, both for the short and long terms, by doing something far more significant than continuing to improve what it is now, essential as that remains. But there are several limitations on what it is possible for music education to become and what it desirable for music education to become. It would be disastrous in every way for us to change simply for the sake of change if doing so were to threaten to diminish our historic mission and our professional integrity. These limitations, which are also our most hallowed obligations, are that we continue to serve the two causes embodied in our name: music and education.

First, we are now and must always continue to be determined in our nature by the nature of the art of music—music as it has existed throughout history, music as it exists now, and music as it might change and develop in the future. Always our mission must remain to understand the art of music as deeply as we are capable and to adapt our practices to best reflect music's artistic essence. It is the power of music that provides our essential energy. We must never betray the art we exist to nurture.

Second, we are now and must always continue to be bounded by the nature of education. We must not forget that teaching and learning are our primary functions, so that we must conform to the best that is known about how to teach effectively and how to provide the most fruitful possible environment for learning to occur. In every instance when we have weakened our bond to education we have weakened our strength as a profession, as, for example, when the entertainment function has superseded the teaching-learning function or when our scholarship has become detached from educational issues. The art of music provides our reason for existence; the process of education determines how we function. Anything we become must preserve those two verities.

What, then, is the alternative between not changing significantly on the one hand or abandoning our inner nature on the other? Only one answer to that question seems possible. That is, that we become an integral part of a field that depends on our essential, authentic character yet is larger than, more important than, more influential than we can ever be by ourselves.

That field is arts education. By allying ourselves with our sister arts, in common cause to establish the arts as a basic subject in the school curriculum, we will be able to achieve a movement upward toward the core of education achievable by no other means within the existing culture.

Why is this so? Why would we be better off as part of an inclusive field of arts education than we can ever be by continuing to go our own way? Several compelling reasons can be offered.

First, we can benefit philosophically. Any claim we can make for the value of music in education can be made equally validly by every other art. Every claim we make for the uniqueness of music as an art can be made as well for the uniqueness of each art. And if it is essential for music to be offered to all students in public education it is just as essential for every other art to be offered. Of course each art has distinctive characteristics, but who would argue that any one of them is more or less suitable for schools than any other? And who would argue that young people should not have equal access to every art, to find pleasure from all and perhaps a special affinity for one or a few? There is simply no philosophical leg to stand on to justify any one art as being essentially more valuable than any other or essentially more appropriate for education than any other. And if we were to be inclusive in our valuing of the arts we would be able to build a philosophical foundation for them that is far more solid than can be built for any one of them alone. Such a philosophy, extending the arguments in this book to cover all the arts, would be an unassailable foundation for claiming a rightful place for the arts in schools, including but exceeding music.

Second, we can benefit politically. Alone, fighting our solitary battles as if we had no allies, we are perceived by people as what we truly are a special interest group among hundreds of other special interest groups, each scrambling to establish a better toe-hold for itself. Caring only for ourselves, as if the broader artistic welfare of young people were less important than our own security, we come across as self-serving, of limited breadth, preoccupied with our special nature to the exclusion of those as special as we. But the arts as a unified field rise above the special interest category. Despite their position below the central core, they are nevertheless too important as a field to be neglected when perceived as a whole. If they were presented as a field of study, with the combined strength of all the separate arts fields working together for the good of their larger cause, their impact would be considerable. The total political clout of the arts as a coalition would be dramatically greater than the sum of its separate parts.

Third, we can benefit psychologically. Our history has been one of almost total isolation from our natural family, and we have suffered in our personality from the selfishness this isolation has caused. We tend, because of our separateness, to be inward looking, defensive, suspicious of whatever might impinge on our own needs. This does not make us generous, even to our students, let alone our professional family. If we were openly and willingly devoted to a cause larger and more important than our narrow self-interest, we would participate in the expansiveness it would allow us to feel. Our image of ourselves, as individuals and as a field, would both deepen and broaden when we understood ourselves to be linked to forces including us but transcending us.

Fourth, we can benefit practically. We will never win for ourselves the amount of time we want to have in the schools because our demands are perceived as being unreasonable and selfish. For example, we have as our standard that around 20–25 minutes a day of music instruction should be offered in each elementary and junior high grade. Why can this standard not apply as well to visual art education? Fine. So now we have 50 minutes a day accounted for. Well, doesn't dance have an equal claim? It would be very difficult not to agree that it does. Good. So now we've used up 75 minutes a day. Now let's add equal time for theater, and for poetry and literature, and for film, all of which have just as good grounds as we for claiming their share of the pie. So far we have scheduled two and a half hours a day, and a few other arts constituencies have yet to get their fingers into the pie.

That way lies madness. And it points up, in bold relief, the narcissism of music education, which blithely claims its share in complete obliviousness to the fact that others have an equal right to the same share. No wonder that we have not gotten anything like what we want. No wonder that, by ourselves, we never will. We must learn the hard lesson that our needs must be met in the context of our family's needs. That reality will not only force use to be more generous to our family, but will, ironically, yield us more minutes per week than we have ever managed or will ever manage to cajole on our own. We have nothing practical to lose by cooperation with the arts and a great deal to gain.

Finally, we can benefit professionally. Most important, our contribution to the quality of young people's lives can be magnified immensely when our goal becomes to introduce all the students to the richness of all the arts. That is a professional stance truly worthy of us. Further, we can learn so much, about the arts and about education, from our colleagues in the other art education fields. Believe it or not those people are often very smart.

Some of them are superlative teachers. Some of them are profound thinkers. Some of them do excellent research, and some are incredibly astute politically, and some have deep insights into children's creative abilities, and some are enormously effective administrators, and a few of them, scattered here and there, are awfully nice human beings. We should know some of these people. And they should know us because we have all those things to offer also. It is a shame that we hardly know our family. It is about time that we all make each other's acquaintance and begin to work together because we all have so much to gain by aiming for the greater good of our larger profession.

Notes

1. An excellent introduction to the monumental work of Jung is Carl G. Jung, ed., *Man and His Symbols* (Garden City, NY: Doubleday, 1964).
2. Also see Arturo B. Fallico, *Art and Existentialism* (Englewood Cliffs, NJ: Prentice Hall, 1962).
3. All the major "isms" in aesthetics are reviewed in Monroe C. Beardsley, *Aesthetics* (University, AL: University of Alabama Press, 1977).

What Knowledge Is of Most Worth in the Arts?: The Arts, Education, and Aesthetic Knowing (1992)

The Claims of Aesthetic Education

. . . Some three decades ago a shift in thinking about education in the arts began to take place in both music and visual arts education. An extensive literature detailing the changes in both theory and practice of music and visual art education during the 1960s and afterward testifies to the magnitude of what occurred.[1] Under the influence of the curriculum reform movement, several educational thinkers began to argue that the qualities of experience mediated by the arts, the meanings they make available through their various modes of representation, and the ways those qualities and meanings are generated and shared, are peculiar to the arts. Thus the aesthetic dimension of human experience is seen as a distinctive cognitive domain requiring to be understood and valued on its own terms and taught in ways relevant to those terms. In addition, creating art, although valuable and necessary as one aspect of experiencing and knowing aesthetically, is not sufficient to gain the breadth and depth and variety of meanings available from the arts. To be literate in the aesthetic domain requires a broad-ranging array of responses to the arts. Such responses depend on refined capacities and dispositions (a) to perceive, discriminate, feel, and evaluate works of art; (b) to understand them as objects and events with distinctive cognitive characteristics; (c) to be aware of the historical, social, cultural, political, and religious contexts in which they reside; and (d) to be cognizant of the many issues and controversies surrounding them. Education in the arts, if it is to influence the development of such learnings, would have to be essentially different from an instrumentality for achieving a variety of aesthetically ancillary values or from professional training to be an artist. Both may be included and provided for, but the broader goal or aim of education in the arts would have to be the development of aesthetic literacy in a sense neither of the previous rationales was able to define. And the question of what is most worth knowing about the arts would have to be addressed by including for consideration a far more comprehensive selection of subject matters than had previously been identified.

The striking movement in the school arts fields over the past three decades toward an image of arts education as focused on the aesthetic nature of the arts, and as responsible for cultivating aesthetic sensitivity/ awareness/literacy as its primary mission, soon began to be known by the term *aesthetic education* (The *Journal of Aesthetic Education* began publishing in 1966). For some this was a confusing phrase in that it seemed to signify an interest in teaching conceptual material from or about the branch of philosophy called aesthetics, which lies outside the training of most arts teachers. But as curricula claiming to be instances of aesthetic education appeared and more books and articles on it were published, the term became ubiquitous and a general sense of its nature became more pervasive. This is not to say that the meaning of the term *aesthetic education* is entirely clear to its theoreticians or to arts teachers in the schools.[2] It is also not to say that its applications in school arts programs have been consistent or unanimous. Many teachers continue to follow models of arts education based on a variety of assumptions including that its purpose is to assist in the promotion of extra-aesthetic values or to train incipient artists (neither of which purposes is necessarily ruled out by many conceptions of aesthetic education). And, of course, some theoreticians simply did not and do not find this point of view attractive.

Several characteristics associated with the term *aesthetic education* became extremely influential in the school arts education fields over the past thirty or so years. Recent important influences have reinforced the belief that education in the arts requires tuition in a broad range of disciplines relevant to the cultivation of the characteristic mode of cognition the arts represent.[3]

The Arts as Cognitive

What knowledge, then, is of most worth in the arts according to the general point of view often called aesthetic education? Another important intellectual movement in recent years bears on how this question might be answered. This is the growing recognition that traditional conceptions of cognition, equating it with verbal and symbolic conceptualization, are inadequate to describe or explain the varieties of modes in which human knowing occurs and by which human knowing may be represented. We can trace to Plato the history of the idea that cognition, to be considered authentic, must be as abstract—that is, free from the vagaries and errors of the senses and the intuitions—as it is possible for rationality to make it. The most dependable, most genuine knowledge therefore is achieved through a movement away from the concrete toward the abstract. "Basic" subjects are those fulfilling the assumption that cognition is essentially a function of abstract thinking achieved through higher and higher levels of verbal and symbolic conceptualization.

In education, the equation of cognition with rational conceptualization is most dramatically apparent in the influential *Taxonomy of Educational Objectives*,[4] in which the "cognitive domain" consists of progressively higher levels of conceptual functioning, ranging from knowledge (of specifics; of ways and means of dealing with specifics; of the universals and abstractions in a field), to intellectual abilities and skills (comprehension; application; analysis), to synthesis, and finally to evaluation. The "affective domain" (construed in the *Taxonomy* to include primarily attitudes and values) and the "psychomotor domain" are not, ipso facto, cognitive. The assumption, then, that cognition exists only when the mind is processing conceptual materials in the ways the "cognitive domain" handbook outlines them is so widespread that few recognize that this is but one way to conceive of cognition. It has, in short, become a dominant myth of our times.

That myth has begun to unravel. Ironically, a major tear in its fabric occurred with the dramatic rise during the 1950s of skepticism about the epistemological foundation of the basic sciences. . . . The notion of aesthetic cognition as one among several bona fide cognitive modes holds great promise, and one is led to ask once more the persistent, contentious, puzzling question, "What is aesthetic cognition?". . . I will concentrate on one dimension of aesthetic cognition, often called "knowing of" or "knowing within." A second dimension, frequently termed "knowing how" (about which I will remark only briefly), is intimately related to "knowing of." The two together, I shall argue, constitute the nature of cognition in the aesthetic domain. Supplementary to these ways of knowing are two further dimensions of cognition relevant to improving the quality of knowing of and knowing how—"knowing about" or "knowing that," and what I will term "knowing why." . . .

General and Special Curricula in the Arts

Given the preceding discussions (about knowing within, knowing how, knowing about, and knowing why), a curriculum in the arts would be the playing out of their implications in the myriad details to be attended to in building a coherent program of instruction. In the context of this chapter only one issue relating to curriculum development can be addressed—the issue of general learnings essential for all students and special learnings for particular students who choose them.

By general education in the arts I mean programs of instruction required of all students in schools, or electives providing the same learnings. By special education in the arts I mean arts electives that concentrate on a particular aspect or related set of aspects of the general arts curriculum and that are conceived to be appropriate only for those students interested in developing particular competencies or understandings.

General education in the arts should be as comprehensive and as extensive as possible. The four basic dimensions of cognition should all be included and should stress the development of each student's capacities to know of and know how. The contexts for such learnings can be single art classes as have traditionally been available or (as I would prefer) comprehensive arts classes in which interdisciplinary learning episodes would be used as (occasional) unifiers for the learnings about particular arts. These classes should concentrate on the unique ways each art functions cognitively, and also call attention at strategic points to the general characteristics of cognition all the arts share.[5]

Whatever the context, learnings related to knowing of or within will provide the unifying core. The experience of many works (from one art if a single art is being taught or from several arts if a comprehensive context exists), representing various historical periods, regions of the world, styles, genres, types, including folk, popular, "classical," ethnic, and so forth, will be the central activity, supported by the knowings about or that and knowings why essential to make aesthetic sense of them. In my view, emphasis should be placed on works of high quality (works demonstrating high levels of imagination, craftsmanship, sensitivity, authenticity) within each type or genre. Comparisons of the relative value of differing types of art should be avoided. Works of lesser quality can be used to heighten the sense that higher and lower levels of aesthetic value exist in particular examples of art.

Knowing how—creating art—serves both as an end and as a means in general education. As an end it engages all students in the mode of cognition called upon to be an artist—a way of thinking and knowing unavailable except by being (or acting as) an artist. All students need to share this cognition for the sake of knowing what it uniquely allows one to know.

In addition, attempts to create art by using qualities one is experiencing in already created works (for example, attempting to paint distorted figures as related to distorted figures one is perceiving in a painting) can illuminate powerfully the meaningful form(s) created by an artist who chose to use distortion as one element. So it is important that creating art be included in general education both as artistically meaningful in and of itself and as adding an educative dimension to aesthetic meaning.

The balances among experiencing and creating works, and of how much and what levels of conceptual learnings about and learnings why will be included, will largely be determined by developmental factors such as those discussed in other chapters in this book. The mix for second graders will be different from the mix for eleventh graders, especially because as students get older their abilities to know of, about, and why will far outstrip in depth and breadth their ability to know how (even if they have chosen to elect special study in creating art). But given that age-related and individual capacity-related factors will be an important influence on the balances among the modes of cognition, the principle for general education in the arts remains to aim for as inclusive a program of studies as is possible.

The special learnings segment of the arts curriculum is, on the other hand, essentially selective and intensive. From the several dimensions of aesthetic and artistic cognition, particular ones are chosen as foci for study. The selective nature of such study allows it to be intensive, with more thorough study of one or a few aspects of art than is possible in the general education segment. What is lost in breadth is gained in depth, but the necessary restrictions on how much and what can be studied in depth makes such study appropriate as electives for particularly interested individuals or groups.

The most popular selection from among the various knowings in art has been and is likely to continue to be knowing how. In special programs devoted to creating art, learnings how will appropriately dominate instruction. Experiences of already created works serve here primarily as a means for heightening growth in the understanding of creating, rather than as an end as they do in the general program. Similarly, knowings about and knowings why are selectively focused toward those relating to and helpful for developing creative abilities. A much more restricted range of styles or types of art will be studied than those encountered in the general program—a chorus, after all, deals with choral music, a ceramics class with shaped clay, a play production with acting and staging—and so on, and each of these with only those instances capable of being handled within the constraints of the students' creative skills and the time available.

All these factors make artistic creation appropriately an elective when conceived as the primary mode of interaction with and study of art. (Most students do not choose to devote the time and energy necessary to achieve even modest levels of success in creating art.) Approaches to general education in an art that consist entirely of creating are misconceived and unfortunate. They narrow unconscionably the range of knowings that general education in the arts should provide and give the impression that arts education consists of a limited set of learnings related to one particular mode of engagement and that the study of art is a special endeavor for only those students especially interested or talented.

Other appropriate special art program electives might emphasize aspects other than creating—a high school course devoted entirely to the plays of Samuel Beckett, or to how to be a music critic, or to the arts of Africa, or to issues of avant-garde art, or to the role of technology in the arts. Such foci could be included as specific *parts* of general education, as, for example, units in a required or elective course on "All About the Arts." What separates special from general education is the difference in *degree* of extensivity, general education aiming toward one end of the whole–part continuum, special education toward the other.

Education in the arts, I suggest, required of and available to all students in schools as part of general education, and available to all those who choose to study particular aspects of art, exists to serve the needs of all to share the cognitions available only from art. Some few students will go on to become professional artists or professionals in other aspects of the arts, and such students need a broad general education in the arts as the foundation for their special study and special vocation. The rest, for whom the arts can provide a singular dimension of cognition in their lives, deserve to be helped to learn what is most worth knowing in the arts—the ways to share the vividness, clarity, significance, and depth of experience the arts provide.

Notes

1. For treatments of the changes that took place in music education, see Michael L. Mark, *Contemporary Music Education* (New York: Schirmer, 1986). For a concise summary of changes in visual art education, see two articles in the *Journal of Aesthetic Education* 21/1 (Summer 1987): Ralph A. Smith, "The Changing Image of Art Education: Theoretical Antecedents of Discipline-based Art Education," 3–34, and Arthur D. Efland, "Curriculum Antecedents of Discipline-based Art Education," 57–94. Both give useful bibliographies.

2. For a discussion of various assumptions about aesthetic education, see Harry S. Broudy, "Some Reactions to a Concept of Aesthetic Education," in *Arts and Aesthetics: An Agenda for the Future*, ed. Stanley S. Madeja (St. Louis: CEMREL, 1977), and Bennett Reimer, "Essential and Nonessential Characteristics of Aesthetic Education," *Journal of Aesthetic Education* 25/3 (1991): 193–214.

3. "Discipline-based art education" is a concept supported by the Getty Center for Education in the Arts, an operating entity of the J. Paul Getty Trust. It is an important attempt to expand traditional curricula in the direction of greater comprehensiveness of learnings. For an overview, see Ralph A. Smith, ed., *Discipline-based Art Education: Origins, Meaning, and Development* (Urbana: University of Illinois Press, 1989).

4. Benjamin S. Bloom et al., ed. *Taxonomy of Educational Objectives, Handbook I: Cognitive Domain* (New York: David Mackay, 1956); David R. Krathwohl, Benjamin S. Bloom, and

Bertram B. Masia, eds., *Taxonomy of Educational Objectives, Handbook II: Affective Domain* (New York: David Mackay, 1964); Anita J. Harrow, *A Taxonomy of the Psychomotor Domain* (New York: David Mackay, 1972).

5. D. C. Phillips, "On What Scientists Know, and How They Know It," in *Learning and Teaching the Ways of Knowing* (*Eighty-fourth Yearbook of the National Society for the Study of Education*, I), ed. Elliot W. Eisner, (Chicago: University of Chicago Press, 1985), 38–39.

Why Do Humans Value Music?:
The Housewright Symposium on the Future of Music Education (2000)

The question of why humans value music has eluded all efforts to answer it conclusively despite many attempts throughout history. However, useful explanations have accumulated over time, serving well to provide enough agreement, or persuasiveness, to allow communities of people, such as music educators, to feel that they share a common belief system upon which they can build cooperative actions.

One significant orientation to the values of music has been toward its role in enhancing the depth, quality, scope, and intensity of inner human experience in ways particular to how music operates; ways that distinguish music from other human endeavors. This orientation has preoccupied philosophers of music whose interests tend to be directed toward understanding the "nature" of music—its particularity as a human creation and the values it serves as such. Taking a philosophical stance, two characteristics of music may be suggested as bases for its values in human life.

1. Music makes human experience "special." It aims to achieve a level of experience different from the commonplace. Music makes ordinary experience extraordinary, or insignificant experience significant. Music creates an alternative to the reality of the everyday; an alternative to the ordinary way of being.

2. Music, unlike all the other arts, depends on the use of sounds, organized in ways various cultures sanction, to create the sense of specialness it adds to human experience. Music is unique in its use of ordered sounds as the basic material by which it accomplishes its "transformation" (passing over from one form to another) of experience.

Five dimensions of musical value may be identified as related to its distinctive nature.

1. Music is end and means

1. All the various ways to be engaged in musical experiences, such as composing, performing, improvising and listening, enable both the creation of musical meanings and the sharing of musical meanings with others. The

value of doing so is in making available an endless source of significant experiences uniquely gained through music. To seek the meaningful satisfactions of musical creating and sharing is to pursue musical value as an end. This end of musically meaningful experience has been sought by humans throughout history.

2. Many positive consequences grow out of the pursuit of musical meaning as an end. To be human is to make meaning and seek meaning. A life full of meaning, including musical meaning, is a life fulfilled in one of its primary needs. The consequence of such fulfillment is a sense of wholeness, wellness, and satisfaction. Effects on individuals' physical, emotional, psychological, and spiritual health are profound. These effects radiate outward to the health of families, communities, nations, and cultures, all of which depend, ultimately, on the well-being of their members.

3. Many values not dependent on the uniqueness of musical experiencing are believed to be gained as a result of involvements with music. When the pursuit of these values requires that musical experiences and leanings be diluted in order to achieve them, music is being used as a means. In most cases the achievement of these values does not require any change from the pursuit of musical values as an end. Such values may then be considered complementary to musical ones, and can be regarded as welcome, positive contributions of programs devoted to musical learning. Music educators may choose to promote such values to gain additional support for music study.

2. Music encompasses mind, body, and feeling.

1. The long-standing idea that "thinking" is the supreme capacity of the human mind, and that thinking is separate and distinct from the body and the feelings, is giving way to the recognition that thinking, knowing, and understanding—what is generally called "intelligence"—takes place in a variety of forms and necessarily includes involvements of the body and feelings.

2. Human intelligence occurs in multiple forms beyond its traditional association with verbal and mathematical thinking. Musical ways of thinking demonstrate intelligence in the fullest sense of that word—the mind functioning in a reasoned way to create meaning. The capacity to think musically is inborn in human beings.

3. Intelligence requires the involvement of the body, and the body-centered imaginative power to form connections among experiences. Musically intelligent functioning is grounded in the body's capacity to undergo the dynamic qualities of sound and their interconnections as imagined by composers, performers, improvisers, and listeners. Sound is a particularly powerful medium for engaging the body in acts of creating meaning.

4. Human intelligence, in addition to taking many forms beyond the verbal and numerical, and in addition to being centered within the realities of

the human body, is saturated with feelings that vivify and color life. Musical meaning arises from the feelings music allows us to create and share. The unification of mind, body, and feeling in the creation of musical meaning adds an indispensable source of value to human life.

3. Music is universal, cultural, and individual.

1. At one level, musical meaning is universally sought by all humans and is cherished universally for the values it adds to life. Music can be conceived, at this level, as a generic possession of the human species.

2. At another level, music can be regarded as a phenomenon particular to the culture in which it exists, both reflecting and creating the values and ways of being in that culture.

3. At still another level the values of music can be understood as the possession of individuals. Only individuals create and respond to music, even if cooperatively. "Universals," or "cultures," are only abstractions from individual experience.

4. These three dimensions of musical value need not be conceived as contradictory. All humans are at the same time, like all other humans, like some other humans, and like no other humans. All three levels of the human condition must be acknowledged as contributing to the values of musical experience: an awareness of all three adds immeasurably to the depth and quality of musical valuing. That music fulfills values at all three levels helps account for its indispensable contribution to the quality of human life.

4. Music is product and process.

1. Successful musical products, whether compositions, performances of them, or improvisations, are precious for the benefits they offer to people as sources of significant meanings. Often a particularly excellent musical product or body of work is considered a cultural treasure, representing the highest achievement of which humans in that culture are capable. Much of music education is devoted to sharing with students the bounties of musical meaning embodied in successful musical products.

2. No product, musical or otherwise, can come into being without the processes that create it. Acts of creative musical imagination, involving mind, body, and feeling, and encompassing universal, cultural, and individual dimensions of experience, engage musical intelligence deeply and powerfully in generating meanings. The experience of musical creativity profoundly satisfies the human need to be generative.

3. Music as process and as product are interdependent: one cannot exist without the other and the values of each depend on the values of the other. An overemphasis of either, at the expense of the other, weakens musical

experience and diminishes its value. Effective education in music continually aims toward a balanced representation of both product and process.

5. Music is pleasurable and profound

1. At one level, music is an essential source of pleasurable experience, either by itself or as allied with a variety of other pursuits of enjoyment. The capacity of music to express the energy, zest, and elation of pleasure is endless, causing music to be treasured as a means for gaining the values of life experienced as joyful.

2. At another level, music serves the need for experience below the surface of the commonplace, in which deep meanings are uncovered—meanings often called sacred, or profound. Such experiences of soulfulness, of spiritual significance, are commonly believed to be among the most precious of which humans are capable. Music's alliance with this level of experience has been acknowledged throughout history as adding a profound realm of value to human life.

3. Music *creates* possibilities of feeling available only from music. It does not simply imitate or reproduce joyful or profound experiences available in other ways. No single kind or style of music has sole possession of this capacity; all musics can serve and have served the values of significant experience. The need for such experience exists for all humans, at every time of life from early childhood to old age.

Music education exists to make musical values more widely and deeply shared. While no single explanation can completely and ultimately define music's values, sufficient agreement to provide a basis for communal action is possible and desirable. At this time in history, a viable belief system for music educators may be achieved if an attitude emphasizing inclusiveness rather than exclusiveness is taken. In this paper an attempt has been made to explain that musical values can be regarded as both end and complementary means; as encompassing the mind, body, and feelings; as being universal, culturally specific, and individual; as deriving from musical products and processes; and as embracing experiences across the entire spectrum of human feeling as made available by the entire array of the world's musics. Each music educator has the responsibility to forge a persuasive professional position from this and other attempts to solve the age-old puzzle of why humans value music.

Mihaly Csikszentmihalyi and Ulrich Schiefele
Arts Education, Human Development, and the Quality of Experience (1992)

Mihaly Csikszentmihalyi is professor of psychology and of education, University of Chicago. Ulrich Schiefele is on the faculty of Social Sciences, University of the Bundeswehr, Munich, Germany.

Aesthetic Cognition and Human Development

Artistic activities, cognitions, and experiences appear to have significant functions in the course of phylogenetic and otogenetic development.[1] Past accounts of human evolution have clearly favored the acquisition of rational knowledge as represented by the sciences and mathematics. It is true that cognition has unequivocally proved its function as a tool for adaptation to the world around us. Rational cognition has made it possible for humankind to predict external events and thus master obstacles and make use of the environment for its own purposes.[2] Its power is very much based on the precision with which phenomena can be analytically defined and labeled, and on the assumption that things in the world can be assigned to single, mutually exclusive categories (i.e., Aristotle's principle of noncontradiction).

These features of rational thought, which contribute a great deal to its usefulness, are at the same time responsible for its constraints. When it comes to basic human affairs, such as feelings and social relationships, a rational system based on precise analytic assumptions ceases to be an adequate representation of reality. A straightforward quantitative approach would disguise these complex and ambiguous phenomena rather than clarify them. Furthermore, seemingly contradictory feelings like love and hate can be experienced almost at the same time. Thus, it seems questionable that the assumption of noncontradiction, which excludes the possibility that a thing can at the same time be its opposite, is a correct model for describing all aspects of reality. The obvious constraints of rational thought led Wittgenstein to demand that "what we cannot speak about we must pass over in silence."[3] He maintained that the rationality of science is not able to deal with those issues that are the most essential to everyday life—such as death, religion, ways of living, the meaning of work and life. It follows that the development of more and more specific rules for scientific reasoning results in the exclusion of ever larger amounts of thought and experience. Although reasoning has proved itself adaptive, there is justified doubt that increasing the powers of reason at the expense of other modes of knowing will ultimately lead to greater understanding.

Some theorists have explored the role of aesthetic cognition as a complementary alternative to rational cognition.[4] It is generally agreed that both science and art are symbolic systems that provide knowledge. However, their respective procedures and the nature of the resulting knowledge are quite different. Unlike science, art represents experienced reality that is ambiguous, contradictory, and partly unconscious. Artistic cognition is based on symbolic rules that are holistic, idiosyncratic, and implicit rather than explicit. The products of art do not represent unequivocal pictures of reality that can be tested empirically.

Were mankind to rely only on this type of knowledge, it would not be able to survive. The merits of aesthetic cognition, however, are as a corrective to an exclusively rational approach. Aesthetic cognition gains its evolutionary value by providing models or descriptions of internal and external realities which cannot be represented by purely rational means. As Getzels and Csikszentmihalyi have shown, artists most often deal with basic existential questions that cannot be answered by scientific reasoning.[5] In *A Portrait of the Artist as a Young Man*, James Joyce provides a nice example for this basic aspect of the artistic endeavor when at the end of the book Stephen Daedalus says: "Welcome, O life! I go to encounter for the millionth time the reality of experience and to forge in the smithy of my soul the uncreated conscience of my race."[6]

In dealing with as yet unexpressed existential human problems, the artist might be regarded as part of the avant garde that creates new concepts and new rules of thinking, and thus may lead rational thought to expand its borders and to reach higher levels. While rational cognition gains control over reality by drastically reducing it to its basic quantifiable aspects, art models phenomena in a more global and analogic way that also tolerates contradictions between constitutive elements.

The contribution of artistic models of reality to the evolution of human thought also appears on the level of individual development. This is especially true for those who actively engage in the creative production of art. Getzels and Csikszentmihalyi have provided numerous examples of painters and sculptors who use their work to express personal problems and basic life themes.[7] The process of visual expression clearly helps gain some control and understanding of barely conscious internal tensions, diffuse problems, or ties. "The key to creative achievement is the transformation of an intangible conflict into a tangible symbolic problem to which creative solution will be the response."[8]

A second function of arts-related activities at the level of individual development is helping the person to maintain the cognitive structure of the self. The sum of all activities a person is engaged in defines a great deal of the person's self. This is especially, and perhaps only, true for intentional and self-determined activities.[9] As the creation of art is by definition an intentional and self-determined activity, it should contribute to what a person defines as his or her being. This contrasts with other ways people strive to reassure themselves that their self is an autonomous and powerful agent, for example, through the possession of material objects, the control of physical energy, and the control of other people's psychic energy.

In this section we have shown that there are important differences between rational thought, as it is represented by the sciences and mathematics, and aesthetic knowledge produced by creating or responding to art. It was our intention to show that the two domains complement each other, by fostering cognizance of different dimensions of reality. Our analysis suggests that creating, responding to, or learning about art have more relevance for people's everyday life experience and their existential struggles than do the natural and technical sciences. If one wants to find a suitable way of living or to understand how another person feels, mathematical equations, physical laws, or sophisticated computer programs won't provide much help. It may be argued that psychological knowledge will bring helpful advice. While this is certainly true for some well-defined problems, psychological knowledge cannot solve many basic existential problems with which we have to struggle. In addition, it is interesting to note that many therapeutic techniques encourage the patient to engage in activities that resemble those of an artist: interpretation of dreams, illogical associative thinking, mental visualization, holistic thinking, painting, psychodrama, and focusing on inner mental and bodily states.[10]

. . . Finally, perhaps the major difference between rational knowledge and artistic knowledge is in terms of their outcomes. Whereas we use reason generally as an instrumental tool in order to achieve some external good (a better prediction, a more efficient procedure), the use of artistic representation is an end in itself; it generates its own enjoyment and its own meaning regardless of future consequences. The enlightenment a work of art produces in the artist and in the viewer enhances the quality of life here and now, and needs no further justification. To the extent that the quality of life is the highest good toward which all our activities tend, it can be argued that art contributes to it directly, whereas sciences and technology do so only indirectly.

If there is validity to these distinctions between rational and artistic cognition, then one would expect that the quality of experience is rather different in these realms. More specifically, we assume that young people engaged in arts-related activities have a more positive experience than when engaged in solving mathematical problems or when learning about physical facts. Whether this is true or not, and what the resulting consequences are for teaching, is the question addressed in the following sections. . . .

The preceding section suggests that involvement in the arts is more enjoyable than engagement in mathematics and science. It is likely that the differences in experience produced by these domains are at least partly a function of their nature. To be able to give further support to this assertion it is useful to specify more clearly those factors that contribute to the quality of subjective experience.

Most people, when they are asked to describe what makes them happy, will first think of something easy and relaxing, like watching TV, having a beer with friends, or having sex. But if they have more time to think, they usually come up with experiences of a different kind, experiences that involve meeting an unusual challenge and require a certain level of skill, such as hiking a treacherous mountain, bowling a perfect game, hearing an outstanding concert, or having an exhilarating conversation with a stimulating friend. None of these activities depends on external reinforcement. People get involved in them because of the quality of experience they provide. Therefore, experience functions in these cases as an autotelic (or intrinsic) reward. But what are the characteristics of such optimal experiences that lead people to get involved in activities just for their own sake?

A line of research that bears on this question was started in the early 1970s at the University of Chicago.[11] In numerous studies hundreds of people have been interviewed who pursued intrinsically rewarding activities such as painting, rock climbing, dancing, playing basketball, playing chess, and composing music. It was found that whenever people deeply enjoy what they are doing, they report a rather similar experiential state. This state has been called a *flow experience*, because many of the respondents said that when what they were doing was especially enjoyable it felt like being carried away by a current, like being in flow. Consequently, the theoretical model that describes optimal experiences is known as the flow model.

At the core, the flow model states that the perception of high challenges (or action opportunities) and high skills can lead people to a state of consciousness (flow) in which high levels of control, concentration, unselfconsciousness, and a strong sense of involvement are experienced. This "negentropic" state of consciousness contrasts with an entropic, confused, or random state of consciousness; persons in flow are deeply concentrated and feel a merging of action and awareness, their attention is centered on a limited stimulus field, and they may experience a "loss of ego" and feel in control of their actions and the environment. A further crucial component of the flow experience is its autotelic nature. In other words, the person in flow does not strive for goals or rewards beyond the activity at hand. The activity provides its own intrinsic rewards.

There is some evidence that flow is most readily experienced in certain kinds of activity. For example, games and play are considered to be ideal flow activities. In our view, typical flow activities provide the acting person with clear goals, well-defined rules, and unambiguous feedback on performance. This also explains why many rituals and other religious practices enable people to go off into trance-like states. However the experience of flow is by no means restricted to games and play. Almost every kind of activity can be structured so as to facilitate the experience of flow.

Research has shown that flow is only possible when a person feels that the opportunities for action in a given situation match his or her ability to master the challenges. The challenge of an activity may be something concrete or physical like the peak of a mountain to be scaled or it can be something abstract and symbolic, like a set of musical notes to be performed, a story to be read, or a puzzle to be solved. Similarly, the skill may refer either to a physical ability or to the mastery of manipulating symbols. More recent research has shown that balance of skill and challenge alone does not necessarily produce a flow experience. Both the challenges and skills must be relatively high (i.e., above a person's average) before a flow experience becomes possible.[12] . . .

Notes

1. Mihaly Csikszentmihalyi, "Phylogenetic and Ontogenetic Functions of Artistic Cognition," in *The Arts, Cognition, and Basic Skills*, ed. Stanley S. Madeja (St. Louis, CEMREL, 1978).

2. Donald T. Campbell, "Evolutionary Epistemology," *The Library of Living Philosophers*, vol. 14, ed P. A. Schilpp (LaSalle, IL: Open Court, 1974), 413–463; Jean Piaget, *Biology and Knowledge* (Chicago: University of Chicago Press, 1971).

3. Ludwig Wittgenstein, *Tractatus Logica–Philosophicus* (London/New York: Routledge & Kegan Paul/Humanities Press, 1969), 151. Originally published in 1921.

4. Robert Collingwood, *The Principles of Art* (New York: Galaxy Books, 1958); John Dewey, *Art as Experience* (New York: Minton Balch, 1934); Howard Gardner, *The Arts and Human Development* (New York: Wiley, 1973); Gardner, *Arts, Mind, and Brain: A Cognitive Approach to Creativity* (New York: Basic Books, 1982).

5. Jacob Getzels and Mihaly Csikszentmihalyi, *The Creative Vision: A Longitudinal Study of Problem Finding in Art* (New York: Wiley, 1976).

6. James Joyce, *A Portrait of the Artist as a Young Man* (New York: Penguin, 1976), 253. Originally published in 1916.

7. Getzels and Csikszentmihalyi, *The Creative Vision*. See also Mihaly Csikszentmihalyi and Olga Beattie, "Life Themes: A Theoretical and Empirical Exploration of Their Origins and Effects," *Journal of Humanistic Psychology* 19 (1979); 45–63.

8. Getzels and Csikszentmihalyi, *The Creative Vision*, 246.

9. Edward L. Deci and R. Michael Ryan, "A Motivational Approach to Self: Integration in Personality," in *Nebraska Symposium on Motivation (Perspectives on Motivation*, 38), ed. Richard A. Dienstbier (Lincoln NE: University of Nebraska Press, 1991).

10. See, for example, Eugene Gendlin, *Focusing* (New York: Everest House, 1978).

11. Mihaly Csikszentmihalyi, *Beyond Boredom and Anxiety* (San Francisco: Jossey-Bass, 1975); Csikszentmihalyi, *Flow: The Psychology of Optimal Experience*, Mihaly Csikszentmi-

halyi and Isabella Csikszentmihalyi, eds., *Optimal Experience: Psychological Studies of Flow in Consciousness* (New York: Cambridge University Press, 1988).

12. Fausto Massimini and Massimo Carli, "The Systematic Assessment of Flow in Daily Experience," in *Optimal Experience: Psychological Studies of Flow in Consciousness*, 266–287.

Wayne D. Bowman
Sound, Society, and Music "Proper" (1994)

Wayne D. Bowman is professor of music at Brandon University, Brandon, Manitoba, Canada.

The conception of musics as autonomous entities endowed with free-standing "absolute" meaning and value is intertwined with the essentialist notion that there must exist in all musical experience an identifiable and philosophically interesting core: a point where all genuine musics overlap, a set of foundational and definitive attributes common to all. This essential core comprises "the" nature and "the" value of music proper, in clear contrast to a merely contingent remainder. But not only does this way of thinking wrongly constrict the range of experience considered "properly" musical, it falsely promises uniform criteria by which the worth of all music (properly so-called) may be evaluated. Essentialism is a conceptual habit from whose comfort we would do well to wean ourselves, for it invariably marginalizes certain musics at the expense of others, silencing many of the aspects necessary for full appreciation of the profound significance of musical experience to human existence.

Efforts to segregate musical values from social ones, to distill a "nature of music" which can stand in clear contrast to the processes of social engagement and interaction in which musical undertakings are invariably embedded, conceal at least as much as they reveal. To the extent that musics are constitutive features of human cultural life, the relegation of their social functions to an extra-musical domain does serious philosophical damage. Music is not the name of a thing whose inherent worth and meaning stand in clear, stable contrast to the contingencies of the social world.

For those determined to defend musics from extra-musical pollutants, conferring socio-political significance to musics is heretical. But musics are definitively human activities whose richness does not survive apart from the human contexts of which they are part. Musics are socially and politically (and by extension, morally) significant enterprises. It is only by a remarkable feat of abstraction that we sustain the image of a pristine domain of music proper, whose boundaries define the limits of the musically relevant and the educationally worthy.

I have suggested that music education philosophy can do without the idea of essential musical attributes. I have suggested that music education

---

philosophy conceive itself as loosely and flexibly tethered to sound, intentionality, and human social relatedness. And I have suggested that we assume a more open minded stance regarding the relationships among the pre-musical, the non-musical, the extra-musical, and the musical. What counts as music is personally and culturally contingent, and the worth of various musical doings is likewise dependent upon a host of contextual concerns. Musical meanings and values are not simply given or absorbed or found; they are negotiated, achieved, constructed. Musics are ways of behaving with roots that extend deeply into instinctive human responses to sound, human interaction, and cultural practices.

These ideas are clearly less friendly to some of music education's traditional assumptions and practices than others. They are, for instance, less inclined to be prescriptive than descriptive; less conservative than liberal in orientation; less concerned to determine once and for all what "music is" than to explore the uses to which musics may be put, the ways musics may be. Those who insist that all musics share certain foundational attributes and conform to certain preordained standards will doubtless respond with dismay to the position outlined here. But those willing to accept its challenges may be rewarded with a breadth of purview that can embrace without distortion the full range of human musical behaviors.[1]

At the least, such a perspective has the salutary effect of reminding us that "our" music and its values are not the only possible ones, not the final resting place to which a process of inevitable and inexorable progress has delivered us. There is no more a final resting place for human musical activity than there is for human thought. There will always be other kinds of songs to be sung, other musics and musical doings that challenge and contradict our predispositions and stereotypes. But that is not cause for despair so much as excitement. An educational community committed to convictions like these would be dedicated to nurturing tolerance and curiosity as well as refining tastes; to enhancing the ability to imaginatively identify with others; to imparting respect for the sonorous world and the sheer joy of musical doings within it; and to nurturing the kind of society in which the musically educated embrace with gratitude startlingly different musics and take pleasure in each other's eccentricities.

Note

1. In an article entitled "The Arts of Music" in *Journal of Aesthetics and Art Criticism*, 50/3, 217–230, Philip A. Alperson suggests that a pluralistic account of "the fine arts of instrumental music 'promises to help us better discriminate' the values according to which musical styles might be judged, and the audiences and traditions to which they appeal" (227). That idea is clearly congruent with the positions advanced here.

Philip A. Alperson
A Praxial View (1994)

Philip A. Alperson is professor of philosophy at the University of Louisville and editor of *The Journal of Aesthetics and Art Criticism*.

The praxial view of art resists the suggestion that art can best be understood on the basis of some universal or absolute feature or set of features such as . . . aesthetic formalism, whether of the strict or enhanced [expressionist] variety. The attempt is made rather to understand art in terms of the variety of meaning and values evidenced in actual practice in particular cultures. . . .

On the praxial view, a music education program which aims to educate students about musical practice in its fullest sense must take into account, not only the history and kind of appreciation appropriate to the musical work of art, but also the nature and significance of the skills and productive human activity that bring musical works into being, if for no other reason than the fact that the results of human action cannot be adequately understood apart from the motives, intentions, and productive considerations of the agents who bring them into being.

David J. Elliott
The Praxial Philosophy of Music Education (1995)

David J. Elliott is professor of music at the University of Toronto and visiting professor at the Irish World Music Centre, University of Limerick.

Chapter 1, Toward a New Philosophy

I wish to suggest that there is a self-evident principle lying behind, beneath, and around our musical involvements that provides us with an indisputable starting point for building a comprehensive concept of music. . . . This self-evident principle is best expressed as an orienting question that Aristotle might have used to get an inquiry such as this under way. Regarding the human phenomenon we call music, let us ask ourselves the following: Is there any sense in which music is a human activity? Both common sense and logic answer yes. Without some form of intentional human activity, there can be neither musical sounds nor works of musical sound. In short, *what music is, at root, is a human activity.* Here is a certain starting point that leads to a multipart way of explaining what music is and why it matters. Let me elaborate.

In the case of Beethoven's "Eroica" Symphony, or the *kete* drumming of the Asante people, or a Zuni lullaby, or Duke Ellington's *Cotton Tail*, and in every example of a musical product that comes to mind, what we are presented with is more than a piece of music, a composition, an improvisation, a performance, or a "work" in the aesthetic sense. What we are presented with is the outcome of a particular kind of intentional human activity. Music is not simply a collection of products or objects. *Fundamentally, music is something that people do.*

In the case of the "Eroica," a human being named Ludwig van Beethoven did something. What he did was to compose and conduct something in the context of a specific time and place and a specific kind of music making. In the case of *Cotton Tail*, a person named Duke Ellington did something. What he did was to compose, arrange, perform, improvise, and record something in the context of another time and place and another kind of music making.

More broadly still, recall that it is entirely possible to have musical sounds without notated compositions, as a glance around the world will quickly confirm. In many cultures, music is not a matter of revered pieces, as Westerners tend to think; music is a matter of singing and playing instruments. And even in the West, where composers and compositions are the norm, there are many kinds of musical situations in which the actions of singing and playing (in the intentional sense) take precedence over music in the narrow sense of esteemed works.

Several points follow from these conclusions. First, if music is essentially a form of intentional human activity, then music must necessarily involve at least three dimensions: a doer or maker; the product he or she makes, and the activity whereby he or she makes the product. But this is obviously incomplete. For in any instance of human activity, doers do what they do in a specific context. (. . . By "context" I shall mean the total of ideas, associations, and circumstances that surround, shape, frame, and influence something and our understanding of that something.)

. . . The springboard principle of music as a human activity provides a self-evident way of beginning to explain the concept of music in all its dimensions, as well as several related ways of proceeding. Which ways shall we select? We have no choice. To select any one direction of thought over another would bias our inquiry from the outset. We must use them all. We must consider all these dimensions and their interrelationships as they contribute to our understanding of the nature and significance of MUSIC as a diverse human practice. Taken together, these various dimensions and directions of thought provide a blueprint for constructing a philosophy of MUSIC on which to base a philosophy of MUSIC EDUCATION.

Chapter 12, Music Education and Schooling

. . . An examination of the tendencies of human consciousness leads to the conclusion that a central goal of each self is to order and strengthen the self. As human beings, we have an innate desire to deploy our conscious powers to bring order to consciousness and achieve self-knowledge. . . . The praxial philosophy I propose suggests that when there is a match or balance between a person's musicianship and the cognitive challenges inherent in constructing musical works (overtly and covertly), musicers and listeners achieve the fundamental values, or "internal goods," of musicing and listening: self-growth, self-knowledge (or constructive knowledge), musical enjoyment (or "flow"), and self-esteem. In this view, musicianship is not only an exquisite form of knowledge, it is a unique source of one of the most important kinds of knowledge humans can achieve: self-knowledge.

In addition to these values, musicing and musical works extend the range of our expressive and impressive powers by providing opportunities to formulate musical expressions of emotions, musical representations of people, places, and things, and musical expressions of cultural-ideological meanings. When this range of opportunities for musical expression and creativity is combined with the opportunities presented by texts in vocal and choral works, music makers gain numerous ways of giving artistic-cultural form to their powers of thinking, knowing, valuing, evaluating, believing, and feeling that, in turn, challenge listeners' conscious powers and musical understandings.

On the basis of the cognitive richness of musicing and listening, this praxial philosophy argues that musical practices are also significant insofar as musical works play an important role (as memes) in establishing, defining, delineating, and preserving a sense of community and self-identify within social groups. Musical practices constitute and are constituted by their cultural contexts.

Teaching and learning a variety of musics comprehensively as music cultures through a praxial approach amounts to an important form of multicultural education. Entering into unfamiliar music cultures activates self-examination and the personal reconstruction of one's relationships, assumptions, and preferences. Students are obliged to confront their prejudices (musical and personal) and to face the possibility that what they may believe to be universal may *not* be so. In the process of inducting learners into unfamiliar musical practices, music educators link the primary values of music and music education to the broader goals of humanistic education. . . .

6. Toward the Future: The Short Term

In the short term, securing the place of music in public education depends on affirming to ourselves and others that MUSIC matters and that the root of our security problem lies principally in the nature of schooling, not in the nature and significance of MUSIC. The security of music education depends upon securing the integrity of MUSIC education. The future depends on making music education more musical, more artistic, and more creative by continuing to improve our philosophical understandings of MUSIC and by continuing to improve the musicianship of pre-service and in-service teachers. The values of music education will be achieved only by deepening and broadening students' musicianship; and the achievement of these values will be demonstrated most effectively to parents, teachers, administrators, and school boards by the quality of our students' musical thinking-in-action.

Our future does not lie in schemes designed to make music education less musical. This may seem too obvious to mention until we remind ourselves that some theorists are serious when they urge music educators to "save" school music programs by teaching music as a scholastic subject or by integrating music with subjects "across the curriculum" or by submerging music in multi-arts courses. These notions are based on false assumptions about the nature and values of MUSIC, about the nature of schooling, and about the nature of the problems we face. By implementing approaches that deny students the opportunity to develop musicianship (and therefore prevent students from achieving the aims of music education), these short-sighted notions jeopardize the efforts they purport to save.

In terms of what our profession can do for itself, securing the place of music education depends on preparing ourselves to explain and demonstrate to others that MUSIC is achievable, accessible, and applicable to all students.

Music Education Processes, Products, and Contexts (1996–97)

How Does the Praxial Philosophy Conceive the Nature of Music?

The praxial philosophy begins from a broad orienting map of music that combines processes (actions), products, and contexts. . . . I summarize this multidimensional concept by combining three related senses of the word itself: (i) MUSIC, (ii) Music, and (iii) music.

MUSIC (uppercase) is a diverse human practice consisting in many different musical practices, music-cultures, or Musics (uppercase M). By "musical practice" or "Music" I mean what musicians, lay people, and scholars routinely mean when they talk about, for example, Jazz, Rock, "Classical music," Irish traditional music, Indian music, and the many subdivisions that experts and lay people commonly make within and between such Musics (e.g., Dixieland and Bop; Acid Rock and Heavy Metal; Medieval chant, Baroque chamber music; Romantic Lied; Donegal fiddling and Connemara sean-nós singing, North Indian drumming and South Indian Carnatic song).

Each and every musical practice or Music is conceived as an artistic–social community, or music-culture. Each musical practice engages music makers and listeners in the corresponding and mutually-reinforcing actions of music making (in all its practice-specific forms) and music listening. These contextualized, practice-specific actions eventuate in *music* (lower-case) in the product sense of musical works that embody the values, standards, and traditions of the given practice or music-culture. (In this view, MUSIC is multicultural in essence.)

Because musical works result from the efforts of musical practitioners (amateur or professional) who compose, arrange, improvise, perform, and/or conduct at particular historical times and places, and in relation to practice-specific musical knowings, values, and traditions, musical works always involve listening *for* several dimensions of musical meaning simultaneously. Making and listening to musical works require us to cognize more than purely auditory information or sound patterns alone. Works of music are multidimensional "thought generators."

One of the fundamental missions of the praxial view is to develop students' abilities to listen *for* and comprehend the full range of meanings that musical works present to our powers of consciousness. What this requires, in turn, is that we replace the nineteenth-century aesthetic concept of esteemed works (i.e., compositions esteemed for their "aesthetic qualities" alone) with a more realistic and comprehensive sense of musical works and musical values. We need to supplant the absolutist claim (at the core of music education as aesthetic education philosophy) that all music everywhere should be understood in the restricted aesthetic sense of "works" and listened to, valued, and taught aesthetically. Instead, musical achievements (compositions, improvisations, renditions, arrangements—all types of "pieces" across all music-cultures) ought to be listened to and esteemed contextually for their *full* range of attributes, meanings, expressions, references, and cultural-ideological aspects. . . .

This is . . . what the praxial philosophy advocates: developing students' listenership (a) in direct relation to the music that students are learning to perform, improvise, compose, arrange, and conduct and (b) in relation to recordings. Moreover, to learn composing/arranging effectively and joyfully, students need continuous opportunities to hear their works interpreted and performed musically (not merely "produced"). Students must also learn actively about the music-culture contexts (including the performing, listening, and evaluating traditions) which surround and inform the two main processes that lie at the heart of composing, arranging, and improvising: generating and selecting original and promising musical ideas.

Thomas A. Regelski
The Aristotelian Bases of Praxis for Music (2000)

Thomas A. Regelski is professor of music at the State University of New York at Fredonia.

Music Education as and for Praxis

To be praxis, the conduct of music education must be "informed" by *theoria* of various kinds. Such pure or basic research already exists in various disciplines, including music research. But as *theoria*, it is by definition "useless" beyond the purely contemplative function it provides for those who create it—mainly academicians in various disciplines. Applied forms of *theoria*, on the other hand, provide the foundational "science" governing the teaching-learning process. *Theoria*, then, provides the formal research base that needs to be distilled into applied and operational terms[1] as the guiding principles and instrumental knowledge of *techne*.

Curriculum theory is also of central importance to teaching. A curriculum is a particular theory of value. It takes the form of a rationally stated hypothesis or proposal concerning what is most worth teaching of all that could be taught—that functions very much as, for example, the ethical philosophies of Aristotle do in hypothesizing the conditions and qualities of the "good life." In music education a praxial curriculum is a theoretical or philosophical hypothesis concerning what formal schooling can contribute to the role music can and *should* properly "play" in life. Such "shoulds" and "oughts" proposed in a curriculum assume that students need to be enabled and empowered to deliberate and choose to be musically active in intentional ways. Deliberation and choice are key ingredients of praxis as Aristotle understood it.[2] Thus, in a praxial theory of music education, musical schooling ought to inform the discernment—the phronesis—at the root of musical choices and taste. And it should increase the range of musical choices by empowering students to be *able* to and to *want* to (i.e., actually choose to) make musical "good time" a central and thus defining condition of the life well-lived. Such curriculum theory is implicit in everything a teacher does but must also take explicit form as the basis for the phronesis upon which teaching as praxis is based. . . .

. . . The omnipresence of music as praxis in human life—the fact that music is so central to so many of life's most important moments—points to its indisputable value, and this ubiquity provides a much stronger rationale for musical schooling than does the claims made by aesthetic education. However, despite the value of music as a social praxis, the level at which most people are able to respond and to make use of music in their lives is typically quite rudimentary. Thus, a formal music education in the schools needs to advance students' competencies in ways that expand their choices and capacities for musical agency *beyond what would have been possible without the formal instruction offered in school.* Music education *as* praxis, then, presumes as an underlying condition the importance of advancing and enhancing music *for* praxisin the lives of *individual* students. This underlying condition is given detailed form as a formal curriculum of action ideals expressed in terms of the particulars of each local teaching situation and serves as the basis by which instruction is organized, guided, and evaluated.

The stipulation of a curriculum in terms of action ideals that will guide instruction is, therefore the first step toward teaching as and for praxis. . . .

Notes

1. "Applied" in this sense refers to "the transformation into useful products of discoveries made at the fundamental research level," and "operational" refers to "finding the most efficient way of achieving goals that are set right from the start and are not problematic" (Clermont Gauthier, "Between Crustal and Smoke—Or, How to Miss the Point in the Debate about Action Research," in *Understanding Curriculum as Phenomenological and Deconstructed Text*, eds. William F. Pinar and William M. Reynolds [New York: Teachers College Press, 1992], 190).

2. David Wiggens, "Deliberation and Practical Reason," in *Essays on Aristotle's Ethics*, ed. A. Rorty (Berkeley: University of California Press, 1908), 221–240.

J. Terry Gates
Why Study Music? (2000)

J. Terry Gates is associate professor of music education at the State University of New York at Buffalo.

Why Should All People in the United States Study Music?

No society lasts for long that fails to maintain a complex and diverse culture and neglects to use it in the general education of its young. The value that we call "free speech" lies at the core of America's strength, and we interpret this now to include all forms of symbolic expression, artistic behavior, and communication. Though this value protects disturbing expression, sometimes, it also permits an open flow of insights. People who sense that change is needed communicate something about their views. Music and the other arts participate in this "landscape of insight." People who are in touch with this landscape, but whose feelings aren't so well formed, can sense when someone else is expressing similar needs. There is communion. Sensitive people can connect, participate, reject, revise, communicate, and advance the insight for themselves others. They can avoid the feeling of being alone with their inchoate perceptions.

This cultural process and the exercise of free expression are critical to the health of our society. The larger, industrialized twentieth-century societies that attempted to control and limit people's cultural resources by the censorship, repression, and politicization of music, the other arts, and religion have collapsed.

However much people often express regret that "things aren't as they used to be" in today's musical participation, we must recognize that culture—music—remains stagnant at the risk of losing its meaning and importance as a social and cultural resource. In fact, school music programs should emphasize musical change and personal creativity. Doing so will go further to strengthen our society and preserve the importance of music in schools than the mindless preservation of bygone skills and repertoires.

Preservation need not be mindless. Our heritage contains monuments of human thought that some call the canon of western civilization, a cultural store that is deemed valuable enough that it ought to be preserved by teaching. Through music study, students gain access to the musical minds of geniuses such as Bach, Mozart, and Beethoven. If music teachers emphasize musical processes that challenge all students to share their musical thoughts, including their musical recreations of the masterworks through their skills, knowledge, and evaluative insights, then music study, even study of the masters, can have a new, stronger focus.

There is an important view that schools should transmit the complex mix of values that define the cultures within our borders, including those values reflected in their musics. At the same time, we expect schools to deliberately model and teach social conventions such as waiting in line, staying to the right, neatness, punctuality, "walk, don't run," polite speech, personal space, empathy for someone hurt, patriotism, individual contributions to group outcomes, and many more. If part of the school's function is to promote a civil society, then these are laudable habits for children to form, whether or not they know why they are forming them. Perhaps music programs reflect a mindless approach to learning social conventions when they emphasize technique over critical insight in learning to perform the musical canon. For example, reinforcing correct, accurate performance and ensemble conformity and discipline at the expense of musical insight, or emphasizing slick public performance as the principal focus of music study for all children may reflect the broader "school values" listed earlier in this paragraph. Alas, in doing so, such programs model for children a disdain for valued musical actions that go beyond correct, prepared performance. Lost are the social and personal values growing out of improvisation, composition and revision, experimentation with musical ideas, and pushing the envelope of one's cognitive and perceptual capacities through music. People who promote correctness and uniformity are disturbed that students can challenge social conventions through the arts. To people disturbed by the authentic music produced by students—much of it exploratory—individual expression is not what these school values and social conventions support. There are good, practical reasons and functions for social conventions; teaching social conventions mindlessly miseducates children on such points.

Musical actions are metaphors of this problem, and music study helps children and young people negotiate the issues that arise from it. Through a good music program, one that emphasizes both individual and group accomplishment, both personal insight and recreative skill, all students can grow in that special value that supports our group preservation of individual "free speech" or, in its more contemporary formulation, "freedom of expression." Music study requires and reinforces individual action that alternatively creates and recreates, expresses and replicates. People who study music for extended periods learn how and when to be themselves and when to be a good group member.

This encourages children to form the dual habit of individual expression and group accomplishment. These interact. Neither trumps the other in our culture. All should study music because there are few other places in their early life experiences where personal sensitivity and contributions to the group are in such consistent, close, and powerful synergy.

At its best, then, music study is both an individual and a communal process. There are many valued musicians (people call them "self-taught") whose study is largely one of individual exploration not only to increase their skills, but also to increase their knowledge of other musicians whose music making they admire. Individual taste guides their study, and some of these musicians contribute significantly to the musical monuments of our culture. Indeed, all active musicians, regardless of the external sources of their expertise, contribute to the society's "landscape of insight" to which I referred earlier.

Far from denigrating the contributions of self-taught musicians, our society values these models and marvels at them. It is instructive that they are held up against the kind of "musical training" that stereotypes many school programs. The fact that self-taught musicians are contrasted with institution-taught musicians should be a warning that music education institutions are losing credibility to the degree that individual musical impulses of children are subjugated to some mistaken notion of group values. We must know more than we do about the music learning strategies of self-taught musicians and bring such strategies into our pedagogy rather than reject them. After all, we leave "formal" instructional we become self-taught. Musical expertise is oriented to self-guided musical study and music making.

For these and other reasons explored here, all persons should study music: a program that challenges both individual musical initiative and communal (group) achievement. In this way, the cultural value that marks our special brand of individual/group integration modeled for children and practiced by them, and is therefore preserved in the schools.

Samuel Hope
Response to J. Terry Gates's "Why Study Music?" (2000)

Samuel Hope is executive director of the National Association of Schools of Music and an executive editor of *Arts Education Policy Review* magazine.

Without question, we live in a context that can be explained from many perspectives. We can consider and argue politically, economically, sociologically, promotionally, and so forth, but none of these perspectives produce a note of music. Virtually none of us are music professionals because, at some time in our past, we made a sociological analysis, much less an economic or political one. At base, we are musicians and teachers of music because our own study has taught us something so valuable that we can do nothing else with our lives except try to pass that value and that opportunity on to others. Our culture regularly invites everyone to feel guilty and walk away from hard focused work and great achievement, to reject that which we don't enjoy immediately. Our policy future on behalf of music study needs to reject these invitations. We must ask and answer the question, "Why study music?" not because we don't have the answers, or even an understanding of other people's answers, but because so many other people don't have the answer, or don't want to hear it—people who make decisions that affect us and our mission of substance. Some want to use the power of music but not give others access to this power. Others want to use music or arts education purely for political, economic, or other purposes. There are hundreds of nonsubstantive agendas.

We satisfy these agendas at the peril of our cause and our professional lives and honor. We will never answer all of the skeptics. Despite all evidence, we in the arts will never convince everyone that intellectual work can be pursued through the still image, the moving image, and sound, as well as it can be pursued through words and numbers. But no matter what anyone says, no matter what anyone funds, no matter what anyone does, the facts of nature, the facts of history, and the facts derived from our own experience reveal fundamental truths about music and its position as a human basic in terms of brain, mind, and heart. As such, everyone who is to be educated must have an introduction to the world of communication, thought, and achievement that is music. Study is the only way to gain a fundamental understanding of this world. Music is not different in this regard than of the other basic modes of thought and action or means of communication. If we are wise, we will render unto politics that which is political; to economics, that which is financial; to sociology, that which is sociological; to demographics, that which is demographic; to advocacy, that which is promotional; and to technology, that which is technical. However, in doing all these things, we will never forget that the center of our purpose is to render unto music that which belongs to music.

Music Education and Society

This section illuminates the changing nature of American society during the second half of the twentieth century, and the ways in which music education has evolved to satisfy the needs of society. The civil rights revolution of the 1950s and 1960s created one of the most profound societal changes that affected music education. New statutory laws, judicial decisions, regulations, and policies required equal treatment in all areas of American life for every American, and by the end of the 1960s, schools were required to provide multicultural education. Now, music teachers were expected to be knowledgeable of musics not in the Western cultural mainstream. As music educators learned musics new to them, they began to incorporate virtually all kinds of music into the curriculum. In 1972, Congress further strengthened the multicultural movement with the passage of Public Law 91-318, the "Ethnic Heritage Program." The introduction to Title IX of the Bill states:

> In recognition of the heterogeneous composition of the Nation and of the fact that in a multiethnic society a greater understanding of the contributions of one's own heritage and those of one's fellow citizens can contribute to a more harmonious, patriotic, and committed populace, and in recognition of the principle that all persons in the educational institutions of the Nation should have an opportunity to learn about the different and unique contributions to the national heritage made by each ethnic group, it is the purpose of this title to provide assistance designed to afford students opportunities to learn about the nature of their own cultural heritage, and to study the contributions of the cultural heritages of the other ethnic groups of the Nation.

John H. Mueller
Music and Education—A Social Approach (1958)

John H. Mueller was chairman of the Department of Sociology at Indiana University, Bloomington.

Function of Education

The continuity between the succeeding generations of society can only be guaranteed if each generation is inducted into the cumulated heritage of its predecessors. The social economy in such a provision is obvious. If each generation were forced to rely on its own resources, to invent a language, experiment with edible food, discover for itself the principles of mechanics, or create its own music, it would literally not get off the ground but be limited to an enduring animal existence. Instead, the experience and lore of thousands of years of costly experimentation is available to endow the newborn generations with ever increasing wealth. There are many vehicles by which this social heritage is passed down: e.g., the family, the church, the community. But society has learned that certain segments of its tradition are best acquired by the new generation if entrusted to a special institution, the school.

If this conception of social continuities is acceptable, it would seem almost redundant to inquire as to the function of education in relation to music. But the query rises out of the fact that the social heritage is extremely abundant, complex, and heterogeneous, and even inharmonious in scope. No given individual will ever encompass it in its entirety. Therefore, the decision must be reached as to which culture traits should be delegated to the schools, and which ones to the other institutions, and which perhaps should be allowed to fend for themselves and randomly perpetuated, if at all.

The schools—if one includes all levels from kindergarten to graduate school—have exerted enormous gravitational force in attracting themselves, in some form or other, nearly every social activity of any dimension. The decline of the family as a socializing agency, together with the growing complexity of our civilization, have conspired to concentrate much of the responsibility for the induction of the young to the specialized institution. What was quite simply and inconspicuously accomplished among the primitives is now a profession in its own right.

There have been many different formulations of the functions of education, couched in language, phrased with nuances, and grounded on ideological foundations of great variety. Essentially, however, they all orient themselves around the objectives of the socialization of the child, and his maturation into a productive member of society. Even the progressive emphasis on individual self-expression of his personality is posited on the assumption that freedom produces a richer social life. Freedom of expression is checked only when it defeats this collective purpose.

Secondly, the function of education is to teach the skills which are necessary for the performance of the higher functions. Thirdly, the educational process takes cognizance of the personality, the individual talents, and disposition. To this has been added, on the higher levels, the professional and vocational training for which a broad base of cumulated knowledge is essential.

How does music fit into this functional format? Music, too, is a profession requiring early training, for which apt recruits must be selected in the elementary grades. It has been one of the objectives of this chapter to delineate the passive presence of music in social life and to demonstrate the pervasiveness is constantly being extended. Music admittedly is part of the cultural amenities of life. Modern life is *not* built on bare appetitive essentials. It does not limit itself to a skeletal existence for animal survival. We do not read basic English, we read literature; we do not dress merely for warmth and protection, we clothe ourselves in style; we do not consume K-rations, we dine with out friends; we do not burn up our biological machine, we intersperse our work with earned leisure.

There are, of course, many embellishments to life. Music is only one. But the heritage is so abundant and its present practice is so widespread in all classes of our stratified society that it takes its place with literature and the humanities in the curriculum.

The multiplicity of aspects of music instruction includes a coterie of skills, not only for actual performance and creativity but also for the enhancement of perspective listening and appreciation. Like every other social practice, musical forms have departed so far from the simplicity of folk art that it would seem necessary to codify these traditions to pass them down to the generality of the citizenry. Musical forms, historical information, styles, and trends of music may quite properly be emphasized for the purpose of inducting the student into such important traditions.

The opinion is often expressed that music, as cultivated by the student in the school, should be self-rewarding. (This corresponds to the "terminal" functions explained previously.) In accordance with this psychological dictum, adverse comment has often been directed against the musical contests because of their emphasis on the desire to "win." But there is no incompatibility between these two positions. Man—and this includes the child—is a social being. He spontaneously measures his own achievement against those of his fellow man. Ambition is essentially a comparative process, which never thrives in isolation. Nor is it a symptom of deterioration of character to desire applause in moderation. Every act, whether musical or economic, is suffused with pluralistic motives. Consequently there is no inner contradiction between legitimate self-expression and a desire of the reward consisting in the esteem of one's fellows. As long as the "desire to win" does not encroach too heavily on the other civic and scholarly duties of the individual, and as long as it does not lead to pathological symptoms of dishonesty, deceit, and other antisocial gestures, it would seem that the musical contest can only be a preparation for life which is, itself, a continuous competitive existence to which everyone must attune himself.

In spire of "progressive" theories enunciated during recent decades, one's measure of value of education is its enrichment of mature life. The various values of music education are, therefore, not restricted to the school itself, but they are planned with the view of carryover into adult activities, for which the school is merely the prelude.

Educational carryover is a very subtle and deceptive phenomenon. In his enthusiastic moments, the music teacher often falls victim to the amiably inflated expectations of a literal continuation of the musical work and activity cultivated in the school. Such expectations are bound to be largely unfulfilled. It must be remembered that, at the end of the educational stage, the youth enters an entirely different schedule of life. He undertakes occupational responsibilities, domestic duties, and civic engagement. The systematic schedule which characterized his socially nonresponsible schooldays has disappeared. Furthermore, other opportunities press in upon them. Therefore, a carrryover may appear in as many different guises as there are phases of musical life itself. The ex-orchestra member now becomes a nucleus for public opinion which may support musical programs in the schools. He becomes a contributor to cultural affairs, in accordance with his sympathies and affluence. But if some supposed musical converts seem to go entirely astray, it is only in conformity to the foibles of human nature and the normal competitive lures of an exceedingly varied and complex culture. The ex-student of chemistry does not invariably proceed to set up a hobby chemical laboratory in the home; the student of languages is likely even to forget his detailed knowledge. Sophistication and erudition are not technical skill or encyclopedic memory, as much as the world may admire these accomplishments in their place. No adult embraces completely the totality of our culture. It is inevitable that this interest in many of the several dozen subjects which he has sampled would seem to lapse entirely.

However, the socialization of the youth should still permit him to move securely and confidently and to range widely among the complexities of our civilization. Indeed, it has been said that a good education will enable one to worry (potentially) about almost anything in the world. Music is one of the achievements of our culture.

John H. Mueller

Max Kaplan
Foundations and Frontiers of Music Education: Goals of Planning (1966)

Max Kaplan was a noted American philosopher and sociologist of leisure. He was Director of the Arts Center at Boston University and co-founder of the Greater Boston Youth Symphony.

Goals of Music Education and the Cultivated Society

1. *To contribute to a dialogue of men's past and future eras.* Art is a dynamic demonstration of previous times, a continuity with the past. The new society, marked particularly by technical changes, will require reminders of excellence in values from the past.

2. *To become the conscience of musical taste for a mass society beset by a popular culture.* . . .

3. *To assume some measure of responsibility for creating those conditions in home, neighborhood, and community life that are conducive to excellence in taste and esthetic participation, and of utilizing the resource of home, neighborhood, and community for the better teaching of music.* . . .

Goals of Music Education and the Status of the Esthetic

1. *To assert itself as an arm of man's esthetic experience, related to other forms of experience, but fundamentally independent as a category of learning and living.* Education in general aims at many sides of the child's growth and personality. As teachers we are aware of the multi-purposes or by-products of any given experience. As musicians our commitment is to music as the basic center of our activity, and we use the social by-products as tools, not as ends.

2. *To contribute to our knowledge of creative persons and the creative act, as cooperation with other disciplines that possess the skills of objective research.* Every class in music and every rehearsal is a laboratory in creativity, operating on three planes: the transmission of gross information, insight, or awareness of subtleties that contribute to the essence of art; the familiarity with the masterpieces that will lead to mature judgment of art; and the development of skills, confidence, and imagination that lead to the creation of art.

3. *To utilize the accumulated insights of the social sciences and humanities wherever they are appropriate, as bases for educational procedures or as tools for the development of conditions outside the school.* . . .

Goals of Music Education Within the Functions and Roles of Music

1. *To uncover, stimulate, and train students so that all will be exposed most fully to the products of the greatest creative minds of past and present, so they will be led toward experiences of their own in creative acts and discoveries.* . . .

2. *To recognize the validity and need of creative persons as participants in serious amateur as well as professional roles in the community and the nation, and to take part in creating the cultural and economic climate in which both may flourish independently and cooperatively. . . .*

3. *To become an experimental distributor so that all styles of music are made available to audiences of the school and the community, and that the school becomes a vital vehicle in encouraging, commissioning, and presenting local and regional composers. . . .*

4. *To undertake the conscious cultivation of audiences and to listen attentively and with discrimination to a variety of mass as well as all live musical media. . . .*

Michael L. Mark
An Appreciation of Diversity (1996)

The population of the United States is extremely diversified, being comprised of people from virtually every national and ethnic background. Most of the early immigrants came from Western Europe, and Africans were brought to America as slaves soon after Europeans started to arrive. Later, Asians, Eastern and Central Europeans, and Hispanics began to immigrate, and by the end of the 19th century, huge waves of immigrants from all parts of the world had poured into the United States. Despite the heterogeneity of the population it served, music education of the nineteenth century, and even of much of the twentieth century, was based on Western art music. Until the 1960s, music teachers attempted to "teach up" to what was considered a "cultured" level, the cultured music of the upper economic class. Western classical music was viewed as the best music, and teachers thought it proper to encourage students to aspire to it.

The acculturation of immigrants into American society, the "melting pot," was one of the goals of music education. The phrase, "melting pot," is derived from the famous line in Israel Zangwill's 1908 play, *The Melting Pot*: "America is God's Crucible, the great Melting-Pot where all the races of Europe are melting and re-forming." The melting pot concept appealed both to Americans who had been here for a long time, and to many new Americans, who were eager to assimilate so they could share in the wealth of their new country. Well-meaning societal leaders attempted to realize their ideal through many of America's societal institutions, including the work place, the military, the streets, the media, and especially the schools. Music education played an important role in trying to homogenize a highly diverse population, and first and second generation Americans accepted the belief that it could help to socially elevate their children. It is not surprising that the national and ethnic musics of the more recent immigrants were not the stuff of school music programs. Most music educators, and probably most Americans whose families had arrived from Europe generations earlier, did not respect the music of the newcomers. Perhaps they were not even aware of it.

At that time, the music education profession did not attempt to find a reasonable balance between what was most meaningful musically to students, and the "cultured" music derived from the European classical music heritage. This unbalanced approach probably failed to interest many pupils in art music, which requires knowledge, experience, and sophistication for most people to appreciate. Music educators were not to blame, though. They were helping to implement the massive social movement to assimilate immigrants and their children.

It has only been in recent years that the American education establishment has come to genuinely respect the heritage of every student. Social movements, legislation, and court decisions have finally persuaded us of the value and significance of social, ethnic, and cultural diversity in American society. Since the 1960s, American schools have attempted to teach about diversity, and the curriculum now is structured to reflect various cultural values and traditions.

Estelle R. Jorgensen
On Spheres of Musical Validity (1997)

Estelle R. Jorgensen is professor of music at Indiana University and the founding editor of Philosophy of Music Education Review.

One of the intriguing aspects of music is the great variety of musical traditions, ways of music making, and transmitting musical knowledge from one generation to another, evident historically and internationally. Why do so many musics coexist, each with a public that identifies with that music and whose culture is partly defined by it? Can this diversity be explained in a way that permits a global and context-sensitive view of world musics? How do these musical traditions maintain themselves, especially in the face of competition or opposition from others? These, among other questions, are especially relevant to music educators whose objective includes musical enculturation.

Music is interrelated with society in multifaceted ways. Of these ways, several tensions seem particularly important. Music is both related to and independent of the other arts. The ancient Greeks thought of music as encompassing poetry, song, dance, drama, and instrumental music. Subsequent specialization in the arts led Western classical musicians to think of music in a much narrower sense, as a separate art form. In *Philosophy in a New Key*, however, Susanne Langer draws attention to the commonalities among music, drama, poetry, dance, myth, and rite, among other non-discursive ways of knowing. She fails to underscore the role of social context in sufficiently understanding musical meaning, yet her analysis of music as closely related to the arts, myth, and religion opens the way for others to explore how music is similar to and different from other ways of knowing. In so doing, she reminds readers that vestiges of an earlier time remain. Music is thought of restrictively and independently of other arts in the abstract instrumental music of a Beethoven symphony; it is also thought of broadly and integratively with other arts in a Wagner opera or Tchaikovsky ballet. So important is the total arts concept of music that opera is regarded as one of the great triumphs of Western music.

Music has form and function. "Form" refers to articulated structure that relies on the skills of the composer, performer, and listener to make and apprehend. "Function" means the use music serves. Philosophers of music have largely overlooked social aspects of musical form and function until recently, when various writers argued that music making is fundamentally a matter of practices motivated and constrained by, and understood within, particular social and cultural contexts. Many world musics are integrated arts that serve myth and rite or mark particular social and political calendars. Rather than being means to their own ends, these musics constitute means to other ends, such as the maintenance of the social structures and processes in which they are found. In the past, rules undergirding Western classical music have been applied indiscriminately to an analysis of the structure and function of all musics. We now recognize that Western norms do not apply to all musics universally, but that many rules govern particular musics. Each must be understood in its own terms, formally and functionally.

Music is a part of society, and musical structures reflect and exemplify social structures. During the past half-century, writers from the social sciences and humanities have advanced the notion of an intimate and intrinsic relationship between music and society. They have argued that music is suffused with meaning that is musically and culturally interpreted and that it contributes in important ways to a sense of shared social consciousness that characterizes a given society. Blacking, for example, has contrasted Western classical music, which reflects Western hierarchical social structures and mores and values individualism and competition, with the indigenous music of the Venda people of South Africa, which reveals egalitarian social values and beliefs and values communalism and cooperation. He believes that music cannot be prophetic of society, but only follow it. On the contrary, the reciprocal interaction between society and music is dynamic; music not

Estelle R. Jorgensen

only follows society but also impacts, portends, and even constructs and reconstructs it. As such, music making involves a dialectic between social conservation and reconstruction.

Music is corporately and individually understood. It is limited to, and transcends, cultural context. Earlier this century, Charles Ives suggested that the reason for this paradox lay in music's possession of both substance and manner: substance is imaginatively grasped in the musical content, and manner is indicated in its style. Substance and manner are inextricably intertwined. Nevertheless, the conceptual distinction between them highlights the importance of, and differences between, personal and social perspectives on music.

Substance, noted Ives, is grasped individually; manner is understood in terms of social expectations. Substance permits music to reach beyond its time and place; manner ties it to a particular time and place. Taken figuratively, a Bach partita seems just as fresh and relevant today as it did three centuries ago, and a Japanese koto ensemble moves an English as well as Japanese audience because of the presence of musical substance, or that which intrigues the imagination more or less independently of the listener's cultural understandings of the music. Listeners can full understand the partita or the koto performance, however, only as they also grasp its manner, its stylistic and contextual aspects. Recognizing the complementary nature of these personal and social understandings about music highlights the importance of studying the interrelationship of music and society from a variety of perspectives, be they social, religious, musical, philosophical, psychological, or physiological.

Patricia Shehan Campbell
Multiculturalism and School Music (1994)

Patricia Shehan Campbell is professor of music at the University of Washington, Seattle.

With growing force and frequency, the issues of multiculturalism that have begun to be woven into the curricular fabric of American schools are facing challenge, if not outright confrontation. Not only are the politically conservative voicing their opinions; many middle-of-the-road teachers and parents are doing the same. Some are frustrated by the disconnected array of experiences students sometimes receive, which stream from curricular attempts to feature too many cultures too quickly. Some are disillusioned by what they see as a hodge-podge of facts and values being presented to students, many of which appear to have no central focal point, nor unifying entities, nor any identifiable overarching purpose. Some are becoming impatient with the superficiality of an educational system that seems unable to define for itself the meaning of an American heritage and that cannot determine a balance between subject-specific knowledge and skills and the multicultural perspectives that can be placed upon them. Some teachers, parents, and concerned citizens are ready to turn back the curricular clock to an earlier time, when the "melting pot" symbolized American unity and a "mosaic" was an artistic work of colored tiles rather than a worn-down-to-meaningless metaphor for multiculturalism.

While education at large is fielding questions that probe the meaning of a multicultural curriculum, music teachers and their programs are just beginning to meet some of the mandates placed upon them in the name of multiculturalism. Music has trailed behind the humanities in its curricular revisions, hanging on to a "school music" heritage of songs, arrangements, and ensemble transcriptions, much of which has been Eurocentric (if not Anglocentric) in nature. Now, as other curricular areas come under fire for superficiality, vocal/choral and instrumental teachers are beginning to enter into an unprecedented period of exploring musical traditions from Africa, Asia, and Latin America, as well as African-American and Native American traditions so integral to the identification as "American." And as these explorations occur, the challenges of educators at large are coming into the range of vision shared by music teachers. . . .

Missing the Mark

The professional stance on multiculturalism in school music instruction has shifted dramatically over the years. While *musica exotica* is still present and is strongly appealing to some . . . a growing commitment to teaching long-standing American musical heritages is evident as well. Music teachers and leaders of their principal professional society have increasingly given their attention to matters of musical repertoire—authenticity, cultural representativeness, and the appropriate age or grade level at which to present and/or perform it.

The Winds of Change

. . . In this land of unparalleled cultural diversity, the time for rhetoric and happenstance is past. If music education is to survive and flourish in the climate of the next century, it will take the full-scale efforts of musicians and educators—in schools and universities, and at the Reston [MENC] headquarters—to activate multiculturalism within the context of music classrooms.

June Boyce-Tillman
Conceptual Frameworks for World Musics in Education (1997)

June Boyce-Tillman is Reader in Community and Performing Arts at King Alfred's College of Higher Education, Winchester, UK.

Within music we have the potential for a world unity based on the valuing of divergent systems. To react to the demands of prevailing political climates rather than to sit about devising a secure philosophical underpinning for our curriculum content and teaching strategies is to yield up our power as music educators to politicians, social engineers, financiers, and psychologists. Higher education needs to enter the debate by questioning the assumptions of the western classical tradition like the need for literacy and the value of notational systems and the decontextualizing effects of concert practices. This will be a step towards respecting other value systems. . . .

There is a saying, "to know all is to forgive all." Musical knowing which includes both experience and understanding can enable existing tensions to be acknowledged and accepted as differences. "If your neighbors appear to be dancing rather strangely, they may be dancing to different drums" (adapted from Thoreau). In the end we all dance to the drums tuned to our own rhythms and the rhythms of the culture that we find ourselves in at any given time. With further work we can create a philosophical frame that values diversity.

Warrick L. Carter
Minority Participation in Music Programs (1993)

Warrick L. Carter was dean of the Berklee School of Music when he wrote this article. He is also the former director of Disney Entertainment Arts for Walt Disney Entertainment.

Regardless of the opportunity for school music instruction, minority students will not participate unless they feel an inviting and supportive environment. Music educators must therefore work to change the climate of school music to be more welcoming for minority students. Although we have little control over the location of our schools, as music educators we do have power over the design of teacher education programs, the curriculum offered in our schools' music programs, and the possibility of these schools' music programs becoming integral parts of the multiple communities they serve. As the current numbers reveal, we have not done a good job

---

thus far, but all is not lost if we start now. Please, no more hyperbole or philosophical papers; rather, we need Herculean deeds and actions to change the situation. If not, school music programs will continue to miss out on the participation of some of the country's best young musical minds. Young minority musicians will continue to make music, but they will not make music in the schools.

Florida Department of Education
Multicultural Arts Education (1993)

This report is a curriculum development and renewal project developed by the Center for Music Research and the Department of Art Education at the Florida State University for the Florida Department of Education, Division of Public Schools.

Rationale for a Multicultural Arts Education

Although it seems ethnocentric and arbitrary, the concept of dividing art into the cultural categories of western and nonwestern may be a useful place to start in western society. This approach corresponds with recognized historical, political, and (to some extent) geographical boundaries. It certainly offers a perspective for thinking about and defining the arts. For example, the western arts tradition can be traced back to at least the classic Greek civilization. Present-day countries and societies that consistently have subscribed to that tradition can be readily identified. The non western tradition, on the other hand, includes all those cultures that do not trace their roots back to the western, or classic Greek foundation. In this context nonwestern means *many* traditions, each with its own cultural foundation. The traditional art of China, for example, is built upon the accumulation of imperial dynasties that defined and valued art in very different ways from their neighbors in India.

In spite of attempts to categorize art, however, we must remember that every art form is a unique expression of a particular culture or society. Each was produced, defined, and valued within the context of the culture and thus cannot be judged *outside* the culture. One cannot say, for example, that ritual performances and the making of containers in tribal societies are not art forms because they serve functional purposes. One should examine the values of those societies and how they mesh with spiritual and historical traditions, as well as with the art forms that serve them. This approach should be the focus of understanding art and teaching it to others.

The aim of multicultural education in Florida is to prepare "students to live, learn, communicate, and work to achieve common goals in a culturally diverse world by fostering understanding, appreciation, and respect for people of other ethnic, gender, socioeconomic, language, and cultural backgrounds."[1]

Note

1. *Multicultural education in Florida: Report of the Multicultural Education Review Task Force* (Orlando, FL: University of Central Florida, 1991) in *Multicultural Arts Education: Guidelines, Instructional Units and Resources for Art, Dance, Music and Theater, Grades K–12* (Tallahassee: Department of Education, Division of Public Schools, 1993), 174–178.

Music Education, Mind, and Brain

At about the time that the aesthetic education movement was maturing, new developments in cognitive psychology and advocacy were also occurring.[1] Howard Gardner, codirector of Project Zero at Harvard University, posed his theory of multiple intelligences, which has provided strong support for the unique value of arts education.[2] Gardner was followed by several others who also identified artistic intelligence as a unique way of knowing.[3] The new theories of learning fueled the advocacy efforts of the Music Educators National Conference, and the entry of neuroscientists into the study of the effects of music on students helped stimulate public support for the profession to a degree that was unanticipated only a few years earlier. The study best known to the public and policy makers, and which music education advocates locked onto, was "Listening to Mozart enhances spatial-temporal reasoning: Towards a neurophysiological basis" by Rauscher, Shaw, and Ky.[4] It was this study that made the public aware of the "Mozart effect," which indicated a relationship between listening to the music of Mozart and increased intelligence in children. This study helped trigger an increased level of public interest in nonmusical outcomes of music education.

The effects of music study on students has become a focus of interest in the fields of cognitive science and behavioral neuroscience, in part because music is an entry point for study of the mind and body. One result of the new scientific focus on music education is the belief and expectation that the study of music supports learning in other subjects. This has led music educators in a new direction—the integration of music in the general curriculum, especially at the elementary school level. Here, music is incorporated into the teaching of such other subjects as science, mathematics, and reading.

Notes

1. See Karen Wolff, "The nonmusical outcomes of music education: A review of the literature," *Bulletin of the Council for Research in Music Education*, 55 (1978), 1–27.

2. Howard Gardner, *Frames of Mind: The Theory of Multiple Intelligences* (New York: Basic Books, 1983).

3. Michael L. Mark, *Contemporary Music Education*, 3rd ed. (New York: Schirmer Books, 1996), 653–64.

4. Frances Rauscher, Gordon Shaw, and Katherine Ky, "Listening to Mozart enhances spatial–temporal reasoning." *Neuroscience Letters* 185 (1995), 44–47.

Howard Gardner
The Theory of Multiple Intelligences (1983)

Howard Gardner, a leading cognitive scientist, is director of Harvard Project Zero, Harvard University. He is affiliated with the Boston University School of Medicine and the Boston Veterans Administration Medical Center.

There is persuasive evidence for the existence of several *relatively autonomous human intellectual competences*, abbreviated hereafter as *human intelligences*. These are the "frames of mind" of my title. The exact nature and breadth of each intellectual "frame" has not so far been satisfactorily established, nor has the precise number of intelligences been fixed. But the conviction that there exist at least some intelligences, that these are relatively independent of one another, and that they can be fashioned and combined in a multiplicity of adaptive ways by individual and cultures, seems to be increasingly difficult to deny. . . . Of all the gifts with which individuals may be endowed none emerges earlier than musical talent.

I submit that both approaches we have contemplated are appropriate. The one that accentuates unfolding displays its particular virtue during the first years of life, from the period of two to seven. With the developmental changes accompanying the years of schooling, a more active and interventionist stance seems advisable, especially in a milieu virtually bereft of societal support for artistic (as opposed to scientific) endeavors. By the time of adolescence, it is in all probability too late to begin a rigorously structured education program, and if natural development has not exerted its effect by then, it never will. Instead, one hopes that by adolescence the child will have attained sufficient skills and a sense of critical awareness, as well as ample ideas and feelings he wishes to express; then he can continue on his own to gain sustenance from whichever artistic medium he selects.

Donald A. Hodges
Neurological Research and Music Education (1996–97)

Donald A. Hodges is professor and director of the Institute for Music Research at the University of Texas at San Antonio.

Implications for Music Education

Keeping in mind the four general discussions placing neuromusical research in perspective (Magic vs. Mystery, Restrictions and Limitations of Neuromusical Research, Basic and Applied Research, and Short-term vs. Long-term Gains), there are some benefits to be had from this line of research. One way to synthesize these benefits is by moving toward the creation of a model of the *Musical Brain*.

Toward a Model of the Musical Brain

Synthesizing neuromusical research leads to a model of the Music Brain with these features:

All human beings are born with a Musical Brain. Wilson[1] states this emphatically when he says that "all human beings have a biologic guarantee of musicianship." Besides supporting this notion with neuromusical research, one can easily look at the anthropological literature. Anthropologists tell us that human beings have always and everywhere engaged in musical behaviors. Blacking[2] said that music, like language, is a species-specific trait of humankind. All human beings—and only human beings (at least to the high degree that we do)—have language and music. They are hallmarks of what it means to be a human being. To be musical is to be human and to be human is to be musical.

To say that all human beings are inherently musical does not mean that all have the potential to become outstanding performers. Rather, it means that we all have the wherewithal to respond to the music of the surrounding culture. Music therapy literature is replete with studies documenting the responsiveness to music among individuals in all handicapping circumstances. While musical behaviors, like any form of human behavior, must be distributed across the population such that there are a wide range of potentials, there are no indications of its missing altogether.

The human Musical Brain is different from other animal brains. Only humans have music—what we call *birdsong* is more communication than music—because only humans are capable of tracking musical elements such as melody, harmony, rhythm, form, and so on. Studying animal sound processing teaches us much about our own sound processing and helps us to define what "extra" neurological resources we have that allow for music.

The Musical Brain operates at birth. The fact that babies respond to music immediately (and, in fact, in the womb during the last three months before birth) gives strong evidence for inherited neural mechanisms devoted to music.

The degree to which the Musical Brain is lateralized is still being debated. Currently, the safest position to take may be that the left hemisphere processes information in more sequential, analytical ways and the right hemisphere in more holistic, intuitive ways. The degree of laterality may depend on the subject (e.g., training), the stimulus (e.g., the kind of music being used), and the task (e.g., listening for global or local features).

The Musical Brain consists of an extensive neural system (or systems) involving widely distributed, but locally specialized regions of the brain. Music is not only in the right side of the brain; rather, it is represented all over the brain. Musical experiences are multimodal, involving auditory, visual, cognitive, affective, motor, and memory systems.

The Musical Brain has cognitive components. Modem neuroscientific techniques (e.g., EEG, ERP, MRI, SQUID, PET) are beginning to identify structures in the brain that carry out specific musical tasks (e.g., absolute pitch in the left temporal lobe) and to look at musical processing (e.g., the electrical activity of sophisticated music listeners is different from naive listeners).

The Musical Brain has affective components. Music medicine is making effective use of music to reduce fear and anxiety. Essentic forms, as identified through the sentograph, show links between music and emotions.

The Musical Brain has motor components. The connection between music and movement holds for both expressive (e.g., musicians as small-muscle athletes) and receptive (e.g., music energizing Parkinsonian and stroke patients) modes.

Early and ongoing musical training affects the organization of the Musical Brain. Musically trained subjects exhibit significantly higher EEG coherence values when compared to controls with limited musical training. An area of the left temporal lobe concerned with sound processing (the planum temporale) is larger in musically trained subjects than in untrained subjects; this is especially true for those who started studying music before the age of seven or who have absolute pitch. Motor cortex areas controlling the fingers increased in response to piano exercises, both actual and imagined. Finally, string players have greater neuronal activity and a larger area in the right primary somatosensory (body mapping) cortex that controls the fingers of the left hand than non-string players. Again, these effects were greater for those who started playing at a young age.

The Musical Brain is highly resilient. Music persists in people who are blind, deaf, emotionally disturbed, profoundly retarded, or afflicted with any number of disabilities or diseases (e.g., Alzheimer's disease, savant syndrome).

This model of a musical brain has rich implications for music education. Some aspects have pedagogical implications, such as the notion of mental rehearsal or the support for early childhood music education. Other aspects might serve to buttress philosophical arguments.

Neuromusical Research Supports Music as Intelligence

By now, most music educators are perhaps aware of Gardner's theory of multiple intelligences.[3] He suggested that rather than thinking of human intelligence as something represented by a single IQ number, we should consider a pantheon of intelligences, including linguistic, musical, spatial, logical-mathematical, bodily-kinesthetic, intra-personal (access to one's own internal world), and interpersonal (ability to notice and make distinctions among other individuals, especially their moods, temperaments, motivations, and intentions) intelligence.

Those who consider these the "sacred seven" intelligences should be aware that Gardner himself states that there may be more or fewer. The seven thus far identified were selected because they meet all eight of the criteria of an intelligence established by Gardner:

1. Potential isolation by brain damage
2. The existence of idiot savants, prodigies, and other exceptional individuals
3. An identifiable core operation or set of operations
4. A distinctive developmental history, along with a definable set of expert "end-state" performances
5. An evolutionary history and evolutionary plausibility
6. Support from experimental psychological tasks
7. Support from psychometric findings
8. Susceptibility to encoding in a symbol system

Although only numbers 1, 2, and possibly 5 are relevant for this discussion, all eight can readily be substantiated for music (see Hodges and Haack, 1996).[5] Previous discussions have provided support for numbers 1 and 2 in music. It is also possible to account for music from an evolutionary standpoint.[6, 7] We live in a universe with many evident periodicities (e.g., phases of the moon, light–dark cycles, etc.) and there are over 100 oscillators in our bodies; it makes sense that we are able to track rhythms. Other ideas focus on:

Mother–infant bonding. As indicated previously, mothers and infants share with one another by manipulating the musical elements (prosody) of speech. Notice that what is being exchanged initially is feelings, not the meanings of words.

Acquisition of language. Rhythm plays an especially crucial role in language acquisition. Newborns move their limbs in rhythm to the speech they hear around them.[8] If they hear a different language, their rhythms will subtly change. Rhythmic activities in the acquisition of language are so important that they form the basis for acquiring cognitive expectancies and for inter-relating cognition and affect.[9]

Social organization. Music may have played a strong role in helping human beings to organize socially[10] Music helps us to express who we are as a people; each social group gains identity, in part, through music. In *How Musical is Man?* Blacking[11] counterbalances the first and last chapters. The first chapter, "Humanly Organized Sound," describes how all human beings organize sounds into a meaningful entity called music. In the last chapter, "Soundly Organized Humanity," he describes how the sounds we create, in turn, create and shape us. Of course, the most important evolutionary reason for music may be that music provides a unique way of knowing. Another way to characterize these multiple ways of knowing is the phrase *human knowledge systems*. A human knowledge system can be defined as a means for knowing, expressing, sharing, and understanding one's inner world, the outer world, and interactions within and between the two. Through the process of evolution, we have developed a variety of knowledge systems, each of which is a unique and equally valuable way of knowing.

It is obvious what kinds of things we can know in the linguistic and mathematical domains. But, more to the point, what can we know, express, share, or understand through music? Among the myriad possibilities, surely the focus must be on feelings or emotions. If we wanted to express ideas about time and distance as they relate to an understanding of the universe, we would resort to the power and economy of mathematics. However, mathematics may not be so useful if we wish to express joy; then we might turn to the power and economy of music. This discussion would take us too far afield if we take time to elaborate on this theme, so let it suffice for now to recognize that human beings are biologically equipped to experience many things of value, primarily feelings, through music.

Neuromusical research will continue to provide support for music as a human knowledge system (or as an intelligence, if that language is preferred), and the possible benefits might be illustrated by two examples. In recent years, American society has seen significant changes with respect to the effects of high-fat diets and smoking. We now have available a variety of low- or no-fat foods and access to non-smoking flights, hotel rooms, and so on. While many individuals may continue to eat fatty foods or smoke, they do so in the face of nearly incontrovertible evidence that these are not healthy habits. All the moralizing and "nagging" has done far less to bring about changes than a body of scientific data.

I do not mean to suggest that neuromusical research will someday be able to "prove" that music is "good" for you. Rather, I am suggesting that neuromusical research may be useful in supporting the important role music plays in human life. To the extent that we are beginning to document neural mechanisms for music, we are saying that music is as biologically inherent in the human system as language. If we are genetically predisposed for musical behaviors, there must be a reason. Just as societal changes have come about in diet and smoking through research, it may be that society will become more strongly supportive of music because of neuromusical research.

Finally, neuromusical research may, in time, provide support for various curricular notions. We are moving toward a time where psychologists and neurobiologists are beginning to work together in a field called cognitive neuroscience. Soon cognitive theories of music and neuromusical research will come together to provide us with more useful models of musical behavior. The previous review of research indicated that musical experiences change the organization of the brain, that the earlier these experiences take place the better, and so on. Just as applications are beginning to be made in music medicine (e.g., enabling stroke patients to walk again, reducing fear and anxiety in surgical patients), we may, in time, have specific pedagogical strategies solidly grounded by research in the cognitive neuroscience of music. In many cases, neuromusical research may merely confirm already established practices; in some cases it may indicate ineffective or incorrect practices, or we may derive entirely new pedagogical strategies. In the meantime, it is hoped that the music education community will be supportive and patiently look to a time when neuromusical research will pay off in significant ways.

Notes

1. F. Wilson, *Tone Deaf and All Thumbs?* (New York: Viking, 1986).

2. J. Blacking, *How Musical Is Man?* (Seattle: University of Washington Press, 1973).

3. Howard Gardner. *Frames of Mind: The Theory of Multiple Intelligences* (New York: Basic Books, 1983).

4. Donald A. Hodges and Paul Haack, "The Influence of Music on Human Behavior," in Hodges, ed., *Handbook of Music Psychology*, 2nd ed. (San Antonio, TX: IMR Press, 1966), pp. 469–555.

5. Donald A. Hodges, "Why Are We Musical? Evolutionary Plausibility for Musical Behaviors (*Bulletin of the Council for Research in Music Education* 99, 1989), pp. 7–22.

6. Donald Hodges, "Human Musicality," in D. Hodges, ed., *Handbook of Music Psychology*, 2nd ed. (San Antonio, TX: IMR Press, 1966), pp. 29–68.

7. P. Bohannon, "That Sync'ing Feeling," *Update: Applications of Research in Music Education* 2 (1); pp. 23–24. First published in *Science* 81, pp. 25–26.

8. D. Stern, "Some Interactive Functions of Rhythm Changes between Mother and Infant," in M. Davis, ed., *Interaction Rhythms: Periodicity in Communication Behavior* (New York: Human Sciences Press, 1982), pp. 101–117.

9. J. Roederer, "The Search for A Survival Value of Music," *Music Perception* 13, pp. 350–356.

10. A. Stiller, "Toward A Biology of Music," *Opus* 35 (1987), pp. 12–15.

11. Blacking.

Frances H. Rausher, Gordon L. Shaw, and Katherine N. Ky
Music and Spatial Task Performance (1993)

This research report, from the Center for the Neurobiology of Learning and Memory, University of California, Irvine, is part of the research literature that was used by advocates for music education. It is part of the body of studies that supported what the public came to think of as the "Mozart effect."

. . . . There are correlational,[1] historical,[2] and anectodal[3] relationships between music cognition and other "higher brain function," but no causal relationship has been demonstrated between music and cognition and cognitions pertaining to abstract operations such as mathematical or spatial reasoning. We performed an experiment in which students were each given three sets of standard IQ spatial reasoning tasks; each task was preceded by 10 minutes of (1) listening to Mozart's sonata for two pianos in D major, K448; (2) listening to a relaxation tape; or (3) silence. Performance was improved for those tasks immediately following the first condition compared to the second two.

Thirty-six college students participated in all three listening conditions. Immediately following each listening condition, the students' spatial reasoning skills were tested using the Stanford-Binet intelligence scale. . . . The music condition yielded a mean standard age score (SAS) of 57.56; the relaxation condition was 54.61 and the mean score for the silent condition was 54.00. To assess the impact of these scores, we "translated" them to spatial IQ scores of 119, 111, and 110, respectively. Thus, the IQs of subjects participating in the music condition were eight to nine points above their IQ scores in the other two conditions. A one-factor (listening condition) repeated measures analysis of variance (ANOVA) performed on SAS revealed that subjects performed better on the abstract/spatial reasoning tests after listening to Mozart than after listening to either the relaxation tape or to nothing. . . .

The enhancing effect of the music condition is temporal, and does not extend beyond the 10–15 minute period during which subjects were engaged in each spatial task. . . .

Notes

1. Hassler, M., Birbaumer, N. & Feil, A. *Psychol. Music* (13), 99-113 (1985).
2. Allman, G.J., *Greek Geometry from Thales to Euclid* (Arno, New York), 1976), 23.
3. Cranberg, L.D. & Albert, M.L. in *The Exceptional Brain*, eds. Obler, L.K. & Fein, D.) (Guilford, New York, 1988), 156.

Robert B. Morrison
Music Education and Areas of Improvement

Robert B. Morrison is vice president of VH1 Save the Music Foundation, a not-for-profit organization dedicated to restoring music education in public schools.

Scientific studies have proven that music participation builds brain power in children by enhancing vital intellectual skills. As a result, music participation increases a child's ability to learn basic math and reading, and students who participate in music programs score significantly higher on standardized tests while at the same time developing crucial skills to be successful in life: self discipline, teamwork, and problem solving skills. Students involved in music are also less likely to be involved in gangs, drugs, or alcohol abuse and have better attendance in school. Most importantly, students enjoy it!

Music education improves:
Early cognitive development
Basic math and reading ability
Spatial reasoning skills
SAT scores
School attendance
Ability to work in teams
Self-esteem
Self-discipline
Creativity
Knowledge of other cultures and history

John Sykes
Strategies for Low-Performing Schools and At-Risk Youth (2001)

John Sykes is president of VH1, a national music television network.

. . . Due to competing demands for time and money in our public schools, music and arts education programs have, in many communities, been eliminated over the past 30 years. The devastation to these programs has been most significant in our more urban and rural schools. One recurring theme I have found . . . in visiting schools across the country . . . is that high-performing schools, without exception, include a robust music and arts education program while low-performing schools in most instances do not.

The elimination of music programs has occurred against the backdrop of a growing body of scientific research that has been reinforcing what many of us in the music community have known all along: *Music education builds brain power*. It is a key to improving academic performance and a key to helping at-risk students and low performing schools. I won't ask you to take my word for it. Let's look at the body of evidence:

In a study released last year, second graders from a low income school in Los Angeles were given eight months of piano keyboard training, as well as timed playing with newly designed music software. The result? These students, taking the Stanford 9 Math Test, went from scoring in the 30th to the 65th percentile. These second graders were performing sixth grade math (*Neurological Research*, March 15, 1999; Gordon Shaw, Ph.D., University of California, Irvine).

A related study by a University of Wisconsin professor, Dr. Frances Rauscher, published in 1997 in the scientific journal *Neurological Research*, showed that children involved with keyboard instruction at an early age showed significantly enhanced abstract reasoning abilities, critical to success in science and complex math. After learning about this research, the Wisconsin School District of Kettle Moraine wanted to see how this concept would work in the real world. They implemented a program that replicated the Rauscher study, using kindergarten students and group piano keyboard instruction. At the end of the school year, students in classes that had received piano keyboard instruction outscored those who received no keyboard instruction by 46 percent! The program has since expanded to K through 6 students across the entire district. The critical point here is the students were not taught math using music . . . they were taught music. It was the process of learning music that helped improve their math skills (*Early Childhood Research Quarterly*, 2000).

One of the issues for at-risk youth is drug and alcohol abuse. A 1999 report released by the Texas Commission on Drugs and Alcohol Abuse found that students involved in band or orchestra (when compared against other student activities) reported the lowest lifetime and current use of all substances (alcohol, tobacco, or drugs; 1999 Texas Commission on Drug and Alcohol Abuse).

According to the College Board, students involved with music score an average of 100 points higher on SAT tests than students who not. The longer a student has been involved with music instruction, the greater the difference (College Board Survey of SAT Test Takers).

In another study, Dr. James Catterall of UCLA analyzed the school records of 25,000 students from the NELL88 Database as they moved through school. He found that students who studied music had higher grades, scored better on standardized tests, and had better attendance records. When he factored in economic status he also found that students from poorer families who studied music improved their overall school performance at the same rate or faster than all others (Dr. James Catterall, UCLA, 1997). . . .

Ellen Winner and Lois Hetland
The Arts and Academic Improvement: What the Evidence Shows (2001)

Ellen Winner and Lois Hetland are researchers at Harvard University Project Zero.

Instrumental Claims for the Arts Are Often Invoked

The arts have typically played a relatively unimportant role in American schools. Arts educators have tried to strengthen the position of the arts in our schools by arguing that the arts can be used to buttress the three Rs. The arts, they said, could help children learn to read and write and calculate and understand scientific concepts. The reasoning was clear: perhaps schools under pressure would value the arts because the arts strengthened skills in valued areas. This approach became a favored strategy in the United States for keeping the arts in schools and for making sure that every child had access to arts education.

Instrumental Claims are a Double-Edged Sword

There is a danger in such reasoning. If the arts are given a role in our schools because people believe the arts cause academic improvement, then the arts will quickly lose their position if academic improvement does not result, or if the arts are shown to be less effective than the three Rs in promoting literacy and numeracy. Instrumental claims for the arts are a double-edged sword. It is implausible to suppose that the arts can be as effective a means of teaching an academic subject as is direct teaching of that subject. And thus, when we justify the arts by their secondary, utilitarian value, the arts may prove to have fewer payoffs than academics. Arts educators should never allow the arts to be justified wholly or even primarily in terms of what the arts can do for mathematics or reading. The arts must be justified in terms of what the arts can teach that no other subject can teach.

What is the Evidence for Instrumental Claims?

What is the research base on which instrumental claims for arts education are made? REAP [Reviewing Education and the Arts Project] has conducted the first comprehensive and quantitative study of what the research on academic outcomes of arts education really shows.

Comprehensive Syntheses of 188 Reports (275 Effect Sizes)

REAP conducted a comprehensive search for all studies from 1950–1999 (published and unpublished, and appearing in English) that have tested the claim that studying the arts leads to some form of academic improvement. Searches turned up 11,467 articles, books, theses, conference presentations, technical reports, unpublished papers, and unpublished data. Irrelevant reports were then weeded out, along with advocacy pieces and program descriptions lacking an empirical test. One hundred eighty-eight reports investigating the relationship between one or more arts areas to one or more academic areas were retained. . . .

We found three areas in which clear causal links could be demonstrated. However, in seven other areas no reliable causal link was found. The lack of findings in these seven areas is attributable to one or more of three factors: in some cases the failure to find a causal link probably reflects the fact that there is in fact no causal link; in some cases a causal link was found but it was not strong enough to be reliably generalized to other studies; and in other cases, the lack of findings may have been due to the small number of studies carried out on a given research question.

Three Areas Where Reliable Causal Links Were Found
Listening to Music and Spatial–Temporal Reasoning

Based on 26 reports . . . a medium-sized causal relationship was found between listening to music and temporary improvement in spatial-temporal reasoning. However, there was wide variation in the studies, with some showing the effect clearly and many not showing the effect at all. Moreover, the existing research does not reveal conclusively *why* listening to music affects spatial-temporary thinking. For education, such a finding has little importance, since it is temporary and not consistently found. Scientifically, however, this finding is of interest because it suggests that music and spatial reasoning are related psychologically and perhaps neurologically as well. Further research is needed to understand the mechanism by which certain types of music influence spatial skills.

Learning to Play Music and Spatial Reasoning

Based on 19 reports . . . a large causal relationship was found between learning to make music and spatial-temporal reasoning. The effect was greater when standard music notation was learned as well, but even without notation the effect was large. The value for education is greater here, since the effect works equally for both general and at risk populations, costs little since it is based on standard music curricula, and influences many students (69 of every 100, 3- to 12-year-old students). Of course we must still determine the value of improved spatial skills for success in school. Spatial skills might or might not be of benefit to students, depending on how subjects are taught. For example, mathematics or geography might be taught spatially, and if they are, then students with strong spatial abilities should have an advantage in these subjects. Sadly, many schools offer few chances to apply spatial abilities.

Classroom Drama and Verbal Skills

Based on 80 reports . . . a causal link was found between classroom drama (enacting texts) and a variety of verbal areas. Most were of medium size (oral understanding/recall of stories, reading readiness, reading achievement, oral language, writing), one was large (written understanding/recall of stories), and one was small and could not be generalized to new studies (vocabulary). In all cases, students who enacted texts were compared to students who read the same texts but did not enact them. Drama not only helped children's verbal skills with respect to the texts enacted; it also helped children's verbal skills when applied to new, non-enacted texts. Thus, drama helps to build verbal skills that transfer to new materials. Such an effect has great value for education: verbal skill is highly valued, adding such drama techniques costs little in terms of effort or expense, and a high proportion of students are influenced by such curricular changes.

Seven Areas Where No Reliable Causal Links were Found

Arts-Rich Education and Verbal and Mathematics Scores/Grades

Based on 31 reports, a small to medium correlation was found between studying the arts and academic achievement as measured primarily by test scores. However, *no* evidence was found that studying the arts *causes* academic indicators to improve. The correlational findings can be explained by non-causal mechanisms. For example, high-achieving students (no matter

Ellen Winner and Lois Hetland

what their ethnic or racial group, no matter what their social class) may choose or be guided to study the arts. This would then result in the finding that students who take arts courses are also high-achieving, hi test-scoring students.

Arts-Rich Education and Creative Thinking

Based on four reports, no relationship was found between studying arts and verbal creativity test measures. A small- to medium-sized relationship was found between studying arts and figural creativity tests (which themselves are visual tests) but this relationship could not be generalized to new studies.

Learning to Play Music and Mathematics

Based on six reports, a small causal relationship was found between music training and math. However, while three of these studies produced medium effects, three produced either very small effects or none at all. Thus, more studies are needed before any firm conclusions can be drawn.

Learning to Pay Music and Reading

Based on six reports, a small relationship was found between music and reading but this relationship could not be generalized to new studies.

Visual Arts and Reading

Based on five reports in which visual arts was taught separately from reading, a very small relationship between visual arts and reading was found, but this relationship could not be generalized to new studies. This effect was entirely due to reading readiness outcomes (which are themselves visual), and did not hold up for reading achievement outcomes. Based on four reports in which visual arts were integrated with reading instruction, a medium-sized relationship was found between integrated arts/reading instruction and reading outcomes. However, this result could not be generalized to new studies.

Dance and Reading

Based on four reports, a small relationship between dance and reading was found, but this relationship could not be generalized to new studies.

Dance and Nonverbal Reasoning

Based on three reports, a small- to medium-sized causal relationship was found between dance and improved visual–spatial skills. The value of this effect is unclear, since it is based on so few reports.

Policy Implications

These mixed findings should make it clear that, even in cases where arts programs add value to non-arts academic outcomes, it is dangerous to *justify* arts education by secondary, non-arts effects. Doing so puts the arts in a weakened and vulnerable position. Arts educators must build justifications based on what is inherently valuable about the arts themselves, even when the arts contribute secondary benefits. Just as we do not (and could not) justify the teaching of history for its power to transfer to mathematics, we must not allow policy makers to justify (or reject) the arts based on their alleged power to transfer to academic subject matters.

A Better Justification for the Arts in Education

Let's stop requiring more of the arts than of other subjects. The arts are the only school subjects that have been challenged to demonstrate transfer as a justification for their usefulness. If we required physical education to demonstrate transfer to science, the results might be no better, and probably would be worse. So, it is notable that the arts can demonstrate any transfer at all. Perhaps with more attention to *how* the arts foster transfer, we can understand how to exploit that capacity further. But even when the relationships are understood, we still maintain that the justification for arts programs must be based on their inherent merit.

Let's stop justifying the arts instrumentally. This is a dangerous (and peculiarly American) practice. Anyone who looks closely, as we have done, will see that these claims do not hold up unequivocally. Those who live by instrumental claims risk dying by such claims.

The arts offer a way of thinking unavailable in other disciplines. The same might be said of athletics. Suppose coaches began to claim that playing baseball increased students' mathematical ability because of the complex score keeping involved. Then suppose researchers set out to test this and found that the claim did not hold up. Would school boards react by cutting the budget for baseball? Of course not. Because whatever positive academic side effects baseball might or might not have, schools believe sports are inherently good for kids. We should make the same argument for the arts: the arts are good for our children, irrespective of any non-arts benefits that the arts may in some cases have. Just as a well-rounded education requires education of the body through physical education, a balanced education requires study of the arts.

Let's bet on history. Of course, we do not know for sure what is the best education for children to ensure that they will grow up to lead productive and happy lives. But the arts have been around longer than the sciences; cultures are judged on the basis of their arts; and most cultures and most historical eras have not doubted the importance of studying the arts. Let's assume, then, that the arts should be a part of every child's education and treat the arts as seriously as we treat mathematics or reading or history or biology. Let's remember why societies have always included the arts in every child's education. The reason is simple. The arts are a fundamentally important part of culture, and an education without them is an impoverished education leading to an impoverished society. Studying the arts should not have to be justified in terms of anything else. The arts are as important as the sciences: they are time-honored ways of learning, knowing, and expressing.

Where Should Researchers Go from Here?

Researchers should try to make sense of the claim frequently made by schools that when the arts are given a serious role in the curriculum, academic achievement improves. While we should never justify the arts on non-arts outcomes, we believe there is value to the search for such links. Researchers should continue to look for, try out, and specify whether—and if so, how—the arts can serve as vehicles for transfer. Educators could then exploit this relationship.

We recommend two kinds of studies to advance our understanding of the relationship between arts and non-arts outcomes: theory-building studies and theory-driven experiments. Both types require rigorous methods. Here is an example of each type.

A Theory-Building Study: What Happens in Schools When the Arts are Given a Prominent Role?

Our research shows that studying the arts does not, in and of itself, lead to improved test scores. Yet schools with strong arts often report a rise in test scores. Why? One possibility is that the same schools that treat the arts seriously institute other kinds of innovations that are favorable to academic learning. For instance, these schools may become more inquiry-oriented, more project-based, more demanding of high standards, and more focused on processes that lead to excellence. Educators and policy makers need to understand what comes along with the arts.

To discover this, researchers need to carry out ethnographic studies of exemplary schools that grant the arts a serious role in the curriculum. What kinds of innovations have been made in these schools to foster excellence? If certain innovations are always found in schools that grant the arts a serious role, this finding could account for why schools with serious arts programs have high academic performance.

A Theory-Drive Experiment: Are the Arts Motivational Entry Points for Non-Academic Students?

While we oppose justifying the arts based on their secondary effects, there may well be educational value in programs that integrate the arts as vehicles that foster understanding of non-arts content. Perhaps the arts *do* cause academic achievement, but only for a certain type of student, and only when the arts are integrated with an academic subject. In schools that make the arts important, academic subjects are often taught "through" the arts.

The arts are used as entry points into academic subjects (e.g., role-playing history courses; analysis of rhythms in a proportions unit in mathematics). Perhaps certain students—those lacking academic interests or strengths in specific subjects—benefit. If these students experience success in the art form linked to the academic subject, they may then believe they can succeed in the academic subject. Or, if they experience success in the subject when it is viewed through an artistic lens, their willingness to stay with the subject may increase. Increased confidence should lead to increased motivation and effort, which in turn should result in higher achievement.

Experimental studies thus far have not tested this hypothesis. What is needed are comparisons of academically strong versus academically at-risk students taught the same subject matter with and without the arts as entry points. Can we identify students who first experience success in the art form, and subsequently go on to show heightened interest and effort in the academic subject matter? And do levels of interest and/or motivation predict later achievement in that subject matter?

It is also possible that all students would benefit from an arts-integrated approach, even those who are high achievers to begin with, simply because an arts-integrated approach makes any subject more interesting. This hypothesis also deserves a rigorous test.

Research in the two directions suggested here can help us to understand the puzzling finding that when the arts are granted a serious role in our schools, academic achievement often rises. It is time to look seriously at the possibility that the arts are associated with academic achievement because of other academic innovations that are made in schools that bring in the arts, and/or because the arts provide engaging and motivational entry points into academic study for the many students who do not thrive in the structures and cultures of our schools today.

Bennett Reimer
Facing the Risks of the "Mozart Effect" (1999)

Reconciling Musical and Other Purposes

The spatial-temporal argument for the value of music study is perhaps the most extreme that the music education profession has ever faced. My analysis of this argument's logical consequences responds directly to its challenge. This forthright response is necessary, given the enormous promotion the "Mozart effect" has received and its imminent potential to force music education over the line that separates its devotion to musical learning, which the National Standards exemplify, and associated learning, which, rather than being comfortably assimilated within the Standards, becomes a replacement for them. It is very tempting for music educators, constantly in the position of having to justify the need for their subject in the schools, to regard a rationale such as improved spatial-temporal reasoning as a gift handed to them on a silver platter. But such a gift . . . is intended to serve only the purpose of the giver, not the receiver. There will be potentially destructive effects if the gift is accepted without a thorough examination of the consequences of accepting it.

How can this unexpected, widely acclaimed benefit of music study be accepted without having it overwhelm musical values? Since the days of the singing school, the music education profession has managed to protect the primary purpose of music study from undue dominance by associated purposes. I would suggest that it can continue to achieve a proper balance through the following two responses.

First of all, music educators must not be rigid about their primary purpose of helping students better create and share the meanings and feelings that only music provides; they need not fear that this purpose is in danger of breaking apart when other interests are also accommodated. A purist, formalistic stance is not possible or desirable in the complex world in which music and music education exists. Music educators can recognize and even call attention to the many diverse benefits that music study offers without giving the impression, by their arguments or educational practices, that such benefits should ever threaten to replace their fundamental mission. By focusing on musical learning goals as stipulated in the Standards and graciously including a variety of purposes reflecting other interests, the profession can both protect the integrity of its musical responsibilities and comfortably serve a variety of associated values.

The key factor in maintaining an acceptable balance is the degree to which the program of musical learning is altered in order to serve other purposes. . . . This kind of dangerous capitulation to other demands can best be deflected by agreeing that music study, such as we music education professionals are obliged to offer, can indeed make such contributions. We are happy that it has such positive effects, and as we go about fulfilling our musical teaching responsibilities, we will be sensitive to and supportive of all the many positive ways in which music study and experience can enhance people's lives.

Second, music educators must continue to learn about, apply, and conscientiously promote the benefits of involvements that are particular to music. As mentioned previously, work in cognitive science has clarified the fact that human knowing and intelligence are multifaceted and that various musical involvements provide opportunities to operate at the highest levels of cognition that humans are capable of—to understand, to create, and to share meanings as only music allows people to do and to exercise the intelligence particular and dependent on each musical role. We have learned that musical doing, thinking, and feeling are essential ways in which humans make contact with, internalize, express, critique, and influence their cultural contexts. We know that musical teachings such as the Standards delineate are necessary if humans are to fully benefit from the opportunities and challenges their innate human capacities and their culture afford them. Such realizations deepen and strengthen the basis for musical learnings as an essential component of education more securely, more convincingly, and more realistically than any others. Our expanding understandings of human knowledge, emotion, expression, and intelligence have solidified the essentiality of music to the human condition. The dog is very healthy. The obligation of the music education profession remains now, as in the past, to keep it so, and to be pleased that it wags its tail, as well.

School Music Program Development

M usic educators, aware that they had to adjust their programs to continue serving a fast-changing society, found direction from many sources. The most potent were general education reform, the civil rights revolution, and the increasing impact of technology on education. Intellectual influences like aesthetic education, the Yale Seminar, and the Tanglewood Symposium helped guide music education, and the adoption of new musics (jazz, popular, folk, ethnic, and others) created a new face for the music education profession—one that looked equally favorably on the music of all cultures.

Yale Seminar on Music Education
Music in Our Schools: A Search for Improvement

The Yale Seminar on Music Education was held at Yale University, from June 17–28, 1963, to identify and examine the problems facing music education. The participants, thirty-one musicians, scholars, and teachers, identified music materials and music performance as primary areas needing improvement. The Seminar did not officially involve MENC [the Music Educators National Conference], and its criticism of the music education profession was a factor in the establishment of the Tanglewood Symposium in 1967.

Musicality

The development of musicality is the primary aim of music education from kindergarten through the 12th grade. It can be accomplished through vocal and instrumental performance; bodily movement in response to music; vocal and instrumental creation, both improvised and written down; and attentive listening and ear training. Creative activities were particularly encouraged by the Seminar participants as a sure means of developing musicality, teaching reading, and stimulating interest in learning. Pupils should perform their own and each other's compositions. The best possible performance should always be expected, and no sloppiness of thinking or action tolerated. From the first grade on, all music teaching should be in the hands of teachers trained in music.

Repertory

The present repertory of school music should be brought in line with contemporary composition and advances in musicology, while being strengthened also in its coverage of the standard concert literature. It should be more representative than it is, not only of our Western musical heritage at its best, but also of jazz and folk music, and of non-Western cultures. Children's potential is constantly underestimated in present educational collections and recordings. Too much of the school repertory now consists of counterfeited and synthetic, rather than genuine, folk and art products. A conscientious and systematic search for authentic sources of suitable repertory is needed. The renewed repertory must be made available in easily accessible forms, such as collections of performing material, special series of recordings, and packages or kits with contents that include teachers' and students' manuals and audiovisual aids.

Music as a Literature

Guided listening as a means to understanding and acquaintance with the monuments of music literature, past and present, deserves a larger place than it occupies today in the elementary and secondary schools. A continuous sequence of graded listening experiences belongs in a balanced elementary and junior high school curriculum. Beyond this, every high school should offer courses in music literature in which the student is given intensive experience with a limited number of representative works. The goal should be to equip the student to listen with understanding to a wide variety of musical genres. A greater emphasis on theoretical and historical studies in teacher-training programs would be needed to support such a curriculum.

Performing Activities

A balanced program of activities should be available in each junior and senior high school. The ensembles most worthy of support are those possessing an authentic, wide-ranging repertory of the highest musical quality, such as the symphony, string, and chamber orchestras; the concert band; and choruses of all sizes. Activities such as the marching band and the "stage," or dance, band are not to be discouraged, since they can lead students to greater participation, but they should not be ends in themselves. Smaller ensembles should be particularly encouraged because they permit greater individual initiative and more intense participation, and are more relevant to later amateur activity. Instruction in vocal and instrumental performance should not neglect keyboard instruments, and should be available free of charge as a regular curricular offering. Such instruction should always be supplemented with classes in basic musicianship and theory, and in the repertory of the instrument as a literature.

Courses for Advance Students

Courses in theory and literature beyond those offered to the average student should be available to those sufficiently advanced musically. Courses in theory should be exploratory, and should lead through the pupil's own discovery of the materials of sound to a gradual understanding of musical resources and their possibilities for composition. Courses in literature should avoid functioning as surveys; rather, they should concentrate on illumination of a few musical works through close analysis and study of other historically and functionally related music.

Musicians in Residence

To combat a growing alienation of the music profession from American life and education, a program of bringing musicians, composers, and scholars into the schools in teaching and nonteaching capacities was recommended. Such a program would provide for (1) performers and conductors in residence; (2) composers and scholars in residence; (3) visits by touring concert artists; and (4) contributions from musicians living in the community. Mutual benefits would be gained from bringing together school youth and practitioners in a stable relationship. To the students it would give an understanding of how a musical artist, a composer, or a scholar thinks and works, To the successful practitioner it would give a share in cultivating musically sensitive audiences and fresh talents. The frequent contact these programs would promote would give the schools a continuing link to contemporary developments in the world of music at large.

Community Resources

Relaxing the certification requirements or otherwise permitting seasoned musicians living in the community to teach in the schools would open a new source of highly qualified music personnel. With timely and appropriate coordination, community-centered ensembles, orchestras, and similar performing groups can contribute much to curricular activities. Community lending libraries of performance and basic research materials should be expanded or founded to bolster school repertories and resources.

National Resources

Opportunities for advanced music study are now available in many metropolitan centers, but not in less populated regions. Several suggested means of making these opportunities more widely available were the creation of regional cadres of skilled teachers; a chain of national or state academies of music, drama, and dance; high schools of performing arts in all large cities; and educational adjuncts to community arts centers.

Audiovisual Aids

Technological advances have created opportunities for audiovisual aids that music teachers have not begun to realize. The successful exploitation of such aids depends ultimately on good teaching, which they cannot replace, and upon their careful preparation by teams of musicians, teachers, and technicians. Although the film sound track is generally poor in fidelity, films are an excellent means to illustrate particular techniques, music in ancient and distant cultures, or such media as opera or ballet that might otherwise be inaccessible. Besides being an excellent means of self-appraisal, tape recording is ideal for programs of self-instruction and for capturing improvisation; it is also a useful aid to composition. Phonograph records would present an immediate means of widening the school reportory if prices could be reduced—perhaps through a national plan of procurement. Television, like film, is handicapped by poor sound reproduction, but under expert control this medium can be of great assistance to the teacher, both in his own training and in the classroom. Radio seems valuable mainly for out-of-school stimulation and for reinforcement of what goes on in school. Because of the technical aspects of audiovisual aids and the need for a considerable amount of expensive equipment, research and development in this field could best be accomplished by a centralized agency; for this reason it was suggested that a national research institute be founded for the development of audiovisual aids for music education.

Teacher Training and Retraining

Essential to the success of a curriculum revision like the one implied in the Seminar's recommendations is an extensive scheme of teacher education. Training in music should be given to teachers who are not musicians, training in teaching to musicians who are not teachers, and retraining in music to teachers now teaching music. Institutes at universities supplied with special facilities and manned by specialized personnel were the means recommended for introducing new curriculum content; regional workshops were suggested as a way of stimulating rebuilding of the repertory. In addition, undergraduate and graduate programs of teacher training should be reexamined in light of the broadened understanding of music and the increased mastery of technique that will be needed by teachers to meet the greater emphasis on creativity and literature.

The College Board
Academic Preparation for College:
What Students Need to Know and Be Able to Do

This report is a part of the College Board Educational Quality Project, a long-term effort to improve the academic quality of secondary education and to assure that all students have equal opportunities for postsecondary education. It identified English, the arts, mathematics, science, social studies, and foreign languages as the basic subjects.

. . . WHY? The arts—visual arts, theater, music, and dance—challenge and extend human experience. They provide means of expression that go beyond ordinary speaking and writing. They can express intimate thoughts and feelings. They are a unique record of diverse cultures and how these cultures have developed over time. They provide distinctive ways of understanding human beings and nature. The arts are creative modes by which all people can enrich their lives both by self-expression and response to the expressions of others.

Works of art often involve subtle meanings and complex systems of expression. Fully appreciating such works requires the careful reasoning and sustained study that lead to informed insight. Moreover, just as thorough understanding of science requires laboratory or field work, so fully understanding the arts involves first-hand work in them.

Preparation in the arts will be valuable to college entrants whatever their intended field of study. The actual practice of the arts can engage the imagination, foster flexible ways of thinking, develop disciplined effort, and build self-confidence. Appreciation of the arts is integral to the understanding of other cultures sought in the study of history, foreign language, and social sciences. Preparation in the arts will also enable college students to engage in and profit from advanced study, performance, and studio work in the arts. For some, such college-level work will lead to careers in the arts. For many others, it will permanently enhance the quality of their lives, whether they continue artistic activity as an avocation or appreciation of the arts as observers and members of audiences.

WHAT? If the preparation of college entrants is in music, they will need the following knowledge and skills:

- The ability to identify and describe—using the appropriate vocabulary—various musical forms from different historical periods
- The ability to listen perceptively to music, distinguishing such elements as pitch, rhythm, timbre, and dynamics
- The ability to read music
- The ability to evaluate a musical work or performance
- To know how to express themselves by playing an instrument, singing in a group or individually, or composing music . . .

The Tanglewood Symposium
A Philosophy of the Arts for an Emerging Society

The Tanglewood Symposium, held in the summer of 1967, was sponsored by the Music Educators National Conference, the Berkshire Music Center, the Theodore Presser Foundation, and Boston University. Its purpose was to consider the role of music in American society during a time of rapid social, economic, and cultural change, and to make recommendations to improve the effectiveness of music education.

. . . 1. We look upon a vast body of social change, as do many in other disciplines, and see enormous upheavals in every phase of life. These changes occur in objective aspects, such as greater abundance in goods, faster travel, quicker communications, more services, decaying cities, civil strife, large-scale cybernated economic production, growing government, and continual international tensions.

2. Perhaps more than in some other fields, leaders in education and in the arts see in these changes the even more disturbing impact on personal and social values, described in such terms as anomie, rootlessness, killing time, waist-high culture, alienation, anonymity, and a whole range of emotional illnesses. Many observers are more deeply concerned with the strengthening of human dignity, love, and self-realization that with the mere accumulation of goods, speed of travel, or televisions sets. They are especially concerned with the strengthening of family ties and the quality of living that would characterize them.

3. In addition to these positive *concerns*, there are elements in the current order of change that can be used to utilize change in support of constructive *values*.

4. Among those means that provide transition to new human conditions are the arts, which reflect positive values, for they are deeply rooted in human needs, in man's nature, in all of his history, and even in his new, post-industrial technology. For example, access has been provided to a broad range of recorded music for almost everyone. Quantitative evidence abounds everywhere of concerts in halls, schools, clubs, parks, and community centers. Qualitative criteria are more subjective and, therefore, the quality of much that is presented may be debatable.

5. It is incumbent upon music educators to bring higher quality into new and familiar contents of quality, by developing audiences as well as performers—audiences that extend far beyond the school, that touch all age groups and all segments of the community.

6. This enlarged commitment of music education comes at a period in American life when there is an increased need to prepare us for more leisure

time. There is a clear need for education, at all levels, to approach music as one major prototype value for leisure alternatives.

7. Thus the statement of "values" that becomes a foundation for articulation and implementing musical experience in the school is increasingly germane and significant for *all* ages, and most especially in an era of revolutionary change. These values, spelled out early in the report, must be grounded on what Northrop calls the "immediately apprehended" as well as the objective or "inferred" meanings. As this eminent philosopher calls for a synthesis between these on the broadest panorama of world cultures in his *Meeting of East and West,* so this duality is dynamic for purposes in music education, and calls equally for a new, conscious synthesis.

8. The emerging world of new social tools, institutions, and sources of power is paralleled in emerging musical forms; and indeed, some of the"new music" is as much a manifestation of intergenerational breakdown of communications as it is of radical sounds per se. Thus, there is need for new aesthetics, or at least a reappraisal of familiar aesthetics, to confront and understand music that now emanates from new technology; there is also need for a close inquiry into the place of musical styles and fads in the value systems of young people. Altogether, music educators must take clear positions about temporary music, characterized by this double-headed fact of life among youth.

9. The reconstruction of schools at all levels is a movement that relates directly from new technology, urban growth, and other external societal changes; but also, from better understanding of young people, theories of learning methods of teacher preparation, and rapport of philosophy and of social sciences with education. It is now incumbent on music education to examine in depth how its characteristic purposes and its inherent nature as an art can best contribute to new educational directions. On the other hand, music and the arts are not only uniquely *creative,* and thus grounded in constant self-change and creative exploration; they are also *preservative* and are, symbolically, direct links with the past. Change may have value for the sake of change, but primarily in a situation of boredom or satiety. Tradition also has value in itself, but primarily in a situation of complacency. What is needed are new formulations or pragmatic directions that recognize continuities and ongoing human and social needs, as well as new, even disturbing tendencies that are irrevocable, provocative, and hopefully significant.

10. The reconstruction of the larger society parallels in many ways the changes close to the teacher and the student. We take the position that the school, and music education, must become more sensitive to social processes and take a more vigorous part in directing social change or in contributing to a recognition of its potentials for good.

11. Finally, we wish to assert a belief that in periods of transition, a national professional organization must itself face a re-examination of its

roles, its strengths, and its potential relationships to all of the issues of the report. . . .

I. Some Considerations Toward a Philosophy of Art in an Emerging Society

The increasing rapidity of change in modern industrial society has many implications for education in the arts but several seem of major importance. Greater productivity is increasing the incomes of the majority of American families with corresponding increase in their aspirations, not only for material goods, but also for the intangible "goods" that have heretofore been largely reserved for the most affluent. We may expect most American families to aspire to participate in the arts and to expect their children to include the arts in their education. In this sense, music education must include all or nearly all children.

New attitudes favoring research, innovation and change, combined with expanding worldwide communication, provide a climate favoring new music; new forms, new sounds (Eastern as well as Western), new musical instruments and techniques, and new contexts in which music will be performed. Music education in the future will be able to draw upon these new developments.

The range of technologies and technological devices available to schools and colleges, and a new interest in research and development of educational procedures, devices, and programs, will furnish music educators with a wider range of means for carrying on education in music.

Increased hours of non-work time, coupled with the lengthening of human life and the higher level of education of adults, will provide a background for continuing education in the arts. The hope that schooling serve only as a new beginning for a lifelong education can become more nearly a reality. Music education can be conceived as a long-term process with the period in school representing the development of interests, initial understanding, and basic skills requisite to carrying on more or less independent learning in the future.

Increasing specialization in occupations and the relative anonymity of modern life afford greater opportunities for the arts to serve in helping the individual find meaning in human life and to share with others by participating in the arts. The realization of such possibilities depends upon relevant selections of musical experiences and musical content, for they will need to lend themselves to these purposes.

The preceding comments are suggested as a general background against which more specific ideas and proposals can be considered. Another general perspective is needed relating to human values, since the arts themselves are valued by many if not most Americans, and they serve to represent and to enhance other values. . . .

Values as means and ends. In addition to the values themselves, human beings direct their behavior in various ways to attain values that are cherished. Thus, to some persons, the way to gain respect and status is to be a patron of the arts. Thus, to some persons, the way to gain respect and status is to be a patron of the arts. Their actions in supporting and attending musical performances reflect this view of art as an instrument of status. This fact has relevance in music education both to indicate objectives and to suggest such additional ways by which students may be initially involved in musical experiences. It is possible for students who enroll in music courses to be motivated initially by values other than those appropriate to music, but it is also possible to plan educational experiences in such a way that some of these students develop genuine interest in music and cherish musical values. Thus, it is important to isolate those values that derive psychologically from the experience of hearing and creating music from those values that relate musical experience sociologically to external or dependent values. Further, each of these types of values have their own criteria and distinctive implications for the teaching of music and for its place in school and society—both of which have always been dynamic factors of music.

As it will be noted in Section V of the report, both dimensions of value are related to trends in the emerging American and world society. It is not the fact that the psychological approach is related to music as an end— music in its "independent" functions—and that the sociological approach lends only to consider music in its dependent, secondary, or referential functions. Both branches of the social sources deal with this duality, for just as individual and social values are functions of each other, ends and means in music blend in the actual experience.

There is, however, a current trend (and, in this committee's judgment, a sound development) to restore some balance in the *validation* of music as an integral body of experience in the school by re-emphasizing the inherent, or aesthetic, values as an educational end.

Developing behavior that is supportive of values. In opening up the consideration of values in relation to music education, it should be clear that teaching values is not necessarily *indoctrinating* or forcing new values on students. But because the meaning of "teaching values" is often unclear, it is less ambiguous to talk about the "learning side"; that is, to consider what students can do that will help them in developing more significant values and in gaining more enjoyment from them. The following partial list will serve to illustrate what students can do in their learning that may be important in the field of values:

Participate in activities that explore values new to the student.
Try to *discover* things in these experiences that are interesting and
    meaningful.

Reflect upon past experiences to *compare, contrast.* Evaluate the things in them that are satisfying, meaningful, or disappointing.

Practice abilities and skills useful in gaining values. (For music, there are likely to be skills involved in identifying aesthetic elements, in gaining understanding of the work, or increasing sensitive apprehension of features in the work.)

Listen, respond, recall other similar or related experiences so as to *enhance* both the meaningfulness of the musical experience and the emotional responses made to it.

Relate the emotional response being made to several kinds of meaning found in the musical experience so as to *discipline* the emotional responses in relation to their meaning and their consequences.

These comments are intended to suggest the relation of values developed by individuals to the dominant values of a society, a culture, or a subculture within that society. From the point of view of educators, their efforts are to assist the individual in developing values that are uniquely his while at the same time they are helpful in enabling him to participate constructively in the common life of the society. *The emphasis should be to help the individual to be able to explore, identify, and develop new values throughout life—ones that help him to be more fully human. . . .*

III. Music in the School

"She Walks in Beauty." If a justification must be constructed for music either as a performing art or an aesthetic experience in the curriculum of American education, it can be done on the basis of postulates regarding the nature of a school, the nature of man, and the relation of music to both:

Schools exist to pass on the cultural heritage of their society. Music is a part of that heritage. Music belongs in the curriculum.

The nature of man demands certain cultural and aesthetic outlets and some means of creative and re-creative expression. Music from earliest history, and apparently in all times and places, has been a major means of experiencing both sensuous-emotional and intellectual-aesthetic feelings and a means of expressing "thoughts that lie too deep for words."

The nature of music is infinite variety and adaptability—qualities assured by the almost limitless scope of sounds audible, malleable, or recognizable, by man.

Thus, if one asks why music should, *nay must*, be part of formal education, if we accept the postulates, then one says that as a subject of study or inquiry: 1) Music belongs with the social and cultural heritage, 2) music is profoundly related to the nature and the man, and 3) music is in itself, by its nature, and by reason of its extraordinary fluidity and plasticity, one of the great challenges to the mind and spirit. Like the arts generally, its province is as wide as the world of man and as deep as the heart of man. . . .

The basic question for the future of music in America is how well prepared the music teacher will be, and how well supported by inner and external strengths. Will tomorrow's music teacher be prepared—that is, not merely *trained* but emotionally and intellectually ready to meet challenges such as:

1. A radically changed society, both in physical terms and in its value system.
2. A radically free state of the art of music.
3. A radically different kind of teaching and performing equipment, including the lavish gifts of technology and sophistication.
4. Students with more musical sophistication as in every other way, by reason of the electronic revolution and the impact of mass media. . . .

The emerging society and purpose in lifelong education. As an educator approaches the task of setting policy for his area of education, he accepts a certain view of the contemporary culture and points his subject area to it. This is particularly so when considering the adult, for he is deep in the affairs of the world. Thus, in deciding what part music should play in education, we begin with one or all of the following characterizations of the contemporary (and emerging) culture, indicating in broad outlines the new demands on education the characterization reveals. One may characterize the contemporary society in a number of ways. Three characterizations seem fruitful and valid:

1) This is an age of science and technology. While the development of science promises a vast number of additional improvements in the life of man, it has challenged man's inner image of himself. Viewed scientifically (mechanistically), man seems in his own eyes a dull creature, surrounded by and limited by machines that diminish his sense of personal worth.

The imperative for music education, as inferred from the above characterization (much oversimplified though it is), is that music, along with other arts and humanities, should be explored by educators as a possible countervailing force to the prevalent emphasis on things and abstractions, restoring a sense of subjective individuality.

2) Modern American society has also been characterized as the "affluent" society, and therefore as the leisure age, or the age of being sought, and a philosophy of leisure is likely to develop.

The imperatives flowing from this characterization of our society are that we need to bring music (and art) into the lives of people so that we help them change the style of life itself. In the affluent society, people need to find in the cultivation of music an occupation that can provide, in part or in whole, the values now derived from work: identity, commitment, a central pole for one's life.

3) Still another way in which the modern age is characterized is as the "age of anxiety." Man is unsure of his ground; he has given up the traditional safeguards against fear and loneliness (religion, rationalism, and so forth), and he has only a vague suspicion of what can comfort him. In the face of an illiberal, even anti-liberal spirit, he seeks in aesthetic experience not only pleasure but also new understanding of himself and his spiritual place in the universe.

Implications. Dealing in broad generalities and attempting no one-to-one relationship between data and implication, one may arrive at a number of inferences for content, audience, and form of music and arts education from the analysis above.

With respect to content, we might say that we must prominently include the contemporary in the curriculum. In selection of educational experiences, we ought to adopt a "now" attitude, not only preparation for the next step but with satisfaction now. But along with this "be" experience, there is need for continuity in learning what must today characterize all education, that is, aiming to go beyond formal schooling.

With respect to audience, the conclusion from the analysis of the modern world given here is that all men (young and old, bright and dull) must have access to music education. But this does not mean that all need the same opportunities, nor want the same things. A comprehensive design is needed that covers all needs, but a flexible approach that makes it possible to fit different kinds of experiences to different needs. Examples of audience groups are: teachers of music; producers and performers; listeners and "friends" of music bodies; amateur performers; and young amateur composers, retired businessmen, and disadvantaged youngsters.

A note on adult and community education. All that has been written above also applies to adult education; but a special note is necessary. First, a special premise has to be accepted: The music educator's philosophy should encompass a responsibility to the adult community in relation to two kinds of educational needs. *Remedial* education is the traditional form of adult education—the school attempts to provide an opportunity for people to "catch up." The aim is to remedy the effects of deprivation, to offer chances that were available to others in an earlier time in life. Students here include new arrivals, second-chance seekers. Education, for them, provides a place to acquire basic skills and information. Another form of education that fits under this heading is the upgrading education, catching-up, keeping-up—all "further" education (for example, professional education for teachers or producers of music).

Already observable and implied in most analyses of the future is the decline of the form of education that provides remedies in favor of a form we may call continuing education—education that provides uninterruptedly throughout life. This kind of education is mainly informal in nature. What was needed and available only to a governing aristocracy in the past is now accessible to wider sections of the population. For the present population, this education must be structured and offered formally through schools and other educational institutions. . . .

David McAllister
Curriculum Must Assume a Place at the Center of Music (1968)

The MENC [Music Educators National Conference] has become increasingly aware that the entire Music Establishment is the perpetrator as well as the victim of a hoax. Ralph Ellison has identified it best in *The Invisible Man*, where he points out that the controlling middle class in the United States does not see the lower classes and the poor among them. Such euphemisms as "the inner city" (slums), "the disadvantaged" (the poor), and "institute for living" (lunatic asylum) are linguistic evidence that the middle class is profoundly unwilling to face the invisible culture.

Most of the Establishment is unaware, or unwilling to admit, that the invisible culture has a rugged vitality of its own. When social workers and crime commissions consider the invisible culture at all, they mistake invisibility (their own inability to see) for emptiness.

In a democracy, class barriers are uncomfortable. The Establishment, seeing that its entertainments, customs, and values are not shared by everybody, makes a limited effort through the schools to impart the love of Shakespeare, T. S. Eliot, and Schubert to the poor. This endeavor is a failure because these great expressions of the cultural heritage of the Establishment have little to do with the cultural heritage of the poor. This endeavor is a hoax because in the name of communication and the elimination of class barriers we insist that only one cultural language be spoken and that the natives on the other side of the barrier do not, in fact, really have a language at all.

We of the Music Establishment believe that there must be a real communication, especially in the arts, between all sectors of a democratic society, if it is to remain healthy. The evidence of a crisis in the health of our society is clear enough. In Dorothy Maynor's words: "It would be tragic indeed if, while we are striving to weave a cloak of democracy for Vietnam and the rest of the world, the fabric of democracy were torn beyond repair right here within our own borders."

In view of these matters, we affirm that it is our duty to seek true musical communication with the great masses of our population. While we continue to develop and make available, to all who are interested, the great musics of the middle class and aristocracy, we must also learn the language of the great musical arts which we have labeled "base" because they are popular.

When we have learned that any musical expression is "music" we hope to be able to reduce the class barriers in our schools and our concert halls. The resulting enrichment of our music will, we hope, give it a new vitality at all levels, and provide a united voice that can speak, without sham, of our democratic ideals.

The Tanglewood Declaration

The intensive evaluation of the role of music in American society and education provided by the Tanglewood Symposium of philosophers, educators, scientists, labor leaders, philanthropists, social scientists, theologians, industrialists, representatives of government and foundations, music educators, and other musicians led to this declaration:

We believe that education must have as major goals the art of living, the building of personal identity, and nurturing creativity. Since the study of music can contribute much to these ends, we now call for music to be placed in the core of the school curriculum.

The arts afford a continuity with the aesthetic tradition in man's history. Music and other fine arts, largely nonverbal in nature, reach close to the social, psychological, and physiological roots of man in his search for identity and self-realization.

Educators must accept the responsibility for developing opportunities which meet man's individual needs and the needs of a society plagued by the consequences of changing values, alienation, hostility between generations, racial and international tensions, and the challenges of a new leisure.

Music educators at Tanglewood agreed that:

(1) Music serves best when its integrity as an art is maintained.
(2) Music of all periods, styles, forms, and cultures belongs in the curriculum. The musical repertory should be expanded to involve music of our time in its rich variety, including currently popular teenage music and avant-garde music, American folk music, and the music of other cultures.
(3) Schools and colleges should provide adequate time for music in programs ranging from preschool through adult or continuing education.
(4) Instruction in the arts should be a general and important part of education in the senior high school.
(5) Developments in educational technology, educational television, programmed instruction, and computer-assisted instruction should be applied to music study and research.
(6) Greater emphasis should be placed on helping the individual student to fulfill his needs, goals, and potentials.

(7) The music education profession must contribute its skills, proficiencies, and insights toward assisting in the solution of urgent social problems as in the "inner city" or other areas with culturally deprived individuals.

(8) Programs of teacher education must be expanded and improved to provide music teachers who are specially equipped to teach high school courses in the history and literature of music and courses in the humanities and related arts, as well as teachers equipped to work with the very young, with adults, with the disadvantaged, and with the emotionally disturbed.

Charles L. Gary
The Needs of Our Students (1975)

Charles L. Gary was executive secretary of the Music Educators National Conference.

For fifty years, music educators have proclaimed "Music for Every Child, Every Child for Music" through their professional organization, the Music Educators National Conference. However, many teachers, as well as principals, have focused on a narrower purpose: the highest possible performance skill to be developed in a few selected students.

Today, this limited purpose—appropriate for professionals—has little relevance to the needs of high school boys and girls in a changing society. The purpose of music education in our time is clear: to reveal to students what music can do for their lives and to offer as many opportunities for musical learning as they desire and are capable of assimilating.

Richard Colwell
Planning and Evaluation: The Evaluation Dilemma (1990)

Richard Colwell was professor of music at the University of Illinois at Urbana-Champaign, the University of Northern Colorado, Boston University, and the New England Conservatory of Music.

Music as a Unique Subject

. . . Music is unique in its bountiful materials. Quality materials, understandable by students, are almost unlimited. Much of the music that you and I would enjoy studying further is also within the comprehension of our students. Advanced study in music does not reflect the same hierarchy as does advanced study in other subjects; to be advanced does not necessarily mean that the materials is more complex. To be sure, there are some recognizable sequences in music instruction and some tasks can be organized in a a hierarchical fashion, but the pedagogical hierarchy is less clearly defined than some would have us believe. The musical learning hierarchy is organized as much from obvious to subtle as it is from simple to complex. Once a student understands a Mozart symphony, transfer of learning allows for many rich and rewarding experiences, experiences that constitute advanced study and experiences that cannot be aligned with the hierarchies in the cognitive, psychomotor, or affective taxonomies.

Music is also unique in that our traditional mode of evaluation, primarily through judging an ensemble concert, does not provide the necessary feedback to improve instruction. Knowing the score of the West German-Argentinian soccer game is not diagnostic; it does not tell the Argentines how to improve. The judging of excellence in a concert, the commendations for students and conductor (mostly for the conductor), the typical reactions to a concert, are so random—random with respect to musical selections as well as random with respect to any errors within any single selection—that no teacher, student, parent, or policy maker recognizes from such an evaluation the contribution of a systematic programme of instruction. Successful performances are attributed to the charisma, personality, and leadership qualities of the teacher. Success in music is also attributed primarily to talent. Ask any adult about the quality of his or her school music instruction; they will have no memory of a systematic curriculum. They will attribute lack of success in school music to their lack of talent, or will assign their success to having a knack for it. Success in performance and creating, whether for the student or the accomplished artist, is in all cultures attributed to musical ability and not to superior instruction.

The view of musical success as relating directly to talent contains disadvantages. Has Howard Gardner[1] helped the arts by suggesting that individuals possess multiple intelligences, one of which is musical intelligence? I think not. He has likely reinforced the idea that one either has musical intelligence or not, that instruction makes little difference, and that the school's primary role is to nourish those students with the musical capacity to excel. Exploratory music courses are also likely to suffer from promotion of the idea that these multiple, but identifiable intelligences are important to educators. The Gardner concept is important to society, but in music education the idea could eliminate exploratory experiences because it implies that administering an aptitude test can discern those students who have musical intelligence and can profit from additional instruction.

Richard Colwell

1. Howard Gardner, *Frames of Mind* (New York: Basic Books Inc., 1983).

Goals 2000
Educate America Act

The Goals 2000 Act of 1994 was the genesis of the national standards for music education.

An Act to improve learning and teaching by providing a national framework for education reform; to promote the research, consensus building, and systemic changes needed to ensure equitable educational opportunities and high levels of educational achievement for all students; to provide a framework for reauthorization of all Federal education programs; to promote the development and adoption of a voluntary national system of skill standards and certifications; and for other purposes.

Be it enacted by the Senate and House of Representatives of the United States of America in Congress assembled . . .

Sec. 2. Purpose.

(1) Promoting coherent, nationwide, systemic education reform;
(2) Improving the quality of learning and teaching in the classroom and in the workplace;
(3) Defining appropriate and coherent Federal, State, and local roles and responsibilities for education reform and lifelong learning;
(4) Establishing valid and reliable mechanisms for
  (A) Building a broad national consensus on American education reform;
  (B) Assisting in the development and certification of high-quality, internationally competitive content and student performance standards;
  (C) Assisting in the development and certification of opportunity-to-learn standards; and
  (D) Assisting in the development and certification of high-quality assessment measures that reflect the internationally competitive content and student performance standards;
(5) Supporting new initiatives at the Federal, State, local, and school levels to provide equal educational opportunity for all students to meet high academic and occupational skill standards and to succeed in the world of employment and civic participation;

(6) Providing a framework for the reauthorization of all Federal education programs by

    (A) Creating a vision of excellence and equity that will guide all Federal education and related programs;

    (B) Providing for the establishment of high-quality, internationally competitive content and student performance standards and strategies that all students will be expected to achieve;

    (C) Providing for the establishment of high-quality, internationally competitive opportunity-to-learn standards that all States, local educational agencies, and schools should achieve;

    (D) Encouraging and enabling all State educational agencies and local educational agencies to develop comprehensive improvement plans that will provide a coherent framework for the implementation of reauthorized Federal education and related programs in an integrated fashion that effectively educates all children to prepare them to participate fully as workers, parents, and citizens;

    (E) Providing resources to help individual schools, including those serving students with high needs, develop and implement comprehensive improvement plans; and

    (F) Promoting the use of technology to enable all students to achieve the National Education Goals;

(7) Stimulating the development and adoption of a voluntary national system of skill standards and certification to serve as a cornerstone of the national strategy to enhance workforce skills; and

(8) Assisting every elementary and secondary school that receives funds under this Act to actively involve parents and families in supporting the academic work of their children at home and in providing parents with skills to advocate for their children at school.

Vision 2020 Symposium
The Housewright Declaration

The Housewright Declaration is the statement of belief that summarized the Vision 2020 Symposium, presented in 2000 at Florida State University, where Wiley Housewright had been dean of the School of Music for many years. Housewright is also a former president of the Music Educators National Conference. The Vision 2020 Symposium was intended to create a vision for music education that would guide the profession for the next 20 years. It was the first such symposium sponsored by MENC since the Tanglewood Symposium of 1967.

Whenever and wherever humans have existed music has existed also. Since music occurs only when people choose to create and share it, and since they always have done so and no doubt always will, music clearly must have important value for people.

Music makes a difference in people's lives. It exalts the human spirit; it enhances the quality of life. Indeed, meaningful music activity should be experienced throughout one's life toward the goal of continuing involvement.

Music is a basic way of knowing and doing because of its own nature and because of the relationship of that nature to the human condition, including mind, body, and feeling. It is worth studying because it represents a basic mode of thought and action, and because in itself, it is one of the primary ways human beings create and share meanings. It must be studied fully to access this richness.

Societal and technological changes have an enormous impact for the future of music education. Changing demographics and increased technological advancements are inexorable and will have profound influences on the ways that music is experienced for both students and teachers.

Music educators must build on the strengths of current practice to take responsibility for charting the future of music education to insure that the best of the Western art tradition and other musical traditions are transmitted to future generations.

We agree on the following:

1. All persons, regardless of age, cultural heritage, ability, venue, or financial circumstance deserve to participate fully in the best music experiences possible.
2. The integrity of music study must be preserved. Music educators must lead the development of meaningful music instruction and experience.
3. Time must be allotted for formal music study at all levels of instruction such that a comprehensive, sequential, and standards-based program of music instruction is made available.
4. All music has a place in the curriculum. Not only does the Western art tradition need to be preserved and disseminated, music educators also need to be aware of other music that people experience and be able to integrate it into classroom music instruction.
5. Music educators need to be proficient and knowledgeable concerning technological changes and advancements and be prepared to use all appropriate tools in advancing music study while recognizing the importance of people coming together to make and share music.
6. Music educators should involve the music industry, other agencies, individuals, and music institutions in improving the quality

and quantity of music instruction. This should start within each local community by defining the appropriate role of these resources in teaching and learning.

7. The currently defined role of the music educator will expand as settings for music instruction proliferate. Professional music educators must provide a leadership role in coordinating music activities beyond the school setting to insure formal and informal curricular integration.

8. Recruiting prospective music teachers is a responsibility of many, including music educators. Potential teachers need to be drawn from diverse backgrounds, identified early, led to develop both teaching and musical abilities, and sustained through ongoing professional development. Also, alternative licensing should be explored in order to expand the number and variety of teachers available to those seeking music instruction.

9. Continuing research addressing all aspects of music activity needs to be supported including intellectual, emotional, and physical responses to music. Ancillary social results of music study also need exploration as well as specific studies to increase meaningful music listening.

10. Music making is an essential way in which learners come to know and understand music and music traditions. Music making should be broadly interpreted to be performing, composing, improvising, listening, and interpreting music notation.

11. Music educators must join with others in providing opportunities for meaningful music instruction for all people beginning at the earliest possible age and continuing throughout life.

12. Music educators must identify the barriers that impede the full actualization of any of the above and work to overcome them.

Advocacy for Music Education

The Music Educators National Conference[1] became the major player in communicating to the public and to policy makers why music education is important to society. Its advocacy efforts began in the 1960s with a new public relations program intended to inform the nation of the forthcoming 1967 Tanglewood Symposium. Print advertisements and radio and television spot announcements blanketed the country. When the international oil crisis of the early 1970s caused a severe economic decline that threatened many music programs, MENC recognized the need to focus on government relations in order to maintain funding for music programs, and since then has become extremely effective in its advocacy efforts. MENC's advocacy, from local to state to national, along with those of other arts and arts education organizations, have had a profound impact on the public's perception of music education.

Note

1. The Music Educators National Conference was renamed in 1998 as the Music Educators National Conference: The National Association for Music Education.

National Association of Secondary School Principals
The Arts in the Comprehensive High School (1962)

Youth today face two radically different forces. Schools push for excellence in all subjects. At the same time, the mass media outside the schools all too frequently focus students' attention on shallow, mediocre models of the good life. Students exercise value standards as they make independent, intellectual judgments about artistic quality in all of their experiences, For example, they identify the characteristic quality in all of their experiences. For example, they identify the characteristics of good theatre in television or motion pictures. They discriminate among the barrage of music that permeates their world. They judge design in the goods they buy and the things they produce.

All secondary-school students, therefore, need experiences in understanding music, the visual arts, the theatre arts, the industrial arts, and home economics. Otherwise they base their decisions on stereotypes and prejudices which can easily be manipulated by the mass media and by superficial shifts in fashion. Students need to learn how to exercise social responsibility in making personal and group decisions about the arts.

The Arts, Education, and Americans Panel
Coming to Our Senses:
The Significance of the Arts for American Education[1] (1977)

The Arts, Education, and Americans Panel, a corporate child of the American Council for the Arts in Education chaired by David Rockefeller, Jr., consisted of twenty-five people selected for their professional arts education experience or for their concern about the arts or about education. All were interested in the way Americans live. They came from several states and represented the arts, education, mass communications, labor, arts patronage, government, and other fields. This report was released at a time when, lacking sufficient funds for complete educational programs, schools were reducing or eliminating their arts programs.

Basics

. . . The arts are a function of life itself, and the process of making art—both creative and recreative—can give insight to all other areas of learning. The arts help people understand themselves in historical, cultural, and aesthetic terms; they provide people with broader choices about their environment and influence the way they do their work and live their lives. Since artistic expression is also truly basic to the individual's intellectual development, it must be included as a component of all education.

The following three principles underlie the fifteen recommendations which follow:

1. The fundamental goals of American education can be realized only when the arts become central to the individual's learning experience, in or out of school and at every stage of life.
2. Educators at all levels must adopt the arts as a basic component of the curriculum deserving parity with all other elements.

3. School programs in the arts should draw heavily upon all available resources in the community: the artists, the materials, the media, and the total environment—both natural and man-made.

Note

1. The Arts, Education, and Americans Panel, *Coming To Our Senses: The Significance of the Arts for American Education* (New York: McGraw-Hill, 1977), pp. 248–263.

Charles Fowler
Can We Rescue the Arts for America's Children?

Charles Fowler was a freelance author on arts education and a former editor of the *Music Educators Journal. Can We Rescue the Arts for America's Children?* was published in 1988, ten years after *Coming to Our Senses* as a follow-up report on the then current state of arts education. Fowler points out that arts education made some gains during that decade, but many weaknesses still existed.

The Rationale Then

. . . *Coming to Our Senses* (CTOS) addressed "the significance of the arts for American education" and was subtitled accordingly. At the outset of the report, the Arts, Education and Americans panel noted a contradictory trend: "On the one hand, the arts are flourishing as never before in American. society. . . . On the other hand, arts education is struggling for its life" (CTOS, 10–11). The report referred to a Harris poll indicating that a majority of the public thought school should offer more courses in the arts.[1] It then stated:

Thus, the American people do appear to believe the arts are important, but simultaneously they are hard put to reconcile that view with their conviction that the schools should concentrate on reading, writing, and arithmetic (CTOS, 54).

The best hint at an explanation for this discrepancy comes from John Goodlad. He noted in the report that, when ranking subjects according to which ones they *liked the best* students ranked the arts at the top; but when rating subjects according to which ones *are most important*, the arts placed near the bottom. The report then asked a very important question: "If arts are the things children like the best, who persuades them they are least important?" (CTOS, 52). The explanation offered is that the arts are viewed by some people as mysteriously subversive, as promoting radical thinking and life styles. The panel concluded that "we have to reassure people that there is a need for this kind of innovative thinking" (CTOS, 53).

Ten years later, this basic contradiction between the importance of the arts in society and the lack of importance accorded the arts in public education remains a pivotal difficulty, even though there is more interaction between the arts and education communities than ever before. . . .

Here we have an important distinction. The public as well as many teachers and educational administrators view the main business of schooling as essentially developing the mind and the power to reason. At the same time, they see the arts as mindless, nonacademic fare, more related to the hand than the head. They associate the arts with entertainment and play, academic subjects with the serious business of life and work. On the practical side, schooling in the minds of many parents is vocational preparation. This helps explain why the public continues to maintain one set of values for the arts in society and another for the arts in education. When it comes to the serious business of education they have other priorities. . . .

Coming to Our Senses, in a direct reference to the work of Harvard psychologist Howard Gardner, says that "the arts specialize in forms of knowledge that cannot be translated or expressed in any other way." Because the arts utilize symbols that are often nonverbal, skill is required to extract that knowledge. "The educational establishment," said Gardner, "is being derelict and delinquent if it neglects ways of knowing."[2]

At the time the report was written, the arts were generally not being taught as forms of knowledge. Dance, music, theater, and visual arts were taught as acts of production. The public and most of the people connected with schools did not view the arts as "ways of knowing." If they had made that connection, the arts would not have been considered extracurricular, nor would they have been treated peripherally. The arts were not thought of as academic, and therefore they were not accorded the status of academic subjects.

The primary rationale for arts education presented in the study was based on the contribution of the arts to the child's cognitive, affective, and psychomotor development. The report stated that the arts "can enrich and accelerate development during early childhood and every subsequent growth stage." They can "help the child move from a reflexive to a reflective human being."[3]

But in terms of constructing a rationale to support and justify their study of the arts as basic in education, the Rockefeller panel set the course for the coming decade with the fundamental viewpoint expressed in this widely quoted paragraph:

> This Panel supports the concept of "basic education," but maintains that the arts, properly taught, are basic to individual development since they more than any other subject awaken all the senses—the learning pores. We endorse a curriculum which puts "basics" first because the arts are basic, right at the heart of the matter. And we suggest not that reading be replaced by art but that the concept of literacy be expanded beyond word skills.[4]

The report went on to say that the arts "provide unique ways of knowing about the world and should be central to learning for this reason alone." Looking back from the perspective of a decade, this view, if not persuasive, was prognostic. It represented a view that would flower in the years ahead into a full-blown, well-substantiated, and well-articulated rationale for the arts in education.

The Rationale Now

It was no coincidence that at the same time as the public's back-to-basics thrust was overtaking and overturning some arts programs, a new and more compelling rationale was in the making. Call it an act of self-survival. A disparate group of educational philosophers, art educators, cognitive psychologists, and other proponents of arts education were reanalyzing the function of the arts and their role in human civilization in the full glare of the aims of American schooling.

Today, this new rationale justifies a far more important role for the arts in education. Increasingly during the past decade, the arts have been promulgated as systems of meaning, as living histories of eras and peoples, and as records and revelations of the human spirit. The arts may well be the most telling imprints of any civilization. For this reason, some prominent educators are viewing the arts as symbol systems that are equal in importance to the symbol systems of science and mathematics.

Human beings are unique among all forms of life because we capture our experience through symbols. Ernest L. Boyer, president of the Carnegie Foundation for the Improvement of Teaching and a former U.S. commissioner of education, reminds us that "the *quality* of a civilization can be measured by the *breadth* of its symbol systems." Only a variety of such systems permits knowledge of every possible kind to be formulated so that it can be conveyed to others. Symbol systems function as both a means to express understandings and to acquire them. They are ways to cast our own perceptions and to encounter the perceptions of others. The symbol systems of the arts permit us to give representation to our ideas, concepts, and feelings in a variety of forms that are understandable and can be "read" by other people.

U.S. Secretary of Education William J. Bennett says, "Great souls do not express themselves by the written work only; they also paint, sculpt, build, and compose." To this we should add dance, act, and sing, for the arts encompass a broad range of expressive media. Bennett goes on to say that an educated person should be able not only to recognize artistic works, but also "to understand why they embody the best in our culture."[5] In a similar vein, Maryland Superintendent of Schools David W. Hornbeck recognizes that the arts constitute one of the main means by which humans communicate. He says:

> One role, if not the central one, of schooling is the development of communication skills. If we are to meet that challenge, we must stretch beyond the traditional spoken and written word. Human feeling and emotion as well as ideas are frequently more forcefully and accurately portrayed through the arts.[6]

In this way of thinking, literacy should not—must not—be limited to the written word. It should also encompass the symbol systems we call the fine arts. Like verbal, mathematical, and scientific symbols, the symbol systems of the arts were invented to enable us to react to the world, to analyze it, and to record our impressions so that they can be shared. If our concept of literacy is defined too narrowly as referring just to the symbol systems of language, mathematics, and science, children will not be equipped with the breadth of symbolic tools they need to represent, express, and communicate the full spectrum of human life. . . .

Science is not the sole conveyance of truth. If humans are to survive, we need all the symbolic forms at our command because they permit us not only to preserve and pass along our accumulated wisdom but also to give voice to the invention of new visions. We need all these ways of viewing the world because no one way can say it all. As Elliot W. Eisner, professor of education and art at Stanford University, reminds us, we need them because "the apotheoses of human achievement have been couched in such forms."[7]

The arts are *acts of intelligence* no less than other subjects. They are forms of cognition every bit as potent as words and scientific symbols. In his study of brain-damaged people, Howard Gardner observed that humans have at least seven basic intelligences that are located in different areas of the brain and operate independently: (1) *linguistic* (the art of creative writing), (2) *musical* (the art of music), (3) *logical-mathematical*, (4) *spatial* (visual arts), (5) *bodily-kinesthetic* (dance), and (6) and (7) the *personal intelligences*—knowledge of self and knowledge of others (theater).[8] He points out that the arts relate directly to six out of seven. Clearly, when we talk about the development of intelligence and the realization of human potential, the arts must be given careful consideration and special attention. While Gardner observes that in today's schools, generally, "spatial, bodily-kinesthetic, and musical forms of knowing will have only an incidental or an optional status,"[9] he acknowledges that

> among those observers partial to spatial, bodily, or musical forms of knowing, as well as those who favor a focus on the interpersonal aspects of living, an inclination to indict contemporary schooling is understandable. The modern secular school has simply—though it need not have— neglected these aspects of intellectual competence.[10]

American schools have systematically devalued certain forms of intelligence in the process of favoring others, thereby *delimiting* the intelligences of students rather than exploring and nurturing all of them. And what are the consequences of this neglect? Gardner says:

> Mastery of different literacies—for example, reading musical *scores*, mathematical proofs, or intricate diagrams—exposes one to once-inaccessible bodies of knowledge and allows one to contribute new knowledge within these traditions.[11]

To be denied the opportunity to develop these various intelligences is a form of mental *deprivation*.

According to Gardner, our intellectual competencies can serve both "as means and as message." For the child who learns to play a musical instrument, musical intelligence becomes a means of transmitting knowledge of music and what music conveys. But musical intelligence opens those doors only if it is exercised. The processes involved in "reading" the arts and deriving meaning from them cannot be taken for granted. The artistic brain—and we all have the physical mechanism—must be educated if it is to function effectively. If education is the means by which each individual realizes his or her inherent potential, then every student should have the opportunity to develop and use all the forms of intelligence. Why should we fix limits on learning?

This view of the arts as forms of human cognition and as systems of meaning important for all students has already begun to have an effect on the curriculum. Cultural literacy is emerging as a fundamental goal of arts education. Accordingly, students should be given the study necessary to assure familiarity with all of a culture's basic symbol systems, the arts included. New entrance requirements in some colleges and universities and new requirements for graduation in some states recognize the need for, and the value of, knowledge and understanding of the arts.

This way of viewing the arts places them squarely within the academic, cognitive priority of American schooling. But this philosophical view must be translated into practice. If the arts do enlighten, then they must be taught so that they enlighten. If they are to become an important part of the serious business we call education, they must be taught as disciplines that develop skill *and* knowledge. Knowledge of the arts must encompass not just the acquisition of facts, but an understanding of how the arts relate to human feeling, intuition, and creativity, areas of focus that are unique to study in the arts. In this view, the arts are "languages" that open vast doors to the stored wisdom of the ages. They serve as vehicles to engage the mind and the imagination with the inner and outer worlds of each person's existence.

This new rationale for the arts brings the field to the precipice. The arts will either be permitted into the club or, much as they are today in many schools, left to muddle along on the sidelines. Logic dictates that they be given more attention and that they be accorded their fair share of resources. But logic is not always the harbinger of change in American education.

A Catastrophe in the Making

It is no happenstance that this rationale—perhaps the most compelling ever formulated—emerged during a decade when arts education programs faced some of their darkest threats. Impending disaster motivates the genius to survive. The arts, which include but are not limited to creative writing, dance, media, music, theater, and visual arts, are a neglected resource in American elementary and secondary education. Their possible significance in the education of America's youth is largely unrecognized, often ignored, generally underrated. Access to this vast treasury of American and world culture is denied to many American children with the result that their education is incomplete, their minds less enlightened, their lives less enlivened. In this educational deprivation, American culture itself is slighted, and whole generations of American youth are permitted to grow up largely unaware of the heritage of human achievement that the arts represent. . . .

In Conclusion

We are on the forefront of turning America's surge of interest in the arts into firm policies to guide the nation's school systems. America's children— all 40 million of them in the public schools—should be able to grow up to participate fully in their culture. As it is now, the arts are a neglected heritage in too many American schools. By and large, America's children are impoverished. That is a national disgrace. Can we persuade those who control the school system of their wrong-headedness ? Can we mobilize the resources ? Can we find the way?

Charles Fowler

Given the fact that large numbers of the youth of future generations are growing up today in urban school systems in which the arts are sorely disregarded, even spurned, the prospects for the arts in American society tomorrow are bleak. If we are not to despair for our culture, present alarms must be translated into redefinitions of what constitutes a great civilization, a fine education, and the good life. We can no longer permit our schools to sell out to the goal of mere employability, our businesses to aspire only to what is expedient, our culture to be satisfied with just the easy and the sensational.

The arts are short-changed in many schools today. The consequences are many children whose possibilities are squandered and whose insights are impeded. But worse, the sheer numbers of these future citizens and their personal barrenness confronts us with prospects of a diminishing cultural future. *Coming to Our Senses* presented us with the alternative to enter the mind through the human sensorium—our capacity to hear, to see, to move, to say, to feel. That is a far more profound idea than it has ever been given credit for. The arts can awaken the learning mechanism because they touch the true inner being, that aspect of the self that is not body, the part that lies outside the domain of science—call it the soul—the wellspring of dreams, caring, daring, and dedication. They are one of the all too rare ways by which humans can experience emotional thrill and fulfillment, powerful stimuli for motivation and inspiration. Because the arts can break the cycle of disaffection and despair that engulfs so many of our inner city children, these children need the arts more, not less, than suburban youth. Yet we know that disadvantaged children often lack even modest access to study of the arts.

If the distribution of the food supply throughout the United States was as erratic as the apportionment of arts education in American schools, the specter of starvation would prompt immediate attention, and the problem would be solved. But starvation of the mind and spirit is evidently a quite different matter altogether. We tend to excuse the fact that some children are well fed artistically and others are without, and we accept this choice as the rightful jurisdiction of local school boards. If a school board does not want the arts, it is because it does not value them or cannot or will not afford them. But should we permit such local discrimination and deprivation? Artistic deficiencies have a detrimental affect on the cultural health of the nation. When we dilute or delete arts programs, we unravel the infrastructure that assures the cultural future of America. By denying children the arts, we starve our civilization. Our citizens lose their sense of cultural cohesiveness, their pride and identity, their ties to the human greatness of the past, and some of their own potential for the future. The hungers of the human being—whether visceral or intellectual or emotional—are ignored at our own peril. This is too big and too important an issue to be left entirely to the whim of local school districts. The fact that some parents and school board members do not happen to value the arts is not sufficient cause for schools to neglect them. There must be a way to assert a higher order of wisdom, whether promulgated at the state or the federal level.

We do not need more and better arts education to develop more and better artists. We need more and better arts education to produce better-educated human beings, citizens who will value and evolve a worthy American civilization. The human capacity to make aesthetic judgments is far too scantily cultivated in public education. As a result, Americans seldom recognize that most of the decisions they make in life—from the kind of environments they create in their communities, offices, and homes to their decisions about the products they buy and the clothing they choose to wear—have an aesthetic component. That component is too seldom calculated when mayors make decisions on public housing (it has been said that we build slums and call them apartment houses), when zoning boards make decisions about appropriate land use, when boards of education approve the architecture of new schools, and when legislators vote on environmental and other issues—the list could go on and on. When the aesthetic component is ignored, we denigrate life. We abuse people with dehumanizing environments, bombard them with insensitivity and ugliness, and deprive them of the comforts and satisfactions they need for their psychological well-being.

But there is a far more important reason for schools to provide more and better education in the arts. Quite simply, the arts are the ways we human beings "talk" to ourselves and to each other. They are the languages of civilization through which we express our fears, our anxieties, our curiosities, our hungers, our discoveries, our hopes. They enable us to express our need for understanding, love, order, beauty, safety, respite, and longevity. They are the means we have invented to listen to our dreams, filling our space and time with what our imagination and feelings tell us. They are the universal ways by which we still play make-believe, conjuring up worlds that explain the ceremonies of our lives. They are the imprints we make that tell us who we are, that we belong, and that we count. The arts are not just important; they are a central force in human existence. Each citizen should have sufficient and equal opportunities to learn these languages, which so assist us in our fumbling, bumbling, and all-too-rarely brilliant navigation through this world. Because of this, the arts should be granted major status in American schooling. That is a cause worthy of our energies.

Basic Concepts in Music Education, II
Finding the Way to Be Basic: Music Education in the 1990s and Beyond

The case for music education is as strong as, perhaps stronger than, it has ever been, Even a cursory reading of Bennett Reimer's *A Philosophy of Music Education*[12] should assure anyone that we are on very firm ground. Basing our educational approach to music in the schools on the aesthetic philosophy of absolute expressionism is basing our practice on the solid foundations of the integrity of music as an art. But translating what we know about the art form into an educational rationale is not easy. Staking our claim that music education is basic education on aesthetic philosophy poses difficulties. The question, as Reimer reminds us, is "how to balance philosophical honesty with practical efficacy." Considering the fact that the curriculum of American schools is justified in largely utilitarian terms, that is excellent advice.

Given the fact that it is the practical (pragmatic) viewpoint of the public and most school administrators and board members that determines what is important in the curriculum, it behooves us to show them in precisely those terms why music is basic. From a pragmatic perspective, music education provides the human family with at least three fundamental and unique functions. These practical and useful functions of music education are true to the nature of music as an art form. In this sense, they represent a meeting and melding of aesthetic and instrumental values. All three can be applied across the other art forms as well, though with somewhat different emphases and interpretations. Because they are indigenous to the arts, music and music teaching do not have to be distorted to teach for these outcomes. These functions could serve as a conceptual framework for music education, providing the foundations and focus of the curriculum and the substantiation for music being included in basic education. They are concepts that could set our course in the years ahead. For the purpose of this overview, *concepts* are defined as those underlying truths that can serve as a rationale for establishing the place of music education in the schools, for formulating its curriculum, and for guiding our actions and advocacy efforts. If, as Harry Broudy suggests, general education should be thought of "as the cultivation of *capacities* for realizing value,"[13] then these functions should lie at the center of education in music.

1. *The study of music provides an essential part of the foundation for humane civilization by encouraging all students to cultivate and refine their sensibilities.*

At its best, arts education opens the door to learning. It awakens our eyes, our ears, our feelings, our minds. Encounters with the arts invite us to explore worlds of meaning that lie right next to the curtain that the old Persian proverb says has never been drawn aside—Rembrandt showing us the soul of his subjects; Mozart showing us the beauty of order; Shakespeare showing us the triumph of the human spirit over adversity. Such insights help students to break through the mathematical, factual, "you name it," and "memorize-this" confines of public education. By intensifying the relationship between our senses and the world around us, the arts quicken our curiosity about the mysteries of the intuitive and imaginative worlds that beckon us beyond the simplistic right and wrong litanies that prevail in so many American classrooms. They put us in touch with our inner being, our real selves. Beeb Salzer, a professor of theater design at San Diego State University, explains it this way: "The arts play a special role in a society such as ours, which is founded on a linear rationality and humanism. They offer a permissible contact with the irrational, the emotional, and the mysterious forces that logic cannot explain." [14]

One's feelings and spirit are part of the cognitive process, but education seldom accords them the attention they deserve. We need to educate the emotive part of our being so that we have clearer perceptions of those fundamental human states that have so much to do with interpersonal relations— love, hate, anxiety, hope, and a host of other feelings. Music is a way we give concrete representation to these inner mental states. Susanne Langer called this process the *"objectification* of subjective life." Just as science captures and represents parts of the world in scientific terms, the arts capture and represent parts of the world in artistic terms. Music expresses a unique realm inexpressible by any other means.

Through music education, students develop their musical intelligence. In defining human cognition, musical intelligence is recognized as one of our autonomous intelligences. The fact that humans can think sound and rhythms and organize them into patterns and forms to give representation to our sentient life is a unique capacity. It permits us to capture, record, store, and share perceptions about our emotive life that might otherwise escape us. Even Stravinsky, recanting his earlier statement to the contrary, stated that "a composer works in the embodiment of his feelings and, of course [music] may be considered as expressing or symbolizing them." [15] Music puts us in touch with our feelings and spirit as they relate to their ideal expressive embodiments in the musical works of the ages. Beethoven's "Ode to Joy" from his Ninth Symphony comes to mind as a prime example of the apotheosis of such expression and a reason our musical heritage is so important.

Should schools provide access to music study because it is a basic intelligence? Gardner points out: "Whereas, in the case of language, there is considerable emphasis in the school on further linguistic attainments, music occupies a relatively low niche in our culture, and so musical illiteracy is acceptable."[16] As an intellectual faculty, musical intelligence has been neglected with little seeming consequence. Or has it?

There are many indications that the failure of schools to cultivate and refine the sensibilities of their students has had adverse effects upon the younger generation. Drugs, crime, hostility, indifference, and insensitivity run rampant in schools that do not provide sufficient instruction in the arts. In the process of overselling science, mathematics, and technology as the salvation of commerce, schools have denied students something more precious—access to their inner beings and their personal spirit. Music speaks through and to a different sensory system than any other subject—that of auditory perception. As Elliot Eisner has pointed out, when we deny children access to a major expressive mode such as music, we deprive them of "the meanings that the making of music makes possible." The result is a form of human deprivation. Without attending to the human spirit, schools tend to turn out insensitive citizens who lack compassion—people whose macho aggressiveness is not tempered by the controlling forces of sensitivity and caring about others. Many of today's schools, devoid of the arts, are cultivating a generation of modern-day barbarians. American society is the victim.

In teaching us to be receptive to our own and other's intuitions, insights, and feelings, the arts teach us something even more valuable: how to be empathetic. Scholastic Aptitude Tests do not measure the heart. Let us always remember that intelligence can be used to deceive and to cheat; it can be used self-servingly as a tool of greed; it can be used cruelly and with indifference; it can cause others to suffer and even to die. Some of Einstein's most important discoveries, born of great intelligence, were put to destructive use. In contrast, empathy intercedes; it reigns in such uses of intelligence. If we have empathy, we can assume another person's point of view. We can put ourselves in their shoes. To the degree that the arts create empathy, they develop a sense of humane responsibility and are a vitally important part of our moral education. Without empathy, we have no compassion for other human beings.

The arts teach children sympathy. They allow children to perceive themselves in relation to other human beings, who also fear, suffer, love, fail, and triumph. That is learning to react and to interact and to project one's own personality into the life of another, and that is basic education.

2. *The study of music provides an essential part of the foundation for humane civilization by establishing a basic relationship between the individual and the cultural heritage of the human family.*

As advancing systems for travel and communication bring the peoples of the world closer, understanding human differences becomes increasingly important. The foundations for peace between peoples depend on intracultural respect and exchange. Recognizing our interdependence as peoples is the backbone of commerce in today's world. By building relationships between the individual and the community we assure the stability of our communal society today is a microcosm of the entire world. Our multiculturalism is an American fact of life, and music is one of the most pervasive and persuasive ways we express it. Immigrant populations are schools to find new ways to study cultural differences and to cultures. Music provides a fundamental way to understand our own and other people's humanness. We neglect such enlightenment our own peril. Schools that do not provide sufficient education in the tradition of community values that unite the society. Nor are they providing a basis to study and appreciate or, at the very least, to understand the values of other societies.

Because music is an expression of the beings that create it, it reflects thinking and values as well as the social milieu from which it originates. Even if it is not the overt intent of the composer, the music we listen to tends to define who we are and give us identity as a social group. . . .

The diversity of music in the world is a richness we share with the human family. The greatest gift one people can give to another is to share its culture, and one of the most revealing ways to do this is through music. If we are not to be a country of many insular groups, we must establish cultural connections. Music provides a way to do this by establishing understanding across our many distinguishable artistic legacies. Music teaches respect for the genius of human musical invention; the *characteristics* that distinguish cultural styles are marvels of human creation. One cannot be moved by the zeal of gospel music without respecting the humanity that created it. To share musical creations across cultures is to share our deepest values. Recognizing our similarities and understanding our differences give us a base to establish cultural cohesiveness and respect, two vitally important values in a shrinking world in which technology seems to doggedly deny our humanness.

Music provides us with another important connection with our communal heritage: it enables us to express the ceremonies of our lives. Music is a fundamental way we express the tragedy of war, the triumph over adversity, consolation in death, our reverence for God, the meaning and value of peace, harmony, and love—universal human states that express the values held by society. The feelings of patriotism and victory, of hope and dignity, of community pride and solidarity are all given clear expression in music. A culture's imprint, its sense of celebrating its own life-style, is inherent in its music.

The extent to which school performing groups, particularly high school bands, have expressed civic homogeneity is the extent to which they have been valued by the community. A high school band marching in a Fourth of July parade celebrates its town's patriotism and hope for the continuity of life tomorrow. Perhaps no group personifies this aspect more than the Harlan (Kentucky) Boys Choir that sang at President George Bush's inaugural ceremony in Washington, D. C., in January 1989. The members of this choir are young men from a coal-mining town in the Appalachian Mountains known for its history of labor violence. Cat Stacey, owner of Cat's Beauty Shop in Harlan, called the choir's performance "one of the highlights of my life. A cold chill just goes through you to hear them." The choir's director, David Davies, said of the students, "[They] represent normal everyday children. We want music to be important to their lives, but not [be] their whole lives." These students are not studying music to become musicians. They are learning that music is a basic way that a society expresses its character and the values it believes in. The people of Harlan support music as a symbol of their indelible community spirit, their pride in who they are. These performers are learning how to communicate, how to "speak" to and for their community—and music is valued in the schools accordingly. . . .

3. *The study of music provides an essential part of the foundation for humane civilization by furnishing students with a crucial aesthetic metaphor of what life at its best might be.*

. . . For a society to have an effective work force, it is essential that it turn out citizens who recognize and respect good craftsmanship, who care about detail and are committed to an artistic result, and who have the ability to judge their own efforts by the highest standards and make corrections accordingly. Music is a celebration of that kind of perfection, that kind of excellence. It is one of the basic ways we learn to release our positive energies toward an aesthetic result. It is one of the essential ways we acquire the habit of thinking aesthetically.

Music provides students with an aesthetic frame of reference that has broad applicability; individuals who are educated musically think differently because of it. Music study transforms the self, providing an aesthetic value orientation. Ideally, the aesthetics of music become the aesthetics of life. Through the study of music we recognize the beauty of order. We understand the striving for perfection. We appreciate how all the elements—the details—make the expressive whole and how important those details are. These conceptual understandings are not discarded when the student leaves the music classroom; these understandings emerge in other settings and are applied there.

The aesthetic awareness we learn through the study of music becomes a way we relate to the world. Personal taste and the expression of it are basic elements of the human condition. Aesthetic considerations are essential to the satisfactory conduct of society and empower us to create our own best state of existence. When the aesthetic component is ignored, we denigrate life: we dehumanize our environments, bombard people with ugliness, and deprive people of the comforts and satisfactions they need for their psychological well-being. Aesthetics is a natural and important part of our encounter with life. It is the way we bring our sensual and rational being to terms with the world around us. . . .

If schools do not provide students with sufficient education in the arts, they deny students opportunities that would enable them to think and operate with an aesthetic frame of reference. The important point here is the significant transfer of aesthetic understanding from music to other realms of life. The quality of aesthetic thought, expectations, and satisfactions learned through music study, applied across the board, can make a substantial difference in the quality of life. That is why the arts are not the domain of only the privileged, the rich, or the talented, but belong to all. The life of every citizen can be enhanced by acquiring an understanding of music. Quality of life and quality of workmanship are concepts that are of fundamental value to American society. They are basic education.

These concepts of music as a means of cultivating and refining our sensibilities, of establishing a basic relationship between the individual and the cultural heritage of the human family, and of furnishing students with a crucial aesthetic metaphor of what life at its best might be constitute basic education at its finest. These goals derive directly from the indigenous nature of music itself. We do not have to distort music and misuse it to achieve these very practical outcomes. But we do have to establish our curricula with these outcomes in mind if we want to claim and achieve them.

Notes

1. *Americans and the Arts* (New York: Associated Councils of the Arts, 1974).

2. *Coming to Our Senses*, p. 53.

3. Ibid., p. 57.

4. Ibid., p. 6.

5. Ibid.

6. David Hornbeck, "Preface," in *Arts, Education, and the States: A Survey of State Education Policies* (Washington, D.C.: Council of Chief State School Officers, 1985), 4.

7. Elliot W. Eisner, *Cognition and Curriculum: A Basis for Deciding What to Teach* (New York: Longman, 1982), 74.

8. Howard Gardner, *Frames of Mind: The Theory of Multiple Intelligences* (New York: Basic Books, 1983).

9. Ibid., p. 358.

10. Ibid., p. 356.

11. Ibid., p. 359.

Charles Fowler

12. Bennett Reimer, *A Philosophy of Music Education*, 2nd edition (Englewood Cliffs, NJ: Prentice-Hall, 1989).

13. Ibid., p. 10.

14. Beeb Salzer, "Teaching Design in a World Without Design," *Theatre Design & Technology*, Winter 1989, p. 64–65.

15. Suzanne Langer, *Problems of Art* (New York: Scribners, 1957), p. 9.

16. Howard Gardner, *Frames of Mind: The Theory of Multiple Intelligences* (New York: Basic Books, 1983), p. 99–127.

National Commission on Music Education
Growing Up Complete: The Imperative for Music Education (1991)

The National Commission on Music Education consisted of leaders from the fields of education, government, business, and the arts.

A Declaration of Concern

During the 1960s, educational reform made it onto the front pages of American newspapers for the first time in decades. Politicians, policy makers, and business figures have been quick to trace the nation's "competitiveness gap" to the schoolhouse door. They have voiced ringing alarms over the declines in math and science scores. But when the discussion has turned to making sure our children learn to understand and participate in music and the other arts, there has been silence. We believe such nearsighted concern shortchanges our children because it leaves them only half-educated. Since the beginnings of civilization, music has been universally recognized as crucial to quality education, for two reasons.

First, every civilization recognizes that both formal and informal music education prepare children for what life ultimately requires. Music education fosters creativity, teaches effective communication, provides basic tools for a critical assessment of the world around us, and instills the abiding values of self-discipline and commitment.

Second, music and the other arts have been recognized as unique to human capabilities, as a means to self-discovery and self-expression, and as a fundamental part of civilization itself.

We, whose lives are marked indelibly by a love for music, and who understand the essential role music education can play in developing the whole human being, call on the parents of our school children, on teachers and school officials, on local and state boards of education, and on the American people, to come to our aid in establishing the rightful place of music in the schools.

Our credo is simple: *Just as there can be no music without learning, no education is complete without music. Music makes the difference.* To that end:

We call on all who care about education to destroy, once and for all, the myth that education in music and the other arts is mere "curricular icing";

We call on all who love the arts to insist that instruction in music and the other arts be reestablished as basic to education, not only by virtue of their intrinsic worth, but because they are fundamental to what it means to be an educated person;

We call on parents, educators, and citizens who know and understand the value of music in our common life to bring the message about the value of music education to decision makers at all levels, and to encourage them to establish music as a priority, so our children can continue to learn and make music; and

We call on those whose livelihoods depend on music—as manufacturers, technicians, teachers, retailers, performers, composers, and others—to lend their support to the cause of music education in our schools. . . .

Part III: Education with Music

What is true of all the arts is supremely true of music. When a child studies music, significant elements of his or her education find focus and expression:

- Developing the ability to understand and use symbols in new contexts;
- Discovering the power, precision, and control of mathematics in unexpected ways;
- Finding and directing personal creativity;
- Exercising the diverse skills of problem-solving;
- Experiencing the joy of self-expression;
- Growing into the liberation acquired through self-discipline; and
- Participating in the deeply human satisfaction of shared work and the gratification of challenges met.

In addition to these characteristics fundamental to education, music shares with the other arts a resource that is of paramount importance to the education of the young: Music is a highway for exploring the emotional and aesthetic dimensions of experience. Indeed, here is where music and the other arts make their unique and most visible contribution. Education *without* music shortchanges our children and their futures. Education *with* music offers exciting possibilities in two directions. As we look to the future, educational research on the nature of intelligence and brain function gives promising indications that could change the face of education. And as we look around us in the present, we see connections between music edu-

ion and changes in students that offer direct and immediate benefits, not
ly to them, but to the educational enterprise as a whole.

National Endowment for the Arts
Toward Civilization: A Report on Arts Education

In 1985, the United States Congress mandated that the National Endowment
for the Arts and the National Endowments "study . . . the state of arts education and humanities education." The National Endowment for the Humanities
published its report, *American Memory*, in 1987. *Toward Civilization* is the report
by the National Endowment for the Arts of its study of arts education, published the following year.

What Is Basic Arts Education?

Basic arts education aims to provide *all* students, not only the gifted and talented, with knowledge of, and skills in, the arts. Basic arts education must
give students the essence of our civilization, the civilizations which have
contributed to ours, and the more distant civilizations which enrich world
civilization as a whole. It must also give students tools for creating, for
communicating and understanding others' communications, and for making
informed and critical choices.

Basic arts education includes the disciplines of literature (from the art of
writing); visual art and design (from the arts of painting, sculpture, photog-
raphy, video, crafts, architecture, landscape and interior design, and product and graphic design); performing art (from the arts of dance, music,
opera, and musical theater and theater); and media art (from the arts of film,
television, and radio).

While each of these arts disciplines differs in character, tradition, and
form, basic arts education must also include art forms that are interdisciplinary: opera and musical theater, which combine vocal and instrumental
music with drama and stage design; film and television, which combine
music, drama, and the visual arts, synthesized by the media arts themselves;
and new work that extends the frontiers of current artistic convention. Just
as artists collaborate to produce interdisciplinary arts, so school faculties
will need to collaborate to teach them.

Like other school subjects, basic arts education must be taught sequentially by qualified teachers; instruction must include the history, critical theory, and ideas of the arts as well as creation, production, and performance;

and knowledge of, and skills in, the arts must be tested. As for other school subjects, appropriate resources—classroom time, administrative support, and textbooks—must be provided to this end.

The problem is: *Basic arts education does not exist in the United States today.*

Why Is Basic Arts Education Important?

Our last seven Presidents have all affirmed the idea that the arts are at the core of what we are and, therefore, of what we should know. President Reagan, after quoting John Adams to the effect that his grandchildren should have "a right to study painting, poetry, music, architecture," urged us to "resolve that our schools will teach our children the same respect and appreciation for the arts and humanities that the Founders had."

A balanced education is essential to an enlightened citizenry and a productive work force, and a balanced education must include comprehensive and sequential study in the three great branches of learning—the arts, humanities, and sciences. It is basic understanding of the combination of these areas of learning that provides for what E. D. Hirsch, Jr. calls "cultural literacy."

There are four reasons why arts education is important: to understand civilization, to develop creativity, to learn the tools of communication, and to develop the capacity for making wise choices among the products of the arts. Lest it be feared that arts education might detract from basic skills thought to be essential to productivity, the example of Japan, whose productivity is without question, is instructive; the Japanese require extensive and sequential arts instruction from kindergarten through twelfth grade.

Very important, arts education is essential for *all* students, not just the gifted and talented. The schools teach reading and writing (including literature) to all students, not just those who are good at these subjects. Just as knowledge of, and skills in, words are essential to functioning in society, so knowledge of, and skills in, nonverbal communication are essential. In order to cope with a twenty-first century permeated by technological change and the electronic media, young Americans need a sense of themselves and their civilization and of the vocabularies of the images on television. Today's kindergartners will be the first graduating class of the twenty-first century.

The first purpose of arts education is to give our young people a sense of civilization. American civilization includes many cultures—from Europe, Africa, the Far East and our own hemisphere. The great works of art of these parent civilizations, and of our own, provide the guideposts to cultural literacy. Knowing them, our young people will be better able to understand, and therefore build on, the achievements of the past; they will also be better able to understand themselves. Great works of art illuminate the constancy of the human condition.

Mere exposure to the best of the arts is not enough. As Elliot Eisner of Stanford University has said, the best of art needs to be "unwrapped," to be studied in order to be understood. The schools already teach the vocabularies and ideas of good writing by including great literature in English studies. But great works of art also communicate in images, sounds, and movements. The schools need to teach the vocabularies of these images, sounds, and movements, as well as of words, if young Americans are to graduate from high school with a sense of civilization. . . .

American civilization has a central core which Henry Geldzahler, the former Fine Arts Commissioner of New York City, describes as a "sleeping giant." The core includes—to name a very few—such diverse artists as Shakespeare, Lao Tse, Cervantes, Melville, and Henry James; Praxiteles, Michelangelo, Velasquez, Frank Lloyd Wright, Winslow Homer, and Jackson Pollock; Bach, Mozart, Beethoven, Aaron Copland, and Duke Ellington; George Balanchine, Martha Graham, and Katherine Dunham; Jan Peerce, Marian Anderson, and Leontyne Price; and John Huston and Katharine Hepburn. The American giant is largely European, but includes strains of Africa, Asia, and the other parts of our own hemisphere.

In designing the contents of arts education, we must set out to make this giant a part of the knowledge and experience of all Americans. The giant *is* American civilization.

Creativity

A second purpose of arts education is to foster creativity. Young people should have the opportunity to emulate master artists—to take blank sheets of paper or rolls of film or video tape and fill them, to blow a trumpet and make melodies and rhythms, to design a house or a city, and to move in dance.

To acquire the skills with which to do this requires hard work and discipline, but to use them to create a personal vision can be a joyful experience. Moreover, whether by inference from a collection of phenomena, or by creating an initial hypothesis from which deductions might flow, learning in the arts can not only develop the discipline and craft necessary to constructive creation, it can also help students to develop reasoning and problem-solving skills essential to a productive work force and to the learning of other subjects.

Trying to create or perform the nonliterary arts without skills and knowledge is like trying to write without vocabulary and syntax. The student is reduced to being the "first artist:" No one would dream of teaching the art of writing that way, just as no one would teach mathematics or physics without the benefit of Euclid or Newton. Arts education must include the vocabularies and basic skills which produced the great works of the past so that young people can build on those who came before.

To create and perform works of art is also to engage actively in the process of worldmaking. As the well-known psychologist Jerome Bruner reminds us, Aristotle in the *Poetics* observed that "the poet's function is to describe, not the thing that has happened, but a kind of thing that might happen." Bruner notes that tyrants hate and fear poets "even more than they fear and hate scientists, who, though they create possible worlds, leave no place in them for possible alternative personal perspectives on those worlds." Such perspectives are very much the domain of the poet, the artist. The function of art is "to open us to dilemmas, to the hypothetical"; it is in this respect "an instrument of freedom, lightness, imagination, and yes, reason."

Communication

A third purpose of arts education is to teach effective communication. As great orators and writers through history have shown, speaking and writing are art forms; the best of writing becomes "literature" and is studied as such. But all writing, whether it is a political speech, advertising copy, a novel, or a poem, is an attempt to communicate to readers. The other art forms also have languages through which artists speak to audiences. The language may be primarily verbal, as in literature, or nonverbal, as in music, dance, or the visual and design arts, or it may be a combination of both, as in drama, opera, and musical theater, and the media arts. Young people must be given an education enabling them to understand these languages and to analyze their meanings.

Their education should include learning elementary artistic skills which can be used in later life—whether visually to express some nonverbal concept in a corporate board room, or to play a phrase on a piano to illustrate tonal differences, or to sing a song, or to use acting techniques to make a point or tell a joke effectively, or to record in words or line an especially memorable personal experience.

Understanding of nonverbal communication is especially important in a time when television has become a principal medium of communication. Television reaches everywhere. It is of prime importance in judging and electing our leaders; its dramas influence the vocabularies of our languages and reinforce or detract from our prejudices; its practitioners' names are household words; young people spend more time watching it than they spend in school. Television may well be the most important innovation in communication since the printing press, and it communicates in images that are as much visual and aural as verbal. It employs all the arts, which in turn are synthesized by the art of television itself. For students, learning the vocabularies of all the arts, including the media arts, is an essential tool for understanding, and perhaps one day communicating, in the medium of television. . . .

National Endowment for the Arts

Choice

A fourth purpose of arts education is to provide tools for critical assessment of what one reads, sees, and hears. It should provide both models and standards of excellence. It should also provide a sense of the emotional power of the arts, their ability to stir an audience, both to inspire it and manipulate it. Arts education can give people the tools to make better choices and even to influence the marketplace of both products and ideas.

Every child growing up in the United States is bombarded from birth with popular art and artful communication over the airways and on the streets. The purpose of arts education is not to wean young people from these arts (an impossible task even if it were desirable) but to enable them to make reasoned choices about them and what is good and bad. . . .

What Is The Problem?

Several impediments stand in the way of arts education. According to a 1986 Gallup poll, Americans generally view job preparation as the principal reason for schooling, and knowledge not obviously related to job skills as relatively unimportant. Our preoccupation with the practical has made education focus on limited basic skills (reading, writing, arithmetic, and now computer literacy) while neglecting education in what those skills are to be used for. Americans also generally confuse the arts with entertainment which can be enjoyed without understanding. Some go so far as to think of the arts as potentially threatening or even blasphemous. Further, because there is little agreement on what arts education should be, there is no agreed course of action to rally those who believe in it.

To sum up, the arts are in triple jeopardy: they are not viewed as serious; knowledge itself is not viewed as a prime educational objective; and those who determine school curricula do not agree on what arts education is.

Richard W. Riley
Music Education

Richard W. Riley, then U.S. Secretary of Education, gave this speech in Washington, D.C., on March 13, 1997, to members of the Music Educators National Conference.

I remember when I was in the third Grade at Donaldson Elementary School in Greenville, South Carolina and we were listening to a concert by Richard Cass, a concert pianist. And my teacher, Miss Bess Allen, leaned over and whispered, "Dick, you too can play like that if you will take your music seriously." And music also played a formative role in my political life. My first

---

political position was in about the sixth or seventh grade when I was elected—unanimously, I might add—as the president of the Woodside Music Club. It was my first political victory. And, I found through music what I was really good at—getting elected. Whether because of this beginning—or in spite of it—I have been a strong supporter of music and the arts throughout my life and career.

And I have long believed in the important role that music can play in helping students learn, achieve, and succeed. Music—as well as theater, dance, and the visual arts—are wonderful forums to exhibit and explore what makes us uniquely human—our creativity. And allowing children to explore their creativity and that of others is an important part of teaching and learning. New studies seem to be coming out every week that demonstrate the crucial link between early music training and academic success.

Why, just today I was in North Carolina with the president. We were riding in a limousine with Secretary of Defense Cohen. They both asked me about my plans this evening. And when I told them I would be with you all tonight they both immediately began discussing the latest research of Drs. Shaw and Rauscher involving music and early childhood development. For them the research results just made sense. It was a wonderful discussion. The recent study by Shaw and Rauscher observed that pre-schoolers who were given keyboard lessons and did group singing scored higher on tests measuring spatial reasoning than those who did not—skills which are essential to later development in math, science, and engineering. Another study showed arts education promoting higher test scores in math and science, as well as reading. And still other studies of arts education show that it increases student and teacher attendance and leads to fewer disciplinary problems and decreased violence among students. The benefits of music and the arts to our society and to the education of the next generation seem unlimited. Now many of you have known all of this for years—and I hope I won't hear too many "I told you so's" going around these days. I hope that all of these studies will convince school administrators and others who must deal with tough budgetary questions concerning education to see that music education and the arts are not a frill. They must be apart of every student's basic education.

A recent report of the President's Committee of the Arts and Humanities warned of dangers of cuts in these areas and called for restoring these funds in schools across the nation. And I think that as more people begin to realize that a curriculum with music and the arts in it is a stronger curriculum, they will heed this advice. Similarly, the president's challenge to have all American students reading well by the end of the third grade, and proficient in math by the end of eighth grade, offers a further rationale to support music and arts education. Because if music education stimulates math, science, and reading achievement, then the one would seem to lay the groundwork for the other.

Your hard work has been so important to spreading the word about the importance of music education. I particularly want to thank you for your support of Goals 2000, your advocacy for music and arts education programs, and your contributions to the development of the National Standards, which I think are excellent. With the standards, for the first time, we have a clear vision of the knowledge, skills, and concepts that all students need to learn through studying the arts.

In closing, I'd like to quote a portion of a letter by John Adams. As you may know, Adams was one of the great letter writers in our nation's history—the correspondence between him and his wife Abigail, in particular, is quite remarkable. Perhaps because my wife Tunky is such an avid fan of music and the arts . . . and because we have shared so many wonderful cultural experiences, I thought it particularly appropriate. In 1780, Adams wrote to his wife (and I abridge it here slightly): "I must study politics and war, so that my sons may have liberty to study mathematics and philosophy . . . in order to give their children a right to study painting, poetry, and music." Adams's words ring truer today than ever.

And I would also like to quote from another writer, Marvin Hamlisch, the composer of *A Chorus Line* and other musicals. He recently described in the *New York Times* how his education in music and the arts—as well as his career teaching music—was such a positive influence on his life. He explained how he was an uninspired student until his third grade teacher allowed him to play the piano at school. When Hamlisch went to college he became a student teacher himself. And using music as an educational tool, he helped turn around the life of a former gang member. This is the power of a music education. In honor of Marvin Hamlisch, the composer of *A Chorus Line* let me say that your award has made me feel, as Marvin's greatest lyric says, "like one singular sensation."

Bill Ivey
Remarks to the National Music Education Summit, Washington, D.C., October 2, 1998

Bill Ivey is chairman of the National Endowment for the Arts.

. . . Many of you know I am a folklorist by training, and I approach life and the arts from the perspective of a folklorist. And, one of the things that folklorists know—at the very core of their being—is that creative expression is central to the lives of individuals and communities. To the folklorist, art is the great window into culture, for societies carry memory and values in images, stories, dances, and songs. Individuals and communities use art to express themselves, and to communicate—to craft a "face" and a "personality" for community life.

The arts are especially important in a complex democracy like ours. Democracy offers the promise of equal participation to hundreds of cultural traditions that share our landscape—Native American to Asian, European, black, and Hispanic—and this promise translates into an endless process of negotiation and accommodation.

We know how tough that negotiation can be, how challenging it can be to the very fabric of our civil society. But art represents a place in which borrowing, blending, and sharing can really work.

Art gives us a place for the guilt-free flow of ideas across cultural lines and cultural barriers. As singer-songwriter Paul Simon wrote several weeks ago, in his insightful *New York Times* essay on George Gershwin, " . . . music is sometimes the only benign avenue of communication between antagonists." What holds for music is true for the full spectrum of artistic endeavor.

We should all note that a recent report to the nation from the Council on Civil Society has called for the return of arts education to our nation's schools as part of a national agenda to bring civility to the lives of our children.

It's time we realized just how much our future depends on how well we integrate the magic and creativity of the arts into the lives of future generations, and that process must begin by ensuring that the arts are essential learning for all children. Your conference is focused on the future, and today, I'd like to talk with you about how far we've come toward realizing goals and how we can work together to make our common vision for the arts an accepted, even sought after, reality for the next century.

The Problem: How Far We've Come

But to know how far we have to go, we have to understand how far we've come. Let's take a brief look at some milestones in education over the last four decades.

In the fifties, faced with Sputnik and our competition with the Russian space program, Americans recognized the importance of science and math and took decisive steps to improve standards in our schools. And, that was right, and good for the country. In fact, a discernable legacy of that Sputnik "scare" is still with us today. It's the more than $600 million that Congress provides to the National Science Foundation annually to improve learning in math, science, and technology in our nation's schools.

In the sixties, our nation placed special emphasis on health through exercise and took steps to raise the level of physical fitness among our school-age children. And, that was right, and good for the country. By the late seventies, we had begun to realize that along with scientific knowledge and physical fitness, we needed to feed the imagination of students with the arts. Reports and studies called for Americans to "come to our senses" and include the arts as part of basic education. And, that was right, and good for the country. But in the early eighties, we were still grappling with the problem. An education report declared that we were "A Nation at Risk," and there was a "rising tide of mediocrity" in our schools. And, by the late eighties, Congress had mandated that NEA report on the status of arts education. In our 1988 report, "Toward Civilization," the Endowment stated that arts education in our schools was in triple jeopardy: The arts were not taken seriously as important subject matter; arts education programs were focused almost exclusively on production and performance and rarely included history, critical judgment, or aesthetics; and there was no common agreement as to what all students should know and be able to do in the arts.

Now, it's been another ten years since "Toward Civilization," and the question is: How far have we come? Have we made progress? Actually, we've made enormous strides in our efforts to address the triple jeopardy issues over the past ten years, and the Endowment is proud to have played a critical federal and national leadership role in those efforts.

In 1992, the Arts Endowment joined forces with the Department of Education and our sister agency, the National Endowment for the Humanities, to fund a two-year process of defining what all students—from kindergarten through twelfth grade—should know and be able to do in the arts. The process, of course, was the development of our national voluntary standards in the arts.

By combining our resources, the three federal agencies made an investment of more than $1 million in the future of arts education. And it turned out to be a good investment—for now, more than 45 states have either adopted or are working toward adoption of content standards that include the arts.

I know there are members of this audience who worked tirelessly to put this national consensus process together. In fact, it was MENC that managed the standards development process for the Consortium of National Arts Education Associations. And, the Arts Endowment was pleased to play a supportive role in this very significant achievement. And the timing could not have been better. Following the signing of the Goals 2000: Educate America Act by President Clinton in 1994—the first federal legislation to declare the arts a "core" subject—the consortium was the first group to present its voluntary national standards to the Secretary of Education.

It's also significant to note that the arts were the first of the core subjects to develop its framework for a national assessment in parallel with its national standards. And, the Arts Endowment was pleased to play an important role in the development of our national assessment framework.

It began with the recommendation in "Toward Civilization" that the arts must be put back into the Nation's Report Card, known more formally as the National Assessment of Educational Progress.

In 1990, my predecessor, John Frohnmayer, learned that the arts could be included in the National Assessment only if money could be found to begin the development process. The Endowment, in collaboration with the Getty Center for Education in the Arts, provided $1.25 million to ensure the return of arts to the Nation's Report Card, and the assessment framework was concluded in 1994. Four years later, we have completed an assessment of America's eighth graders. And, on November 10, I will have the pleasure of joining Secretary of Education Riley to announce the results of the Nation's Report Card on the arts—the first such report in nearly twenty years.

The National Education Goals, the Goals 2000: Educate America Act, voluntary national standards, and a pending national Report Card on the arts provide us with both a policy framework and a "window of opportunity" to secure a more solid place for the arts in our schools. This "window of opportunity" was the catalyst for the Arts Endowment to invite the Department of Education to join us in developing the Goals 2000 Arts Education Partnership.

Now, the partnership is a national-level consortium that brings together more than 140 disparate groups, representing arts education and arts groups, school principal and administrator associations, business and private sectors, as well as parent and civic groups, to work together to grow and improve arts education.

MENC has been an important partner in this effort, and one sign of our success occurred just two weeks ago, when the First Lady hosted an Arts Education event at the White House to praise the Partnership for coming together to work toward the promise of Goals 2000.

Here, at the end of the decade, we're experiencing an abundance of policy development in favor of arts education. To these accomplishments, we can add more and more research that supports what those of us in the arts have known for years: that education in the arts improves the intellectual, emotional, and social development of our children.

As those of you who work with state and local school boards know, there is an accepted maxim in education, "In God we trust, and everybody else had better bring their data." We are bringing our data.

Many of our leading scientists and researchers are lending their support for arts as a part of basic education. I'm sure all of you are familiar with the research of Drs. Frances Rauscher and Gordon Shaw, into the connection between music instruction for young children and their abilities in spatial-temporal reasoning, which is important for their later achievement in math and science. MENC and the music industry have both played an important leadership role in supporting these critical research initiatives.

Our case for the essential nature of the arts is also bolstered by the College Board report that students who study the arts in general, and music in particular, score considerably higher on both the verbal and math portions of the Scholastic Achievement Test (SAT).

Members of Congress, too, have added their voices to the chorus of experts speaking out in favor of arts education. Last year, when the Senate discussed the future of the Arts Endowment, leaders from both sides of the aisle, specifically Senators James Jeffords and Edward Kennedy, spoke forcefully about the need to help improve the quantity, and quality, of arts education.

At the state level, an increasing number of legislatures and school boards are calling for inclusion of the arts in high-school graduation and college entrance requirements. At the local level, the source of most of the public funds that pay for K–12 education in our country, there's good news to report, as well. In places like New York City, local leaders, including the mayor and school superintendent, are committing substantial amounts of public funds to the hiring of art and music specialists.

With less fanfare, schools in Sarasota, Florida, lost—and then regained—music and art specialists in their elementary schools. This was thanks to an extraordinary advocacy campaign mounted by the local arts council in partnership with the arts educators, parents, and local business and civic leaders. And, in Nashville, Tennessee, I'm proud to say that 184 art and music teachers were hired during the past two years.

Why is all this so important? Because we know that making art—and consuming art—and learning about art automatically brings into play the finest of our democratic values: tolerance, generosity, fairness, openness, opportunity, freedom of expression, and creativity. These are some of the deepest philosophical principles on which our nation was founded. These values are imbedded in the work of artists, and in America's unique arts process.

What is the value of this arts process to our citizens? I would argue, that above all, this potent manifestation of our democracy has made us a creative people. How could it be otherwise? We draw from, and have access to, the very best of virtually every culture and every nation on earth. And, I would argue that this creativity is possibly our greatest national resource, and because it is so valuable to our nation, it must be encouraged, preserved, and nurtured. And, it must be passed on to each succeeding generation of Americans if our democracy is to remain strong and viable. . . .

Conclusion

In 1998, with the millennium only two years away, we have unprecedented opportunities to shape the future as we continue to reform and improve education in this country.

It has been said that "education is simply the soul of a society as it passes from one generation to another." Let us continue to work toward ensuring that by the time we honor the high school graduates of the Class of 2011— the kindergarten children of today—we will have:

- Nourished their creativity with the arts so that they are strong and imaginative contributors to our society;
- Provided them with an appreciation for the democratic nature of American arts, a heritage that places no one tradition above or below another, but understands the arts across disciplines and cultures; and
- Instilled in them the importance of participating in and preserving America's living cultural heritage, which will strengthen our families and communities.

When our children have this knowledge about the arts and their world, then our efforts today will have succeeded.

Then, as a nation, we can say, that the state of the arts in education is right and good in our country.

The 106th Congress of the United States
Resolution on Music Education (2000)

Expressing the sense of the Congress regarding the benefits of music education:

Whereas there is a growing body of scientific research demonstrating that children who receive music instruction perform better on spatial-temporal reasoning tests and proportional math problems;

Whereas music education grounded in rigorous instruction is an important component of a well-rounded academic program;

Whereas opportunities in music and the arts have enabled children with disabilities to participate more fully in school and community activities;

Whereas music and the arts can motivate at-risk students to stay in school and become active participants in the educational process;

Whereas according to the College Board, college-bound high school seniors in 1998 who received music instruction scored 53 points higher on the verbal portion of the Scholastic Aptitude Test and 39 points higher on the math portion of the test than college-bound high school seniors with no music or arts instruction;

Whereas a 1999 report by the Texas Commission on Drug and Alcohol Abuse states that individuals who participated in band or orchestra reported the lowest levels of current and lifelong use of alcohol, tobacco, and illicit drugs; and

Whereas comprehensive, sequential music instruction enhances early brain development and improves cognitive and communicative skills, self-discipline, and creativity:

Now, therefore, be it Resolved by the House of Representatives (the Senate concurring), That it is the sense of the Congress that—

(1) music education enhances intellectual development and enriches the academic environment for children of all ages; and

(2) music educators greatly contribute to the artistic, intellectual, and social development of American children, and play a key role in helping children to succeed in school.

June M. Hinckley
Testimony to Congress (1999)

June M. Hinckley is the Arts Education Specialist for the Florida Department of Education. At the time of this testimony to Congress, she was president of the Music Educators National Conference: The National Association for Music Education.

Mr. Chairman and members of the Subcommittee, I am June Hinckley, president of MENC: The National Association for Music Education, which represents over 70,000 music educators across the country. I am also the Arts Education Specialist for the Florida Department of Education. In that capacity, I help develop and coordinate the arts education curricula for Florida schools. I am pleased to have this opportunity to share with you my experience and observations on the importance of music and arts education for all children.

A Statement of Principles on the Value of Arts Education

Last year, all of the major professional education associations, representing over nine million teachers, parents, school board members, school administrators, and principals, joined together to endorse a set of principles that articulate the meaning and value of arts education. A copy of this statement is attached to my testimony, but the principles may be summarized as follows:

Every student in the nation should have an education in the arts.

To ensure a basic education in the arts for all students, the arts should be recognized as serious, core academic subjects. As education policy-

---

makers make decisions, they should incorporate the multiple lessons of recent research concerning the value and impact of arts education.

Qualified arts teachers and sequential curriculum must be recognized as the basis and core for substantive arts education for all students.

Arts education programs should be grounded in rigorous instruction, provide meaningful assessment of academic progress and performance, and take their place within a structure of direct accountability to school officials, parents, and the community.

Community resources that provide exposure to the arts, enrichment, and entertainment through the arts all offer valuable support and enhancement to an in-school arts education.

What inspired these organizations to make such strong statements in support of arts education for every child? Certainly, they share our collective belief in the power of music and the other arts to communicate the emotions of the human spirit and connect us to our history, traditions, and heritage. But they also understand the direct link between arts education and academic achievement as documented by a growing body of research. This research has important implications for the future of education policy.

The Research: Music and the Brain

There is an exciting body of research that indicates that music instruction at an early age actually wires the brain for learning. According to psychologist Frances Rauscher of the University of Wisconsin at Oshkosh, "Children are born with all the nerve cells, or neurons, they will ever have. However, connections between neurons, called synapses, are sparse and unstable. Synaptic connections largely determine adult intelligence. During the first six years of life, the number of synapses increases dramatically, and synapses already in place are stabilized. This process occurs as a result of experience or learning. Those synapses that are not used are eliminated—a 'use it or lose it' situation. Music training appears to develop the synaptic connections that are relevant to abstract thought. . . ."

Additional Evidence

Beyond the work of Dr. Rauscher and her colleagues, there also is considerable research and anecdotal evidence that supports the important role of arts education classes in keeping students in school, particularly at the high school level. In Florida, we have found that students identified as potentially at-risk, but who are active in music programs, are more on task in school, identify strongly with their schools, and indicate that participation in music programs was an important factor in their decision to stay in school. Administrators confirm this data.

According to The College Board (*Profiles of SAT and Achievement Test Takers*), there is a direct correlation between improved SAT scores and the length of time spent studying the arts. Those children who studied the arts for four or more years scored 60 points higher on verbal and 41 points higher on math portions of the SAT (for a combined total of 101 points) than students with no coursework or experience in the arts.

For many disadvantaged students, participation in music and arts programs helps to break the cycle of failure they have so often encountered in life. While study after study demonstrates that participation by disadvantaged children in a well-developed, sequential music program can be extremely beneficial academically, socially, and emotionally, these are the very students who are most often denied this instruction. Middle- and upper-income parents who have the resources are able to provide private instruction for their children. But not all children have that luxury, and many are denied access to the benefits of education in music and the other arts if their schools do not provide it.

Implications for Education Reform

The research clearly shows that music instruction, taught by qualified teachers, produces measurable enhancements in the development of children's brains, resulting in significant educational benefits. It is important to note, however, that the cognitive and academic improvements highlighted by the research come about only with sequential instruction in music provided by qualified teachers, not through mere exposure to music. Music exposure and enrichment programs, such as trips to hear performances of the local symphony, are the types of activities that are funded under Title X of the Elementary and Secondary Education Act. They are vital because of the pleasure they provide and the critical role they play in enhancing education. They often furnish the spark that inspires a child to pursue formal study in the arts and should continue to be funded and supported. Yet, they cannot substitute for formal instruction as part of the regular school day. Dr. Rauscher emphasized this when she noted that "there is no scientific data indicating that, when provided in isolation from music instruction, enrichment and exposure programs induce long-term cognitive benefits. It is important not to confuse these forms of musical involvement." For this reason, it is not sufficient to support only arts exposure and enrichment programs under the guise of "arts education." In order to realize the cognitive and academic benefits illustrated by the research, federal support must also be directed to schools to help them establish, retain, and strengthen arts education programs.

Unfortunately, this needed support does not currently exist. Because of the misperception that music and the other arts are "frills," school arts programs are the first to be eliminated when budgets are restricted. The problem is most acute in poor urban and rural areas, but it is a problem shared by virtually all school districts to one degree or another. Just recently, the San Francisco School District made the tragic decision to eliminate its elementary school arts programs.

One contributing factor in the decision to cut music and arts classes from the school curriculum is the ever-present quest to improve standardized test scores, particularly in reading and math. This has led many principals to choose more time for instruction in reading and math at the expense of the arts. This choice is an error rooted in lack of awareness of the latest research and failure to appreciate the power of the arts to positively impact student self-esteem, self-worth, as well as student performance in other academic subjects.

We have to be concerned about the culture of our schools. Music programs can make the school a more humane learning environment because they invite cooperation rather than confrontation. Music connects students to schools in a wonderfully positive way. That connection is needed more today than ever before. And, it is a connection that we must make in every school. Too often, it is the children who would most benefit from instruction in music and the other arts (children in schools characterized by low achievement) who do not have access to the artistic, academic, and personal benefits of music education. . . .

What Congress Can Do
Elementary and Secondary Education Act (ESEA) Reauthorization

As Congress considers legislation to reauthorize ESEA, MENC asks that you work with us to:

Reinforce the concept of music and arts education as part of the core curriculum. Music and the other arts are core academic subjects and have been recognized as such by Congress and the Administration in Goals 2000. This status should be confirmed and reinforced in ESEA legislation. Incorporating the Statement of Principles into ESEA is one way to accomplish this.

Strengthen music and arts education programs authorized under Title X by establishing a formal consultative role for arts educators in determining the nature, scope, and direction of these programs. Currently, no such role exists in the statute. It makes no sense for education policy to be determined and executed without the involvement of educators.

Ensure greater access to school music programs for at-risk students. Special efforts are needed to make certain that disadvantaged students have the same access to comprehensive, balanced, and sequential instruction in music as students in more affluent districts. MENC would be pleased to work with the Subcommittee to identify school programs that are making successful use of music with disadvantaged children to determine what they are doing,

June M. Hinckley

how it has led to their success, and how these programs can be replicated throughout the country.

Prioritize funding so that arts education grants are available to schools. We understand the budget constraints that Congress faces. All disciplines and programs must compete for scarce dollars. However, simply re-ordering priorities in light of the scientific research on the link between music education and higher achievement potential in math and science would be an effective beginning.

Make certain that federal funds that are directed to after-school arts activities are not used to replace in-school music and arts classes. Investing in after-school programs is sound policy. There appears to be an urgent need for these programs, and MENC fully supports this type of investment. But if the arts become relegated to an after-school activity, they lose their rightful status as a core academic subject. And, children who cannot take advantage of after-school programs because of conflicts with sports or work commitments or for other reasons will be denied access to the significant benefits achieved through arts education.

The Congressional Bully Pulpit

Beyond what Congress can accomplish through legislation, Congress can exercise a leadership role in disseminating to parents, school administrators, and state education officials information on the music/brain research and its implications for education reform. Congress can accomplish this task through hearings, town hall meetings, floor statements, media outreach, and other effective uses of the powerful Congressional bully pulpit. As Congress places greater emphasis on state and local flexibility, its role as communicator and disseminator of information becomes even more crucial. Parents, school boards, and state policymakers want to do what is best for our children, but their decisions must be based on the best information available.

Conclusion

MENC stands ready to work with this Subcommittee and with Congress as you consider ways to strengthen educational opportunities and achievement for all children. We would like to serve as a resource to you as you develop legislation and hopefully undertake to spread the message to your constituents about the importance of music and arts education.

Arts Education Partnership and
The President's Committee on the Arts and the Humanities
Champions of Change: The Impact of the Arts on Learning (2000)

Preface

When young people are involved with the arts, something changes in their lives. We've often witnessed the rapt expressions on the faces of such young people. Advocates for the arts often use photographs of smiling faces to document the experience.

But in a society that values measurements and uses data-driven analysis to inform decisions about allocation of scarce resources, photographs of smiling faces are not enough to gain or even retain support. Such images alone will not convince skeptics or even neutral decision-makers that something exceptional is happening when and where the arts become part of the lives of young people.

Until now, we've known little about the nature of this change, or how to enable the change to occur. To understand these issues in more rigorous terms, we invited leading educational researchers to examine the impact of arts experiences on young people. We developed the *Champions of Change: The Impact of the Arts on Learning* initiative in cooperation with The Arts Education Partnership and The President's Committee on the Arts and the Humanities to explore why and how young people were changed through their arts experiences.

. . . We invited the initial *Champions of Change* researchers to examine well-established models of arts education. We then added research efforts that looked beyond specific programs to larger issues of the arts in American education. Finally, we expanded our concept beyond classrooms and schools to include out-of-school settings. We wanted to better understand the impact of the arts on learning, not just on formal education.

Executive Summary

What the Arts Change About the Learning Experience

As a result of their varied inquiries, the *Champions of Change* researchers found that learners can attain higher levels of achievement through their engagement with the arts. Moreover, one of the critical research findings is that the learning in and through the arts can help "level the playing field" for youngsters from disadvantaged circumstances.

James Catterall . . . demonstrates that students with high levels of arts participation outperform "arts-poor" students by virtually every measure. Since arts participation is highly correlated with socioeconomic status, which is the most significant predictor of academic performance, this comes as little surprise. [He] . . . showed that high arts participation makes a more significant difference to students from low-income backgrounds than for high-income students. Catterall also found clear evidence that sustained involvement in particular art forms—music and theater—are highly correlated with success in mathematics and reading.

These findings are enriched by comparisons of student achievement in fourteen high-poverty schools in which the Chicago Arts Partnerships in Education (CAPE) has developed innovative arts-integrated curricula. The inspiring turnaround of this large and deeply troubled school district is one of the important education stories of this decade. Schools across Chicago, including all those in this study, have been improving student performance. But, when compared to arts-poor schools in the same neighborhoods, the CAPE schools advanced even more quickly and now boast a significant gap in achievement along many dimensions.

Schools are not the only venue in which young people grow, learn, and achieve. Shirley Brice Heath ["Imaginative Actuality: Learning in the Arts during the Nonschool Hours"] spent a decade studying dozens of after-school programs for disadvantaged youth. These programs were broadly clustered into three categories—sports/academic, community involvement, and the arts. This research shows that the youth in all these programs were doing better in school and in their personal lives than were young people from the same socioeconomic categories.

To the researchers' surprise, however, the youth in the arts programs were doing the best. Skeptical about this finding, Heath and her colleagues looked more closely at the arts programs and the youth participating in them. Although the youth in the arts programs were actually at greater "risk" than those in the other programs, the researchers found that characteristics particular to the arts made those programs more effective. They now believe that a combination of "roles, risks, and rules" offered in the arts programs had a greater impact on these young lives.

Another broad theme emerges from the individual *Champions of Change* research findings: the arts no longer need to be characterized solely by either their ability to promote learning in specific arts disciplines or by their ability to promote learning in other disciplines. These studies suggest a more dynamic, less either–or model for the arts and overall learning that has more of the appearance of a rotary with entrances and exits than of a linear one-way street.

This rotary of learning provides the greater access to higher levels of achievement. "Learning in and Through the Arts" (LITA) and other *Champions of Change* studies found much evidence that learning in the arts has significant effects on learning in other domains. LITA suggests a dynamic model in which learning in one domain supports and stimulates learning in others, which in turn supports and stimulates learning in a complex web of influence described as a "constellation." LITA and the other researchers provide compelling evidence that student achievement is heightened in an environment with high-quality arts education offerings and a school climate supportive of active and productive learning.

Why the Arts Change the Learning Experience

When well taught, the arts provide young people with authentic learning experiences that engage their minds, hearts, and bodies. The learning experiences are real and meaningful for them.

While learning in other disciplines may often focus on development of a single skill or talent, the arts regularly engage multiple skills and abilities. Engagement in the arts—whether the visual arts, dance, music, theater or other disciplines—nurtures the development of cognitive, social, and personal competencies. Although the *Champions of Change* researchers conducted their investigations and presented their findings independently, a remarkable consensus exists among their findings:

The arts reach students who are not otherwise being reached.

Young people who are disengaged from schools and other community institutions are at the greatest risk of failure or harm. The researchers found that the arts provided a reason, and sometimes the only reason, for being engaged with school or other organizations. These young people would otherwise be left without access to any community of learners. The studies concerning ArtsConnection, CAPE, and learning during non-school hours are of particular significance here.

The arts reach students in ways that they are not otherwise being reached.

Other recent educational research has produced insights into different styles of learning. This research also addresses examples of young people who were considered classroom failures, perhaps "acting out" because conventional classroom practices were not engaging them. These "problem" students often became the high achievers in arts learning settings. Success in the arts became a bridge to learning and eventual success in other areas of learning. The ArtsConnection study provides case studies of such students; the LITA research examines the issue of learner self-perception in great depth.

The arts connect students to themselves and each other.

Creating an artwork is a personal experience. The student draws upon his or her personal resources to generate the result. By engaging his or her whole person, the student feels invested in ways that are deeper than "knowing the answer." Beyond the individual, Steve Seidel ["Stand and Unfold Yourself: A Monograph on the Shakespeare & Company Research Study"] and Dennie Palmer Wolf ["Why the Arts Matter in Education: or Just What Do Children Learn When They Create an Opera"] show how effective arts learning communities are formed and operated. James Catterall also describes how the attitudes of young people toward one another are altered through their arts learning experiences.

The arts transform the environment for learning.

When the arts become central to the learning environment, schools, and other settings become places of discovery. According to the Teachers College research team and those examining the CAPE schools, the very school culture is changed, and the conditions for learning are improved. Figurative walls between classrooms and disciplines are broken down. Teachers are renewed. Even the physical appearance of a school building is transformed through the representations of learning. The Heath research team also found "visible" changes in nonschool settings.

The arts provide learning opportunities for the adults in the lives of young people.

Those held responsible for the development of children and youth—teachers, parents, and other adults—are rarely given sufficient or significant opportunities for their own continuing education. With adults participating in lifelong learning, young people gain an understanding that learning in any field is a never-ending process. The roles of the adults are also changed—in effective programs, the adults become coaches, active facilitators of learning. Heath and other researchers here describe the altered dynamics between young and less young learners.

The arts provide new challenges for those students already considered successful.

Boredom and complacency are barriers to success. For those young people who outgrow their established learning environments, the arts can offer a chance for unlimited challenge. In some situations described in the research, older students may also teach and mentor younger students. In others, young people gain from the experience of working with professional artists. The ArtsConnection researchers in general, and James Catterall ["Involvement in the Arts and Human Development: General Involvement and Intensive Involvement in Music and Theater Arts"] in particular, explored the impact of intensive involvement in specific art disciplines.

The arts connect learning experiences to the world of real work.

The world of adult work has changed, and the arts learning experiences described in the research show remarkable consistency with the evolving workplace. Ideas are what matter, and the ability to generate ideas, to bring ideas to life, and to communicate them is what matters to workplace success. Working in a classroom or a studio as an artist, the young person is learning and practicing future workplace behaviors. A company is a company, whether producing an opera or a breakthrough technological service.

How the Arts Change the Learning Experience

The programs and schools examined by the *Champions of Change* researchers were selected because they appeared to be models of excellence that were making a real difference to young people. Their research helps us identify the principles and requirements that make these arts learning models work. By helping to better define the characteristics of effective arts learning programs, the *Champions of Change* researchers have also done a great service.

Education reformers and researchers have learned a great deal about "what works" in recent years. In examining the work of Shakespeare & Company, Steve Seidel cites the general characteristics of "project-based learning" as factors that also support effective arts learning. In *Real Learning, Real Work,* author Adria Steinberg identifies six elements that are critical to the design of project-based learning: authenticity, academic rigor, applied learning, active exploration, adult relationships, and assessment practices. Seidel also emphasizes that the best assessment of a person's understanding is a product that "puts that understanding to work": Learning is deepest when learners have the capacity to represent what they have learned, and the multiple disciplines of the arts all provide modes of representation. . . .

What Are the Implications of This Research?

This paper presents observations from a large-scale data base of U.S. secondary school students suggesting positive associations between involvement in various arts and academic and social outcomes. The work supports strong suggestions, but is not definitive. No one study ever decides issues in this sort of research. Our knowledge base grows incrementally with the accumulation of consistent studies, and with the accumulation of professional knowledge by educators, school leaders, parents, students, and in this case artists involved in the schools.

The main implication of this work is that the arts appear to matter when it comes to a variety of non-arts outcomes, some of them intended and some not. The advantages accruing to arts involvement show up as both a general relationship as well as in relations between specific art forms, such as instrumental music and theater, and specific developments for youngsters.

In addition, although not the main theme of this paper, our data support long-held concerns that access to the arts is inequitably distributed in our society. Students from poor and less educated families are much more likely to record low levels of participation in the arts during the middle and high school years; affluent youngsters are much more likely to show high, rather than low engagement the arts. If our analysis is reasonable, the arts do matter—not only as worthwhile experiences in their own right for reasons not addressed here, but also as instruments of cognitive growth and development and as agents of motivation for school success. In this light, unfair access to the arts for our children brings consequences of major importance to our society.

Sources and Permissions

Part I. European Views

1. Greece and Rome

Plato: *The Collected Dialogues of Plato*, ed. Edith Hamilton and Huntington Cairns, 322; and 643–47, 654–56. Copyright © 1961 by Princeton University Press. Reprinted by permission of Princeton University Press.

Aristotle: *Politica*, book VIII, from *The Works of Aristotle*, vol. X, ed. W. D. Ross (London: Oxford University Press, 1921), 1336–442.

Quinitilian: *Instituto Oratoria*. From William M. Smail, trans., *Quintilian on Education* (Oxford: Clarendon Press, 1938), book I., ch. 1, 47–55.

St. Augustine: F. J. Sheed, trans., *The Confessions of St. Augustine* (New York: Sheed & Ward, 1943), 242–44.

2. The Middle Ages

Boethius: Calvin Martin Bower, "Boethius' *The Principles of Music*, an Introduction, Translation, and Commentary," Ph.D. dissertation, George Peabody College for Teachers, 1967, 31-44. University Microfilms no. 67-15,005.

Charlemagne: *Monumenta Germania historica*, Leges II, Capitularia regum Francorum I, in Gerald Ellard, Master Alcuin, *Liturgist* (Chicago: Loyola University Press, 1956) 54–55.

St. Odo of Cluny: Oliver Strunk, ed., *Source Readings in Music History* (New York: Norton, 1950), 103–04.

3. Later European Views

Frank Ll. Harrison: "The Musical Impact of Exploration and Cultural Encounter," in *Musical Repercussions of 1492: Encounters in Text and Performance*, ed. Carol E. Robertson (Washington, DC: Smithsonian Institution, 1992), 171–73.

Martin Luther: F. V. N. Painter, *Luther on Education* (Philadelphia: Lutheran Publication Society, 1889), 165–66; Ulrich S. Leupold, ed., *Luther's Works*, vol. 53, Liturgy and Hymns (Philadelphia: Fortress Press, 1965), 321–24.

Calvin: Joseph Haroutunian and Louise Smith, "Ethics and the Common Life," in *Calvin: Commentaries*, vol. XXIII, The Library of Christian Classics (Philadelphia: The Westminster Press, 1958), 354–55.

Mulcaster: *Elementare* (1582) (London: Oxford University Press, 1925), 5–6.

Comenius: Will S. Monroe, *Comenius' School of Infancy* (D. C. Heath, 1896), 48–9. John Amos Comenius, *The Great Didactic*, trans. and ed. M. W. Keatinge (London: A. & C. Black, Ltd., 1923), 194–202, 259–261, 268.

Locke: *Some Thoughts Concerning Education* (Cambridge: Cambridge University Press, 1913), 174–5; letter to Edward Clark from James L. Axtell, March 15, 1686, in *The Educational Writings of John Locke* (Cambridge: Cambridge University Press, 1968), 358–59.

Pestalozzi: Letter XXIII, *Pestalozzi's Educational Writings*, ed. by J. A. Green (New York: Longmans, Green & Co., 1916), 228–32.

Froebel: *The Education of Man* (New York: D. Appleton and Company, 1908), 225–29.

Spencer: *Literary Style and Music* (New York: Philosophical Library, 1951), 69–76, "What Knowledge is of Most Worth?" *Education: Intellectual, Moral, and Physical* (New York: D. Appleton and Company, 1890), 28–33, 70–81.

Jaques-Dalcroze: *Rhythm, Music and Education* (New York City: G. P. Putnam's Sons, 1921), 13–26.

Neill: *Summerhill: A Radical Approach to Child Rearing* (New York: Hart Publishing Company, Inc., 1960), 12.

Part II. American Views, *1750–1950*

Mather: *The Accomplished Singer* (Boston: 1721), in *Music in Boston*, ed. John C. Swan, (Boston: Trustees of the Public Library of the City of Boston, 1977), 10–11.

Billings: *The Singing Master's Assistant* (Boston: Draper and Folsom, 1778), 16–17, quoted in McKay and Crawford, *William Billings of Boston* (Princeton: Princeton University Press, 1975).

Brown: *The Musician and Intelligencer* (Cincinnati, 1848), in Michael L. Mark and Charles L. Gary, *A History of American Music Education* (Reston, VA: Music Educators National Conference, 1999), 90.

Mason: *Manual of the Boston Academy of Music for Instruction in the Elements of Vocal Music on the System of Pestalozzi* (Boston: Boston Academy of Music, 1834).

"School Committee Report," *Boston Musical Gazette: Devoted to the Science of Music*, (December 5, 1838, 123; December 12, 1838). Report concluded December 26, 1838, 137–38.

Superintendent's Annual Report for 1843, Buffalo Public Schools (Buffalo, NY, 1843), in Michael L. Mark and Charles L. Gary, *A History of American Music Education*, 2nd ed. (Reston, VA: Music Educators National Conference, 1992), 167.

Mann: *Life and Works of Horace Mann: Annual Reports of the Secretary of the Board of Education of Massachusetts for the Years 1839–1844* (Boston: Lee and Shepherd Publishers, 1891), 445–63.

Mayo: "Methods of Moral Instruction in Common Schools" (lecture), *The Addresses and Journal of Proceedings of the National Education Association* (Philadelphia: National Education Association, 1873), 21–22.

Tomlins: Lecture presented to grade teachers, music supervisors and school superintendents, various locations, ca. 1900, in William Bailey Birge, *History of Public School Music in the United States* (Washington, DC: Music Educators National Conference, 1966), 151–52.

Cole: *Journal of Proceedings and Addresses of the 42nd Annual Meeting* National Education Association (Winona, MN: National Education Association, 1903), 695–99.

Winship: *Journal of Proceedings and Addresses of the 44th Annual Meeting*, National Education Association (Winona, MN: National Education Association, 1905) 630–33.

Parker, McConathy, Birge, and Miessner: *The Progressive Music Series*, Teacher's Manual, vol. II (Boston: Silver, Burdett and Company, 1916), 9.

Clark: *Response to Address of Welcome at the Twelfth Annual Meeting of the Music Supervisors National Conference* (St. Louis, 1919), in Hazel Nohavec Morgan, *Music in American Education* (Chicago: Music Educators National Conference, 1955), 4–5. Copyright© 1955 Music Educators National Conference. Reprinted with permission.

Cundiff and Dykema: *School Music Handbook: A Guide for Teaching School Music* (Boston: C. C. Birchard & Company, 1923), 3–7.

Damrosch, Gartlan, and Gehrkens: *The Universal School Music Series*, Teacher's Book (New York: Hayden and Eldredge, Inc., 1922), 1–2.

Buescher Saxophones: Advertisement in *The Etude*, (February 1928), 146.

Earhart: *A Steadfast Philosophy* (Washington: Music Educators National Conference, 1962), 80–83. Copyright© 1962 Music Educators National Conference. Reprinted with permission.

Dewey: "The Aesthetic Element in Education, " *Addresses and Proceedings of the National Education Association* (Winona, MN: National Education Association, 1897), 329–30; Dewey, *Art as Experience* (New York: Minton, Balch & Company, 1934), 80–81.

Handlin: "John Dewey's Challenge To Education." Lecture presented to the 1959 meeting of the John Dewey Society (New York; Harper and Brothers, 1959), 29–32. Copyright © renewed 1987 by Oscar Handlin. Reprinted by permission of HarperCollins Publishers, Inc.

Gehrkens: "The Ultimate Aim of Music Teaching in the Public Schools." Statement published in the *Music Supervisors' Bulletin* (vol. I, 1915, n. 1) in Edward Bailey Birge, *History of Public School Music in the United States* (Washington, DC: Music Educators National Conference, 1934, 249–50.

Dykema and Gehrkens: *The Teaching and Administration of High School Music* (Boston: C. C. Birchard, 1941), xix–xxiv.

Mursell and Glenn: *The Psychology of School Music Teaching* (New York City: Silver Burdett Company, 1938), 365–77.

Nohavec Morgan: *Music Education Source Book* (Chicago: Music Educators National Conference, 1947), iv, xi–xiii. Copyright © 1947 Music Educators National Conference. Reprinted with permission.

Mursell: "Principles of Music Education," *The Thirty-Fifth Yearbook*, National Society for the Study of Education (Bloomington, IL: Public School Publishing Company, 1936), 10–11. Reprinted with permission of the National Society for the Study of Education; James L. Mursell, *Music in American Schools* (New York City: Silver Burdett Company, 1943).

Part III. American Views since 1950

1. Philosophy of Music Education

Clippinger: "Collective Voice Training." *Music Supervisors Journal*, 12/1 (October 1925), 10.

Mark: "Public Policy and the Genesis of Aesthetic Education," *Philosophy of Music Education Review* 6/1 (Spring 1998), 107–12. Reprinted with permission of *Philosophy of Music Education Review*.

Morgan: *Music: A Living Power in Education* (New York: Silver Burdett Company, 1953), 1–7.

Harper: Address given at the MENC Biennial Convention, Chicago, 1954, reprinted in Hazel Nohavec Morgan, *Music in American Schools* (Chicago: Music Educators National Conference, 1955), 5–8. Copyright © 1955 Music Educators National Conference. Reprinted with permission.

Willis: Address given at the MENC Biennial Convention, Chicago, 1954, in Hazel Nohavec Morgan, *Music in American Education* (Chicago: Music Educators National Conference, 1955), 1–4. Copyright © 1955 Music Educators National Conference. Reprinted with permission.

Broudy: "A Realistic Philosophy of Music Education," in *Basic Concepts in Music Education*, ed. Nelson B. Henry (Chicago: National Society for the Study of Education, 1958), 65–68, 86–87. Reprinted with permission of the National Society for the Study of Education.

Burmeister: "The Role of Music in General Education," *Basic Concepts in Music Education, The Fifty-seventh Yearbook*, National Society for the Study of Education, ed. Nelson B. Henry (Chicago: The University of Chicago Press, 1958) 218–21. Reprinted with permission of the National Society for the Study of Education.

Leonhard and House: *Foundations and Principles of Music Education* (New York: McGraw–Hill, 1959), 1–6, 96–102.

Schwadron: *Aesthetics: Dimensions for Music Education* (Washington, DC: Music Educators National Conference, 1967), iv–v, 93–95. Copyright © 1967 Music Educators National Conference. Reprinted with permission.

Knieter: "The Nature of Aesthetic Education," in *Toward an Aesthetic Education* (Washington, DC: Music Educators National Conference, 1971), 3–8, 18–19. Copyright © 1971 Music Educators National Conference. Reprinted with permission.

Ball: "Thoughts on Music as Aesthetic Education," in *Toward An Aesthetic Education* (Washington, DC: Music Educators National Conference, 1971), 60–62. Copyright © 1971 Music Educators National Conference. Reprinted with permission.

Reimer: *A Philosophy of Music Education*, 2nd ed. (Englewood Cliffs, NJ: Prentice–Hall, 1989), xi–xii, 14–16, 226–29. Reprinted by permission of Pearson Education, Inc., Upper Saddle

River, NJ; "What Knowledge Is of Most Worth in the Arts?" in *The Arts, Education, and Aesthetic Knowing*, ed. Bennett Reimer and Ralph A. Smith (Chicago: National Society for the Study of Education, 1992), 25–29, 45–48. Reprinted with permission of the National Society for the Study of Education; "Why Do Humans Value Music?" in *Vision 2020: The Housewright Symposium on the Future of Music Education* (Reston, VA: Music Educators National Conference–The National Association for Music Education, 2000), 43–46. Copyright © 2000 Music Educators National Conference–The National Association for Music Education. Reprinted with permission.

Csikszentmihalyi and Schiefele: "Arts Education, Human Development, and the Quality of Experience," in *The Arts, Education, and Aesthetic Knowing*, Ninety-first Yearbook of the National Society for the Study of Education, ed. Bennett Reimer and Ralph A. Smith (Chicago: National Society for the Study of Education, 1992), 170–73, 180–82. Reprinted with permission of the National Society for the Study of Education.

Bowman: "Sound, Society, and Music 'Proper,'" *Philosophy of Music Education Review* 2/1, (Spring 1994), 22–23.

Alperson: *What is Music? An Introduction to the Philosophy of Music* (University Park, PA: The Pennsylvania State University Press, 1994), 233, 235–36.

Elliott: *Music Matters: A New Philosophy of Music Education.* (New York: Oxford University Press, 1995), 39–45, 296–97, 305–06. Copyright © 1995 by David J. Elliott; used by permission of Oxford University Press, Inc; "Putting Matters In Perspective: Reflections On A New Philosophy," *The Quarterly Journal of Music Teaching and Learning* 7/2–4 (trilogy issue, 1996–97), 23, 25, which was published by the School of Music of the University of Northern Colorado.

Regelski: "The Aristotelian Bases of Praxis for Music and Music Education as Praxis," *Philosophy of Music Education Review*, 6/1, (Spring 1998), 44–45.

Gates: "Why Study Music?" *Vision 2020: The Housewright Symposium on the Future of Music Education* (Reston, VA: Music Educators National Conference–The National Association for Music Education, 2000), 70–72. Copyright © 2000 Music Educators National Conference–The National Association for Music Education. Reprinted with permission.

Hope: "Response to J. Terry Gates' 'Why Study Music?' *Vision 2020: The Housewright Symposium on the Future of Music Education* (Reston, VA: Music Educators National Conference–The National Association for Music Education, 2000), 85–86. Copyright © 2000 Music Educators National Conference–The National Association for Music Education. Reprinted with permission.

2. Music Education and Society

Mueller: "Music and Education," *Basic Concepts in Music Education*, The Fifty-seventh Yearbook, National Society of the Study of Education, ed. John H. Mueller (Chicago: The University of Chicago Press, 1958), 119–122. Reprinted with permission of the National Society for the Study of Education.

Kaplan: *Foundations and Frontiers of Music Education* (New York: Holt, Rinehart and Winston, Inc., 1966), 200–202.

Mark: *Contemporary Music Education* (New York City: Schirmer Books, 1996), 9–10.

Jorgensen: *In Search of Music Education* (Urbana and Chicago: University of Illinois Press, 1997), 33–43. Used with permission of the University of Illinois Press.

Shehan Campbell: "*Musical Exotica, Multiculturalism, and School Music.*" *The Quarterly Journal of Music Teaching and Learning* 5/2 (Summer 1994), 65–66, 72, 74, which was published by the University of Northern Colorado.

Boyce-Tillman: "Conceptual Frameworks for World Musics in Education," *Philosophy of Music Education Review*, 5/1, Spring 1997, 12.

Carter: "Personal Observations On Integration and School Music Programs." *The Quarterly Journal of Music Teaching and Learning* 4/2, (Summer 1993), 10, which was published by the School of Music of the University of Northern Colorado.

Florida Dept. of Education: *Multicultural Arts Education: Guidelines, Instructional Units and Resources for Art, Dance, Music and Theater, Grades K–12* (Tallahassee, FL: Department of Education, Division of Public Schools, 1993).

3. Music Education, Mind, and Brain

Gardner: *Frames of Mind: The Theory of Multiple Intelligences* (New York City: Basic Books, 1983), 99.

Hodges: "What Neuromusical Research Has To Offer Music Education," *The Quarterly Journal of Music Teaching and Learning* 7/2–4 (Trilogy issue, 1996–97), 43–46, which was published by the University of Northern Colorado.

Rausher, Shaw, and Ky: "Music and Spatial Task Performance," *Nature* (October 14, 1993), n. 611. Reprinted by permission from *Nature* (October 14, 1993), Macmillan Magazines Ltd.

Morrison: Unpublished letter to the 1998 Music Education Summit, Washington, DC. VH1 Save the Music Foundation.

Sykes: Unpublished speech to National Governors Association, Washington, DC, February 25, 2001. VH1 Save the Music Foundation.

Winner and Hetland: "Reviewing Education and the Arts Project." *The Arts and Academic Improvement: What the Evidence Shows*, executive summary. From the website of Project Zero, Harvard University: http://pzweb.harvard.edu/Research/REAP.htm. Published by permission of the authors.

Reimer: "Facing the Risks of the 'Mozart Effect,'" in *Music Educators Journal*, 86/1 (July 1999), 37–43. Copyright © 1999 Music Educators National Conference–The National Association for Music Education. Reprinted with permission.

4. School Music Program Development

Yale Seminar on Music Education: In *Music In Our Schools: A Search for Improvement*, ed. Claude V. Palisca. (Washington, DC: U.S. Department of Health, Education, and Welfare, Office of Education, OE-33033, 1964), 53–56.

College Board: *Academic Preparation for College* (Princeton, NJ: College Entrance Examination Board, 1983), in Michael L. Mark, *Contemporary Music Education*, 3rd ed. (New York: Schirmer Books, 1996), 21–22.

Tanglewood Symposium: *Documentary Report of the Tanglewood Symposium*, ed. by Robert Choate (Washington: Music Educators National Conference, 1968), 110–15, 138–39. Copyright © 1968 Music Educators National Conference. Reprinted with permission.

Gary: "Why Music Education?" *NASSP* [National Association of Secondary School Principals] *Bulletin*, 1975), iii.

Colwell: "Planning and Evaluation: The Evaluation Dilemma," in *Music Education: Facing the Future* (Christchurch, New Zealand: International Society for Music Education, 1990), 33–34. Copyright is vested in the International Society for Music Education.

Goals 2000: Public Law 103-227—March 31,1994, 103d Congress (Washington, DC: Government Printing Office, 1994).

The Housewright Declaration: *Vision 2020: The Housewright Symposium on the Future of Music Education* (Reston, VA: Music Educators National Conference–The National Association for Music Education, 2000), 219–20. Copyright © 2000 Music Educators National Conference–The National Association for Music Education. Reprinted with permission.

5. Advocacy for Music Education

National Association of Secondary-School Principals: *The Arts in the Comprehensive Secondary School* (Washington: National Association of Secondary School Principals, 1962), 4–5.

The Arts, Education and Americans Panel: *Coming to Our Senses: The Significance of the Arts for American Education* (New York: McGraw-Hill, 1977), 248–63.

Fowler: *Can We Rescue the Arts for America's Children?: Coming to Our Senses—10 Years Later* (New York: American Council for the Arts, 1988), 2–19; "Finding the Way to Be Basic: Music Education in the 1990s and Beyond," in *Basic Concepts in Music Education*, ed. Richard Colwell (Niwot, CO: University Press of Colorado, 1991), 16–24.

National Commission on Music Education: "Education with Music," *Growing Up Complete: The Imperative for Music Education* (Reston, VA: MENC, 1991), vii–viii, 17–18. Copyright © 1991 Music Educators National Conference. Reprinted with permission.

National Endowment for the Arts: *Toward Civilization: A Report on Arts Education* (Washington, DC: National Endowment for the Arts, 1988), 13–19.

Riley: Transcript of speech to Music Educators National Conference, Washington, DC, March 13, 1997.

Ivey: Transcript of unpublished speech to National Music Educators Summit, Washington, DC, October 2, 1998.

106th Congress, 2d Session, H. Con. Res. 266, passed the House of Representatives June 13, 2000, The Senate of the United States June 14, 2000.

Hinckley: Testimony on "Elementary and Secondary Education Act—Educating Diverse Populations" to the House Subcommittee on Early Childhood, Youth and Families, July 15, 1999.

Arts Education Partnership and The President's Committee on the Arts and the Humanities: *Champions of Change: The Impact of the Arts on Learning*, ed. Edward B. Fiske (Washington, DC: Arts Education Partnership and President's Committee on the Arts and the Humanities, 2000), iv, viii–xii.

Index

Commission on Church Music, 153
Common Schools, 93
community songs, 106
Conceptual Frameworks for World Musics in Education, m June Boyce-Tillman, 227
Confessions, St. Augustine, 23
Congress, 303
Connemara sean-nós singing, 209
Constitution, 131
constructive knowledge, 208
consumption, 72
Cooper, Dr. William John, 109
Copland, Aaron, 289
Cotton Tail, Duke Ellington, 206, 207
Council on Civic Society, 294
Couperin harpsichord pieces, 183
Cousin, 85
creating art, 192
Crotch, 71
cultural literacy, 275, 288
cultural representativeness, 226
curriculum theory, 211
Curriculum Must Assume a Place at the Center of Music, David McAllister, 261
Cushing, Mr., 81

Daedalus, Stephen, 200
Damrosch, Walter, 145
dances, 102
dancing, 37
Dante, 65
David, 32
David's Psalter, 24
Davies, David, 283
Davis, T. Kemper, 86
Davison, 122
De Institutione Musica, Boethius, 25
De Magisero, St. Augustine, 23
Declaration of Faith, Purpose and Action, 124
Derby, England, 47
Dewey, 145
Dewey, John, 119, 120, 121
Dewey, John, 115
divergent systems, 227
Dixieland and bop, 209
dominance and subordination, 137
Donaldson Elementary School, 291
Donegal fiddling, 209

Dorian, 19
Dorian, 15, Phrygian mode, 15
drama, 53
drawing, 11, 42, 80
Dunham, Katherine, 289
Duskin, Joel, 67
Dykema, Peter, 145

Earhart, Will, 145
Early Childhood Research Quarterly, 239
Ecphantikes, 17
education through music, 119
EEG coherence values, 233
efflorescence of civilized life, 52
Einstein, 281
Eisenhower, Dwight D., 65
Eisleben, Germany, 31
Eisner, Elliot, W., 274, 281, 289
Elementary and Secondary Education Act, Title X, 301; reauthorization, 302
Eliot of Harvard, 130
Ellington, Duke, 289
Enchiridion musices, St. Odo of Cluny, 28
England, 84
enrichment of home life, 127
era of aesthetic education philosophy, 144
Eroica Symphony, Beethoven, 206, 207
esoteric or elitist view, 183
Essentialism, 204
esthetic experience, 221
Euclid, 289
Euripides, 13
Evansville College, 150
Evenus, 20
existentialist aesthetics, 185
Experimentation, 115

Facing the Risks of the "Mozart Effect," Bennett Reimer, 246
Factual Compared with Aesthetic, 108
Farnsworth, Charles Hubert, 119
Fellenberg, 85
Ferdinand of Austria, 35
Finding the Way to be Basic: Music Education in the 1990s and Beyond, 279
Florence, Italy, 65
Florida State University, 228, 266; Department of Education, 228, 299

VH1 Save the Music, 67; Foundation, 238, 239
Victor Talking Machine Company, 100
Villa-Lobos, Heitor, 1
virtue and piety, 73
Vision 2020 Symposium, 266
vocational education, 103
Voice Culture, 100

Wagner, 99, 224
Walt Disney Entertainment, 227
Washington, D.C., 291
Washington, George, 65
W.C.T.U., 131
Western cultural mainstream, 217
Western norms, 224
What Knowledge Is of Most Worth in the Arts? The Arts, Education, and Aesthetic Knowing, Bennett Reimer, 189
White House, 296; Panel on Education Research and Development, 139
Why Do Humans Value Music?, Bennett Reimer, 195
Why study music?, 215
Why Study Music?, J. Terry Gates, 212
Willard, Reverend Joseph, 65
Wolf, Dennie Palmer, 306

Woodbridge, William, 79, 80
Woodside Music Club, 292
work lesson, 105
works of lesser quality, 192
world at peace, 125
World Music Centre, University of Limerick, 206
World War II, 128
World Through Sense Pictures, The, Comenius, 35
Worship and the Fine Arts, 153
worthless ballads, 53
Wright, Frank Lloyd, 289
Wrington, England, 37
Wyse, Mr., 84

Xenophon, 99

Yale University, 68, 249; Seminar on Music Education, 249
Yankee Doodle, 159
Yankee Peddlars, 70

Zeus, 14
Zumárraga, Juan de, 30
Zuni lullaby, 206
Zurich, Switzerland, 38